Understanding Quarkus 2.x

Quarkus

Antonio Goncalves

2021-11-29

D1730103

Table of Contents

Understanding Quarkus 2.x

The distribution of the book is made through Amazon KDP (*Kindle Direct Publishing*[1]).

Any source code referenced by the author in this text is available to readers at https://github.com/agoncal/agoncal-fascicle-quarkus/tree/2.0. This source code is available for reproduction and distribution as it uses an MIT licence[2].

- www.antoniogoncalves.org
- agoncal.teachable.com
- www.amazon.com/author/agoncal

You can find two different formats of this fascicle:

- eBook (PDF/EPUB) at https://agoncal.teachable.com/p/ebook-understanding-quarkus
- Paper book (ISBN: 9798775773083) and eBooks at https://www.amazon.com/gp/product/B0993R88N3

Version Date: 2021-11-29

To my wonderful kids, Eloise, Ligia and Ennio, who are the best thing life
has given me.

Foreword

Hi there, I'm Emmanuel Bernard, co-founder of Quarkus. I am Chief Architect at Red Hat overseeing part of the Middleware portfolio. But, at heart, I'm an Open Source developer (of projects and communities). I contributed to, and led, the Hibernate projects as well as many others. Recently, I was lucky enough to be in the right place at the right time with the right people in order to co-found Quarkus. Since then, I have been leading it since then on its mission to deliver Java for the cloud era.

I've known Antonio for a long time now. We have watched the various evolutions of the Java ecosystem together over the years. I trust his expertise in figuring out where technology is going and avoiding the latest shiny object distraction. So when a seasoned developer like him jumps on Quarkus, loves it and wants to invest his time in it, that, to me is a ringing endorsement that the project is doing something right and addressing key problems.

I'm really pleased Antonio embarked on this Quarkus book adventure. He has a deep understanding of the developer community: from customers to community members, from freelancers to big enterprise development teams. I trust his ability to explain technology in a practical way and he offers readers the knowledge and building blocks to solve their problems.

Fun fact about Quarkus: we knew we needed to strike a balance between "*new + revolutionary*" and "*familiar + boring*". One key aspect of Quarkus is how it offers very familiar APIs and programming concepts but it's packaged with boosted usefulness. Antonio is one of the most expert people I know on the APIs and technologies Quarkus exposes: CDI, RESTEasy, Hibernate, Eclipse MicroProfile and many more.

One of Quarkus' philosophies is "*Developer Joy*". This is realised, in part, by making developers deliver their applications faster, by being more practical. But it is also built on a very solid technological foundation. This book is written with the same philosophy, it gets you to solve the concrete problems you have while distilling the fundamental knowledge you need to go to the next level.

When we released Quarkus to the community, we thought we were onto something. But what you think and what the world thinks are often distinctly different. It's amazing how Quarkus caught fire. More importantly, I am really happy when I hear users telling me how Quarkus has addressed their key Cloud Native needs and concerns: short development cycles, the need for high density deployments (less RAM per instance), and the need for fast startup times - for microservices or functions. Even better, they love the experience of using it.

The future of Java as a solution for writing Cloud Native applications deployed in Kubernetes had been questioned. This is no longer the case and I think Quarkus is the answer. I hope this book will spread the word far and wide and help more developers and more teams be productive with Java and our new way of writing modern applications.

Emmanuel Bernard
Co-founder of Quarkus at Red Hat
@emmanuelbernard

[1] **KDP** https://kdp.amazon.com

About the Author

I am a senior software architect living in Paris. Having been focused on Java development since the late 1990s, my career took me to many different countries and companies where I now work as a recognised consultant. As a former employee of BEA Systems (acquired by Oracle), I developed a very early expertise on distributed systems. I am particularly fond of open source and I am a member of the OSSGTP[3] (*Open Source Solution Get Together Paris*). I love to create bonds with the community. So, I created the Paris Java User Group[4] in 2008 and co-created Devoxx France[5] in 2012 and Voxxed Microservices in 2018[6].

I wrote my first book on Java EE 5[7], in French, in 2007. I then joined the JCP[8] to become an Expert Member of various JSRs (Java EE 8, Java EE 7, Java EE 6, CDI 2.0, JPA 2.0, and EJB 3.1) and wrote *Beginning Java EE 6* and *Beginning Java EE 7* with Apress[9]. Still hooked on sharing my knowledge, I decided to then self-publish my later fascicles as well as on-line video courses.

For the last few years, I have given talks at international conferences, mainly on Java, distributed systems and microservices, including JavaOne, Devoxx, GeeCon, The Server Side Symposium, Jazoon, and many JUGs (*Java User Groups*). I also wrote numerous technical papers and articles for IT websites (DevX) and IT magazines (Java Magazine, Programmez, Linux Magazine). Since 2009, I have been part of the French Java podcast called *Les Cast Codeurs*[10].

In recognition of my expertise and all of my work for the Java community, I was elected **Java Champion**[11].

I am a graduate of the *Conservatoire National des Arts et Métiers*[12] (CNAM) in Paris (with an engineering degree in IT), *Brighton University*[13] (with an MSc in object-oriented design), *Universidad del Pais Vasco*[14] in Spain, and *UFSCar University*[15] in Brazil (MPhil in Distributed Systems). I also taught for more than 10 years at the Conservatoire National des Arts et Métiers where I previously studied.

Follow me on Twitter (@agoncal) and on my blog (www.antoniogoncalves.org).

[3] OSSGTP https://www.ossgtp.org

[4] Paris JUG https://www.parisjug.org

[5] Devoxx France https://devoxx.fr

[6] Voxxed Microservices https://voxxeddays.com/microservices

[7] Amazon https://www.amazon.com/author/agoncal

[8] JCP https://jcp.org

[9] Amazon https://www.amazon.com/author/agoncal

[10] Les Cast Codeurs https://lescastcodeurs.com

[11] Java Champions https://developer.oracle.com/javachampions

[12] CNAM https://www.cnam.eu/site-en

[13] Brighton University https://www.brighton.ac.uk

[14] Universidad del Pais Vasco https://www.ehu.eus/en/en-home

[15] UFSCar https://www.ufscar.br

Acknowledgments

In your hands, you have a technical fascicle that comes from my history of writing, learning and sharing. When writing, you need a dose of curiosity, a glimpse of discipline, an inch of concentration, and a huge amount of craziness. And of course, you need to be surrounded by people who help you in any possible way (so you don't get totally crazy). And this is the space to thank them.

First of all, it is a great honour to have **Emmanuel Bernard** writing the foreword of this book. Thank you for this difficult exercise that is writing foreword for a technical book.

Then, I really want to thank my proofreading team. I was constantly in contact with them during the writing process. They reviewed the book and gave me precious advice. I have to say, it was a real pleasure to work with such knowledgeable developers.

Georgios Andrianakis[16] is a Senior Software Engineer at Red Hat where he works on Quarkus and Spring-related technologies. As one of the most active Quarkus contributors, Georgios has spoken at various conferences, such as Devoxx, spreading his enthusiasm for Quarkus. Moreover, he is also a co-organiser of the Athens Kubernetes Meetup. He lives in Athens, Greece.

Roberto Cortez[17] is a professional Java Developer working in the software development industry for more than 10 years. He is involved within the Open Source Community in helping other individuals spread the knowledge about Java technologies. He is a regular speaker at conferences suc as JavaOne, Devoxx, Devnexus, JFokus and others. He leads the Coimbra JUG and founded the JNation Conference in Portugal. When he is not working, he hangs out with friends, plays computer games and spends time with his family. Currently, he leads the SmallRye initiative at Red Hat.

From deep in the Nice mountains, **Stéphane Épardaud**[18] works for Red Hat on the Vert.x, RESTEasy, MicroProfile Context Propagation and Quarkus projects. He is a passionate hacker in Java, C, Perl or Scheme. He likes web standards, languages and databases. Eager to share, he is a frequent speaker at various conferences, co-leads the Riviera Java User Group and co-created the Riviera DEV conference.

George Gastaldi[19] is a Principal Software Engineer working remotely for Red Hat from Brazil. George has been an experienced Java developer and architect since 2000 and was introduced to the Open Source world in 2006. Since 2019, he has enjoyed spending his time as a core developer in Quarkus.

Youness Teimouri[20] is currently a Senior Software Developer in Silicon Valley with over 15 years of development experience, particularly in Java, across various countries. He has utilised Java stack to help numerous companies scale in a variety of industries such as Telecoms, ERP systems, Mobile Banking, and Payment systems, etc. He has co-authored and contributed to some papers on Cloud-Computing and some of my previous books. Youness is fascinated by the endless possibilities of Java in different industries and enjoys mentoring junior developers, inspiring them to develop their own Java skill-set. And thank you Youness for still being around (this is the 7th book he has reviewed).

Nicolas Martignole[21] is currently a Principal Engineer at Doctolib in Paris. He is also a Senior Java/Scala developer. He co-created Devoxx France with Antonio after a few years as one of the core members of the Paris JUG. He discovered Quarkus and with his strong background as a Play Framework developer, he was really impressed by the ideas and the developer experience. He co-authored TimeKeeper[22], an open-source project based on Quarkus, Keycloak and React.

Thanks to my proofreader, **Gary Branigan**, who added a Shakespearean touch to the fascicle.

I could not have written this fascicle without the help and support of the Java community: blogs, articles, mailing lists, forums, tweets etc.

The fascicle you have in your hands uses a rich Asciidoctor[23] toolchain, making it possible to create PDF, EPUB and MOBI files. I am really grateful to the entire Asciidoctor community, and to Dan Allen[24] and Marat Radchenko in particular, who helped me in sorting out a few things so that the end result looks so great. PlantUML[25] is an amazing tool with a very rich syntax for drawing diagrams, etc. and sometimes, you need a bit of help. So, thanks to the PlantUML community. As for the text editor used to write this fascicle, you might have guessed: it's an IDE! Thank you JetBrains for providing me with a free licence for your excellent IntelliJ IDEA[26].

Living in Paris, I also have to thank all the bars who have given me shelter so that I could write while drinking coffee and talking to people: La Fontaine, Le Chat Bossu, La Grille, La Liberté and Bottle Shop.

As you might have guessed, I have a passion for IT. But I have other passions such as science, art, philosophy, cooking, Tango dancing and music (I even play jazz guitar). I cannot work without listening to music, so while I was writing this fascicle, I spent most of my time listing to the best radio ever: FIP[27]. Thank you FIP.

And a big kiss to my wonderful kids, **Eloise**, **Ligia** and **Ennio**. They are the best present life has given me.

Thank you all!

[16] Georgios Andrianakis https://twitter.com/geoand86

[17] Roberto Cortez https://twitter.com/radcortez

[18] Stéphane Épardaud https://twitter.com/unfromage

[19] George Gastaldi https://twitter.com/gegastaldi

[20] Youness Teimouri http://www.youness-teimouri.com

[21] Nicolas Martignole https://twitter.com/nmartignole

[22] TimeKeeper https://github.com/lunatech-labs/lunatech-timekeeper

[23] Asciidoctor http://asciidoctor.org

[24] Dan Allen https://twitter.com/mojavelinux

[25] PlantUML http://plantuml.com

[26] IntelliJ IDEA https://www.jetbrains.com/idea

[27] FIP https://www.fip.fr

Introduction

In the late 90s, I was working on J2EE 1.2: the very first release of the *Java Enterprise Edition*. It was also the time where companies started to realise the potential of the Internet for their business. For a few months, I worked for a famous English airline company setting up their e-commerce website. Yes, it was a time where you would usually buy a flight or train ticket at a travel agency. This revolutionary move (buying flights online) came at a technical cost: a cluster for static content (HTML, CSS, images), a cluster for the web tier (Servlets and JSPs), a cluster for Stateless EJBs, a cluster for Entity Beans, and a cluster for the database. And as you can imagine, load balancing, failover and sticky sessions for every tier were loaded with application servers. This e-commerce website went live... and it worked!

Then came Struts, Spring and Hibernate. Full J2EE application servers shrank down to servlet containers such as Tomcat or Jetty. We could see things moving, such as architectures becoming stateless, failover being abandoned, migrations from SOAP to REST and mobile devices taking over web crawling. Then came the *Internet of Things* (IoT), the cloud, microservices, *Function as a Service* (FaaS), and it never stops moving. Other things didn't change, like the good old *Gang of Four* design patterns, architecture design patterns, unit testing frameworks and building tools. We reinvented some wheels and gave them different names, but we also learnt dozens of new promising programming languages (running on top of the JVM or not) and agile techniques. Thanks to these evolutions that I have witnessed, today you can sit down, read this fascicle and write some code.

Where Does This Fascicle Come From?

Involved in J2EE since 1998, I followed its evolution and joined the Java EE expert group from version 6 to version 8. During that time, I wrote a book in French called "*Java EE 5*"[28]. The book was published by a French editor and got noticed. I was then contacted by Apress, an American editor, to work on an English version. I liked the challenge. So, I changed the structure of the book, updated it, translated it, and I ended up with a "*Beginning Java EE 6*" book. A few years later, Java EE 7 was released, so I updated my book, added a few extra chapters, and ended up with a "*Beginning Java EE 7*"[29] that was 500 pages long. This process of writing got a bit painful (some text editors shouldn't be used to write books), inflexible (it's hard to update a paper book frequently) and I also had some arguments with my editor[30].

Parallel to that, the history of Java EE 8 was also somewhat painful and long[31]. I was still part of the Expert Group, but nobody really knew why the experts' mailing list was so quiet. No real exchange, no real vision, no real challenges. That's when I decided not to work on a Java EE 8 book. But the community said otherwise. I started receiving emails about updating my book. I used to always meet someone at a conference going "*Hey, Antonio, when is your next book coming out?*" My answer was "*No way!*"

I decided to take stock. What was holding me back from writing? Clearly it was my editor and Java EE 8. So, I decided to get rid of both. I extracted the chapters I wanted from my Java EE 7 book and updated them. That's where the idea of writing "*fascicles*", instead of an entire book, came from. Then, I looked at self-publishing, and here I am on my own publishing platform[32] as well as on Amazon Kindle Publishing[33].

After self-publishing a few fascicles, I saw that Red Hat was working on a game changer: Quarkus. I started to look at it at a very early stage, and got the idea of creating a workshop. I contacted the Quarkus team to submit my idea: Emmanuel Bernard and Clement Escoffier liked it, and we put together a workshop[34] and gave it at a few conferences. This workshop inspired a first fascicle: *Practising Quarkus 2.x*. I liked Quarkus so much that I started using it at customers for proof of concepts and then bringing it to production. I started to write a few blogs, a few articles and then I decided to write a fascicle on Quarkus as well as created a few online courses. The fascicle you have in your hands is for you to have an understanding of what Quarkus is and how you can use it for your microservice architecture.

I hope you'll find this fascicle useful.

Who Is This Fascicle For?

Quarkus has its genesis in the JBoss community. JBoss has a long expertise on running applications on application servers (JBoss EAP, WildFly) or building reactive applications on the JVM (with Eclipse Vert.x for example). Due to its extension mechanism, Quarkus supports several Java frameworks (e.g. Hibernate, Camel, etc.) as well as specifications (e.g. a subset of Jakarta EE, or MicroProfile which is a set of specifications to develop microservices in Java).

So, this fascicle is for the Java community as a whole and for those of you interested in microservice architectures. The only requirement to follow and understand this fascicle is to know Java and have some knowledge of relational databases and Docker.

How Is This Fascicle Structured?

This fascicle uses Quarkus 2.5.0.Final. Its structure will help you to discover this technology as well as helping you to further dive into it if you already have some experience of it.

This fascicle starts with Chapter 1, *First Look at Quarkus* by showing a few lines of Quarkus code. That's because, as developers, we like to read code first when learning a new technology.

Chapter 2, *Understanding Quarkus* sets up some terminology (Microservices, Reactive Systems, MicroProfile, Cloud Native, GraalVM) and briefly presents Quarkus, the problems it addresses and explains the common concerns discussed throughout the fascicle.

Chapter 3, *Getting Started* is all about showing some basic code running on Quarkus and explaining how to run and test such application before building and packaging a native executable version of it.

Quarkus has a powerful extension mechanism for integration with many technologies. Chapter 4, *Core Quarkus* focuses on the core technologies of Quarkus such as injection, configuration and profiles.

Microservices are trendy and use all sorts of design patterns. But all in all, most microservices need to interact with data. Chapter 5, *Data, Transactions and ORM* covers data validation, object-relational mapping and transactions. In this chapter, you will also see ORM with Panache which is an easy way to manipulate persistent data.

When it comes to microservices, the first thing that comes to our minds is: HTTP microservices.

Chapter 6, *HTTP Microservices* presents most of the HTTP-related technologies such as RESTful web services, OpenAPI v3 and JSON manipulation.

One microservice does not make a microservice architecture. You need several of them talking to each other. Chapter 7, *Communication and Fault Tolerance* is all about microservices invoking each other through HTTP and making sure they can fallback if communication does not work.

Reactive programming and reactive messaging are covered in Chapter 8, *Event-Driven Microservices*.

When you have several microservices, observability becomes a real challenge. So you need to know which microservices are alive and ready, and expose some metrics so you know they are performing as expected. Chapter 9, *Observability* covers the MicroProfile specifications dealing with observability: Health and Metrics.

When there are many microservices, you need to package them into containers and orchestrate them with an orchestrator. In Chapter 10, *Cloud Native* you'll see the different formats used by Quarkus to package your code, and then how Quarkus extensions make it easy to interact with Docker and Kubernetes.

One thing that Quarkus is really good at, is testing. Chapter 11, *Tests* digs into JVM and Native Mode testing in Quarkus, as well as all the testing and mocking frameworks it supports.

In Chapter 12, *Putting It All Together*, you'll build a more complex application with several concepts that have been introduced throughout this fascicle.

Chapter 13, *Summary* wraps up with a summary of what you've learnt in this fascicle.

Appendix A, *Setting up the Development Environment on macOS* highlights the tools used throughout the fascicle and how to install them.

Appendix B, *Quarkus Versions* lists all the Quarkus releases.

Appendix C, *Eclipse MicroProfile Specification Versions* lists all the revisions of the MicroProfile specification.

Appendix D points to some external references which are worth reading if you want to know more about Quarkus.

Thanks to self-publication and electronic format, I can update this fascicle regularly when typos or bugs are discovered. Appendix E, *Revisions of the Fascicle* gives you the revision notes of each version of this fascicle.

This is not the only fascicle I have written. You'll find a description of the other fascicles I wrote and online courses I created in Appendix F:

- *Understanding Bean Validation 2.0*
- *Understanding JPA 2.2*
- *Understanding Quarkus 2.x*
- *Practising Quarkus 2.x*

Conventions

This fascicle uses a diverse range of languages, mostly Java, but also JSON, XML, YAML or shell scripts. Each code example is displayed appropriately and appears in `fixed-width font`. All the included code comes from a public Git repository and is continuously tested. Therefore, you shouldn't have any problem with code that is not syntactically correct. In some cases, the original source code has been specially formatted to fit within the available page space, with additional line breaks or modified indentation. To increase readability, some examples omit code where it is seen as unnecessary. But always remember that you can find the entire code online at https://github.com/agoncal/agoncal-fascicle-quarkus/tree/2.0.

Italics are used to *highlight an important word for the first time*, or to give the definition of an abbreviation or *acronym*. Bold is **rarely used**.

 Some useful information.

 Something you really should do if you want the code to work properly.

 Warns you of a possible technical problem.

The Sample Application

Throughout the book, you will see snippets of code all belonging to the Vintage Store application. I created this application for my very first book a long time ago, and I still use it as an example. This application is an e-commerce website allowing users to browse a catalogue of vintage stuff (vinyl, tapes, books and CDs). Using a shopping cart, they can add or remove items as they browse the catalogue and then check out so that they can pay and obtain a purchase order. The application has external interactions with a bank system to validate credit card numbers.

The actors interacting with the system are:

- *Employees* of the company who need to manage both the catalogue of items and the customers' details. They can also browse the purchase orders.
- *Users* who are anonymous persons visiting the website and who are consulting the catalogue of books and CDs. If they want to buy an item, they need to create an account to become customers.
- *Customers* who can login to the system, browse the catalogue, update their account details, and buy items online.
- The external *Bank* to which the system delegates credit card validations.

Figure 1 depicts the use case diagram which describes the system's actors and functionalities.

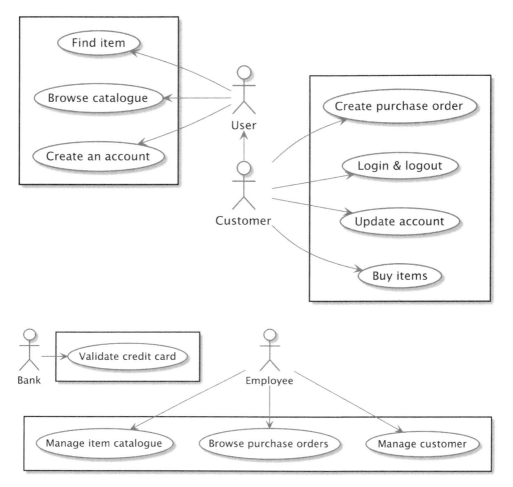

Figure 1. Use case diagram of the Vintage Store application

The Vintage Store application manipulates a few domain objects that are described in Figure 2. Vinyl, tapes, books and CDs, of course, but also chapters, authors, purchase orders, invoices and shopping carts. Don't spend too much time on this diagram for now as you will come across most of these objects throughout this fascicle.

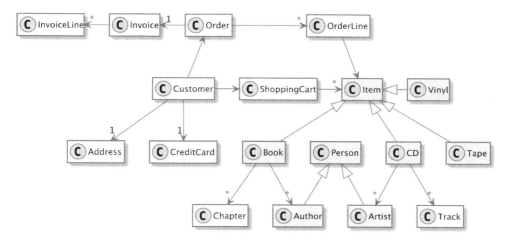

Figure 2. Class diagram of the Vintage Store application

 The code you'll see in this fascicle gets its inspiration from the Vintage Store application, but it's not the original application per-se. You can download the code of the original application if you want, but it's not necessary in order to follow the code[35] of this fascicle.

Downloading and Running the Code

The source code of the examples in the fascicle is available from a public Git repository and can be cloned, downloaded or browsed online at https://github.com/agoncal/agoncal-fascicle-quarkus/tree/2.0. The code has been developed and tested on the macOS platform but should also work on Windows or Linux. The examples used in this fascicle are designed to be compiled with Java 11, to be built with Maven 3.8.3 and to be tested with JUnit 5.x and to store data in a relational database (H2 and PostgreSQL). GraalVM 21.3.0 is used to build native images. Appendix A shows you how to install all of these software packages which will be used in most of the chapters to build, run and test the code.

Getting Help

Having trouble with the code, the content or the structure of the fascicle? Didn't understand something? Not clear enough? I am here to help! Do not hesitate to report issues or any questions at https://github.com/agoncal/agoncal-fascicle-quarkus/issues. I'll do my best to answer them. This will also allow me to improve the content of this fascicle, and upload a new version through Amazon Kindle Publishing.

Contacting the Author

If you have any questions about the content of this fascicle, please use the instructions above and use the GitHub issue tracker. But if you feel like contacting me, drop me an email at agoncal.fascicle@gmail.com or a tweet at @agoncal. You can also visit my blog at:

- www.antoniogoncalves.org

- agoncal.teachable.com

[28] Antonio's books http://amazon.com/author/agoncal

[29] Antonio's Books https://antoniogoncalves.org/category/books

[30] The Uncensored Java EE 7 Book https://antoniogoncalves.org/2014/09/16/the-uncensored-java-ee-7-book

[31] Opening Up Java EE https://blogs.oracle.com/theaquarium/post/opening-up-java-ee-an-update

[32] Antonio Goncalves https://antoniogoncalves.org

[33] Amazon Kindle Publishing https://kdp.amazon.com

[34] Quarkus workshop https://quarkus.io/quarkus-workshops/super-heroes

[35] Code of the Vintage Store application https://github.com/agoncal/agoncal-application-cdbookstore

Chapter 1. First Look at Quarkus

If you are reading this fascicle, it's because you are a developer. And like most developers, when you learn a new technology or framework, you like to see some code first. So here is the very first step with Quarkus.

Listing 1 shows a Java class representing an *Author* REST resource. This resource "*listens*" to HTTP requests on the /authors URL and has two methods: one returning the entire list of sci-fi authors, and another one returning a single author giving the index of the array.

Listing 1. Java Class with JAX-RS Annotations

```java
@Path("/authors")
@Produces(MediaType.TEXT_PLAIN)
public class AuthorResource {

  String[] scifiAuthors = {"Isaac Asimov", "Nora Jemisin", "Douglas Adams"};

  @GET
  public String getAllScifiAuthors() {
    return String.join(", ", scifiAuthors);
  }

  @GET
  @Path("/{index}")
  public String getScifiAuthor(@PathParam("index") int index) {
    return scifiAuthors[index];
  }
}
```

If you look carefully at Listing 1, you can see a few JAX-RS annotations (@Path, @Produces, @GET, and @PathParam) but no specific Quarkus code (don't worry if you don't know JAX-RS, Chapter 6 covers it). So where is Quarkus?

Actually, you can find a little bit of Quarkus in Listing 2 (because most of the code is from REST Assured, which you will see in Chapter 11). Here, we use the @QuarkusTest annotation to let Quarkus test the *Author* REST resource. We target the URL /authors with an HTTP GET method (with and without an index parameter), and we make sure the HTTP status code is 200-OK and that the content of the HTTP body is correct.

Listing 2. Test Class with a Quarkus Annotation

```java
@QuarkusTest
public class AuthorResourceTest {

  @Test
  public void shouldGetAllAuthors() {
    given()
      .header(ACCEPT, TEXT_PLAIN).
    when()
      .get("/authors").
    then()
      .assertThat()
        .statusCode(is(200))
      .and()
        .body(is("Isaac Asimov, Nora Jemisin, Douglas Adams"));
  }

  @Test
  public void shouldGetAnAuthor() {
    given()
      .header(ACCEPT, TEXT_PLAIN)
      .pathParam("index", 0).
    when()
      .get("/authors/{index}").
    then()
      .assertThat()
        .statusCode(is(200))
      .and()
        .body(is("Isaac Asimov"));
  }
}
```

You didn't understand all the code? You did understand it but you feel there is more to it than that? The fascicle you have in your hands is all about Quarkus. Thanks to the chapters that follow, you will understand the basics of this technology and will have plenty of examples so that you can dive into more complex topics.

Chapter 2. Understanding Quarkus

In the previous *First Step with Quarkus* chapter, you've already seen some code. But before going further into more code, we need to step back and define some concepts. This *Understanding* chapter gives you some terminology that will be used in the rest of the fascicle so you don't get lost.

So, what is Quarkus? Quarkus[36] is *A Kubernetes Native Java stack tailored for OpenJDK HotSpot & GraalVM, crafted from the best of breed Java libraries and standards*. In practice, Quarkus is an Open Source stack for writing Java applications, specifically back end applications. So Quarkus is not limited to microservices, even though it is highly suited for it.

Just by reading the definition of Quarkus, you can see that there are many technologies involved: Java, of course, but also GraalVM, Reactive Systems and Kubernetes. For the standards, Quarkus supports some Jakarta EE and MicroProfile specifications. Let's have a look at all these pieces.

2.1. Understanding Microservices

Microservices[37] is *the* most popular architecture style when creating cloud native applications. It significantly shortens the time to market of new application features by changing, testing and deploying each service, individually, without affecting other services. A well-designed and right-sized microservice architecture can help engineer an application that is stable, scalable and fault tolerant.

2.1.1. Monolith

When talking about microservices, we need to understand its counterpart: the monolith[38]. A few decades ago, it was common to develop an application that could fulfil all your business needs while running isolated on a single machine. Such applications had a graphical interface, processed business operations, stored data in a local database, accessed custom files, but also took advantage of various remote code operations (e.g. accessing remote data stores, remote services, etc.). These *Monoliths*, as shown in Figure 3, are built as a single unit and deployed as a single logical executable.

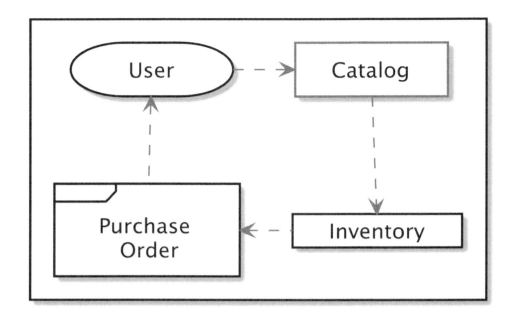

Figure 3. Monolith

2.1.2. Microservices

The difficulties associated with developing, testing, fixing, and updating applications have relegated big monolithic applications to the past. Today, application architecture must support agile and continuous development by decomposing systems into smaller services focused on specific business domains. These domain-specific services can then be developed and modified independently according to evolving business needs, without impacting the system as a whole.

Decomposing a monolith into independent microservices (see Figure 4), on the whole or only partially while leaving the remaining functionality unchanged, has many advantages. For example, each microservice is easy to understand, develop and maintain. A microservice can be deployed, scaled and run independently. Changes to one microservice can be done without the risk of side effects on other microservices. Such advantages help shorten the time to market by facilitating advanced agility.

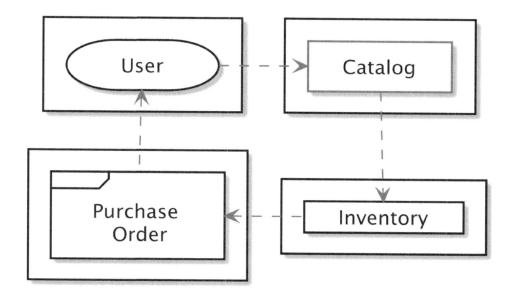

Figure 4. Microservices

As shown in Figure 5, microservice architectures tend to use external services, possibly controlled by a third-party provider. Examples would be delegating authentication to popular account providers like Google, Facebook or Twitter, email processing to MailChimp or MailJet, payments to Paypal or Strip, invoices to and.co, etc.

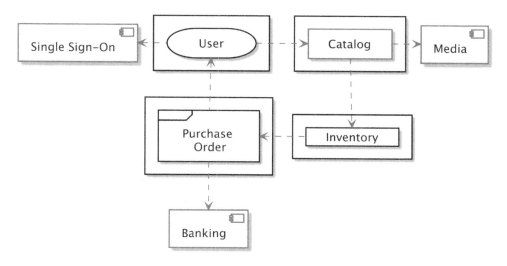

Figure 5. Microservices invoking external services

2.1.3. Pros and Cons

Like any architectural style, microservices bring costs and benefits[19]. So before diving into microservices, you have to understand these and apply them to your specific context. Microservices provide the following benefits:

- *Strong Module Boundaries*: Microservices reinforce modular structure, which is particularly important for larger teams.
- *Independent Deployment*: Simple services are easier to deploy, and since they are autonomous, are less likely to cause system failures when they go wrong.
- *Technology Diversity*: You can mix multiple languages, development frameworks and data-storage technologies (i.e. each team working on a microservice has more flexibility to employ different technologies without affecting other teams).

But microservices also come with costs:

- *Distribution*: Distributed systems are harder to program since remote calls are slow and are always at risk of failure.
- *Eventual Consistency*: Maintaining strong consistency is extremely difficult for a distributed system, which means everyone has to manage eventual consistency.
- *Operational Complexity*: You need a mature operations team to manage lots of services which are being redeployed regularly.

That's when Quarkus comes into play. Quarkus brings a set of functionalities to reduce these costs and lets you focus on the benefits of a microservice architecture. When reading about microservices, you might come across the word *Reactive Systems* which embeds a few other techniques. That's because microservices and reactive systems go hand in hand. To help you in building reactive microservices, Quarkus integrates reactive messaging and reactive programming.

2.2. Understanding Reactive

The term *Reactive* has been around for a few decades, but it has gained momentum lately with cloud native microservices. *Reactive* means that you *show a response to a stimulus*. With this definition, you can think of a keyboard that responds to a pressed key, a spreadsheet cell that recalculates itself when another cell changes, etc. Reactive is everywhere. But *Reactive* often comes associated with other words such as *"Manifesto"*, *"Systems"*, *"Streams"*, *"Programming"*, or *"Messaging"*:

- *Reactive systems*: Systems that are modelled to *react to a stimulus*, such as a message, a request, a metric, etc.
- *Reactive streams*: Stream processing with non-blocking backpressure.
- *Reactive programming*: Programming model (based on *Reactive streams*) on which reactive systems depend on.

Before defining these concepts, let's first introduce the *Reactive Manifesto*.

2.2.1. Reactive Manifesto

The *Reactive Manifesto*[40] is a document that defines the core principles of reactive systems. It was first released in 2013 by a group of developers explaining the reasons behind the manifesto[41]. The four properties of reactive systems are: responsive, resilient, elastic and message-driven as shown in Figure 6.

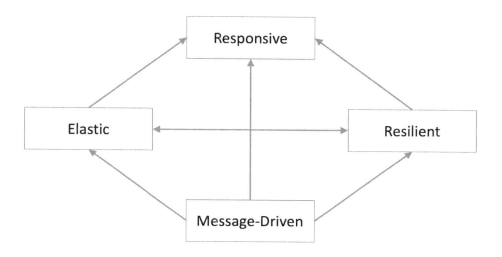

Figure 6. Reactive Manifesto

The manifesto defines each property as:

- *Elastic*: Is the ability of an application to work with a variable number of instances. This is useful as elasticity allows responding to traffic spikes by starting new instances, and load-balancing traffic across instances.

- *Resilient*: When one instance in a group of elastic instances crashes, then traffic is redirected to other instances (and a new instance can be started).

- *Responsive*: Is the result of combining elasticity and resiliency to respond in a timely manner.

- *Message-Driven*: Using asynchronous messages is the key enabler for elasticity and resiliency, and this leads to responsivity.

Reactive Principles

The *Reactive Principles*[42] is also an important source of inspiration for designing distributed applications. This document is a companion to the Reactive Manifesto as it incorporates the ideas, paradigms, methods and patterns from both Reactive Programming and Reactive Systems into a set of practical principles.

With these definitions in mind, let's see why and how we can apply them to an entire system.

2.2.2. Reactive Systems

Our world is changing! In 2005, an application would use a dozen servers hosted internally, the response time would be counted in seconds, we would use a few hours a year for offline maintenance, and we would handle a few gigabytes of data. Today we handle thousands of multicore processors somewhere in a datacentre, response time is in milliseconds, we need 100% uptime, and we have changed our metrics to petabytes for data. This all demands that applications a written in a fundamentally different way than what most programmers were used to. Today, systems are designed with multicore and cloud computing architectures, as well as user requirements, low latency and higher throughput in mind. That's when reactive systems can help.

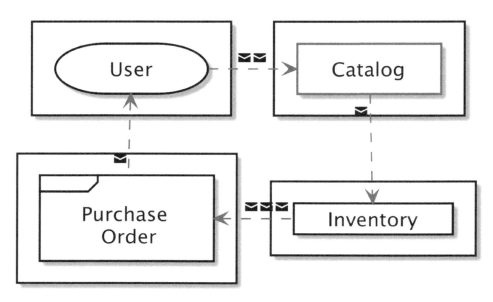

Figure 7. Reactive microservices

As shown in Figure 7, reactive systems rely on asynchronous messages (a.k.a. events) to communicate between microservices. This ensures loose coupling between microservices, but also isolation and location transparency. Employing messages enables load management, elasticity, and flow control by monitoring the message queues in the system and applying backpressure when necessary. Messages can be dispatched to more instances (making the system elastic), and we can control the flow between message producers and message consumers (this is *backpressure*[13]). Location transparency makes it possible for the management of failure to work either across a cluster or within a single host. Non-blocking communication allows recipients to only consume resources while active, leading to less system overhead. This has an interesting impact on the code where reactive streams and reactive programming are needed.

2.2.3. Reactive Streams

Everything in the reactive world is accomplished with the help of *Reactive Streams*[14]. Reactive streams is a standard specification created in 2013 as the reactive programming model was beginning to spread, and more frameworks for reactive programming were starting to emerge in various languages. It is now implemented across various frameworks and platforms. The core goal is to standardise the exchange of asynchronous data between software components with non-blocking backpressure.

Reactive streams is a very low-level contract, expressed as a handful of concepts applicable in many languages, including Java:

- *Publisher*: Publishes an unlimited number of sequenced messages according to the demand received from its subscriber(s).
- *Subscriber*: Subscribes to a given publisher and then receives messages.
- *Subscription*: Represents a one-to-one life cycle of a subscriber subscribing to a publisher.
- *Processor*: If an entity is both a publisher and a subscriber, it is called a processor. A processor commonly acts as an intermediary between another publisher and subscriber.

Figure 8 shows the sequence of interactions between a subscriber and a publisher. A subscriber informs a publisher that it is willing to accept a given number of messages (a.k.a. events, items, records). Then, the publisher notifies the subscriber of the subscription that was created. Once this notification process is completed, the subscriber can inform the publisher that it is ready to receive *n* number of messages. The publisher pushes the maximum receivable number of messages to the subscriber. The process of restricting the number of messages that a subscriber is willing to accept is called backpressure: it is essential in prohibiting overloading the subscriber.

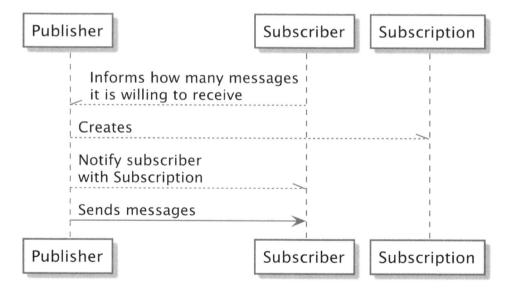

Figure 8. Subscriber and publisher interacting

 Reactive Streams interfaces have been added to the Java platform since version 9. They include basic interfaces for each of the fundamental Reactive Stream concepts in the `Flow` concurrency[45] library. This allows all Java applications to depend on these interfaces rather than using a specific implementation.

In Chapter 8, you will see how Quarkus makes reactive programming easy with Mutiny and how it handles reactive messages.

2.3. Understanding MicroProfile

Having an extension mechanism (described below), Quarkus implements many features and integrates with many external frameworks. Furthermore, being microservices-oriented, Quarkus integrates the entire set of specifications of Eclipse MicroProfile through *SmallRye*.

Eclipse MicroProfile[46] addresses the need for enterprise Java microservices. It is a set of specifications for handling microservices design patterns. MicroProfile enables Jakarta EE developers to leverage their existing skill set while shifting their focus from traditional monolithic applications to microservices. MicroProfile APIs establish an optimal foundation for developing microservices-based applications by adopting a subset of the Jakarta EE standards and extending them to address common microservices patterns. *Eclipse MicroProfile* is specified under the *Eclipse Foundation* and is implemented by *SmallRye*.

Jakarta EE

Even if Quarkus does not rely on Jakarta EE, it supports some of its specifications, and so does Eclipse MicroProfile. So it's worth mentioning it.

Created in 1998, Java EE (*Java Enterprise Edition*[47]) can be seen as an extension of the *Java Standard Edition* (Java SE). It is a set of specifications intended for enterprise applications in order to facilitate the development of distributed, transactional, and secure applications. It is developed using the JCP (*Java Community Process*[48]), with contributions from industry experts and commercial and open source organisations.

In 2017, with version 8 of the platform, Java EE was donated to the Eclipse Foundation[49] and renamed *Jakarta EE*[50]. Jakarta EE is the name of the platform governed by the Jakarta EE Working Group. The first version is Jakarta EE 8, which is based on the Java EE 8 technologies. Future versions will not be driven by the JCP but through the open *Eclipse Foundation*.

2.3.1. Eclipse Foundation

The *Eclipse Foundation*[51] is an independent, non-profit entity that acts as a steward for the Eclipse open source software development community. The Foundation focuses on key services such as: intellectual property management, ecosystem development, development process, and IT infrastructure. It was created by IBM in 2001 and is now supported by a consortium of several software vendors (Red Hat, Huawei, Bosch, Fujitsu, SAP, Oracle, etc.).

2.3.2. SmallRye

SmallRye[52] is an open source project that implements the Eclipse MicroProfile specifications. It is community-driven and everyone is welcome to contribute to it. SmallRye implementations are tested against the Eclipse MicroProfile TCKs (*Technology Compatibility Kits*). Several open source projects integrate SmallRye such as Thorntail, WildFly, WebSphere Liberty and Quarkus.

2.3.3. MicroProfile Specifications

Quarkus integrates version 4.1 of MicroProfile (see Appendix C if you want to see all the previous revisions of the specification). MicroProfile 4.1 specifications are described in Table 1. You'll find specifications that come from Jakarta EE (e.g. CDI, JAX-RS, etc.) as well as brand new specifications that were created with microservices in mind.

Table 1. MicroProfile 4.1 Specifications

Specification	Version	URL
Context and Dependency Injection (CDI)	2.0	https://jcp.org/en/jsr/detail?id=365
Java API for RESTful Web Services (JAX-RS)	2.1	https://jcp.org/en/jsr/detail?id=370
JSON Binding (JSON-B)	1.0	https://jcp.org/en/jsr/detail?id=367
JSON Processing (JSON-P)	1.1	https://jcp.org/en/jsr/detail?id=374
Common Annotations	1.3	https://jcp.org/en/jsr/detail?id=250
Configuration	2.0	https://microprofile.io/project/eclipse/microprofile-config
Fault Tolerance	3.0	https://microprofile.io/project/eclipse/microprofile-fault-tolerance
Health	3.1	https://microprofile.io/project/eclipse/microprofile-health
JSON Web Token (JWT)	1.2	https://microprofile.io/project/eclipse/microprofile-jwt-auth
Metrics	3.0	https://microprofile.io/project/eclipse/microprofile-metrics
OpenAPI	2.0	https://microprofile.io/project/eclipse/microprofile-open-api
OpenTracing	2.0	https://microprofile.io/project/eclipse/microprofile-opentracing
REST Client	2.0	https://microprofile.io/project/eclipse/microprofile-rest-client

CDI

Context and Dependency Injection[53] (CDI) is a central technology in Jakarta EE or in MicroProfile. Its programming model turns nearly every component into an injectable, interceptable and manageable bean. CDI is built on the concept of "*loose coupling, strong typing*", meaning that beans are loosely coupled, but in a strongly-typed way. Decoupling goes further by bringing interceptors, decorators and events to the entire platform. CDI homogenises scopes among beans, as well as context and life cycle management. Quarkus uses CDI extensively. However, it is not a full CDI implementation verified by the TCK. CDI being runtime based and not compile time based, Quarkus decided to only implement the most useful CDI features that could be generated at compile time. Chapter 4 covers how to use CDI injection within Quarkus.

JAX-RS

Java API for RESTful Web Services[54] (JAX-RS) is a specification that provides support for creating web services according to the Representational State Transfer (REST) architectural style. JAX-RS provides a set of annotations and classes/interfaces to simplify the development and deployment of REST endpoints. It also brings a client API to programmatically invoke REST endpoints. Chapter 6 covers how to use JAX-RS to expose RESTful web services. In Chapter 7, you will see how HTTP microservices can invoke each other using REST Client (which is based on JAX-RS).

JSON-B

JSON Binding[55] (JSON-B) is a standard binding layer for converting Java objects to/from JSON documents. It defines a default mapping algorithm for converting existing Java classes to JSON while enabling developers to customise the mapping process through the use of Java annotations. JSON-B is used in Chapter 6 to customise the JSON output of RESTful web services.

JSON-P

JSON Processing[56] (JSON-P), is a specification that allows JSON processing in Java. The processing includes mechanisms to parse, generate, transform, and query JSON data. JSON-P provides a standard to build a Java object in JSON using an API similar to DOM for XML. At the same time, it provides a mechanism to produce and consume JSON by streaming in a manner similar to StAX[57] (*Streaming API for XML*) for XML. JSON-P is also used in Chapter 6 to produce JSON output for RESTful web services.

Common Annotations

Common Annotations[58] provides annotations for common semantic concepts across a variety of individual technologies in the Java SE, Jakarta EE and MicroProfile platforms. Table 2 lists a subset of the most commonly used annotations.

Table 2. Main Common Annotations

Annotation	Description
@DenyAll, @PermitAll, @RolesAllowed, @RunAs	Standard annotations based on a simple role-based security model
@Priority	Can be applied to classes or parameters to indicate in what order they should be used
@PostConstruct, @PreDestroy	Used on a method that needs to be executed after being created or before being removed by the container
@Generated	Marks the source code that has been generated by some other API

Configuration

In a microservice architecture, the fact that there is no central runtime implies that there is no single point of configuration, but several points. Each microservice has its own configuration. But sometimes two microservices might want to share a common configuration. In that case, it can be helpful that they access configurations from multiple sources homogeneously and transparently. *Eclipse MicroProfile Configuration*[59] provides applications and microservices with the means to obtain configuration properties through several sources (internal and external to the application), through dependency injection or lookup. Chapter 4 covers configuration in depth.

Fault Tolerance

As the number of services grows, the odds of any service failing also grows. If one of the involved services does not respond as expected, e.g. because of fragile network communication, we have to compensate for this exceptional situation. *Eclipse MicroProfile Fault Tolerance*[60] allows us to build up our microservice architecture to be resilient and fault tolerant by design. This means we must not only be able to detect any issue but also to handle it automatically. Chapter 7 covers different fault tolerance patterns.

Health

Eclipse MicroProfile Health[61] provides the ability to probe the state of a computing node from another machine. The Eclipse MicroProfile Health APIs allow applications to provide information about their state to external viewers which is typically useful in cloud environments where automated processes must be able to determine whether the application should be discarded or restarted. Chapter 9 is all about observability, so that's where you will find Eclipse MicroProfile Health.

Metrics

Eclipse MicroProfile Metrics[62] provides a unified way for MicroProfile servers to export monitoring data to management agents. Metrics will also provide a common Java API for exposing their telemetry data. MicroProfile Metrics allows applications to gather various metrics and statistics that provide insights into what is happening inside the application. The metrics can be read remotely using a JSON or OpenMetrics format to be processed by additional tools such as Prometheus, and stored for analysis and visualisation. MicroProfile Metrics is covered in Chapter 9 as it is related to observing the performance of your microservices.

OpenAPI

Exposing RESTful APIs has become an essential part of all modern applications. From the microservices developer's point of view, it is important to understand how to interact with these APIs and how to test that they are still valid and backward compatible. For that, there needs to be a clear and complete contract. Therefore a standard API documentation mechanism is required and can also be used for API testing. That's when *OpenAPI*[63] comes along.

Eclipse MicroProfile OpenAPI[64] provides a Java API for the OpenAPI v3 specification that all application developers can use to expose their API documentation. It aims to provide a set of Java interfaces and programming models which allow Java developers to natively produce OpenAPI v3 documents from their JAX-RS endpoints. Chapter 6 covers OpenAPI as well as Swagger UI.

REST Client

Eclipse MicroProfile REST Client[65] provides a type safe approach using proxies and annotations for invoking RESTful services over HTTP. The Eclipse MicroProfile REST Client builds upon the JAX-RS

2.1 APIs for consistency and ease-of-use. REST Client will be covered in Chapter 7. Meanwhile, Chapter 6 covers JAX-RS and its client API.

JWT

In a microservice architecture, we need a mechanism to handle distributed authentication and authorisation. *Eclipse MicroProfile JWT Auth*[66] provides *Role-Based Access Control* (RBAC) using *OpenID Connect* (OIDC) and *JSON Web Tokens*[67] (JWT). Due to the stateless character of microservices, the solution must offer security context propagation in an easy way. This is done by passing tokens around microservices invocations.

OpenTracing

In a microservice architecture, requests often span multiple services (e.g. database queries, publishing messages, etc.). *Eclipse MicroProfile OpenTracing*[68] defines an API that allows services to easily participate in a distributed tracing environment. But this API has been deprecated in MicroProfile 4.1 and will be replaced by OpenTelemetry in a future release.

2.3.4. Standalone Releases

The previous specifications are part of MicroProfile. But under the MicroProfile umbrella, other specifications are either being incubated or still in progress. Some might get into the future releases of MicroProfile, while others might disappear. But some have made some notable progress and made their way to Quarkus.

Context Propagation

When using a reactive model which executes upon completion of prior stages, the context under which dependent stages execute is unpredictable. Dependent stages might run with the context of a thread that awaits completion. *Eclipse Context Propagation*[69] allows transferring thread context.

Reactive Messaging

Eclipse Reactive Messaging[70] is made for building event-driven, data streaming, and event-sourcing applications. It lets your application interact with various messaging technologies such as Apache Kafka, AMQP or MQTT. The framework provides a flexible programming model bridging CDI and event-driven APIs.

Mutiny

Eclipse Mutiny[71] is a reactive programming library. Mutiny provides a guided API, making reactive programming easy. It avoids having classes with hundreds of methods that are not always very explicit (e.g. `map()` or `flatmap()` on other reactive frameworks). But Mutiny has several converters from and to other reactive programming libraries, so you can always pivot and use the `map()` method if you really wish.

Mutiny was designed years after existing reactive programming libraries. It is based on the experience of many developers, lost in an endless sequence of `map` and `flatMap` operators. Mutiny does not provide as many operators as the other reactive libraries, focusing instead on the most used operators. Furthermore, it helps developers by providing a more guided API, which avoids having classes with hundreds of methods to choose from. Chapter 8 covers both Mutiny and Reactive Messaging.

2.4. Understanding Cloud Native Computing

The old way to deploy applications was to use physical hardware. Once this physical hardware was purchased, it wouldn't matter if we used all the machine resources or just a small amount. In most cases, we wouldn't care that much, as long as we could run the application. If we needed to scale, we could either buy more physical hardware or install several copies of the same application in the same box.

However, in the Cloud, we pay exactly for what we use. So we have become pickier with our hardware usage. If the application takes 10 seconds to start, or consumes a lot of memory or CPU, we have to pay for these resources. And if we need to scale, then we will pay for these 10 seconds, memory and CPU again.

Cloud Native Computing[72] (CNC) is an approach that utilises cloud computing to build and run scalable applications in modern, dynamic environments such as public, private, and hybrid clouds. Technologies such as containers, microservices, serverless functions, service meshes and immutable infrastructure are common elements of this architectural style. These techniques enable loosely coupled systems that are resilient, manageable, and observable. The *Cloud Native Computing Foundation*[73] (CNCF) seeks to drive adoption of this paradigm by fostering and sustaining an ecosystem of open source, vendor-neutral projects.

 I would recommend having a look at the *Cloud Native Interactive Landscape*[74] map. It is a very well designed and interactive map with all the cloud native, serverless and member landscapes that make the CNCF. You will see how huge and diverse this ecosystem is.

In Cloud Native Computing each (micro)service is packaged into its own container, and those containers are then dynamically orchestrated in order to optimise resource utilisation. So let's focus on these last two technologies that we will be using in this fascicle: containers and orchestrators. Or, if we want to name the implementations, *Docker* and *Kubernetes*.

2.4.1. Docker

Docker[75] is a set of *Platform-as-a-Service* (PaaS) products that use OS-level virtualisation to deliver software. It makes it easier to create, deploy and run applications by using containers. Containers are isolated from one another and bundle their own software, libraries and configuration files; they can communicate with each other through well-defined channels. Containers allow developers to package an application with all its dependencies and ship it all out as one package.

To understand why we created containers, we need to go back in history and see how running applications has evolved. Figure 9 shows how we used to run applications on bare metal, then on VMs, and today, containers. By 2000, we were mostly deploying one application per server. So when a company needed a new application, you needed a new server, make sure the server was up and running, administer it, etc. Because this was a new application, we didn't really know how big the server needed to be, how fast, how much memory, how many CPUs. So we usually ended up with an expensive big server with this new application using 5% of the resources.

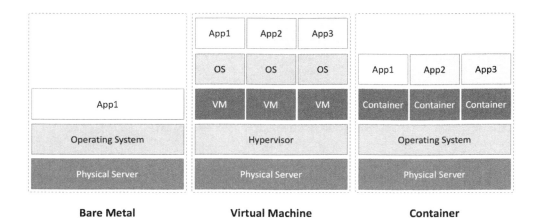

Bare Metal   **Virtual Machine**   **Container**

Figure 9. From bare metal to VMs to containers

Then came virtualisation. With virtualisation, we could have multiple applications deployed on a single server, totally isolated one from another. If a new application was coming along, we didn't need to buy a new server, we could just reuse an existing one. Servers were now more used (80% instead of 5%) On a virtual machine, each application gets a percentage of the real server's resources and each virtual machine needs an operating system with a licence. So when you have several virtual machines, you end up with several operating systems that need to be administered, patched, etc.

A container runs on a physical server, it doesn't need virtualisation (even if it can technically run on a virtual machine, but doesn't need to). Instead of installing several operating systems per application, we install only one operating system per server, and then a container per application. Therefore, each application starts quickly because there is no need to start the operating system, it's already started.

Docker has its own terminology when talking about packaging and running an application. A *Docker Image* is a read-only template with instructions for creating a Docker container. It is a combination of file system and parameters. Often, an image is based on another image with some additional customisation. We can use existing images or create our own images. A *Docker Container* is a runnable instance of an image. We can create as many containers as we want from an image. A container is isolated from the host by default. We can modify its behaviour using network, volume, etc. When a container is created, we can stop, restart or remove it.

Executing a container on a single machine is one thing, but having to execute dozens, hundreds of containers, manage them, restart them if they fail, scale them if needed, that is another story. That's why you need an orchestrator such as Kubernetes.

2.4.2. Kubernetes

Kubernetes[76] (a.k.a. K8s) is an orchestrator for containerised applications. It takes its name from a Greek word meaning *helmsman,* or *captain*: if Docker packages applications inside containers, Kubernetes is the captain sailing those containers. Kubernetes can schedule, scale, heal, update, start or stop several containers.

Kubernetes is platform agnostic (bare metal, VM, cloud, etc.): as long as you can install an agent, it works! Package your application in a container, declare the desired state of your application on a manifest file, give the all lot to Kubernetes and it will manage it. It will decide on which node to run the container (depending if the container needs a lot of CPU or ram) and also how many instances of the container. That's because Kubernetes is watching the state of the cluster, and instantiates more containers (without a human getting involved) if the instances are under heavy load. If the load gets lower, Kubernetes can get rid of containers, and if a node fails, it instantiates another one.

For this reason, as shown in Figure 10, a Kubernetes cluster is made up of a *master*, one or several *nodes* where one or several *pods* are deployed. Kubernetes runs your application by placing containers into *Pods* to run on *Nodes*. A pod is a sandbox to run multiple containers and contains a network, kernel namespaces, volumes, etc. All containers in a single pod share the same pod environment.

A *node* may be a virtual or physical machine, depending on the cluster.

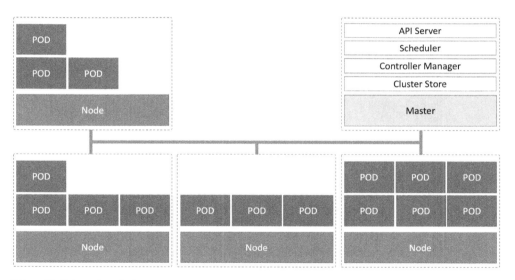

Figure 10. Kubernetes cluster

A Kubernetes cluster has a minimum of one *Master*. A master (a.k.a. *master node*) is not supposed to run workload but, instead, it controls and manages a set of nodes (a.k.a. *worker nodes*). A master is made of:

- *API Server*: Front controller to which we talk to (through a rest API, or command line interface) when managing the entire cluster.

- *Scheduler*: Watches the API Server for new pods, assigns work to nodes, etc.
- *Controller Manager*: Manages all the controllers (node controller, endpoint controller, namespace controller, etc.).
- *Cluster Store*: Cluster storage, state and configuration (uses etcd[77], the open source key/value store).

 You will see in Chapter 10 how Quarkus helps you in packaging a microservice into a Docker image and deploying it to a Kubernetes cluster. Go to Appendix A if you want to setup Docker and Kubernetes and learn how to manage a cluster using Minikube.

It's good to have orchestrators managing containers so our applications can scale and heal. But one reason for them is also related to startup time: how fast can an orchestrator instantiate a container and start a new instance of a Java application? The answer is usually that, no matter how fast the orchestrator works, the JVM will always take long to startup. GraalVM is a technology that can shorten this startup time by building native images out of Java code.

2.5. Understanding GraalVM

Quarkus targets the HotSpot VM, of course, but it was built with GraalVM in mind. *GraalVM*[78] is an extension of the *Java Virtual Machine* (JVM) to support more languages and several execution modes. It is itself implemented in Java. GraalVM supports a large set of languages: Java, of course, other JVM-based languages (such as Groovy, Kotlin etc.) but also JavaScript, Ruby, Python, R and C/C++.

But it also includes a new high performance Java compiler, itself called *Graal*. Running your application inside a JVM comes with startup and footprint costs. GraalVM has a feature to create *native images* for existing JVM-based applications. The image generation process employs static analysis to find any code reachable from the main Java method and then performs full *Ahead-Of-Time* (AOT) compilation on the *Substrate VM*[79]. The resulting native binary contains the whole program in machine code form for its immediate execution. This improves the performance of Java to match the performance of native languages for fast startup and low memory footprint.

2.5.1. JIT and AOT

The HotSpot uses a Just-in-Time compiler while GraalVM uses the Ahead-of-Time compilation. *Just-in-Time*[80] (JIT) compilation compiles code at runtime, rather than before at build time. That means that the HotSpot interprets bytecode, and for optimisation purposes, compiles some methods at runtime.

On the other hand, *Ahead-of-Time*[81] (AOT) compilation is done at build time, and not at runtime. That means that the compilation process is longer, but then, the code is compiled into binary. This improves the startup time and the compiler does not need to be invoked during runtime.

2.5.2. Architecture

Figure 11 depicts a high-level view of the GraalVM stack. The *Graal Compiler* is a high performance

JIT compiler written in Java. It accepts the JVM bytecode and produces the machine code. It uses the new *JVM Compiler Interface* (JVMCI) to communicate with the *Java HotSpot VM*. On top of all that, you will find the *Truffle* framework that enables you to build interpreters and implementations for other languages except JVM-based languages (such as Java, Groovy or Scala). If you want to run a new programming language, you will just have to integrate it with Truffle and the framework will produce the optimised machine code for you. As you can see, there are already language implementations for R, Ruby, or JavaScript. For LLVM-based languages (e.g. C/C++, Fortran), *Sulong* guarantees memory safety.

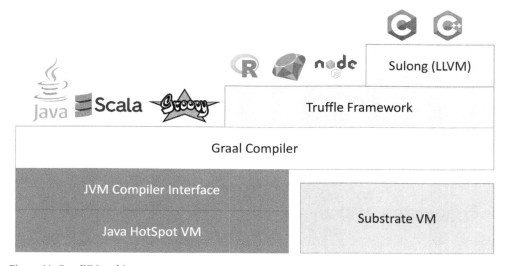

Figure 11. GraalVM architecture

The major differentiators of GraalVM compared to the base JDK are:

- *Sulong*[82]: Guarantees memory safety for C/C++ and other LLVM-based languages (e.g. Fortran).
- *Truffle*[83]: A language implementation framework for creating languages and instrumentations for GraalVM (e.g. R, Ruby, Python, NodeJS, etc.).
- *Graal Compiler*[84]: Written in Java and supports both dynamic and static compilation.
- *JVM Compiler Interface*[85] (JVMCI): Is part of the regular JDK and allows us to plug-in additional Java compilers (such as Graal) to the JVM.
- *Java HotSpot VM*: Runtime with the GraalVM compiler enabled as the top tier JIT compiler for JVM-based languages.
- *Substrate VM*[86]: Allows AOT compilation for applications written in various languages.

GraalVM allows you to ahead-of-time compile Java code to a standalone executable, called a *native image*. This executable includes the application classes, classes from its dependencies, runtime library classes from the JDK and statically linked native code from the JDK. It does not run on the Java VM, but includes necessary components like memory management and thread scheduling from a different virtual machine, called *Substrate VM*. Substrate VM is the name for the runtime components. Chapter 10 will cover native compilation. You will also see a glimpse of native

2.5.3. A Brief History of GraalVM

The history of Graal dates back to the research works on *MaxineVM*[87] in 2013, also known as a *meta-circular virtual machine* because this JVM is actually written in Java itself. Oracle invested in this research project and then released it under the name of GraalVM. GraalVM is a production-ready software and is available as a *Community Edition* (open source license) and as an *Enterprise Edition* (OTN License[88]). Oracle Corporation announced the release of Oracle GraalVM Enterprise Edition in May 2019. GraalVM has become an important part of the Quarkus story, and Red Hat is committed to its success. Therefore, Red Hat sits on the *GraalVM Project Advisory Board*[89] and regularly contributes features and fixes to GraalVM.

2.5.4. Mandrel

The history of GraalVM does not stop here. In June 2020 Red Hat announced the project *Mandrel*[90]. Mandrel is a distribution of a regular OpenJDK with a specially-packaged GraalVM native image. On the technical side, Mandrel's GitHub repository[91] represents a fork of GraalVM. It is a downstream distribution of GraalVM where Red Hat can continue to innovate in the open with an "*upstream-first*" mentality, preferring not to deviate from the upstream GraalVM. The primary driver behind Red Hat's introduction of Mandrel is to drive the speed and efficiency of the Quarkus framework, especially on the native-image feature.

2.6. Quarkus Overview

Java was born in 1995 and, at the time, was mostly used to write GUI applications and Applets. The language was based on the available hardware using single cores and multi-threads. Quickly, the language moved to the servers, and we started developing monolithic applications, designed to run on huge machines 24/7 for months (even years), with lots of CPU and memory. The JVM startup time was not an issue, the memory used by the JVM was huge, but we just let the JIT optimise the execution over time and left the GC manage the memory efficiently. Slow startup time and resource consumption don't fit well in our new environment where we need to deploy hundreds of microservices into the cloud, move them around and stop and start them quickly. Instead of scaling an application by adding more CPU and memory, we now scale microservices dynamically by adding more instances. That's where Quarkus, GraalVM, Kubernetes and other projects come into play.

Quarkus tailors applications for HotSpot and GraalVM. The result is that your application will have amazingly fast boot time and incredibly low RSS memory (*Resident Set Size*[92]) offering high density memory utilisation in container orchestration platforms like Kubernetes.

From a developer's point of view, Quarkus proposes a nice developer experience: it gives you fast live reload, unified configuration and hides the complexity of GraalVM, allowing you to easily generate native executables. All this without reinventing the wheel by proposing a new programming model, Quarkus leverages your experience in standard libraries that you already know (e.g. CDI, JPA, Bean Validation, JAX-RS, etc.) as well as many popular frameworks (e.g. Eclipse Vert.x, Apache Camel, etc.).

If you like the format of this fascicle and are interested in Quarkus, check out the references for my *Practising Quarkus 2.x* fascicle in Appendix F. In this *Practising* fascicle, you will develop, test, build, package and monitor an entire microservice application.

2.6.1. A Brief History of Quarkus

Quarkus made its debut in 2019 and is driven by Red Hat. But to tell the history of Quarkus, we first need to quickly go through the history of Red Hat; or I should say JBoss.

JBoss[93] was created in 1999 and started developing the JBoss Application Server[94] (later known as JBoss EAP, or *Enterprise Application Platform*). JBoss EAP is a runtime environment, implemented in Java, supporting all the Jakarta EE (a.k.a. Java EE or *Java Enterprise Edition*) specifications. The company acquired expertise in the middleware industry by supporting JBoss EAP and developing other middleware-related services. Thanks to this expertise, JBoss was acquired by Red Hat in 2006.

Red Hat, known for its enterprise operating system *Red Hat Enterprise Linux*[95] (RHEL), built on JBoss expertise by developing a lighter application server (WildFly Swarm, renamed as Thorntail[96]), getting involved in the MicroProfile consortium, and being a committer on the Java HotSpot project. Red Hat continued developing and contributing to the monolithic world of application servers, but also knew how to reinvent itself by creating a family of containerisation software called *OpenShift Container Platform*[97].

Moving to the cloud made sense for Red Hat. They had a Linux operating system, a JVM they contributed to, and a container platform. But the cloud environment has some costs and constraints that typical application servers do not handle well (slow startup time, heavy memory consumption, mutable environments, etc.). So the company decided to create a runtime environment that would fit well in this cloud environment: *Quarkus*.

Even if Quarkus was created in 2019, it came from a company that had a long history with open source, the Java ecosystem, distributed environments (Jakarta EE), ORM mapping (Hibernate), reactive programming (Vert.x), microservices (MicroProfile), and so on. If you come from this history, you can say that you have a few decades of expertise in Quarkus.

 The code in this fascicle relies on Quarkus 2.5.0.Final. Appendix B lists all the revisions and major changes of Quarkus since its very first release.

2.6.2. Architecture

Let's have a look at the internal architecture of Quarkus. As you will see in this fascicle, Quarkus does a lot of things! From persistence, to transactions, to fault-tolerance, to reactive messaging, etc., you might think of it as a huge application server that implements hundreds of features. Well, this is not the case. As shown in Figure 12, Quarkus is made of a small *core* that orchestrates the other pieces. And that's all. The power of Quarkus is its *extension mechanism*[98]. Persistence, transactions, fault-tolerance, etc. are all external extensions that can be added to your application only if needed. This extension mechanism is heavily based on ArC, a lightweight dependency injection framework.

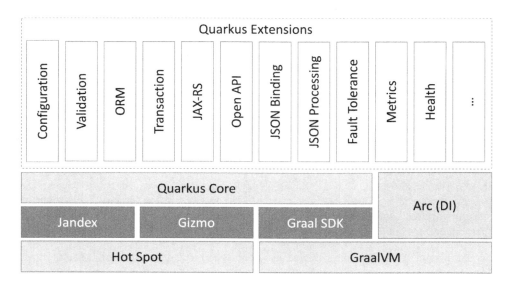

Figure 12. Quarkus internal architecture

The core component of Quarkus also does the hard work of rewriting applications in the build phase so that native executable and Java-runnable applications can be generated. For that it uses a set of tools such as *Jandex*[99], a Java annotation indexer and reflection library, to optimise annotation processing. *Gizmo*[100] is a library used to produce Java bytecode. Also, to overcome other limitations of GraalVM, thanks to the Graal SDK API[101], Quarkus uses a single-pass, single class loader and dead-code elimination mechanism (substantially cutting down the size of the executable file).

2.6.3. Imperative and Reactive Programming

One of the goals of Quarkus is to unify both imperative and reactive programming models seamlessly. Thanks to its reactive core based on Netty and Eclipse Vert.x, everything in Quarkus is non-blocking.

Netty[102] is a non-blocking I/O framework which enables development of network applications. Vert.x[103] is a reactive and polyglot development toolkit. It uses an event bus, to communicate with different parts of the application and passes events, asynchronously to handlers.

Non-blocking means that the same thread can handle multiple concurrent requests: while a process is waiting for some IO, the thread is released and so can be used to handle another request. With non-blocking IO, the number of cores becomes the essential setting as it defines the number of *IO threads*[104] you can run in parallel. Used properly, it efficiently dispatches the load on the different cores, handling more with fewer resources.

But that requires the application code to be non-blocking and avoid blocking the IO thread. This is a very different development model and you would have to use reactive programming in your code, not imperative. That would mean that you would not be able to use any of your legacy imperative code such as REST endpoints, database access or file systems. So having the ability to mix both reactive and imperative code is essential for Quarkus.

The secret behind this is to use a single reactive engine for both imperative and reactive code as shown in Figure 13. Quarkus uses Eclipse Vert.x and Netty at its core. Netty is an asynchronous event-driven framework. That means that every request is handled by an event loop (the IO thread) and then, depending on the destination, it can invoke the imperative code on a *worker thread* (e.g. servlet, Jax-RS) or the reactive code on an IO thread (reactive route). Thus, Quarkus is also a solution that lets you write imperative code and/or non-blocking code in the same application. Specific solutions such as non-blocking database drivers can be used, but they're not mandatory.

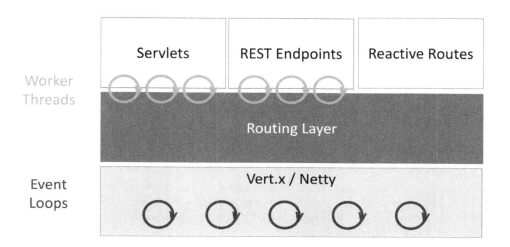

Figure 13. Quarkus reactive core

Reactive programming and reactive messaging are covered in Chapter 8.

2.6.4. Augmentation

If you come from the Jakarta EE or Spring world, you know that most of the work of an application server is performed at runtime. You compile and package an application into a JAR file, deploy it, and then wait for the application server to do all the XML parsing, annotation discovery, classpath scanning, and so on. Then, finally, the application is ready.

Quarkus goes the other way round and proposes to generalise ahead-of-time[105] techniques. When a Quarkus application is built, some work that usually happens at runtime is moved to the build time. Thus, when the application runs, most of it has been pre-computed, and all the annotation scanning, XML parsing, and so on won't be executed anymore. This is called *augmentation*[106] as shown in Figure 14. This means that Quarkus brings an infrastructure for other frameworks to embrace build time metadata discovery (like annotations), declares which classes need reflection at runtime and generates static proxies to avoid reflection (not to be confused with dynamic proxies that are created by traditional servers at runtime). This has two direct benefits: faster startup time and lower memory consumption.

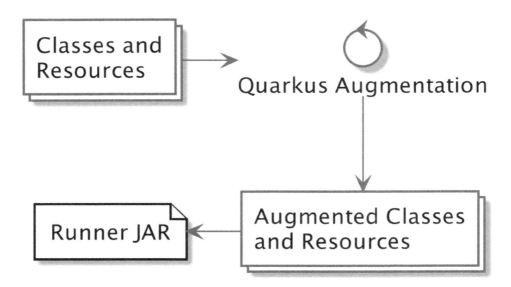

Figure 14. Quarkus augmentation

But Quarkus can also use GraalVM to generate native executables. Thanks to an aggressive dead-code elimination process (see Figure 15), the final executable is smaller, faster to start and uses a smaller amount of memory. This makes Quarkus a great runtime environment for containers, as well as cloud native and serverless deployments.

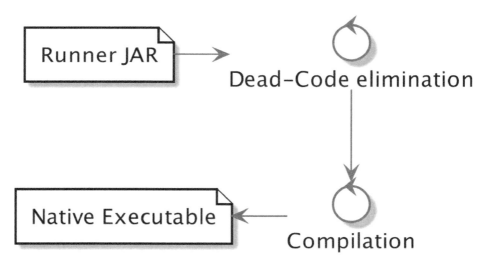

Figure 15. Native compilation

2.6.5. Extensions

Quarkus does so many things that we could thing of it as a huge piece of software implementing thousands of features. It's not the case. As shown in Figure 16, Quarkus is made of a small core, and then uses an extension mechanism to bring as many functionalities as possible.

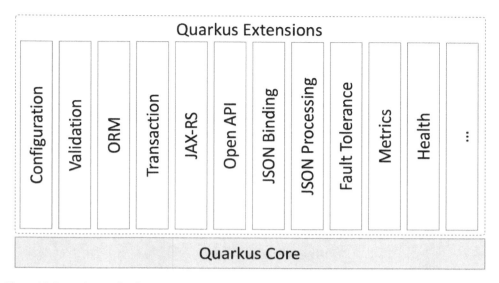

Figure 16. Extension mechanism

But not every external framework or library is an extension. Quarkus works with any external library in JVM mode, so you are not restricted to Quarkus extensions. But the advantage of an extension over a third-party library, is that the extension integrates seamlessly into the Quarkus architecture as it can be processed at build time and be built in native mode. Then, you only pick the extensions you need on your application and Quarkus will make sure it works.

 Quarkus has hundreds of extensions, and every release brings new ones. One way to keep up to date is to go to https://code.quarkus.io and check if the technology/framework that you are looking for has been integrated as a Quarkus extension. You can also use the Maven command `mvn quarkus:list-extensions` These are the extensions maintained by the Quarkus team. But you can also go to *Quarkiverse*[107] where you will find extensions maintained by the community. Quarkiverse is a GitHub organization where any contributor can host their Quarkus extensions.

I won't go through all the Quarkus extensions, just the ones used directly or indirectly in this fascicle (see Table 3).

Table 3. Some Quarkus Extensions

Extension	Description
Agroal[108]	Datasource connection pool implementation that integrates with transactions, security and other systems
Hibernate ORM[109]	Object/Relational Mapping (ORM) framework implementing Java Persistence API
Hibernate Validator[110]	Reference implementation of Bean Validation

Extension	Description
Narayana[111]	Transaction manager with over 30 years of expertise in the area of transaction processing
SmallRye Mutiny[112]	Reactive programming library
Vert.x[113]	Event-driven and non-blocking tool-kit for building reactive applications on the JVM

When it comes to implementing MicroProfile, Quarkus uses several implementations that come either from Jakarta EE or SmallRye. The MicroProfile implementations used by Quarkus are listed in Table 4).

Table 4. Quarkus MicroProfile Extensions

Extension	Description
ArC[114]	Context and Dependency Injection implementation
RESTEasy[115]	Java API for RESTful Web Services implementation
Yasson[116]	JSON Binding implementation
Glassfish JSON-P[117]	JSON Processing implementation
RestEasy Client Microprofile[118]	Implementation of Eclipse MicroProfile REST Client
SmallRye Config[119]	Implementation of Eclipse MicroProfile Configuration
SmallRye Fault Tolerance[120]	Implementation of Eclipse MicroProfile Fault Tolerance
SmallRye Health[121]	Implementation of Eclipse MicroProfile Health
SmallRye JWT[122]	Implementation of Eclipse MicroProfile JWT Auth
SmallRye Metrics[123]	Implementation of Eclipse MicroProfile Metrics
SmallRye OpenAPI[124]	Implementation of Eclipse MicroProfile OpenAPI

2.6.6. What's New in Quarkus 2.x?

Quarkus 2.0 Final was released in June 2021. You should see the 2.x version as a continuation of 1.x. In fact, if you migrate from 1.x to 2.x you won't have to do big refactorings, nor will you have to learn something totally new. These are mostly internal changes. The migration of most applications will be a no-brainer.

The major new features are:

- The JDK 11 is now the minimal version to use Quarkus 2.x as JDK 8 is not supported anymore (use Quarkus 1.13.x instead).
- GraalVM 21.1 is the recommended version for Quarkus 2.x.
- Integration of MicroProfile 4 and Vert.x 4.
- Continuous Testing to improve developer productivity.
- A new Quarkus command line tool to create projects, manage extensions and builds.

Most of these novelties will be discussed in the chapters that follow.

 Appendix B lists all the revisions and major changes of the Quarkus specification.

2.7. Summary

This *Understanding* chapter gave you most of the required terminology around Quarkus. There is less code in this chapter than in the following ones, but we needed to make sure you understand all the concepts around Quarkus before going any further.

Quarkus is not just about microservices but it was built with microservices in mind. So this chapter started introducing this architectural style, its pros and cons, and put it in perspective with the monolithic approach. Microservices are not just HTTP based (more in Chapter 6, *HTTP Microservices*), so this chapter also had to introduce reactive systems that you will be developing in Chapter 8, *Event-Driven Microservices*.

When it comes to microservices, Quarkus tends to integrate with the MicroProfile set of specifications. Supported by the independent Eclipse Foundation, MicroProfile adopts a small subset of Jakarta EE standards (CDI, JAX-RS, JSON-B and JSON-P), and adds new ones to address common microservices patterns (Configuration, Fault Tolerance, Health, Metrics, etc.).

Microservices are perfect for cloud native applications. So this chapter also had to explain what containers and orchestrators are, so you will have all the knowledge to follow Chapter 10, *Cloud Native*. But using Docker and Kubernetes might not be enough for certain application constraints. By using GraalVM, you can take your Quarkus microservice, build a native image out of it so you can get fast startup time and lower resource consumption.

This chapter finishes with an overview of what Quarkus is, what it brings you as a developer, and how its internal structure is based on a powerful and rich extension mechanism.

The next chapter *Getting Started* is about setting up your development environment to make sure you can follow the samples of all the following chapters. You will develop a very simple example, but you will use most of the technology presented here: bootstrapping a Quarkus application, testing it, building a native image with GraalVM and packaging it in a Docker container.

[36] Quarkus https://quarkus.io

[37] Microservices https://en.wikipedia.org/wiki/Microservices

[38] Monolith https://en.wikipedia.org/wiki/Monolithic_system

[39] Microservice Trade-offs https://martinfowler.com/articles/microservice-trade-offs.html

[40] Reactive Manifesto https://www.reactivemanifesto.org

[41] Why Do We Need a Reactive Manifesto? https://www.lightbend.com/blog/why-do-we-need-a-reactive-manifesto

[42] Reactive Principles https://principles.reactive.foundation

[43] Backpressure https://medium.com/@jayphelps/backpressure-explained-the-flow-of-data-through-software-2350b3e77ce7

[44] Reactive Streams http://www.reactive-streams.org

[45] Flow Concurrency library https://docs.oracle.com/javase/9/docs/api/java/util/concurrent/Flow.html

[46] MicroProfile https://microprofile.io

[47] Jakarta EE https://en.wikipedia.org/wiki/Jakarta_EE

[48] JCP https://jcp.org

[49] Eclipse Foundation https://www.eclipse.org/org/foundation/

[50] Jakarta EE https://jakarta.ee

[51] Eclipse Foundation https://www.eclipse.org/org/foundation

[52] SmallRye https://github.com/smallrye

[53] CDI https://jcp.org/en/jsr/detail?id=365

[54] JAX-RS https://jcp.org/en/jsr/detail?id=370

[55] JSON-B https://jcp.org/en/jsr/detail?id=367

[56] JSON-P https://jcp.org/en/jsr/detail?id=374

[57] StAX https://en.wikipedia.org/wiki/StAX

[58] Common Annotations https://jcp.org/en/jsr/detail?id=250

[59] Configuration https://microprofile.io/project/eclipse/microprofile-config

[60] Fault Tolerance https://microprofile.io/project/eclipse/microprofile-fault-tolerance

[61] Health https://microprofile.io/project/eclipse/microprofile-health

[62] Metrics https://microprofile.io/project/eclipse/microprofile-metrics

[63] OpenAPI Specification https://github.com/OAI/OpenAPI-Specification

[64] OpenAPI https://microprofile.io/project/eclipse/microprofile-open-api

[65] REST Client https://microprofile.io/project/eclipse/microprofile-rest-client

[66] JWT https://microprofile.io/project/eclipse/microprofile-jwt-auth

[67] JWT https://tools.ietf.org/html/rfc7519

[68] OpenTracing https://microprofile.io/project/eclipse/microprofile-opentracing

[69] Context Propagation https://microprofile.io/project/eclipse/microprofile-context-propagation

[70] Reactive Messaging https://github.com/eclipse/microprofile-reactive-messaging

[71] Mutiny https://github.com/smallrye/smallrye-mutiny

[72] Cloud Native Computing https://github.com/cncf/toc/blob/master/DEFINITION.md

[73] CNCF https://www.cncf.io

[74] CNCF Landscape https://landscape.cncf.io

[75] Docker https://www.docker.com

[76] Kubernetes https://kubernetes.io

[77] etcd https://etcd.io

[78] GraalVM https://www.graalvm.org

[79] SubstrateVM https://github.com/oracle/graal/tree/master/substratevm

[80] JIT https://en.wikipedia.org/wiki/Just-in-time_compilation

[81] AOT JEP 295 https://openjdk.java.net/jeps/295

[82] Sulong https://github.com/oracle/graal/tree/master/sulong

[83] Truffle https://github.com/oracle/graal/tree/master/truffle

[84] Graal Compiler https://github.com/oracle/graal/tree/master/compiler

[85] JVM Compiler Interface https://openjdk.java.net/jeps/243

[86] Substrate VM https://github.com/oracle/graal/tree/master/substratevm

[87] MaxineVM https://dl.acm.org/doi/10.1145/2400682.2400689

[88] OTN License https://www.oracle.com/downloads/licenses/graalvm-otn-license.html

[89] GraalVM Project Advisory Board https://www.graalvm.org/community/advisory-board

[90] Red Hat announces Mandrel https://developers.redhat.com/blog/2020/06/05/mandrel-a-community-distribution-of-graalvm-for-the-red-hat-build-of-quarkus

[91] Mandrel repository https://github.com/graalvm/mandrel

[92] RSS memory https://en.wikipedia.org/wiki/Resident_set_size

[93] JBoss https://en.wikipedia.org/wiki/Red_Hat#History

[94] JBoss EAP https://en.wikipedia.org/wiki/JBoss_Enterprise_Application_Platform

[95] RHEL https://www.redhat.com/en/technologies/linux-platforms/enterprise-linux

[96] Thorntail https://thorntail.io

[97] OpenShift https://www.openshift.com

[98] Quarkus extensions https://quarkus.io/guides/writing-extensions

[99] Jandex https://github.com/wildfly/jandex

[100] Gizmo https://github.com/quarkusio/gizmo

[101] Graal SDK API https://www.graalvm.org/sdk/javadoc

[102] Netty https://netty.io

[103] Vert.x https://vertx.io

[104] IO Thread Benchmark https://quarkus.io/blog/io-thread-benchmark

[105] Ahead-of-Time https://www.graalvm.org/reference-manual/native-image

[106] Augmentation https://quarkus.io/guides/reaugmentation

[107] Quarkiverse https://github.com/quarkiverse

[108] Agroal https://agroal.github.io

[109] Hibernate https://hibernate.org/orm

[110] Hibernate Validator http://hibernate.org/validator

[111] Narayana https://github.com/jbosstm/narayana

[112] SmallRye Mutiny https://github.com/smallrye/smallrye-mutiny

[113] Vert.x https://github.com/eclipse-vertx/vert.x

[114] ArC https://github.com/quarkusio/quarkus/tree/master/independent-projects/arc

[115] RESTEasy https://github.com/resteasy/Resteasy

[116] Yasson https://projects.eclipse.org/projects/ee4j.yasson

[117] Glassfish JSON-P https://github.com/eclipse-ee4j/jsonp

[118] RestEasy Client Microprofile https://github.com/resteasy/resteasy-microprofile

[119] SmallRye Config https://github.com/smallrye/smallrye-config

[120] SmallRye Fault Tolerance https://github.com/smallrye/smallrye-fault-tolerance

[121] SmallRye Health https://github.com/smallrye/smallrye-health

[122] SmallRye JWT https://github.com/smallrye/smallrye-jwt

[123] SmallRye Metrics https://github.com/smallrye/smallrye-metrics

[124] SmallRye OpenAPI https://github.com/smallrye/smallrye-open-api

Chapter 3. Getting Started

In the previous *Understanding Quarkus* chapter, you learnt about Quarkus, Microservices, MicroProfile, GraalVM and Cloud Native. You've also looked at what Quarkus is and where it comes from. Time to see some code.

To get started with a new technology, there is nothing better than a simple "*Hello World*" kind of example. In this *Getting Started* chapter, you will be developing your very first Quarkus sample application. It is a simple application made up of only a few classes with not much business logic but with some technical complexity. The idea is to develop something simple to understand and to set up so that you are sure you have the basis to follow the chapters coming up.

 Make sure your development environment is set up to execute the code in this chapter. You can go to Appendix A to check that you have all the required tools installed, in particular JDK 11.0.13 or higher, GraalVM 21.3.0 (with Native Image), Maven 3.8.3, cURL 7.64.1 and Docker. The code in this chapter can be found at https://github.com/agoncal/agoncal-fascicle-quarkus/tree/2.0/getting-started

3.1. Developing Your First Quarkus Application

Let's develop a simple application that highlights some of the key features of Quarkus. In this chapter, we'll use the Quarkus Maven Plugin to generate a simple Quarkus application. We will end-up with a Maven directory structure with a set of test classes and business classes that define a RESTful web service which produces a JSON representation of an *Artist*. We'll use cURL to interact with this RESTful web service. Finally, thanks to GraalVM, we will build an executable out of our code and containerise it with Docker. We use Maven[123] to build this project because it is the most commonly used build system these days. Plus, we can use Maven in the command line and most IDEs support it.

3.2. Bootstrapping the Application

Let's first bootstrap a Quarkus application. For that, we have different ways to start a project with a minimum amount of code: a web interface, an IDE plugin, or a Maven plugin. Let's quickly see these different options before bootstrapping the application with the Maven plugin.

3.2.1. Web Interface

If you want to use a web interface, go to https://code.quarkus.io. As shown in Figure 17, you can choose your build tool (Maven or Gradle), set the `groupId` and `artifactId`, but most importantly, select the extensions you need. For our first application, we just need a REST endpoint and some JSON Binding, so we can tick two boxes, set all the Maven coordinates, and click on the "*Generate your application*" button. This action will download a zip file containing enough code to bootstrap an application.

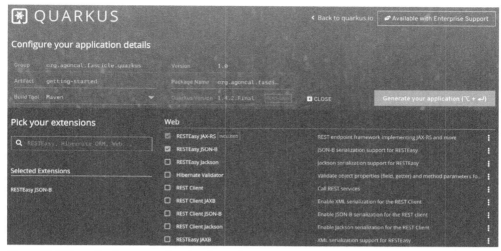

Figure 17. Web application generating Quarkus code

3.2.2. IntelliJ IDEA Plugin

If you want to use your IDE, you will find that Quarkus is integrated into many of them[120]. Here, I am showing how to bootstrap an application in IntelliJ IDEA, but IDEs such as VSCode or Eclipse can do the same. In fact, the IntelliJ IDEA plugin is based on https://code.quarkus.io. So if you invoke the menus **File** › **New** › **Module** › **Quarkus** you end up with a wizard shown in Figure 18.

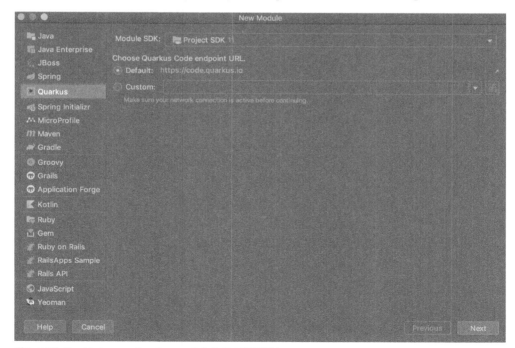

Figure 18. Creating a new Quarkus module in IntelliJ IDEA

The project wizard will guide you through the selection of the Maven coordinates of your project (shown in Figure 19) and the extensions you want to have included in it.

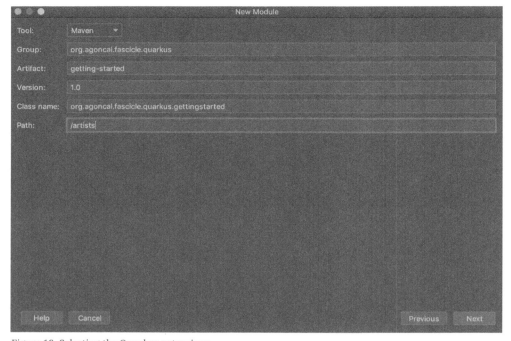

Figure 19. Selecting the Quarkus extensions

3.2.3. Maven Plugin

We can also bootstrap a Quarkus application by means of its Maven plugin[127]. This plugin provides a set of goals that can be executed to create, compile and build an application, and even extend the project with some features. The Quarkus plugin is based on the following Maven coordinates: `io.quarkus:quarkus-maven-plugin`. You can check the available goals and the latest version of it with the following command:

```
$ mvn -Dplugin=io.quarkus:quarkus-maven-plugin:2.5.0.Final help:describe

This plugin has 24 goals:
  quarkus:add-extension
  quarkus:analyze-call-tree
  quarkus:build
  quarkus:create
  quarkus:create-extension
  quarkus:dependency-tree
  quarkus:dev
  quarkus:help
  quarkus:list-categories
  quarkus:list-extensions
  quarkus:list-platforms
  quarkus:remote-dev
  quarkus:test
  ...
```

 Another way to bootstrap a Quarkus application is to use the Quarkus blueprint for the *JHipster* generator[128]. This is a community-driven effort to be able to generate an entire application, the JHipster way, using Quarkus.

3.2.4. Generating Some Code

As you've just seen, we have several choices to bootstrap a Quarkus application, but let's use the Maven plugin from the command line. The following command uses the Quarkus Maven plugin to generate a REST endpoint called ArtistResource located at the /artists path. Because we will need some JSON Binding, we add the JSON-B extension:

```
mvn io.quarkus:quarkus-maven-plugin:2.5.0.Final:create \
    -DplatformVersion=2.5.0.Final \
    -DprojectGroupId=org.agoncal.fascicle.quarkus \
    -DprojectArtifactId=getting-started \
    -DprojectVersion=2.0.0-SNAPSHOT \
    -DclassName="org.agoncal.fascicle.quarkus.gettingstarted.ArtistResource" \
    -Dpath="/artists" \
    -Dextensions="resteasy-jsonb"
```

Generated Classes and Directory Structure

As a result of the preceding command, the following directory structure has been generated in the getting-started folder:

```
.
├── README.md
├── mvnw
├── mvnw.cmd
├── pom.xml
└── src
    ├── main
    │   ├── docker
    │   │   ├── Dockerfile.jvm
    │   │   ├── Dockerfile.legacy-jar
    │   │   ├── Dockerfile.native
    │   │   └── Dockerfile.native-distroless
    │   ├── java
    │   │   └── org/agoncal/fascicle/quarkus/gettingstarted
    │   │       └── ArtistResource.java
    │   └── resources
    │       ├── META-INF
    │       │   └── resources
    │       │       └── index.html
    │       └── application.properties
    └── test
        └── java
            └── org/agoncal/fascicle/quarkus/gettingstarted
                ├── ArtistResourceTest.java
                └── NativeArtistResourceIT.java
```

The Maven directory structure ensures we put the business code under src/main/java while the test code goes under src/test/java. But the Quarkus Maven plugin goes further as it also includes a set of files and configurations to package the application in a Docker image and to generate a native executable using GraalVM. You will find:

- A readme file,
- A Maven wrapper file (mvnw and mvnw.cmd) to allow execution of Maven goals without installing it,
- A Maven pom.xml file (*Project Object Model*) with the project configuration and dependencies,
- Docker files so that we can create a container out of our application,
- A sample REST service named ArtistResource.java and its test class named ArtistResourceTest.java, as well as a wrapper class named NativeArtistResourceIT.java for executing the test against the native executable application,
- A configuration file called application.properties,
- An index.html file to indicate where we can add static web content.

Generated Maven POM

At the root of the generated code, you will find the pom.xml file. The pom.xml is the fundamental unit of work in Maven that will be used to build our project. Next, I am going to break down the pom.xml file into several parts so you can understand it better. First, Listing 3 shows the header of the pom.xml with the groupId and artifactId. It also defines the properties used in the project. This is where you find the version of Quarkus, for example.

Listing 3. Header of the pom.xml

```
<project xsi:schemaLocation="http://maven.apache.org/POM/4.0.0
https://maven.apache.org/xsd/maven-4.0.0.xsd" xmlns="
http://maven.apache.org/POM/4.0.0"
    xmlns:xsi="http://www.w3.org/2001/XMLSchema-instance">
  <modelVersion>4.0.0</modelVersion>

  <groupId>org.agoncal.fascicle.quarkus</groupId>
  <artifactId>getting-started</artifactId>
  <version>2.0.0-SNAPSHOT</version>

  <properties>
    <compiler-plugin.version>3.8.1</compiler-plugin.version>
    <maven.compiler.parameters>true</maven.compiler.parameters>
    <maven.compiler.source>11</maven.compiler.source>
    <maven.compiler.target>11</maven.compiler.target>
    <project.build.sourceEncoding>UTF-8</project.build.sourceEncoding>
    <project.reporting.outputEncoding>UTF-8</project.reporting.outputEncoding>
    <quarkus.platform.artifact-id>quarkus-bom</quarkus.platform.artifact-id>
    <quarkus.platform.group-id>io.quarkus.platform</quarkus.platform.group-id>
    <quarkus.platform.version>2.5.0.Final</quarkus.platform.version>
    <surefire-plugin.version>3.0.0-M5</surefire-plugin.version>
  </properties>
```

 Notice that Quarkus version 2.5.0.Final is used in this fascicle.

Then comes the dependencyManagement section, shown in Listing 4, which imports Quarkus' *Bill of Materials*. This allows us to automatically link the exact version of each Quarkus extension.

Listing 4. Quarkus Bill of Materials

```
<dependencyManagement>
  <dependencies>
    <dependency>
      <groupId>${quarkus.platform.group-id}</groupId>
      <artifactId>${quarkus.platform.artifact-id}</artifactId>
      <version>${quarkus.platform.version}</version>
      <type>pom</type>
      <scope>import</scope>
    </dependency>
  </dependencies>
</dependencyManagement>
```

The dependencies section in Listing 5 gives us all of the required dependencies to compile and execute the *ArtistResource* REST API. This section declares the following dependencies:

- quarkus-resteasy-jsonb: JSON-B serialisation support for RESTEasy.
- quarkus-arc: Context and Dependency Injection implementation.
- quarkus-resteasy: REST framework implementing JAX-RS.

Listing 5. Maven Dependencies

```
<dependencies>
  <dependency>
    <groupId>io.quarkus</groupId>
    <artifactId>quarkus-resteasy-jsonb</artifactId>
  </dependency>
  <dependency>
    <groupId>io.quarkus</groupId>
    <artifactId>quarkus-arc</artifactId>
  </dependency>
  <dependency>
    <groupId>io.quarkus</groupId>
    <artifactId>quarkus-resteasy</artifactId>
  </dependency>
```

Testing an application with Quarkus is very easy. For that, you need to add the dependencies listed in Listing 6:

- quarkus-junit5: JUnit 5 support in Quarkus.
- rest-assured: Framework to easily test REST endpoints.

 If you want to know more about JUnit and REST Assured, you can check out Chapter 11, *Tests*.

Listing 6. Test Dependencies

```
<dependency>
  <groupId>io.quarkus</groupId>
  <artifactId>quarkus-junit5</artifactId>
  <scope>test</scope>
</dependency>
<dependency>
  <groupId>io.rest-assured</groupId>
  <artifactId>rest-assured</artifactId>
  <scope>test</scope>
</dependency>
```

The next parts of the pom.xml in Listing 7 and Listing 8 show the plugins needed to execute and test our code:

- quarkus-maven-plugin: The Quarkus plugin is responsible for creating the final jar and for running the development mode.

- `maven-compiler-plugin`: The Maven compiler plugin is used to compile the sources of the project.

- `maven-surefire-plugin`: The Surefire plugin is used during the test phase to execute the unit tests of the application.

Listing 7. Building Steps

```xml
<build>
  <plugins>
    <plugin>
      <groupId>${quarkus.platform.group-id}</groupId>
      <artifactId>quarkus-maven-plugin</artifactId>
      <version>${quarkus.platform.version}</version>
      <extensions>true</extensions>
      <executions>
        <execution>
          <goals>
            <goal>build</goal>
            <goal>generate-code</goal>
            <goal>generate-code-tests</goal>
          </goals>
        </execution>
      </executions>
    </plugin>
    <plugin>
      <artifactId>maven-compiler-plugin</artifactId>
      <version>${compiler-plugin.version}</version>
      <configuration>
        <parameters>${maven.compiler.parameters}</parameters>
      </configuration>
    </plugin>
    <plugin>
      <artifactId>maven-surefire-plugin</artifactId>
      <version>${surefire-plugin.version}</version>
      <configuration>
        <systemPropertyVariables>
          <java.util.logging.manager>
org.jboss.logmanager.LogManager</java.util.logging.manager>
          <maven.home>${maven.home}</maven.home>
        </systemPropertyVariables>
      </configuration>
    </plugin>
  </plugins>
</build>
```

Notice that we also set the `org.jboss.logmanager.LogManager` system property to make sure that the tests will use the correct logging manager. With all these test dependencies and plugins in place, a simple `mvn compile` will compile the Java code, and `mvn test` will execute the Quarkus tests.

The last part of the `pom.xml` shown in Listing 8 declares the `native` profile that will execute the test on the native executable. It configures the `maven-failsafe-plugin` so it runs the integration tests against the native executable.

Listing 8. Maven Profile to Test Native Images

```xml
<profiles>
  <profile>
    <id>native</id>
    <activation>
      <property>
        <name>native</name>
      </property>
    </activation>
    <build>
      <plugins>
        <plugin>
          <artifactId>maven-failsafe-plugin</artifactId>
          <version>${surefire-plugin.version}</version>
          <executions>
            <execution>
              <goals>
                <goal>integration-test</goal>
                <goal>verify</goal>
              </goals>
              <configuration>
                <systemPropertyVariables>
<native.image.path>${project.build.directory}/${project.build.finalName}-runner</native.image.path>
                  <java.util.logging.manager>
org.jboss.logmanager.LogManager</java.util.logging.manager>
                  <maven.home>${maven.home}</maven.home>
                </systemPropertyVariables>
              </configuration>
            </execution>
          </executions>
        </plugin>
      </plugins>
    </build>
    <properties>
      <quarkus.package.type>native</quarkus.package.type>
    </properties>
  </profile>
</profiles>
```

 At this point, you can import the Maven project into an IDE (most modern Java IDEs include built-in support for Maven).

Now we can list the libraries that our project depends on. If you execute the `quarkus:dependency-`

tree goal, in Listing 9 you will see that several dependencies were not explicitly defined in the pom.xml in Listing 5 and Listing 6. That's because Maven transitively pulls all the required dependencies automatically. That's why we end up with the Eclipse Vert.x or Netty APIs, for example.

Listing 9. Simplified Maven Dependencies Tree

```
$ mvn -Dplugin=io.quarkus:quarkus-maven-plugin:2.5.0.Final quarkus:dependency-tree

org.agoncal.fascicle.quarkus:getting-started:pom:2.0.0-SNAPSHOT
├── io.quarkus:quarkus-resteasy-jsonb-deployment:jar:2.5.0.Final
│   ├── io.quarkus:quarkus-resteasy-jsonb:jar:2.5.0.Final
│   │   ├── io.quarkus:quarkus-jsonb:jar:2.5.0.Final
│   │   │   ├── org.eclipse:yasson:jar:1.0.9
│   │   │   └── io.quarkus:quarkus-jsonp:jar:2.5.0.Final
│   └── io.quarkus:quarkus-jsonb-deployment:jar:2.5.0.Final
│       ├── io.quarkus:quarkus-jsonb-spi:jar:2.5.0.Final
│       └── io.quarkus:quarkus-jsonp-deployment:jar:2.5.0.Final
├── io.quarkus:quarkus-arc-deployment:jar:2.5.0.Final
│   ├── io.quarkus:quarkus-vertx-http-dev-console-spi:jar:2.5.0.Final
│   │   └── io.vertx:vertx-web:jar:4.1.5
│   │       └── io.vertx:vertx-core:jar:4.1.5
│   ├── io.quarkus:quarkus-arc:jar:2.5.0.Final
└── io.quarkus:quarkus-resteasy-deployment:jar:2.5.0.Final
    ├── io.quarkus:quarkus-resteasy-server-common-deployment:jar:2.5.0.Final
    │   └── io.quarkus:quarkus-undertow-spi:jar:2.5.0.Final
    ├── io.quarkus:quarkus-vertx-http-deployment:jar:2.5.0.Final
    ├── io.quarkus:quarkus-resteasy:jar:2.5.0.Final
    └── io.quarkus:quarkus-security-spi:jar:2.5.0.Final
        └── io.quarkus.security:quarkus-security:jar:1.1.4.Final
```

 Appendix A has an entire chapter on Maven, explaining the scopes (runtime, test etc.) and the goals you can use on a pom.xml. Please refer to it if you need more in-depth information on Maven.

3.3. Developing the Application

It's time to develop our simple REST endpoint that will return a JSON representation of artists. For that, we need to change the generated code of the ArtistResource class as well as its test class ArtistResourceTest.

3.3.1. The Artist Resource

The ArtistResource in Listing 10 uses some JAX-RS annotations (more on Java API for RESTful Web Services in Chapter 6). As you can see, ArtistResource is a very simple REST endpoint, returning a JSON representation of artists on the /artists path (that we previously defined in the Quarkus Maven plugin). It first declares an ArrayList of four artists, and then defines a few methods:

• getAllArtists(): Returns the entire list of artists in a JSON format.

- `countArtists()`: Returns the number of artists in a text format.

Listing 10. REST Endpoint Returning Artists

```
@Path("/artists")
public class ArtistResource {

  private static final List<Artist> artists = List.of(
    new Artist().id(UUID.randomUUID()).firstName("John").lastName("Lennon"),
    new Artist().id(UUID.randomUUID()).firstName("Paul").lastName("McCartney"),
    new Artist().id(UUID.randomUUID()).firstName("George").lastName("Harrison"),
    new Artist().id(UUID.randomUUID()).firstName("Ringo").lastName("Starr")
  );

  @GET
  @Produces(MediaType.APPLICATION_JSON)
  public Response getAllArtists() {
    return Response.ok(artists).build();
  }

  @GET
  @Path("/count")
  @Produces(MediaType.TEXT_PLAIN)
  public Integer countArtists() {
    return artists.size();
  }
}
```

3.3.2. The Artist Class

The getAllArtists() method of the ArtistResource returns a list of Artist objects defined in Listing 11. As you can see, Artist is just a simple POJO (*Plain Old Java Object*) with attributes, getters and setters. It holds the values of a music artist.

Listing 11. Java Class Holding Artists

```
public class Artist {

  @JsonbTransient
  private UUID id;
  @JsonbProperty("first_name")
  private String firstName;
  @JsonbProperty("last_name")
  private String lastName;

  // Constructors, getters, setters
}
```

If you look carefully at Listing 11, you will see some JSON-B mapping annotations. The

`@JsonbProperty` annotation tells the JSON-B provider to change the name `firstName` to `first_name` when a JSON output is generated. As for `@JsonbTransient`, it prevents the identifier from being present on the JSON output. Don't worry about JSON-B (JSON Binding) for now, Chapter 6 covers it.

3.3.3. Running the Application

Time to run the application. For that, it's just a matter of executing the `quarkus:dev` Maven goal. This builds and runs the application:

```
getting-started$ ./mvnw quarkus:dev
```

After a few seconds, the application will be compiled and executed, as shown in Listing 12.

Listing 12. Quarkus Starting Up

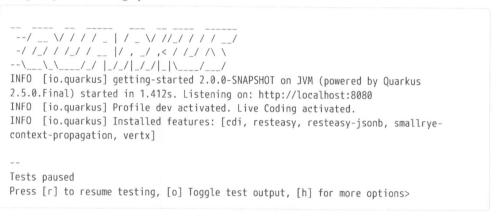

```
    __  ____  __  _____   ___  __ ____  _____
 --/ __ \/ / / / _ | / _ \/ //_/ / / / __/
 -/ /_/ / /_/ / __ |/ , _/ ,< / /_/ /\ \
--_____/_/ |_/_/|_/_/|_|\____/___/
INFO  [io.quarkus] getting-started 2.0.0-SNAPSHOT on JVM (powered by Quarkus
2.5.0.Final) started in 1.412s. Listening on: http://localhost:8080
INFO  [io.quarkus] Profile dev activated. Live Coding activated.
INFO  [io.quarkus] Installed features: [cdi, resteasy, resteasy-jsonb, smallrye-
context-propagation, vertx]

--
Tests paused
Press [r] to resume testing, [o] Toggle test output, [h] for more options>
```

You can stop the application with `Ctrl + C`. But leave it running for now as we will be testing the hot reload feature soon! Now, execute the following cURL commands to invoke our two methods:

```
$ curl http://localhost:8080/artists/count
4

$ curl http://localhost:8080/artists | jq

[
  {
    "first_name": "John",
    "last_name": "Lennon"
  },
  {
    "first_name": "Paul",
    "last_name": "McCartney"
  },
  {
    "first_name": "George",
    "last_name": "Harrison"
  },
  {
    "first_name": "Ringo",
    "last_name": "Starr"
  }
]
```

If you get the same output for these commands, that means that everything is running correctly. But let's go further with hot reloading the application and testing our endpoint.

 jq is a nice tool to manipulate JSON in the shell. If you want to know more about jq and install it, see Appendix A.

3.3.4. Live Reload

So far we've been using mvn quarkus:dev to execute our application. This command runs Quarkus in development mode. This enables hot reload with background compilation, which means that when you modify your Java files and/or your resource files and invoke a REST endpoint, these changes will automatically take effect. This works also for resource files like the configuration property and HTML files. Invoking a cURL command or refreshing the browser triggers a scan of the workspace, and if any changes are detected, the Java files are recompiled and the application is redeployed; your request is then serviced by the redeployed application. Let's see this live reload in action. For that, make sure mvn quarkus:dev is still running.

With Quarkus running, update the artists list in ArtistResource. Remove two or three artists from the ArrayList, and execute the cURL command again. As you can see, the output has changed without you having to stop and restart Quarkus:

```
$ curl http://localhost:8080/artists | jq

[
  {
    "first_name": "Paul",
    "last_name": "McCartney"
  },
  {
    "first_name": "Ringo",
    "last_name": "Starr"
  }
]
```

Undo your changes, you get your four artists back, access the endpoint with cURL again, the JSON representation of the four artists is back.

3.3.5. Configuring the Application

As you will see in Chapter 4, Quarkus is highly configurable. You can configure its core mechanism as well as most of its extensions in the single application.properties file located under the src/main/resources directory. To configure Quarkus logs, just add the properties listed in Listing 13 to the application.properties file. No need to stop and restart Quarkus: re-execute the cURL command and the new log format will automatically be applied.

Listing 13. Configuring Quarkus Logs

```
quarkus.log.level=DEBUG
quarkus.log.console.format=%d{HH:mm:ss} %-5p [%c{2.}] %s%e%n
quarkus.log.console.level=DEBUG
```

3.3.6. Testing the Application

So far so good, but wouldn't it be better with a few tests, just in case? How is it possible to test our REST endpoints then? Do we need to run the application with the tests? The answer is yes. In Listing 14, we use the QuarkusTest runner to instruct JUnit to start the application first, and then execute the tests. We then have two test methods:

- The shouldGetAllArtists() method checks the HTTP response status code (200) and the size of the JSON array.

- The shouldCountArtist() method checks that the response contains the number 4 (because we have four artists).

Notice that these tests use REST Assured[129]. More on REST Assured, Hamcrest and testing Quarkus applications in Chapter 11.

Listing 14. Testing the Artist REST Endpoint

```java
@QuarkusTest
public class ArtistResourceTest {

  @Test
  public void shouldGetAllArtists() {
    given().
    when()
      .get("/artists").
    then()
      .assertThat()
        .statusCode(is(200))
      .and()
        .body("size()", equalTo(4));
  }

  @Test
  public void shouldCountArtist() {
    given().
    when()
      .get("/artists/count").
    then()
      .assertThat()
        .statusCode(is(200))
      .and()
        .body(is("4"));
  }
}
```

Now execute the test with `./mvnw test` or from your IDE. The test should pass and you should see similar logs to those in Listing 15.

Listing 15. Tests Successful Output

```
[INFO] ------------------------
[INFO] Building Getting Started
[INFO] ------------------------
[INFO]
[INFO] --- quarkus-maven-plugin:2.5.0.Final:generate-code
[INFO]
[INFO] --- maven-compiler-plugin:3.8.1:compile
[INFO]
[INFO] --- quarkus-maven-plugin:2.5.0.Final:generate-code-tests
[INFO]
[INFO] --- maven-surefire-plugin:3.0.0-M5:test
[INFO]
[INFO] ------------------------
[INFO]  T E S T S
[INFO] ------------------------
[INFO] Running org.agoncal.fascicle.quarkus.gettingstarted.ArtistResourceTest
[INFO] [io.quarkus] Quarkus started in 1.100s. Listening on: http://0.0.0.0:8081
[INFO] [io.quarkus] Profile test activated.
[INFO] [io.quarkus] Installed features: [cdi, resteasy, resteasy-jsonb]
[INFO] Tests run: 2, Failures: 0, Errors: 0, Skipped: 0, Time elapsed: 2.642 s
[INFO] [io.quarkus] (main) Quarkus stopped in 0.032s
[INFO]
[INFO] Results:
[INFO]
[INFO] Tests run: 2, Failures: 0, Errors: 0, Skipped: 0
[INFO]
[INFO] ------------------------
[INFO] BUILD SUCCESS
[INFO] ------------------------
[INFO] Total time:  5.945 s
[INFO] ------------------------
```

There are a few interesting pieces of information in these logs. First of all, you'll notice that Quarkus starts and runs the application. Thanks to @QuarkusTest you get real integration tests with the Quarkus runtime. And when you look at the timestamps, you can see that starting and shutting down the application is quite quick. Quarkus makes your integration tests run quickly. While Quarkus will listen on port 8080 by default, when running tests it defaults to 8081. This allows you to run tests while having the application running in parallel.

3.3.7. Continuous Testing

If you look at the output on Listing 12 when Quarkus starts, you'll notice this message:

```
Tests paused
Press [r] to resume testing, [o] Toggle test output, [h] for more options>
```

This means that Quarkus has paused the tests and is ready for continuous testing. Continuous testing means that tests are executed immediately after code changes have been saved. This allows you to get instant feedback on your code changes. Quarkus detects which tests cover which code, and uses this information to only run the relevant tests when code is changed.

If you press r, the tests are executed and you will get the following:

```
All 2 tests are passing (0 skipped), 2 tests were run in 381ms. Tests completed at
09:29:59 due to changes to ArtistResource.class and 1 other files.
Press [r] to resume testing, [o] Toggle test output, [h] for more options>
```

Now, break a test, save the file, and let Quarkus recompile the code and execute the tests. You'll get the following:

```
ERROR [io.qua.test] ===================== TEST REPORT #3 =====================
ERROR [io.qua.test] Test ArtistResourceTest#shouldGetAllArtists() failed
: java.lang.AssertionError: 1 expectation failed.
Expected status code is <300> but was <200>.

ERROR [io.qua.test] >>>>>>>>>>>>>>>>>>>>> 1 TEST FAILED <<<<<<<<<<<<<<<<<<<<<

--
1 test failed (1 passing, 0 skipped), 2 tests were run in 431ms. Tests completed at
09:31:02 due to changes to ArtistResourceTest.class.
Press [r] to re-run, [o] Toggle test output, [h] for more options>
```

Continuous testing is one numerous gem brought by Quarkus when it comes to developer's joy.

3.3.8. Debugging the Application

If you again at the logs in Listing 12, you'll notice that Quarkus, by default, uses the port 5005 for debugging purposes. The port 5005 is where Quarkus, through JPDA (*Java Platform Debugger Architecture*[130]), listens to the socket transport dt_socket allowing communication between a debugger and the virtual machine that is being debugged. When running in development mode (./mvnw quarkus:dev), Quarkus will configure the JVM to automatically listen on this port. You can check that the debugging is active with the following shell command:

```
$ lsof -i tcp:5005

COMMAND   PID     USER    FD   TYPE  NAME
java    70796 agoncal    4u   IPv4  *:avt-profile-2 (LISTEN)
```

Now, it's just a matter of attaching the IDE to the debugger. The process is different for each IDE but I'll show you how to do it with IntelliJ IDEA. In order to attach IntelliJ IDEA to the debugger, add a new configuration called *Remote*, and set all the required values as shown in Figure 20.

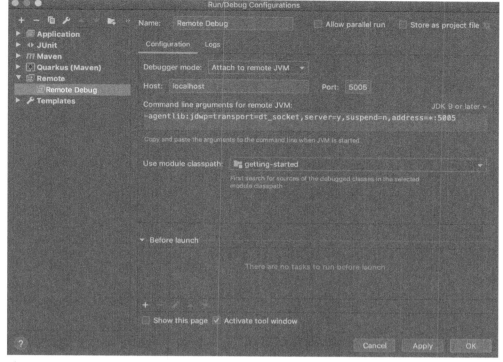

Figure 20. Remote debugging in IntelliJ IDEA

Select the *Remote Debug* configuration and click on *Debug* while Quarkus is still up and running. Place a breakpoint somewhere in the `ArtistResource` and invoke the application (using cURL). From the debugger prompt, you can inspect the class and method variables from its console. You can also control the execution path (*Step Over*, *Step Into*, etc.) by clicking on the buttons located on the *Debugger Console*.

 IntelliJ IDEA has a nice integration with Quarkus that eases debugging. The Quarkus plugin goes through all the configuration that we've done, with just one click. Don't hesitate to check the Quarkus plugins[13] if you are using IntelliJ IDEA.

3.3.9. Checking the Development Console

In development mode, Quarkus comes with a lot of great features from the console: terse, nicely coloured logs, as well as continuous testing reports and commands. But not everything can be displayed in the console. That's why Quarkus comes with a *Dev UI*.

Dev UI is a graphical interface that lists all the extensions that are installed on a running Quarkus application. It is available on the `/q/dev` endpoint. Along with each extension, you get links to their documentation and specific pages, such as the Swagger UI to test REST endpoints, for example. You also have the list of installed CDI beans, or continuous testing presented in a graphical manner.

While Quarkus is running, go to http://localhost:8080/q/dev. You should see a web console similar to the one shown in Figure 21.

Figure 21. Development console

Click on the *Config Editor* box and you will get all the properties that configure your application (see Figure 22).

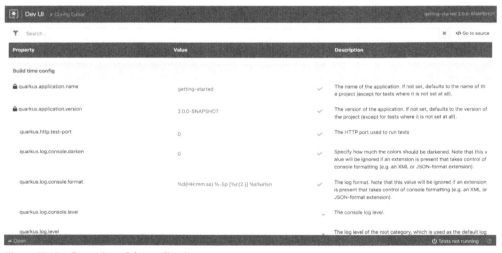

Figure 22. Configuration of the application

3.4. Running the Application

So far we've been running the `ArtistResource` endpoint using `./mvnw quarkus:dev`. This development mode is really handy as it brings us live reload: we can execute the application, change some code, and Quarkus automatically restarts taking into account our changes. But this has a cost as the startup time is slower.

3.4.1. Building an Executable JAR

To execute our endpoint in production mode, first, we need to package it with the `./mvnw package` command. If we do so, it produces two JAR files under the `target` directory:

```
getting-started$ ./mvnw package
getting-started$ ls -lh target

-rw-r--r-- 603B  quarkus-app/quarkus-run.jar
-rw-r--r-- 7.5K  getting-started-2.0.0-SNAPSHOT.jar
```

As you can see, these two JAR files have different sizes (more on executable JARs in Chapter 10), therefore their content is different:

- `getting-started-2.0.0-SNAPSHOT.jar`: Contains just the classes and resources of the projects, it's the regular artifact produced by the Maven build.

- `quarkus-app/quarkus-run.jar`: Is an executable jar.

3.4.2. Executing the Executable JAR

With an executable JAR, you can run the application using the following command:

```
getting-started$ java -jar target/quarkus-app/quarkus-run.jar
```

But be aware that `quarkus-run.jar` is an executable JAR, not an Uber-JAR[132]. An Uber-JAR contains both the code of our application and all its dependencies in one single JAR file. This is not the case here. Quarkus copies all the dependencies into the `target/quarkus-app/lib` directory and `quarkus-run.jar` depends on this `target/quarkus-app/lib` directory. If you remove the `target/quarkus-app/lib` and re-run the application with `java -jar target/quarkus-app/quarkus-run.jar` it won't work (as you will get a `ClassNotFoundException`).

By executing the executable JAR, you will get traces that look like the ones in Listing 16.

Listing 16. Startup with Production Profile

```
getting-started$ java -jar target/quarkus-app/quarkus-run.jar


__  ____  __  _____   ___  __ ____  _____
 --/ __ \/ / / / _ | / / _ \/ //_/ / / / __/
 -/ /_/ / /_/ / __ |/ /, _/ ,< / /_/ /\ \
--_____/_/ |_/_/|_/_/|_|\____/___/
INFO  [io.quarkus] getting-started 2.0.0-SNAPSHOT on JVM (powered by Quarkus
2.5.0.Final) started in 0.693s. Listening on: http://0.0.0.0:8080
INFO  [io.quarkus] Profile prod activated.
INFO  [io.quarkus] Installed features: [cdi, resteasy, resteasy-jsonb, smallrye-
context-propagation, vertx]
```

You'll notice a few things here. First of all, the application has started slightly faster than in development mode. Then, Port 5005 is not opened by default. Also notice that the logs show the message "*Profile prod activated*" and the message "*Live Coding activated*" has disappeared (more on profiles in Chapter 4). Invoke a cURL command on the following URL http://localhost:8080/artists and you will get the same JSON representation of artists as before.

 When you execute a Quarkus application in production mode, the Dev UI is not accessible. If you go to http://localhost:8080/q/dev you will notice that there is no more graphical interface.

3.5. Going Native

Let's now produce a native executable for our REST endpoint. Thanks to GraalVM, Quarkus is able to generate native executables. Just like Go, native executables don't need a Virtual Machine (VM) to run, they contain the whole application, like an .exe file on Windows. Native executables improve the startup time of the application, memory consumption, and produce a minimal disk footprint. The executable has everything to run the application including the JVM (shrunk to be just enough to run the application), and the application itself.

3.5.1. Building a Native Executable

Building an executable JAR, as we just did, is one thing. But Quarkus, with the help of GraalVM, can go further: it can build a native executable. Before building the executable, verify that you have set GRAALVM_HOME in your environment, as described in Appendix A.

Thanks to the built-in Maven native profile, you can easily create a native executable using the following command.

```
getting-started$ ./mvnw package -Pnative
```

The plugin will start analysing the classes and packaging what's used by the application. By executing this command, you should have a similar output:

```
[getting-started-2.0.0-SNAPSHOT-runner]    classlist:    3 179,28 ms
[getting-started-2.0.0-SNAPSHOT-runner]        (cap):    1 238,43 ms
[getting-started-2.0.0-SNAPSHOT-runner]        setup:    2 226,59 ms
[getting-started-2.0.0-SNAPSHOT-runner]     (typeflow):    9 376,87 ms
[getting-started-2.0.0-SNAPSHOT-runner]     (objects):   12 031,39 ms
[getting-started-2.0.0-SNAPSHOT-runner]    (features):      553,82 ms
[getting-started-2.0.0-SNAPSHOT-runner]     analysis:   23 048,54 ms
[getting-started-2.0.0-SNAPSHOT-runner]      (clinit):      680,90 ms
[getting-started-2.0.0-SNAPSHOT-runner]     universe:    1 445,67 ms
[getting-started-2.0.0-SNAPSHOT-runner]        (parse):      982,12 ms
[getting-started-2.0.0-SNAPSHOT-runner]      (inline):    3 537,58 ms
[getting-started-2.0.0-SNAPSHOT-runner]    (compile):   16 089,81 ms
[getting-started-2.0.0-SNAPSHOT-runner]      compile:   22 338,84 ms
[getting-started-2.0.0-SNAPSHOT-runner]        image:    2 984,38 ms
[getting-started-2.0.0-SNAPSHOT-runner]        write:      729,42 ms
[getting-started-2.0.0-SNAPSHOT-runner]      [total]:   56 189,06 ms
[INFO] Quarkus augmentation completed in 58205ms
```

In addition to the regular files, the build also produces the `getting-started-2.0.0-SNAPSHOT-runner` file (notice that there is no `.jar` file extension). It is an executable that contains just a thin JVM layer (slim enough to just execute the application) and the application itself. And if you check the permissions of the files, you can notice that `getting-started-2.0.0-SNAPSHOT-runner` is executable (x allowing executable permissions).

```
getting-started$ ls -lh target/getting-started*

-rwxr-xr-x   44M   getting-started-2.0.0-SNAPSHOT-runner*
-rw-r--r--   7.5K   getting-started-2.0.0-SNAPSHOT.jar
```

 Creating a native executable requires a lot of memory and CPU. It also takes a few minutes, even for a simple application like the *ArtistResource* REST endpoint. Most of the time is spent during the dead-code elimination, as it traverses the whole closed-world[133].

3.5.2. Executing the Native Executable

Now you can simply execute the file like any other native executable with `./target/getting-started-2.0.0-SNAPSHOT-runner`.

```
getting-started$ ./target/getting-started-2.0.0-SNAPSHOT-runner


__  ____  __  _____   ___  __ ____  _____
 --/ __ \/ / / / _ | / _ \/ //_/ / / / __/
 -/ /_/ / /_/ / __ |/ , _/ ,< / /_/ /\ \
--_____/_/ |_/_/|_/_/|_|\____/___/
INFO  [io.quarkus] getting-started 2.0.0-SNAPSHOT native (powered by Quarkus
2.5.0.Final) started in 0.023s. Listening on: http://0.0.0.0:8080
INFO  [io.quarkus] Profile prod activated.
INFO  [io.quarkus] Installed features: [cdi, resteasy, resteasy-jsonb, smallrye-
context-propagation, vertx]
```

One thing to notice when doing so is the startup time. Depending on your machine, starting the native executable is 4 to 6 times faster that executing the executable JAR. The memory footprint is also smaller. And also notice that the log displays getting-started 2.0.0-SNAPSHOT native: we know it's the native executable that is being executed.

3.5.3. Testing the Native Executable

Interestingly, native executable code can be tested. Producing a native executable can lead to a few issues (more on that in Chapter 11), and so it's also a good idea to run some tests against the application running in the native file. In the pom.xml file in Listing 8, the native profile instructs the failsafe-maven-plugin[134] to run integration-test and indicates the location of the produced native executable. When we generated our project, a NativeArtistResourceIT class name was included in the test folder. As you can see in Listing 17, this class extends our original test (ArtistResourceTest) and is annotated with the @NativeImageTest annotation.

Listing 17. Native Test

```
@NativeImageTest
public class NativeArtistResourceIT extends ArtistResourceTest {

    // Execute the same tests but in native mode.
}
```

Now, you can test the native executable application by using the native profile in the following Maven command:

```
getting-started$ ./mvnw verify -Pnative

[INFO] --- maven-surefire-plugin:3.0.0-M5:test (default-test)
[INFO]
[INFO] -------------------------------------------------------
[INFO]  T E S T S
[INFO] -------------------------------------------------------
[INFO] Running org.agoncal.fascicle.quarkus.gettingstarted.ArtistResourceTest
[INFO]
[INFO] Results:
[INFO] Tests run: 2, Failures: 0, Errors: 0, Skipped: 0
[INFO]
[INFO] --- maven-failsafe-plugin:3.0.0-M5:integration-test (integration-test)
[INFO]
[INFO] -------------------------------------------------------
[INFO]  T E S T S
[INFO] -------------------------------------------------------
[INFO] Running org.agoncal.fascicle.quarkus.gettingstarted.NativeArtistResourceIT
[INFO] Results:
[INFO] Tests run: 2, Failures: 0, Errors: 0, Skipped: 0
```

Great! We have just managed to test our application in both scenarios: JVM and native executable.

3.6. Containerising the Application

When we bootstrapped our application, the Quarkus Maven plugin generated a few Dockerfiles for us under the src/main/docker directory:

- Dockerfile.jvm: Containerises the application using the JAR produced by the Quarkus Maven Plugin.

- Dockerfile.legacy-jar: Containerises the application using a legacy format generated JAR.

- Dockerfile.native: Containerises the application using the native executable and a Linux distribution.

- Dockerfile.native-distroless: Containerises only the application native executable without any distribution (package managers, shells or ordinary programs commonly find in a standard Linux distribution are removed).

We could containerise the application using the executable JAR (using Dockerfile.jvm), but let's focus on creating a container image using the produced native executable.

3.6.1. Building the Native Executable Image

Now, let's see how to build a native executable for the container and include it in the image. The native executable we just built is specific to the operating system we are on (Linux, macOS, Windows etc.). Because the container may not use the same executable format as the one produced by your operating system, we first need to instruct the Maven build to produce an executable from inside a container. This is done using the following command which sets the `quarkus.native.container-build` attribute to `true`:

```
getting-started$ ./mvnw package -Pnative -Dquarkus.native.container-build=true

[INFO] --- quarkus-maven-plugin:2.5.0.Final:build (default)
[INFO] Building native image from target/getting-started-2.0.0-SNAPSHOT-native-image-
source-jar/getting-started-2.0.0-SNAPSHOT-runner.jar
[INFO] Using docker to run the native image builder
[INFO] Checking image status quay.io/quarkus/ubi-quarkus-native-image:21.3.0-java11
[INFO] Pulling image quay.io/quarkus/ubi-quarkus-native-image:21.3.0-java11
[INFO] Status: Downloaded newer image for quay.io/quarkus/ubi-quarkus-native-
image:21.3.0-java11
[INFO]
[INFO] Running Quarkus native-image plugin on GraalVM 21.3.0 Java 11 CE
[INFO] docker run -v target/getting-started-2.0.0-SNAPSHOT-native-image-source-jar
[INFO] Quarkus augmentation completed in 136499ms
[INFO] ----------------------------
[INFO] BUILD SUCCESS
[INFO] ----------------------------
```

The produced executable `target/getting-started-2.0.0-SNAPSHOT-runner` is a 64-bit Linux executable, so depending on your operating system it may no longer be runnable. For example, if you try to execute this file on macOS you will get the following error:

```
getting-started$ ./target/getting-started-2.0.0-SNAPSHOT-runner

Failed to execute process './target/getting-started-2.0.0-SNAPSHOT-runner'
Reason: exec: Exec format error
The file './target/getting-started-2.0.0-SNAPSHOT-runner' is marked as an executable
but could not be run by the operating system
```

However, it's not an issue as we now have to build a Docker image with this 64-bit Linux executable. That's the purpose of the generated `Dockerfile.native` described in Listing 18. Notice the `FROM` statement in the Dockerfile. UBI, or *Red Hat Universal Base Image*[135], is a subset of the *Red Hat Enterprise Linux* operating system, stripped down to the bare essentials, and is perfect for containers.

Listing 18. Dockerfile for the Native Image

```
FROM registry.access.redhat.com/ubi8/ubi-minimal:8.4
WORKDIR /work/
RUN chown 1001 /work \
    && chmod "g+rwX" /work \
    && chown 1001:root /work
COPY --chown=1001:root target/*-runner /work/application

EXPOSE 8080
USER 1001

CMD ["./application", "-Dquarkus.http.host=0.0.0.0"]
```

To build the image with the declarations of the Dockerfile in Listing 18, use the following docker image build command:

```
getting-started$ docker image build -f src/main/docker/Dockerfile.native -t
quarkus/getting-started .

[1/4] FROM registry.access.redhat.com/ubi8/ubi-minimal:8.4
[2/4] WORKDIR /work/
[3/4] RUN chown 1001 /work     && chmod "g+rwX" /work     && chown 1001:root /work
[4/4] COPY --chown=1001:root target/*-runner /work/application
exporting to image
=> exporting layers
=> writing image sha256:440248ad225fbe27ce9951
=> naming to docker.io/quarkus/getting-started
```

If you want to check that the image has been successfully created, use the docker image ls command as follows:

```
getting-started$ docker image ls | grep getting-started

REPOSITORY                 TAG      IMAGE ID      SIZE
quarkus/getting-started    latest   1e28e9a16045  148MB
```

3.6.2. Executing the Container Image

Now that we have built a 64-bit Linux executable of our application, and included it in a Docker image, let's run it. For that, we use the following docker container run command to execute our image and expose the port 8080:

```
getting-started$ docker container run -i --rm -p 8080:8080 quarkus/getting-started

 __  ____  __  _____   ___  __ ____  _____
 --/ __ \/ / / / _ | / / _ \/ //_/ / / / __/
 -/ /_/ / /_/ / __ |/ , _/ ,< / /_/ /\ \
 --_____/_/ |_/_/|_/_/|_|\____/___/
INFO  [io.quarkus] getting-started 2.0.0-SNAPSHOT native (powered by Quarkus
2.5.0.Final) started in 0.029s. Listening on: http://0.0.0.0:8080
INFO  [io.quarkus] Profile prod activated.
INFO  [io.quarkus] Installed features: Installed features: [cdi, resteasy, resteasy-
jsonb, smallrye-context-propagation, vertx]
```

Like previously, notice the log `getting-started 2.0.0-SNAPSHOT native`: it's the native executable that is being executed. Now, execute the following cURL commands to invoke our `ArtistResource` endpoint:

```
$ curl http://localhost:8080/artists/count
4
```

Good! Everything is running as expected. If you want further information on packaging, native image, performances and containers, you can check out Chapter 10.

3.7. Summary

If you've managed to execute all the code in this chapter, then it means that your development environment is all setup. You are ready to follow the next chapters and execute the samples.

In this chapter, we went through our first Quarkus project, which was generated through the `quarkus-maven-plugin`. The default bootstrapped application is a REST endpoint with minimal functionalities, a `pom.xml`, a few test classes as well as Docker files. We've progressively enriched this default application to develop a REST endpoint that would return a JSON representation of artists. After developing with live reload, debugging with remote debug and testing our code, we've executed our application in several flavours (development environment and executable JAR). We turned the Java code into a thin native executable using the appropriate `native` profile of `quarkus-maven-plugin`, we ended up containerising and executing it with Docker.

Now that you know the basis of Quarkus, microservices, MicroProfile, and GraalVM, and have run a "*Hello World*" example from code to a native executable, let's use the following chapters to dig more into Quarkus. Next, *Core Quarkus* focuses on some core technologies that most applications or extensions get out of the box. That is, injection (with Context and Dependency Injection), configuration, profiles, logs and application life cycle.

[125] Maven https://maven.apache.org

[126] Quarkus support in IDEs https://quarkus.io/blog/march-of-ides

[127] Quarkus Maven plugin https://github.com/quarkusio/quarkus/tree/master/devtools/maven

[128] JHipster Quarkus https://github.com/jhipster/jhipster-quarkus

[129] REST Assured http://rest-assured.io

[130] JPDA https://docs.oracle.com/en/java/javase/11/docs/specs/jpda/jpda.html

[131] Quarkus IntelliJ IDEA Plugin https://plugins.jetbrains.com/plugin/14242-quarkus-integration

[132] Uber-JAR https://stackoverflow.com/questions/11947037/what-is-an-uber-jar

[133] Closed-World Assumption https://www.graalvm.org/community/opensource

[134] Maven Failsafe Plugin https://maven.apache.org/surefire/maven-failsafe-plugin

[135] UBI https://www.redhat.com/en/blog/introducing-red-hat-universal-base-image

Chapter 4. Core Quarkus

In the previous *Getting Started* chapter, you made sure you could run a Quarkus application. This means that your environment is up and running and you've already caught a glimpse of what Quarkus does. As explained in the *Understanding Quarkus* chapter, Quarkus has a powerful extension mechanism for integrating many technologies. The chapters coming up will show you some of these extensions and how to use them.

This *Core Quarkus* chapter focuses on the core technologies that you first need to know because they will be used throughout this fascicle. First, *Context and Dependency Injection*, because Quarkus makes heavy use of injection. Injection is actually used in *Eclipse MicroProfile Configuration* which configures most parts of Quarkus, including its *profile* mechanism or *logging*. This chapter will end explaining the *lifecycle* of a Quarkus application and how it initialises and terminates.

 The code in this chapter can be found at https://github.com/agoncal/agoncal-fascicle-quarkus/tree/2.0/core

4.1. Context and Dependency Injection

Injection is at the core of Quarkus. From injecting a bean into another one, injecting configuration into a component, or injecting a resource to a component, injection is everywhere. CDI is the MicroProfile specification taking care of dependency injection. But CDI comes with other features that are heavily used in Quarkus: scopes or event management.

 Quarkus is based on a CDI implementation called ArC[136]. ArC does not fully implement CDI, only the most commonly used subset of the specification is implemented. Therefore, there are a few limitations[137] that you need to take into account if you come from a full-CDI world.

Context and Dependency Injection[138] (CDI) is a central technology in Jakarta EE or in MicroProfile. Its programming model turns nearly every component into an injectable, interceptable and manageable bean. CDI is built on the concept of "*loose coupling, strong typing*", meaning that beans are loosely coupled, but in a strongly-typed way. Decoupling goes further by bringing interceptors, decorators and events to the entire platform. CDI homogenises scopes among beans, as well as context and life cycle management.

The Context and Dependency Injection APIs and annotations are defined under several root packages: javax.inject, javax.enterprise and javax.interceptor. Table 5 lists the main subpackages defined in CDI 2.0.

Table 5. Main CDI Subpackages

Subpackage	Description
javax.inject	Root package of the CDI APIs
javax.enterprise.inject	Core dependency injection APIs
javax.enterprise.context	Scope and contextual APIs

Subpackage	Description
javax.enterprise.event	Event and observer APIs
javax.enterprise.util	Utility package
javax.interceptor	Interceptor APIs (JSR 318)

Along with APIs, CDI comes with a set of annotations. Table 6 lists a subset of the most commonly used annotations.

Table 6. Main CDI Annotations

Annotation	Description
@Inject	Identifies injectable constructors, methods, and fields
@Qualifier	Identifies qualifier annotations
@ApplicationScoped, @SessionScoped, @RequestScoped, @Singleton, @Dependent	Set of annotations defining the life cycle of a bean
@Observes	Identifies the event parameter of an observer method

CDI is part of the core of Quarkus and most extensions need it. So, most of the time, you don't have to explicitly add the CDI extension, it will be resolved recursively. But if you need it, you must add the extension defined in Listing 19 to your pom.xml

Listing 19. CDI Extension

```
<dependency>
    <groupId>io.quarkus</groupId>
    <artifactId>quarkus-arc</artifactId>
</dependency>
```

4.1.1. Understanding Beans

The word *Bean* might be interpreted in different ways. Java SE has JavaBeans. *JavaBeans*[139] are just POJOs (*Plain Old Java Object*) that follow certain patterns (e.g. a naming convention for accessors/mutators (getters/setters) for a property, a default constructor...) and are executed inside the JVM. In a managed environment such as Quarkus, we have *CDI Beans* which are a sort of *Managed Beans*.

Managed Beans are container-managed objects that support only a small set of basic services: resource injection, life cycle management, and interception. They provide a common foundation for the different kinds of components that exist in managed platforms (such as Spring, Jakarta EE or MicroProfile). For example, a RESTful web service can be seen as a Managed Bean with extra services. A transactional service can also be seen as a Managed Bean with extra services (different from the RESTful web service), and so on.

CDI Beans (or *Beans* for short) are objects that are built on this basic Managed Bean model. CDI

Beans have an improved life cycle management for stateful objects; are bound to well-defined contexts; bring a typesafe approach to dependency injection, interception, and decoration; are specialised with qualifier annotations; and can be used in *Expression Language*[140] (EL). In fact, with very few exceptions, potentially every Java class that has a default constructor and runs inside a container is a Bean.

4.1.2. Injecting Beans

In a managed environment, you don't need to construct dependencies by hand but can leave the container to inject a reference for you. In a nutshell, CDI dependency injection is the ability to inject beans into others in a typesafe way, which means annotations rather than XML. With CDI, you can inject nearly anything anywhere thanks to the @Inject annotation.

Listing 20 shows how you would inject a reference of the NumberGenerator into the BookService using the CDI @Inject.

Listing 20. BookService Using @Inject to Get a Reference of NumberGenerator

```
public class BookService {

  @Inject
  NumberGenerator numberGenerator;

  public Book createBook(String title, Float price, String description) {
    Book book = new Book(title, price, description);
    book.setIsbn(numberGenerator.generateNumber());
    return book;
  }
}
```

As you can see in Listing 20, a simple @Inject annotation on the property will inform the container that it has to inject a reference of a NumberGenerator implementation into the numberGenerator property. This is called the injection point (the place where the @Inject annotation is). Listing 21 shows the IsbnGenerator implementation. As you can see, there are no special annotations and the class implements the NumberGenerator interface.

Listing 21. The IsbnGenerator Bean

```
public class IsbnGenerator implements NumberGenerator {

  public String generateNumber() {
    return "13-84356-" + Math.abs(new Random().nextInt());
  }
}
```

Quarkus is designed with GraalVM in mind so it can build native executables. One of the limitations of GraalVM is the use of reflection. Reflective operations are supported in Quarkus, but all relevant members must be explicitly registered for reflection (which results in a bigger native executable). And if you use injection in a private member, reflection is used. For this reason, you are encouraged to use package-private scope instead of private when using injection.

Injection Points

The `@Inject` annotation defines an injection point that is injected during bean instantiation. Injection can occur via three different mechanisms: property, setter, or constructor.

Property injection is when you annotate an attribute (a.k.a. property) with `@Inject`.

```
@Inject
NumberGenerator numberGenerator;
```

Notice that it isn't necessary to create a getter and a setter method on an attribute to use injection. CDI can access an injected field directly (even if it's private), which sometimes helps eliminate some wasteful code. But instead of annotating the attributes, you can add the `@Inject` annotation on a constructor as follows:

```
@Inject
public LegacyBookService(NumberGenerator numberGenerator) {
  this.numberGenerator = numberGenerator;
}
```

But the rule is that you can only have one constructor injection point. The container is the one doing the injection, not you (you can't invoke a constructor in a managed environment); therefore, there is only one bean constructor allowed so that the container can do its work and inject the right references.

The other choice is to use setter injection, which looks like constructor injection. You just need to annotate the setter with `@Inject`.

```
@Inject
public void setNumberGenerator(NumberGenerator numberGenerator) {
  this.numberGenerator = numberGenerator;
}
```

You may ask, "*When should I use a field over a constructor or setter injection?*" There is no real technical answer to that question; it's a matter of your own personal taste. In a managed environment, the container is the one doing all the injection's work; it just needs the right injection points.

Quarkus simplifies the injection model even more. When using constructor or setter injection, you can even skip the @Inject annotation. Quarkus will know how to inject the reference of NumberGenerator automatically.

```
public PrestigiousBookService(NumberGenerator numberGenerator) {
  this.numberGenerator = numberGenerator;
}
```

Default Injection

Assume that, as shown in Figure 23, the NumberGenerator interface only has one implementation: IsbnGenerator. CDI will then be able to inject it simply by using @Inject on its own.

```
@Inject
NumberGenerator numberGenerator;
```

This is termed *default injection*. Whenever a bean or injection point does not explicitly declare a qualifier, the container assumes the qualifier @javax.enterprise.inject.Default. In fact, the following code is identical to the previous one:

```
@Inject @Default
NumberGenerator numberGenerator;
```

@Default is a built-in qualifier that informs CDI to inject the default bean implementation. If you define a bean with no qualifier, the bean automatically has the qualifier @Default. So the code in Listing 22 uses @Default but it could be omitted.

Listing 22. The IsbnGenerator Bean with the @Default Qualifier

```
@Default
public class IsbnGenerator implements NumberGenerator {

  public String generateNumber() {
    return "13-84356-" + Math.abs(new Random().nextInt());
  }
}
```

If you only have one implementation of a bean to inject, the default behaviour applies and a straightforward @Inject will inject the implementation. The class diagram in Figure 23 shows the @Default implementation (IsbnGenerator) as well as the default injection point (@Inject @Default).

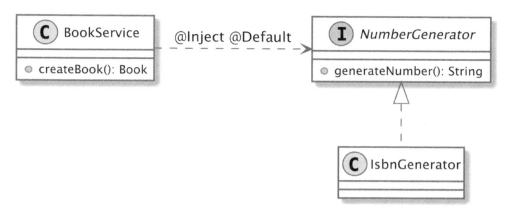

Figure 23. Class diagram with @Default injection

But sometimes you have to choose between several implementations. That's when you need to use qualifiers.

Injecting Qualified Beans

At system initialisation time, the container must validate that exactly one bean satisfying each injection point exists. Meaning that, if no implementation of NumberGenerator is available, the container will inform you of an unsatisfied dependency and will not deploy the application. If there is only one implementation, injection will work using the @Default qualifier. If more than one default implementation were available, the container would inform you of an *ambiguous dependency* and would not deploy the application. That's because the typesafe resolution algorithm fails when the container is unable to identify exactly one bean to inject.

So how does a component choose which implementation (IsbnGenerator or IssnGenerator) should get injected? Most frameworks heavily rely on external XML configuration to declare and inject beans. CDI uses qualifiers, which are basically Java annotations that bring typesafe injection and disambiguate a type without having to fall back on String-based names.

There are several book number formats, the most common are:

- ISBN (*International Standard Book Number*[141]): Thirteen-digit book identifier which is intended to be unique.

- ISSN (*International Standard Serial Number*[142]): Eight-digit serial number used to uniquely identify a serial publication.

Let's say we have an application with a BookService that creates books with a 13-digit ISBN number and a LegacyBookService that creates books with an 8-digit ISSN number. As you can see in Figure 24, both services inject a reference of the same NumberGenerator interface. The services distinguish between the two implementations by using qualifiers.

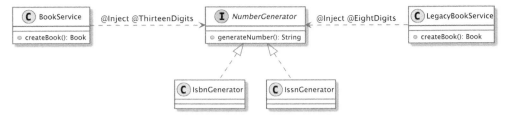

Figure 24. Services using qualifiers for non-ambiguous injection

A qualifier represents some semantics associated with a type that is satisfied by some implementation of that type. It is a user-defined annotation, itself annotated with @javax.inject.Qualifer. For example, we could introduce qualifiers to represent 13- and 8-digit number generators, both shown in Listing 23 and Listing 24.

Listing 23. The ThirteenDigits Qualifier

```
@Qualifier
@Retention(RUNTIME)
@Target({FIELD, TYPE, METHOD})
public @interface ThirteenDigits {
}
```

Listing 24. The EightDigits Qualifier

```
@Qualifier
@Retention(RUNTIME)
@Target({FIELD, TYPE, METHOD})
public @interface EightDigits {
}
```

Once you have defined the required qualifiers, they must be applied on the appropriate implementation. As you can see in both Listing 25 and Listing 26, the @ThirteenDigits qualifier is applied to the IsbnGenerator bean and @EightDigits to IssnGenerator.

Listing 25. The IsbnGenerator Bean with the @ThirteenDigits Qualifier

```
@ThirteenDigits
public class IsbnGenerator implements NumberGenerator {

  public String generateNumber() {
    return "13-84356-" + Math.abs(new Random().nextInt());
  }
}
```

Listing 26. The IssnGenerator Bean with the @EightDigits Qualifier

```java
@EightDigits
public class IssnGenerator implements NumberGenerator {

  public String generateNumber() {
    return "8-" + Math.abs(new Random().nextInt());
  }
}
```

These qualifiers are then applied to injection points to distinguish which implementation is required by the client. In Listing 27, the BookService explicitly defines the 13-digit implementation by injecting a reference of the @ThirteenDigits number generator and, in Listing 28, the LegacyBookService injects the 8-digit implementation.

Listing 27. BookService Using the @ThirteenDigits NumberGenerator Implementation

```java
public class BookService {

  @Inject
  @ThirteenDigits
  NumberGenerator numberGenerator;

  public Book createBook(String title, Float price, String description) {
    Book book = new Book(title, price, description);
    book.setIsbn(numberGenerator.generateNumber());
    return book;
  }
}
```

Listing 28. LegacyBookService Using the @EightDigits NumberGenerator Implementation

```java
public class LegacyBookService {

  @Inject
  @EightDigits
  NumberGenerator numberGenerator;

  public Book createBook(String title, Float price, String description) {
    Book book = new Book(title, price, description);
    book.setIsbn(numberGenerator.generateNumber());
    return book;
  }
}
```

For this to work, you don't need external configuration; that's why CDI is said to use strong typing. You can rename your implementations to whatever you want and rename your qualifier - the injection point will not change (that's loose coupling). As you can see, CDI is an elegant way to have typesafe injection.

As shown in Listing 29, Quarkus simplifies the CDI specification by allowing you to inject qualified beans without using the @Inject annotation.

Listing 29. Injecting Qualified Beans without @Inject

```
public class LegacyBookService {

  @EightDigits
  NumberGenerator numberGenerator;

  public Book createBook(String title, Float price, String description) {
    Book book = new Book(title, price, description);
    book.setIsbn(numberGenerator.generateNumber());
    return book;
  }
}
```

Injecting Alternative Beans

Qualifiers let you choose between multiple implementations of an interface at development time. But sometimes you want to inject an implementation depending on a particular deployment scenario. For example, you may want to use a mock number generator in a testing environment.

Alternatives are beans annotated with the special qualifier javax.enterprise.inject.Alternative. By default, alternatives are disabled and need to be enabled to make them available for instantiation and injection. Listing 30 shows a mock number generator alternative.

Listing 30. A Mock Generator Alternative

```
@Alternative
public class MockGenerator implements NumberGenerator {

  public String generateNumber() {
    return "MOCK";
  }
}
```

As you can see in Listing 30, the MockGenerator implements the NumberGenerator interface as usual. It is annotated with @Alternative, meaning that CDI treats it as the default alternative of the NumberGenerator. This default alternative could have used the @Default built-in qualifier as shown in Listing 31.

Listing 31. A Default Mock Generator Alternative

```
@Alternative
@Default
public class MockGenerator implements NumberGenerator {

  public String generateNumber() {
    return "MOCK";
  }
}
```

Instead of a default alternative, you can specify the alternative by using qualifiers. For example, the following code tells CDI that the alternative of a 13-digit number generator is the mock:

```
@Alternative @ThirteenDigits
public class MockGenerator implements NumberGenerator {...}
```

By default, `@Alternative` beans are disabled and you need to explicitly enable them using configuration. For that, declare the alternative using the property `quarkus.arc.selected-alternatives` in the `application.properties` file as shown in Listing 32.

Listing 32. Enabling an Alternative

```
quarkus.arc.selected-
alternatives=org.agoncal.fascicle.quarkus.core.cdi.alternatives.MockGenerator
```

In terms of injection point, nothing changes. So your client code is not impacted. The code that follows injects the default implementation of a number generator. If the alternative is enabled, then the `MockGenerator` defined in Listing 30 will be injected.

```
@Inject
NumberGenerator numberGenerator;
```

You can have several alternatives enabled in the `application.properties` configuration file.

4.1.3. Scopes

CDI is about *Dependency Injection* but also *Context* (the "*C*" in CDI). Every bean has a well-defined scope and life cycle that is bound to a specific context. In Java, the scope of a POJO is pretty simple: you create an instance of a class using the new keyword and you rely on the garbage collection to get rid of it and free some memory. With CDI, a bean is bound to a context and it remains in that context until the bean is destroyed by the container. There is no way to manually remove a bean from a context. CDI defines the following scopes:

- Normal scopes:
  - *Application scope* (`@ApplicationScoped`): Spans for the entire duration of an application. The

bean is created only once for the duration of the application and is discarded when the application is shut down. This scope is useful for utility or helper classes, or objects that store data shared by the entire application (but you should be careful about concurrency issues when the data have to be accessed by several threads).

- *Session scope* (@SessionScoped): Spans across several HTTP requests or several method invocations for a single user's session. The bean is created for the duration of an HTTP session and is discarded when the session ends. This scope is for objects that are needed throughout the session such as user preferences or login credentials.

- *Request scope* (@RequestScoped): Corresponds to a single HTTP request or a method invocation. The bean is created for the duration of the method invocation and is discarded when the method ends. It is used for service classes that are only needed for the duration of an HTTP request.

- Pseudo scopes:

  - *Dependent scope* (@Dependent): The life cycle is the same as that of the client. A dependent bean is created each time it is injected and the reference is removed when the injection target is removed. This is the default scope for CDI.

  - *Singleton scope* (@Singleton): Identifies a bean that CDI only instantiates once.

As you can see, all the scopes have an annotation you can use on your beans (all these annotations are in the javax.enterprise.context package). The first three scopes are well known. For example, if you have a session scoped shopping cart bean, the bean will be automatically created when the session begins (e.g. the first time a user logs in) and automatically destroyed when the session ends.

```
@SessionScoped
public class ShoppingCart implements Serializable {...}
```

An instance of the ShoppingCart bean is bound to a user session and is shared by all requests that execute in the context of that session. If you don't want the bean to sit in the session indefinitely, consider using another scope with a shorter life span, such as the request scope.

If a scope is not explicitly specified, then the bean belongs to the dependent pseudo-scope (@Dependent). Beans with this scope are never shared between different clients or different injection points. They are dependent on some other bean, which means their life cycle is bound to the life cycle of that bean. A dependent bean is instantiated when the object it belongs to is created, and destroyed when the object it belongs to is destroyed. The code that follows shows a dependent scoped ISBN generator with a qualifier:

```
@Dependent @ThirteenDigits
public class IsbnGenerator implements NumberGenerator {...}
```

Being the default scope, you can omit the @Dependent annotation and write the following:

```
@ThirteenDigits
public class IsbnGenerator implements NumberGenerator {...}
```

Scopes can be mixed. A `@SessionScoped` bean can be injected into a `@RequestScoped` or `@ApplicationScoped` bean and vice versa.

4.1.4. Events

In a few sections, you will learn about Quarkus life cycle, which is based on CDI events. So let's first discover CDI events. CDI events allow beans to interact with no compile time dependency at all. One bean can define an event (using the `javax.enterprise.event.Event` interface), another bean can fire the event (by calling the `fire()` method), and yet another bean can handle the event (using the `@Observes` annotation). The beans can be in separate packages and even in separate JARs of the application. This basic schema follows the observer/observable design pattern[143] from the *Gang of Four*.

Event producers fire events using the `javax.enterprise.event.Event` interface. A producer raises events by calling the `fire()` method, passes the event object, and is not dependent on the observer. In Listing 33, the `BookService` fires an event (`bookAddedEvent`) each time a book is created. The code `bookAddedEvent.fire(book)` fires the event and notifies any observer methods observing this particular event. The content of this event is the `Book` object itself that will be carried from the producer to the consumer.

Listing 33. The BookService Fires an Event Each Time a Book Is Created

```
@ApplicationScoped
public class BookService {

  @Inject
  NumberGenerator numberGenerator;

  @Inject
  Event<Book> bookAddedEvent;

  public Book createBook(String title, Float price, String description) {
    Book book = new Book(title, price, description);
    book.setIsbn(numberGenerator.generateNumber());
    bookAddedEvent.fire(book);
    return book;
  }
}
```

Events are fired by the event producer and subscribed to by event observers. An observer is a bean with one or more observer methods. Each of these observer methods takes an event of a specific type as a parameter that is annotated with the `@Observes` annotation and optional qualifiers. The observer method is notified of an event if the event object matches the event type and all the qualifiers. Listing 34 shows the inventory service whose job is to keep the inventory of available books by increasing the book stock. It has an `addBook()` method that observes any event typed with `Book`. The annotated parameter is called the event parameter. So once the event is fired from the `BookService` bean, the CDI container pauses the execution and passes the event to any registered observer. In our case, the `addBook()` method in Listing 34 will be invoked and the inventory updated, and the container will then continue the code execution where it paused in the

`BookService` bean. This means that events in CDI are not treated asynchronously.

Listing 34. Service Observing the Book Event

```
@Singleton
public class InventoryService {

  List<Book> inventory = new ArrayList<>();

  public void addBook(@Observes Book book) {
    inventory.add(book);
  }
}
```

Like with most of CDI, event production and subscription are typesafe and allow qualifiers to determine which events observers will be observing. An event may be assigned one or more qualifiers, which allows observers to distinguish it from other events of the same type. Listing 35 revisits the `BookService` bean by adding an extra event. When a book is created, it fires a `bookAddedEvent` and when a book is removed it fires a `bookRemovedEvent`, both of type `Book`. To distinguish both events, each is qualified either by `@Added` or by `@Removed`. The code of these qualifiers is identical to the code in Listing 23: an annotation with no members annotated with `@Qualifier`.

Listing 35. The BookService Firing Several Events

```
@ApplicationScoped
public class BookService {

  @Inject
  NumberGenerator numberGenerator;

  @Inject @Added
  Event<Book> bookAddedEvent;

  @Inject @Removed
  Event<Book> bookRemovedEvent;

  public Book createBook(String title, Float price, String description) {
    Book book = new Book(title, price, description);
    book.setIsbn(numberGenerator.generateNumber());
    bookAddedEvent.fire(book);
    return book;
  }

  public void deleteBook(Book book) {
    bookRemovedEvent.fire(book);
  }
}
```

The InventoryService in Listing 36 observes both events by declaring two separate methods observing either the book added event (@Observes @Added Book) or the book removed event (@Observes @Removed Book).

Listing 36. The InventoryService Observing Several Events

```
@Singleton
public class InventoryService {

  @Inject
  Logger LOGGER;

  List<Book> inventory = new ArrayList<>();

  public void addBook(@Observes @Added Book book) {
    LOGGER.info("Adding book " + book.getTitle() + " to inventory");
    inventory.add(book);
  }

  public void removeBook(@Observes @Removed Book book) {
    LOGGER.info("Removing book " + book.getTitle() + " to inventory");
    inventory.remove(book);
  }
}
```

4.1.5. Configuring ArC

What you've just seen is the default behaviour of CDI in Quarkus. But being highly configurable, you can tweak the CDI behaviour a little bit by changing the properties in the application.properties file. In the application.properties file, you can use several quarkus.arc.* properties[144] defined in Table 7 to change the behaviour of ArC (the CDI implementation in Quarkus).

Table 7. Some Quarkus ArC Configuration Properties

Property	Default
quarkus.arc.remove-unused-beans	all
If set to all the container will attempt to remove all unused beans	
quarkus.arc.config-properties-default-naming-strategy	kebab-case
The default property naming strategy (from-config, verbatim, kebab-case)	
quarkus.arc.selected-alternatives	
The list of selected alternatives for an application	
quarkus.arc.auto-producer-methods	true
If true then javax.enterprise.inject.Produces is automatically added to all methods that are annotated with a scope annotation	

Property	Default
`quarkus.arc.auto-inject-fields`	`true`

If set to `true` `@Inject` is automatically added to all non-static fields that are annotated with one of the annotations defined by `AutoInjectAnnotationBuildItem`.

4.2. Eclipse MicroProfile Configuration

You've just seen that Quarkus allows some sort of configuration through the `application.properties` file. But it goes way beyond that. SmallRye Config implements Eclipse MicroProfile Configuration for configuring applications (and profiles as you'll see in next section). In a microservice architecture, the fact that there is no central runtime implies that there is no single point of configuration, but several points. Each microservice has its own configuration. But sometimes two microservices might want to share a common configuration. In that case, it can be helpful that they access configurations from multiple sources homogeneously and transparently. *Eclipse MicroProfile Configuration*[145] provides applications and microservices with the means to obtain configuration properties through several sources (internal and external to the application), through dependency injection or lookup.

The Eclipse MicroProfile Configuration APIs and annotations are all defined under the `org.eclipse.microprofile.config` package. Table 8 lists the main subpackages defined in Eclipse MicroProfile Configuration version 2.0 (under the root `org.eclipse.microprofile.config` package[146]).

Table 8. Main org.eclipse.microprofile.config Subpackages

Subpackage	Description
root	Root package of the Configuration APIs
`inject`	CDI support
`spi`	Internal SPIs (*Service Provider Interfaces*) implemented by the provider

In these packages, you'll find all the APIs and annotations. Table 9 shows a few Configuration APIs.

Table 9. Main Configuration APIs

API	Description
`ConfigProvider`	Central class to access a `Config`
`Config`	Resolves the property value by searching through all the configuration sources
`ConfigBuilder`	A builder for manually creating a configuration instance
`ConfigSource`	Provides configuration values from a specific place (a source)
`Converter`	Mechanism for converting configured values from a String to any Java type

Along with APIs, Configuration comes with a set of annotations. Table 10 lists a subset of the most commonly used annotations.

Table 10. Main Configuration Annotations

Annotation	Description
@ConfigProperty	Binds the injection point with a configured value

There is no Quarkus extension per-se for configuration as it is part of its core. So you have configuration for free in all Quarkus extensions and applications. But Quarkus comes with YAML support that needs the extension defined in Listing 37 to be added to your pom.xml.

Listing 37. Configuration Extension

```xml
<dependency>
    <groupId>io.quarkus</groupId>
    <artifactId>quarkus-config-yaml</artifactId>
</dependency>
```

4.2.1. Understanding Configuration

An application usually needs to change some data or behaviour depending on some technical or business requirements, or based on the running environment. You might want to change the VAT percentage depending on the country where you deploy your application; or depending on your environment (development, production, etc.) you might need to change the URL of a database or the credentials of an external service. It must be possible to modify configuration data from outside an application so that the application itself does not need to be repackaged. So, hard coding these values is not a good idea.

As shown in Figure 25, the configuration data can come from different locations and in different formats (e.g. system properties, system environment variables, external files, databases, .properties, .xml, .yaml). We call these configuration locations *configuration sources*.

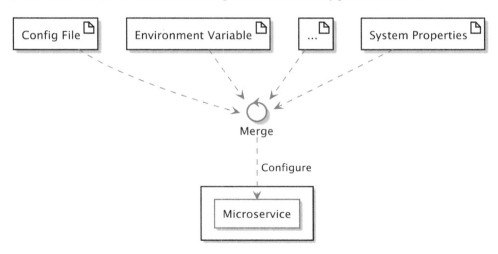

Figure 25. Several sources configuring a microservice

4.2.2. Configuring Data

Eclipse MicroProfile Configuration allows you to easily configure an application either programmatically or using injection. It also allows you to have several configuration sources, from environment variables to external files.

Injecting Configuration

Let's say we have an invoice. And depending on the country within which the application is deployed, the invoice has a different VAT rate, allows discounts or not, and has different terms and conditions or penalties. For that, Eclipse MicroProfile Configuration can inject an external configuration thanks to the `@ConfigProperty` annotation. As seen in Listing 38, `Invoice` is a bean containing several attributes, and some of these attributes are configurable. The semantics are:

- `subtotal` is not a configurable attribute,
- `vatRate` is configurable and its default value is `10`,
- `terms` is configurable but it has no default value.

Listing 38. Bean Injecting Configuration

```java
package org.agoncal.fascicle;

public class Invoice {

  Float subtotal;
  @Inject @ConfigProperty(defaultValue = "10")
  Float vatRate;
  Float vatAmount;
  Float total;
  @Inject @ConfigProperty(defaultValue = "true")
  Boolean allowsDiscount;
  @Inject @ConfigProperty(defaultValue = "2.5")
  Float discountRate;
  @Inject @ConfigProperty
  String terms;
  @Inject @ConfigProperty
  String penalties;
}
```

Then it's just a matter of configuring these attributes. Listing 39 shows an external property file. By default, the configuration key uses dot-separated blocks to prevent name conflicts and is similar to the Java package namespacing: *<fully qualified package name>.<bean name>.<attribute name>*.

Listing 39. Configuration File

```
org.agoncal.fascicle.Invoice.vatRate=10
org.agoncal.fascicle.Invoice.allowsDiscount=false
org.agoncal.fascicle.Invoice.terms=Payment upon receipt
org.agoncal.fascicle.Invoice.penalties=Penalty in case of late payment
```

As shown in Listing 40, the @ConfigProperty annotation actually has two optional members:

- The key of the configuration property used to look up the configuration value (e.g. invoice.vatRate or invoice.terms),
- The default value if the configured property value does not exist.

So if you want to change the key of the configuration property, you can easily customise it as shown in Listing 40.

Listing 40. Injecting Configuration Using Different Keys

```java
public class Invoice {

    Float subtotal;
    @Inject
    @ConfigProperty(name = "invoice.vatRate", defaultValue = "10")
    Float vatRate;
    Float vatAmount;
    Float total;
    @Inject
    @ConfigProperty(name = "invoice.allowsDiscount", defaultValue = "true")
    Boolean allowsDiscount;
    @Inject
    @ConfigProperty(name = "invoice.discountRate", defaultValue = "2.5")
    Float discountRate;
    @Inject
    @ConfigProperty(name = "invoice.terms")
    String terms;
    @Inject
    @ConfigProperty(name = "invoice.penalties")
    String penalties;
}
```

Then you rename the properties accordingly in the configuration file (see Listing 41).

Listing 41. Configuration File

```
invoice.vatRate=10
invoice.allowsDiscount=false
invoice.terms=Payment upon receipt
invoice.penalties=Penalty in case of late payment
```

If you do not provide a value for a property (as a default value or as an external property), the application startup fails with a deployment exception. That is because CDI cannot inject a value:

```
Failed to start application: javax.enterprise.inject.spi.DeploymentException:
No config value of type [java.lang.String] exists for: invoice.terms
```

By default, Quarkus reads the `application.properties` file. In the Maven directory structure, the file is under `src/main/resources`.

`@ConfigProperty` is a CDI qualifier. As we've seen in the previous section, Quarkus simplifies injection by allowing us to inject a qualified bean without using the `@Inject` annotation. So, when injecting a configured value, you can use `@Inject @ConfigProperty` or just `@ConfigProperty` as seen in Listing 40.

Listing 42. Injecting Configuration without @Inject

```
public class Invoice {

    Float subtotal;
    @ConfigProperty(name = "invoice.vatRate", defaultValue = "10")
    Float vatRate;
    Float vatAmount;
    Float total;
    @ConfigProperty(name = "invoice.allowsDiscount", defaultValue = "true")
    Boolean allowsDiscount;
    @ConfigProperty(name = "invoice.discountRate", defaultValue = "2.5")
    Float discountRate;
    @ConfigProperty(name = "invoice.terms")
    String terms;
    @ConfigProperty(name = "invoice.penalties")
    String penalties;
}
```

Programmatic Configuration

Configuration can be accessed programmatically. This can be handy when classes are not CDI beans and cannot use injection, for example. Programmatic configuration is accessed from the `Config` API, either by injection, or via the `ConfigProvider` API.

Listing 43 shows how to get an instance of `Config` using the `ConfigProvider`. Once you have an instance of `Config`, it's just a matter of invoking the method `getValue()` passing the configuration key and the datatype of the value (e.g. `String`, `Float`, etc.) as parameters.

Listing 43. Programmatic Configuration Using ConfigProvider

```
Config config = ConfigProvider.getConfig();

invoice.vatRate = config.getValue("invoice.vatRate", Float.class);
invoice.allowsDiscount = config.getValue("invoice.allowsDiscount", Boolean.class);
invoice.terms = config.getValue("invoice.terms", String.class);
invoice.penalties = config.getValue("invoice.penalties", String.class);
```

In a bean, you can use injection. So a simple `@Inject` will give you an instance of `Config` as shown in Listing 44.

Listing 44. Programmatic Configuration Using Injection

```
@Inject
Config config;

public void calculateInvoice() {
    invoice.vatRate = config.getValue("invoice.vatRate", Float.class);
    invoice.allowsDiscount = config.getValue("invoice.allowsDiscount", Boolean.class);
    invoice.terms = config.getValue("invoice.terms", String.class);
    invoice.penalties = config.getValue("invoice.penalties", String.class);
}
```

If a property is optional (e.g. Optional<String> terms instead of String terms), you can instead use the getOptionalValue() method as shown in Listing 45.

Listing 45. Optional Values

```
invoice.terms = config.getOptionalValue("invoice.terms", String.class);
invoice.penalties = config.getOptionalValue("invoice.penalties", String.class);
```

Type Safe Configuration

When you use the @ConfigProperty annotation, the property name is represented as a String (e.g. @ConfigProperty(name = "invoice.vatRate"). As an alternative to injecting Strings, you can use a more type-safe way using a Java interface, thanks to the @ConfigMapping annotation. So let's take our Invoice bean again, and get rid of all the @ConfigProperty annotations. We end up with the code shown in Listing 46: a bean with attributes and no annotations, that's all.

Listing 46. Invoice with No Configuration

```
public class Invoice {

    Float subtotal;
    Float vatRate;
    Float vatAmount;
    Float total;
    Boolean allowsDiscount;
    Float discountRate;
    String terms;
    String penalties;
}
```

To externalise the configuration, it's just a matter of creating a new interface, let's say InvoiceConfiguration, and only having the configured attributes. Listing 47 shows the configuration interface annotated with @ConfigMapping. Notice that the interface declares all the properties as methods.

Listing 47. Invoice Configuration

```java
@ConfigMapping(prefix = "inv", namingStrategy = NamingStrategy.VERBATIM)
public interface InvoiceConfiguration {

  Float vatRate();
  Boolean allowsDiscount();
  Float discountRate();
  String terms();
  String penalties();
}
```

The `prefix` member of `@ConfigMapping` is optional. If set, the configuration keys will use this prefix (see Listing 48), if not, then the prefix to be used will be determined by the class name (e.g. `invoice.vatRate` instead of `inv.vatRate`).

Listing 48. Property File

```
inv.vatRate=10
inv.allowsDiscount=false
inv.discountRate=2.5
inv.terms=Payment upon receipt
inv.penalties=Penalty in case of late payment
```

And to use it, it's very straight forward: you inject the interface, and invoke the methods to get the configured value (see Listing 49).

Listing 49. Type-Safe Configuration

```java
@Inject
InvoiceConfiguration invoiceConfiguration;

  invoice.vatRate = invoiceConfiguration.vatRate();
  invoice.allowsDiscount = invoiceConfiguration.allowsDiscount();
  invoice.terms = invoiceConfiguration.terms();
  invoice.penalties = invoiceConfiguration.penalties();
```

Notice the `namingStrategy` member in Listing 47 that is set to `VERBATIM`. Actually there are two naming strategies you can use:

- `VERBATIM`: takes the attribute name as it is for the configuration key (e.g. the attribute `vatRate` has a configuration key called `vatRate`).

- `KEBAB_CASE`: hyphenates the attribute name (e.g. the attribute `vatRate` has a configuration key called `vat-rate`).

If you change the naming strategy to `KEBAB_CASE` as shown in Listing 50, then all your properties should be hyphenated (see Listing 51) in the property file.

Listing 50. Kebab Case

```
@ConfigMapping(prefix = "inv", namingStrategy = NamingStrategy.KEBAB_CASE)
```

Listing 51. Kebab Case Property File

```
inv.vat-rate=10
inv.allows-discount=false
inv.discount-rate=2.5
inv.terms=Payment upon receipt
inv.penalties=Penalty in case of late payment
```

4.2.3. YAML Support

You might want to use YAML over properties for configuration. In fact, Quarkus will choose an application.yaml over an application.properties (but make sure to keep just one configuration type to avoid errors). Listing 52 shows an example of a YAML file to configure the application.

Listing 52. application.yaml File

```
app:
  invoice:
    vatRate: 10
    allowsDiscount: false
    terms: Payment upon receipt
    penalties: Penalty in case of late payment
```

Then, as shown in Listing 53, it's just a matter of using @ConfigProperty to inject a property (or using programmatic configuration).

Listing 53. Injecting YAML Configuration

```java
public class Invoice {

    Float subtotal;
    @ConfigProperty(name = "app.invoice.vatRate", defaultValue = "10")
    Float vatRate;
    Float vatAmount;
    Float total;
    @ConfigProperty(name = "app.invoice.allowsDiscount", defaultValue = "true")
    Boolean allowsDiscount;
    @ConfigProperty(name = "app.invoice.discountRate", defaultValue = "2.5")
    Float discountRate;
    @ConfigProperty(name = "app.invoice.terms")
    String terms;
    @ConfigProperty(name = "app.invoice.penalties")
    String penalties;
}
```

4.2.4. Configuration Sources

By default, Quarkus reads the configuration of an application by reading the `application.properties` file located under the `src/main/resources` directory. Eclipse MicroProfile Configuration also allows you to configure the application by using several sources for configured values, a.k.a. `ConfigSource`. A `ConfigSource` provides configuration values from a specific place, from files to system properties. Each configuration source has a specified ordinal, which is used to determine the importance of the values taken from the associated source. A higher ordinal means that the values taken from this source will override values with a lower priority. Properties can be set (in decreasing ordinal priority) as:

- System properties (`-Dinvoice.vatRate=50`)
- Environment variables (`INVOICE_VATRATE=50`)
- Environment file named `.env` placed in the current working directory (`INVOICE_VATRATE=50`)
- External config directory under the current working directory (`config/application.properties`)
- Resources `src/main/resources/application.properties`

If the same property is defined in multiple configuration sources, a policy to specify which one of the values will effectively be used is applied. Therefore, the default values can be specified in a file packaged with the application, and the value can be overwritten later for each deployment, using system properties for example. And of course, you can create your own source. Eclipse MicroProfile Configuration has a set of APIs for that.

4.2.5. Configuring Quarkus

We've just seen how to configure our application. But Quarkus itself is configured via the same mechanism. In fact, Quarkus is highly configurable with hundreds of configuration keys you can tweak. Quarkus reserves the `quarkus.` namespace for its own configuration. Table 11 shows a very small subset of these configuration keys[144], but you can easily find the ones you are looking for on the Quarkus website.

Table 11. Some Quarkus Configurations

Property	Default
`quarkus.http.root-path` The HTTP root path. All web content will be served relative to this root path.	/
`quarkus.http.port` The HTTP port	8080
`quarkus.http.test-port` The HTTP port used to run tests	8081
`quarkus.http.ssl.protocols` The list of protocols to explicitly enable.	TLSv1.3,TLSv1.2
`quarkus.http.auth.form.login-page` The login page	/login.html

Property	Default
quarkus.http.auth.form.error-page The error page	/error.html
quarkus.http.auth.form.landing-page The landing page to redirect to if there is no saved page to redirect back to	/index.html
quarkus.http.cors Enables the CORS filter	false

To access these configuration keys, you can use injection or programmatic configuration as shown in Listing 54.

Listing 54. Getting Quarkus Properties

```
Config config = ConfigProvider.getConfig();

LOGGER.info(config.getValue("quarkus.banner.enabled", Boolean.class));
LOGGER.info(config.getValue("quarkus.default-locale", String.class));
LOGGER.info(config.getValue("quarkus.http.port", String.class));
LOGGER.info(config.getValue("quarkus.http.test-port", String.class));
LOGGER.info(config.getValue("quarkus.http.ssl.protocols", String.class));
LOGGER.info(config.getValue("quarkus.http.read-timeout", String.class));
LOGGER.info(config.getValue("quarkus.log.level", String.class));
LOGGER.info(config.getValue("quarkus.log.min-level", String.class));
```

4.3. Profiles

Quarkus supports the notion of configuration profiles. This allows you to have multiple configurations in the same file and to select them via a profile name.

By default, Quarkus has three profiles, although it is possible to create your own, as many as you like. The built-in profiles are:

- dev: Activated when in development mode (when running mvn quarkus:dev).

- test: Activated when running tests.

- prod: The default profile when not running in development or test mode.

The syntax is %{profile}.config.key=value. So if our application needs a variable called isbn.prefix (see Listing 55) specific to the development mode, it needs to be defined as %dev.isbn.prefix in the application.properties file.

Listing 55. Injecting a Property Key

```
@ApplicationScoped
public class IsbnGenerator implements NumberGenerator {

  @ConfigProperty(name = "isbn.prefix")
  String prefix;

  public String generateNumber() {
    return prefix + Math.abs(new Random().nextInt());
  }
}
```

As we've seen in the previous section, for this property injection to work, it's just a matter of defining the key isbn.prefix and a value in the application.properties file.

```
isbn.prefix=13
```

But if we need to have different values depending on the environment, profiles are here to help. Let's say we want a different prefix in development mode. When executing mvn quarkus:dev, the dev profile is automatically enabled, so we prefix all the configuration keys with %dev. Notice how we can use profiles to have different log levels as well.

```
%dev.isbn.prefix=DEV
%dev.quarkus.log.category."org.agoncal".level=INFO
```

Accordingly, when you run your tests, the test profile is enabled, and the prod profile is enabled when building an executable JAR or a native executable.

```
%test.isbn.prefix=TST
%test.quarkus.log.category."org.agoncal".level=DEBUG

%prod.isbn.prefix=PRD
```

Quarkus comes with 3 profiles (dev, test, prod) but you might need other profiles. This is quite easy to do as Quarkus will simply use the quarkus.profile system property (or the QUARKUS_PROFILE environment variable). Let's say you have a staging environment and want to set some specific values for this environment. It's just a matter of adding these variables with the prefix %staging in the application.properties:

```
%staging.isbn.prefix=STAG
%staging.quarkus.log.category."org.agoncal".level=INFO
```

Then, you set the system variable depending on your needs:

- Use `mvn -Dquarkus.profile=staging quarkus:dev` if you are developing,

- Or `java -Dquarkus.profile=staging -jar myapp.jar` if you are running your executable JAR.

4.3.1. Configuring Profiles

Quarkus being really highly configurable, you can even tweak some properties so the configuration strategy is changed accordingly. Table 12 shows some properties related to the profiles configuration.

Table 12. Some Quarkus Profile Configuration Properties

Property	Default
`quarkus.profile` Profile that will be active when Quarkus launches	prod
`quarkus.test.native-image-profile` The profile to use when testing the native image	prod
`quarkus.test.profile` The profile to use when testing using `@QuarkusTest`	test

4.4. Logging

When developing an application, we know that there are chances that it won't work as expected. In order to check what went wrong, we can use debuggers while developing, but not in production (most debuggers won't be available in production). Hence, adding logging statements in the source code to help finding potential bugs is handy.

Logging is so common, that Java provides a built-in framework in the `java.util.logging` package. But throughout the history of the Java platform, many more logging frameworks have appeared, making it difficult sometimes to integrate well with each other. Quarkus acknowledges this diversity and integrates the following APIs for logging:

- *Java Util Logging*[147] (JDK JUL)

- *JBoss Logging*[148]

- *Simple Logging Facade for Java*[149] (SLF4J)

- *Apache Commons Logging*[150]

Listing 56 shows some code that uses all these supported logging frameworks.

Listing 56. Using Several Loggers

```
// JBoss Logging
org.jboss.logging.Logger JBOSS_LOGGER =
  org.jboss.logging.Logger.getLogger(LoggingResource.class);
// JUL
java.util.logging.Logger JUL_LOGGER =
  java.util.logging.Logger.getLogger(LoggingResource.class.getName());
// Commons Logging
org.apache.commons.logging.Log COMMONS_LOGGING =
  org.apache.commons.logging.LogFactory.getLog(LoggingResource.class);
// SLF4J
org.slf4j.Logger SLF4J_LOGGER =
  org.slf4j.LoggerFactory.getLogger(LoggingResource.class);

JBOSS_LOGGER.info("Trace produced by JBoss Logger");
JUL_LOGGER.info("Trace produced by JUL");
COMMONS_LOGGING.info("Trace produced by Commons Logging");
SLF4J_LOGGER.info("Trace produced by SLF4J");
```

No matter which one you use, or which one a third-party framework uses, all the logs will be merged by Quarkus:

```
[INFO] Trace produced by JBoss Logger
[INFO] Trace produced by JUL
[INFO] Trace produced by Commons Logging
[INFO] Trace produced by SLF4J
```

The fact that Quarkus supports all these loggers is very important. When you build an application, you tend to embed third-party libraries, and each one of them uses one of these logger frameworks. And if within your own application you use one of these loggers, you know your traces will be handled by Quarkus.

To get a logger, all these frameworks use the factory pattern, such as the JBoss logger:

```
org.jboss.logging.Logger JBOSS_LOGGER =
  org.jboss.logging.Logger.getLogger(LoggingResource.class);
```

But if you use the JBoss logger, you can actually inject it. The code in Listing 57 uses the CDI @Inject annotation to inject the logger without using the factory.

Listing 57. Injecting the JBoss Logger

```
@Inject
Logger JBOSS_LOGGER;

@GET
public void displayLogs() {
    JBOSS_LOGGER.info("Trace produced by JBoss Logger");
}
```

But be careful, logger injection only works with the JBoss logger, not the others. If you start an application from scratch, you might as well choose the JBoss Logger.

4.4.1. Log Levels

Log levels provide a way to categorise logs by their severity, or their impact on the overall health and stability of the application. JBoss Logger provides different levels described in Table 13.

Table 13. JBoss Logger Levels

Level	Description
FATAL	A critical service failure/complete inability to service requests of any kind
ERROR	A significant disruption in a request or the inability to service a request
WARN	A non-critical service error or problem that may not require immediate correction
INFO	Service life cycle events or important related very-low-frequency information
DEBUG	Messages that convey extra information regarding life cycle or non-request-bound events which may help debug
TRACE	Messages that convey extra per-request debugging information that may be very high frequency

The way to use these levels is quite simple. The API has several methods (e.g. fatal(), info(), etc.), each one corresponding to one level (e.g. FATAL, INFO, etc.). As shown in Listing 58, it's just a matter of invoking these methods and passing a message (with or without parameters).

Listing 58. Invoking Log Levels Methods

```
Logger LOGGER = Logger.getLogger(LoggingResource.class);

LOGGER.fatal("Fatal", exception);
LOGGER.error("Error");
LOGGER.warn("Warning");
LOGGER.info("Information");
LOGGER.debug("Debug");
LOGGER.trace("Trace");
```

4.4.2. Configuring Logging

You can configure how Quarkus logs. In fact, you can configure almost everything: from the format of the log entry, the format of the date of the log entry, to the appender to use. Quarkus can even integrate with external formats or systems such as *GELF*[151], *Sentry*[152] or *Syslog*[153]. The logging configuration is under the `quarkus.log.` namespace[144]. Table 14 shows only a subset of the properties you can use to customise logging.

Table 14. Some Quarkus Logging Configuration Properties

Property	Default
`quarkus.log.handler.gelf.enabled` Determine whether to enable the GELF logging handler	false
`quarkus.log.console.json` Determine whether to enable the JSON console formatting	true
`quarkus.log.console.json.pretty-print` Enable *"pretty printing"* of the JSON record	false
`quarkus.log.level` The log level of the root category (FATAL, ERROR, WARN, INFO, DEBUG, TRACE)	INFO
`quarkus.log.min-level` The default minimum log level	INFO
`quarkus.log.category."categories".level` The log level for this category	inherit
`quarkus.log.category."categories".handlers` The names of the handlers to link to this category	
`quarkus.log.handler.console."console-handlers".enable` If console logging should be enabled	true
`quarkus.log.handler.console."console-handlers".format` The log format	%d{yyyy-MM-dd HH:mm:ss,SSS} %-5p [%c{3.}] (%t) %s%e%n

Logging configuration uses the same configuration mechanism we just saw in the previous section. So Listing 59 shows some code where we programmatically get the value of these property keys.

Listing 59. Getting Logging Configuration

```
Config config = ConfigProvider.getConfig();

LOGGER.info(config.getValue("quarkus.log.level", String.class));
LOGGER.info(config.getValue("quarkus.log.min-level", String.class));
LOGGER.info(config.getValue("quarkus.log.console.json", Boolean.class));
LOGGER.info(config.getValue("quarkus.log.console.json.pretty-print", Boolean.class));
```

The logging configuration goes in the `application.properties` file. The configuration below displays log entries up to DEBUG level to the console, in a specific format:

```
quarkus.log.console.enable=true
quarkus.log.console.level=DEBUG
quarkus.log.console.format=%d{HH:mm:ss} %-5p [%c{2.}] %s%e%n
quarkus.log.console.darken=5
```

The following configuration writes the log entries up to INFO level to the /tmp/quarkus.log file, with a different format:

```
quarkus.log.file.enable=true
quarkus.log.file.path=/tmp/quarkus.log
quarkus.log.file.level=INFO
quarkus.log.file.format=%d %-5p [%c{2.}] (%t) %s%e%n
```

4.4.3. Logging Categories

Logging is done on a per-category basis and each category can be independently configured. The root logger category (quarkus.log) sits at the top of the logger hierarchy, and then you can have zero or several categories, depending on your needs. For example, the configuration below sets a different log level to different categories (notice that the quotes shown in the property name are required, as categories normally contain "." which must be escaped):

```
quarkus.log.level=TRACE
quarkus.log.category."org.agoncal".level=INFO
quarkus.log.category."io.quarkus.resteasy".level=DEBUG
quarkus.log.category."io.quarkus.arc".level=DEBUG
quarkus.log.category."org.jboss".level=WARN
```

A configuration which applies to a category will also apply to all sub-categories of that category, unless there is a more specific matching sub-category configuration.

4.4.4. Logging Format

By default, the log entry displays the timestamp, the log level, the class name, the thread id and the message. But this logging string can be customised through a set of symbols. Only a subset of these symbols is listed in Table 15 (you can find the entire list on the Quarkus website[154]).

Table 15. Some Logging Format Symbols

Symbol	Description
%c	Category name
%C	Source class name
%d{xxx}	Date with the given date format string defined by java.text.SimpleDateFormat[155]
%e	Renders the thrown exception, if any
%h	System host name

Symbol	Description
%i	Current process PID
%l	Source location (source file name, line number, class name, and method name)
%L	Source line number
%m	Renders the log message plus exception (if any)
%M	Source method name
%n	Renders the platform-specific line separator string
%p	Log level of the message
%s	Renders just the log message, with no exception trace
%t	Thread name

Then it's just a matter of using these symbols in the .format configuration key. Below we configure the log entry to display the timestamp, the level, the class name and the message, and we add a newline at the end of the entry:

```
quarkus.log.console.format=%d %p %c %s %n

2020-06-09 09:40:36,013 INFO org.agoncal.fascicle.quarkus.core.logging.LoggingResource
Information
```

The date (%d) follows the java.text.SimpleDateFormat. So below we only display the hour, minute and second of the log entry date:

```
quarkus.log.console.format=%d{HH:mm:ss} %p %c %s %n

09:41:08 INFO org.agoncal.fascicle.quarkus.core.logging.LoggingResource Information
```

We can also add text symbols, if we want, or use a regular expression. Below we add square brackets to the log level, and we only display the first 2 characters of the package name:

```
quarkus.log.console.format=%d{HH:mm:ss} [%p] [%c{2.}] %s %n

09:42:38 [INFO] [or.ag.fa.qu.co.lo.LoggingResource] Information
```

Below we add the method name and line number of where the log is produced:

```
quarkus.log.console.format=%d{HH:mm:ss} [%p] [%c{2.}] [%M:%L] %s %n

09:42:58 [INFO] [or.ag.fa.qu.co.lo.LoggingResource] [displayLogs:40] Information
```

4.4.5. JSON Format

It is possible to change the output format to JSON. This can be useful in environments where the logs of the application are captured by a service which can, for example, process and store the log information for later analysis. With JSON, a log entry can be read by any number of JSON interpreters as parsing a JSON log is far easier than parsing a plain text log. To do that, it's just a matter of adding a specific dependency to your pom.xml

```xml
<dependency>
    <groupId>io.quarkus</groupId>
    <artifactId>quarkus-logging-json</artifactId>
</dependency>
```

The presence of this extension means that you will be able to activate and configure the JSON format output. The configuration below activates the JSON logging and the pretty-print:

```
quarkus.log.console.json=true
quarkus.log.console.json.pretty-print=true
```

This will produce the following log entry:

```json
{
    "timestamp": "2020-06-08T16:53:13.304+02:00",
    "sequence": 8658,
    "loggerClassName": "org.jboss.logmanager.Logger",
    "loggerName": "org.agoncal.fascicle.quarkus.core.logging.LoggingResource",
    "level": "INFO",
    "message": "Trace produced by Commons Logging",
    "threadName": "executor-thread-159",
    "threadId": 279,
    "mdc": {
    },
    "ndc": "",
    "hostName": "imac-pro-de-antonio.local",
    "processName": "logging-dev.jar",
    "processId": 94651
}
```

4.5. Application Initialisation and Termination

In the *Getting Started* chapter, we developed a REST endpoint and Quarkus executed it: we didn't code an entry point per-se (e.g. a static main method), the application is executed as a whole. But sometimes you need to specify such an entry point. You also often need to execute custom actions when the application starts and clean up everything when the application stops. Quarkus lets you take control of the initialisation and termination of an application.

Quarkus comes with a set of APIs (listed in Table 16) that you can use, extend or observe to manage the application life cycle.

Table 16. Main Life Cycle APIs

API	Description
Application	Responsible for starting and stopping the application, but not managing the application life cycle
Quarkus	The entry point for applications that use a main method
QuarkusApplication	Interface allowing the execution of business logic at startup
StartupEvent	Event class that is fired on startup
ShutdownEvent	Event that is fired before shutdown
ApplicationLifecycleManager	Manages the lifecycle of a Quarkus application

Table 17 lists some annotations that deal with application life cycle. Some of these annotations are Quarkus specific (such as @QuarkusMain or @Startup) but others can be used anywhere as they come from Context and Dependency Injection and Common Annotations.

Table 17. Main Life Cycle Annotations

Annotation	Description
@QuarkusMain	Annotates the default main class of a Quarkus application
@Startup	Used to initialise a CDI bean at application startup
@PostConstruct	Marks a method to be invoked immediately after the bean instance is created
@PresDestroy	Marks a method to be invoked immediately before the bean instance is destroyed
@Priority	Can be applied to classes or parameters to indicate in what order they should be used

4.5.1. Entry Point

There is a way in Quarkus to develop an entry point. Listing 60 shows what an entry point looks like. The Main class is annotated with @QuarkusMain and implements QuarkusApplication. This annotation indicates the default entry point of the application. By implementing the interface you need to override the run() method. This is where you can add any custom code and then launch Quarkus with the waitForExit() method, otherwise it will just exit without starting Quarkus. In fact, if no main class is specified, then one is generated automatically and will simply wait to exit after Quarkus is booted.

Listing 60. Entry Point

```
@QuarkusMain
public class Main implements QuarkusApplication {

  @Override
  public int run(String... args) throws Exception {
    System.out.println("Running main method...");
    Quarkus.waitForExit();
    return 0;
  }
}
```

Another convenient way to start Quarkus is by having a `public static void main` entry point and starting Quarkus with a `run()` method (see Listing 61). Notice that this method is not supposed to be used for packaging or production, it is just a convenient way to execute or debug an application from an IDE.

Listing 61. Convenient Main for IDEs

```
@QuarkusMain
public class ConvenientMain {

  public static void main(String... args) {
    System.out.println("Convenient to run inside an IDE");
    Quarkus.run(args);
  }
}
```

The `io.quarkus.runtime.Quarkus` API has several methods to start Quarkus in different ways.

- `run()` starts a Quarkus application, that will run until it either receives a signal (e.g. pressing `Ctrl + C`) or one of the exit methods is called,

- `waitForExit()` blocks until the Quarkus shutdown process is initiated.

4.5.2. Application Life Cycle

You can be notified when the application starts/stops by observing specific CDI events. Thanks to the CDI `@Observes` annotation, the `ApplicationLifecycle` in Listing 62 can observe events and react in a certain way. That's because Quarkus fires CDI events at startup and shutdown:

- On startup with the `StartupEvent` so it can execute code when the application is starting,

- On shutdown with the `ShutdownEvent` before the application is terminated.

Listing 62. Listening to Events

```java
@ApplicationScoped
public class ApplicationLifecycle {

  @Inject
  Logger LOGGER;

  void onStart(@Observes StartupEvent ev) {
    LOGGER.info("The application is starting...");
  }

  void onStop(@Observes ShutdownEvent ev) {
    LOGGER.info("The application is stopping...");
  }
}
```

There is another way to execute custom code at startup: by using the @Startup annotation (see Listing 63). The behaviour of the @Startup annotation is similar to a declaration of a StartupEvent observer. The value of this annotation is an integer and is used to specify the priority of the observer and thus affect observer ordering.

Listing 63. Startup with Priority

```java
@Startup(Interceptor.Priority.LIBRARY_BEFORE)
@ApplicationScoped
public class LibraryStartupBefore {

  private static final Logger LOGGER = Logger.getLogger(LibraryStartupBefore.class);

  public LibraryStartupBefore() {
    LOGGER.info("LIBRARY_BEFORE");
  }
}
```

@javax.interceptor.Interceptor.Priority takes an integer that can be any value. The rule is that values with a lower priority are called first. The javax.interceptor.Interceptor annotation defines the following set of constants:

- PLATFORM_BEFORE = 0: Start of range for early interceptors defined by the platform,

- LIBRARY_BEFORE = 1000: Start of range for early interceptors defined by extension libraries,

- APPLICATION = 2000: Start of range for interceptors defined by applications,

- LIBRARY_AFTER = 3000: Start of range for late interceptors defined by extension libraries, and

- PLATFORM_AFTER = 4000: Start of range for late interceptors defined by the platform.

If we execute the Main class with the ApplicationLifecycle and LibraryStartupBefore classes, we get the following output. The Main class is executed first ("*Running main method*"), then comes the library priority ("*LIBRARY_BEFORE*") and then the StartupEvent ("*The application is starting...*"):

```
Running main method

--/ __ \/ / / / _ | / _ \/ //_/ / / / __/
-/ /_/ / / /_/ / __ |/ , _/ ,< / /_/ /\ \
--_____/_/ |_/_/|_/_/|_|\____/___/
INFO [org.LibraryStartupBefore] LIBRARY_BEFORE
INFO [org.ApplicationLifecycle] The application is starting...
INFO [io.quarkus] Quarkus on JVM started in 1.384s. Listening on: http://0.0.0.0:8080
INFO [io.quarkus] Profile dev activated. Live Coding activated.
INFO [io.quarkus] Installed features: [cdi]
INFO [org.ApplicationLifecycle] The application is stopping...
INFO [io.quarkus] Quarkus stopped in 0.002s
```

Notice than in Listing 62 we inject the logger. That's because the application is already started, all the CDI beans are discoverred, therefore we have all the CDI beans available for injection. On the other hand, in Listing 63 we create the logger manually. That's because at that moment, the application is not entirely started and we don't have all the CDI beans available yet and can't inject them.

4.6. Summary

In this chapter, you saw some core functionalities of Quarkus. Why are they called *core*? Because you will see injection, configuration and profiles in most of the following chapters.

First, Context and Dependency Injection. CDI, with its implementation ArC, is used in Quarkus to inject beans into other beans, or configuration values into beans. CDI qualifiers and events are also heavily used in MicroProfile and in Quarkus.

As for Eclipse MicroProfile Configuration, Quarkus can be configured through several sources, but comes with a default one: the `application.properties` file. This is where you will be configuring logs, datasources, database creation or the URL of external microservices. And of course, you can have other configuration sources to override any property, such as passing system variables, for example. And remember that these sources can make use of the Quarkus profiles where the same property can have different values in dev, test or prod.

Quarkus also allows you to hook business code at different stages of the application life cycle: before it starts, after, or before shutting down. You can even have a main entry point to execute your Quarkus application programmatically.

The next chapter is about *Data, Transactions and ORM*. Yes, Quarkus is not only about microservices. As you will see, it also integrates a set of specifications and technology to easily map your object into a relational database in a transactional way.

[136] **ArC** https://github.com/quarkusio/quarkus/tree/master/independent-projects/arc

[137] **CDI limitations** https://quarkus.io/guides/cdi-reference#limitations

[138] **CDI** https://jcp.org/en/jsr/detail?id=365

[139] **JavaBeans** https://en.wikipedia.org/wiki/JavaBeans

[140] **Expression Language** https://jakarta.ee/specifications/expression-language

[141] **ISBN** https://www.isbn-international.org

[142] ISSN https://www.issn.org

[143] Observer Pattern https://en.wikipedia.org/wiki/Observer_pattern

[144] Quarkus Configuration https://quarkus.io/guides/all-config

[145] Configuration https://microprofile.io/project/eclipse/microprofile-config

[146] Configuration GitHub https://github.com/eclipse/microprofile-config

[147] JUL https://docs.oracle.com/en/java/javase/11/docs/api/java.logging/java/util/logging/package-summary.html

[148] JBoss Logging https://github.com/jboss-logging/jboss-logging

[149] SLF4J http://www.slf4j.org/

[150] Commons Logging https://commons.apache.org/proper/commons-logging

[151] GELF https://www.graylog.org/features/gelf

[152] Sentry https://sentry.io

[153] Syslog https://en.wikipedia.org/wiki/Syslog

[154] Logging format string https://quarkus.io/guides/logging#format-string

[155] SimpleDateFormat https://docs.oracle.com/en/java/javase/11/docs/api/java.base/java/text/SimpleDateFormat.html

Chapter 5. Data, Transactions and ORM

The previous *Core Quarkus* chapter gave you a good understanding of what makes up the basis for Quarkus. From what you've already read in the previous chapters, Quarkus is about microservices, Kubernetes, Cloud Native or GraalVM. But not only that. Quarkus is built by the open source company that created transaction management in JBoss EAP, the object-relational mapping tool Hibernate ORM, and specified Bean Validation from their Hibernate Validator implementation. So Quarkus integrates well with all these tools.

Your applications usually manipulate data, validate data and store it in relational databases in a transactional way. You can use Quarkus as a runtime environment for data centric applications. This chapter starts with *Bean Validation* and shows how to constrain data so it's valid. *Java Persistence API* with *Java Transaction API* and datasources make a perfect environment to map objects into a relational database with transactions. Last but not least, this chapter will illustrate how *Hibernate ORM with Panache* makes database access easier.

 The code in this chapter can be found at https://github.com/agoncal/agoncal-fascicle-quarkus/tree/2.0/data

5.1. Bean Validation

As you will see in this chapter, JPA, JTA and Hibernate ORM with Panache are about accessing data from a relational database. Bean Validation has nothing to do with databases, but it does with data: valid data. You want your REST endpoints to process valid data or your databases to store valid data. So let's start this chapter with Bean Validation.

Validating data is a common task that developers have to do and it is spread throughout all layers of an application (from client to database). This common practice is time-consuming, error prone, and hard to maintain in the long run. Besides, some of these constraints are so frequently used that they could be considered standard (checking for a null value, size, range, etc.). It would be good to be able to centralise these constraints in one place and share them across layers. That's where Bean Validation comes into play.

Bean Validation[156] allows you to write a constraint once and reuse it in different application layers. It is layer agnostic, meaning that the same constraint can be used from the presentation to the business model layer. Bean Validation is available for server-side applications as well as rich Java client graphical interfaces (Swing, Android, JavaFX etc.).

Bean Validation allows you to apply already-defined common constraints to your application, and also to write your own validation rules in order to validate beans, attributes, constructors, method return values and parameters. The API is very easy to use and flexible as it encourages you to define your constraints using annotations or XML descriptors.

The Bean Validation APIs and annotations are all defined under the `javax.validation` package. Table 18 lists the main subpackages defined in Bean Validation 2.0 (under the root `javax.validation` package[157]).

Table 18. Main javax.validation Subpackages

Subpackage	Description
root	Root package of the Bean Validation APIs
bootstrap	Classes used to bootstrap Bean Validation and to create a provider agnostic configuration
constraints	This package contains all the built-in constraints
constraintvalidation	Package containing constructs specific to constraint validators
executable	Package related to the control and execution of validation on constructors and methods
groups	Bean Validation groups for defining a subset of constraints
metadata	Metadata repository for all defined constraints and query API
spi	Internal SPIs (*Service Provider Interfaces*) implemented by the provider
valueextraction	Package dedicated to extracting values to validate container elements

In these packages, you'll find all the APIs and annotations. Table 19 shows a few Bean Validation APIs.

Table 19. Main Bean Validation APIs

API	Description
Validation	This class is the entry point for Bean Validation and is used to build a ValidatorFactory
ValidatorFactory	This interface acts as a factory for returning initialised Validator instances
Validator	The implementation of this interface is used to validate bean instances
ExecutableValidator	Validates parameters and return values of methods and constructors
ConstraintViolation	Describes a constraint violation exposing the constraint violation context as well as the message describing the violation
ConstraintValidator	Defines the logic to validate a given @Constraint
MessageInterpolator	Builds a given constraint violation message when a constraint fails
ConstraintValidatorContext	Provides contextual data and operation when executing a given constraint validator
ValidationException	Base exception of all Bean Validation "expected" problems
ConstraintViolationException	Reports the result of constraint violations

Along with APIs, Bean Validation comes with a set of annotations. Table 20 lists a subset of the most commonly used annotations.

Table 20. Main Bean Validation Annotations

Annotation	Description
@Constraint	Marks an annotation as being a Bean Validation constraint

Annotation	Description
@Email	The string has to be a well-formed email address
@Max, @Min	The annotated element must be a number whose value is lower or equal, or higher or equal to the specified value
@Null, @NotNull	The annotated element must be null or not null
@Past, @Future	The annotated element must be an instant, date or time in the past or in the future
@Valid	Marks a property, method parameter or method return type for validation

 If you like the format of this fascicle and are interested in Bean Validation, check out the references for my *Understanding Bean Validation 2.0* fascicle in Appendix F.

To have access to all the Bean Validation APIs and annotations, you need to add the appropriate extension to your pom.xml (see Listing 64).

Listing 64. Bean Validation Extension

```
<dependency>
  <groupId>io.quarkus</groupId>
  <artifactId>quarkus-hibernate-validator</artifactId>
</dependency>
```

5.1.1. Understanding Constraints

Application developers spend a considerable amount of time making sure the data they process and store is valid. They write data constraints, apply these constraints to their logic and model, and make sure the different layers validate these constraints in a consistent manner. This means applying these constraints in their client application (e.g. web browser, JavaFX etc.), presentation layer, business logic layer, domain model (a.k.a. business model), database schema, and, to some degree, the interoperability layer (see Figure 26). And, of course, for consistency, they have to keep all these rules synchronised across all layers.

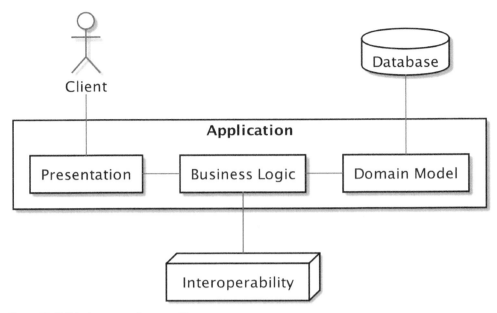

Figure 26. Validation occurs in several layers

In heterogeneous applications, developers have to deal with several technologies and languages. So even a simple validation rule, such as "*this piece of data is mandatory and cannot be null,*" has to be expressed differently in Java, JavaScript, database schema, or XML schema.

5.1.2. Constraining Data

Bean Validation solves the problem of code duplication by allowing developers to write a constraint once, use it, and validate it in any layer. Bean Validation implements a constraint in plain Java code and then defines it by an annotation (metadata). This annotation can then be used on your bean, properties, constructors, method parameters, and return value. In a very elegant yet powerful way, Bean Validation exposes a simple API to help developers write and reuse business logic constraints.

Built-in Constraints

Bean Validation is a specification that allows you to write your own constraints and validate them. But it also comes with some common built-in constraints. Table 21 gives you an exhaustive list of all the built-in constraints (i.e. all the constraints that you can use out of the box in your code without developing any annotation or implementation class). All of the built-in constraints are defined in the `javax.validation.constraints` package. Being part of the specification, you can use them in a portable way across all the Bean Validation implementations.

Table 21. Exhaustive List of Built-in Constraint Annotations

Constraint	Accepted Types	Description
`@Null`, `@NotNull`	`Object`	The annotated element must be null or not

Constraint	Accepted Types	Description
@NotBlank	CharSequence	The element must not be null and must contain at least one non-whitespace character
@NotEmpty	CharSequence, Collection, Map, arrays	The annotated element must not be null or empty
@Size	CharSequence, Collection, Map, arrays	The element size must be between the specified boundaries
@Max, @Min	BigDecimal, BigInteger, byte, short, int, long, and their wrappers	The element must be greater or lower than the specified value
@DecimalMax, @DecimalMin	BigDecimal, BigInteger, CharSequence, byte, short, int, long, and their respective wrappers	The element must be greater or lower than the specified value
@Negative, @NegativeOrZero, @Positive, @PositiveOrZero	BigDecimal, BigInteger, byte, short, int, long, and their wrappers	The element must be negative or positive, including zero or not
@Digits	BigDecimal, BigInteger, CharSequence, byte, short, int, long, and respective wrappers	The annotated element must be a number within the accepted range
@AssertFalse, @AssertTrue	Boolean, boolean	The annotated element must be either false or true
@Future, @FutureOrPresent, @Past, @PastOrPresent	Calendar, Date and types of the Java 8 date and time API (JSR 310)	The annotated element must be a date in the future or in the past, including the present or not
@Email	CharSequence	The string has to be a well-formed email address
@Pattern	CharSequence	The element must match the specified regular expression

Applying Built-in Constraints

These built-in constraints can be applied to different parts of our code. As an example, Listing 65 shows an Order class that uses constraint annotations on attributes, containers (List), constructors, and business methods.

Listing 65. A POJO Using Constraints on Several Element Types

```java
public class Order {

  @NotNull @Pattern(regexp = "[CDM][0-9]+")
  public String orderId;
  @NotNull @Min(1)
  public BigDecimal totalAmount;
  @PastOrPresent
  public Instant creationDate;
  @Future
  public LocalDate deliveryDate;

  @NotNull
  public List<OrderLine> orderLines;

  public Order(@PastOrPresent Instant creationDate) {
    this.creationDate = creationDate;
  }

  @NotNull
  public Double calculateTotalAmount(@Positive Double changeRate) {
    return complexCalculation();
  }

}
```

As you can see, Bean Validation is flexible enough to apply the same built-in constraints on different element types.

Constraining Attributes

Bean Validation takes its name from the Java Bean[158] design pattern. A Java Bean has properties, getters, setters, and methods. The most common use case of Bean Validation is constraining the attributes of a class. Listing 66 shows a Book class, containing attributes annotated with Bean Validation built-in constraints.

Listing 66. A Book Constraining Its Properties

```
public class Book {

  @NotNull
  public String title;
  @Digits(integer = 4, fraction = 2)
  public Float price;
  @Size(max = 2000)
  public String description;
  public Integer isbn;
  @Positive
  public Integer nbOfPages;
  @Email
  public String authorEmail;
}
```

Thanks to Bean Validation, the Book class in Listing 66, adds semantic to its properties. Instead of just saying that the price attribute is a Float, it actually expresses that the price of a book can have 4 numbers and 2 fractions. This is how we can read this code:

- A book must have a title (@NotNull),

- The price of a book must have maximum 4 digits for the number and maximum 2 digits for the fraction,

- The description of the book can be null, and if not, its length cannot be greater than 2000 characters,

- The number of pages must be a positive integer, and

- The author's email must be well-formed if not null. If you need the email to be not null and well-formed, then you need to use both the @NotNull and @Email annotations.

Constraining Methods

Method-level constraints are declared on methods as well as constructors (getters are not considered constrained methods by default). These constraints can be added to the method parameters (called parameter constraints) or to the method itself (called return value constraints). In this way, Bean Validation can be used to describe and validate the contract applied to a given method or constructor. This enables utilising the well-known *Programming by Contract*[159] paradigm.

- *Preconditions* must be met by the caller before a method or constructor is invoked, and

- *Postconditions* are guaranteed to the caller after a method or constructor invocation returns.

Listing 67 shows how you can use method-level constraints in several ways. The CardValidator service validates a credit card through a specific validation algorithm. This algorithm is passed to the constructor and cannot be null. For that, the constructor uses the @NotNull constraint on the ValidationAlgorithm parameter. Then, the two validate() methods return a boolean (indicating the validity of the credit card) with an @AssertTrue constraint on the returned type. In our example, this is to ensure the credit card is always valid (postcondition). The `validate()` methods also have some constraints like `@NotNull` and `@Future` on the method parameters to validate input parameters (preconditions).

Listing 67. A Service with Constructor and Method-level Constraints

```java
public class CardValidator {

  private ValidationAlgorithm algorithm;

  public CardValidator(@NotNull ValidationAlgorithm algorithm) {
    this.algorithm = algorithm;
  }

  @AssertTrue
  public boolean validate(@NotNull CreditCard creditCard) {
    return algorithm.validate(creditCard.getNumber(), creditCard.getControlNumber());
  }

  @AssertTrue
  public boolean validate(@NotNull String number,
                          @Future  Date expiryDate,
                          @NotNull Integer controlNumber) {
    return algorithm.validate(number, controlNumber);
  }
}
```

5.1.3. Validating Data

So far, we've been applying constraints on attributes, constructors, method parameters and return values. But for validation to occur on all these element types, you need to use validation APIs. In fact, the validation runtime uses a small set of APIs to be able to validate constraints. The main one is the `javax.validation.Validator` interface. It holds the methods to validate objects and graphs of objects independently of the layer in which it is implemented (presentation layer, business layer, or business model).

Like the `Config` object that we saw in the previous chapter, Quarkus allows the injection via `@Inject`. So you can inject a `Validator` as follows:

```java
@Inject Validator validator;
```

Quarkus looks after the life cycle of the validator, so you do not need to manually create or close it.

Validating Beans

Once the `Validator` is obtained programmatically or by injection, we can use its methods to validate either an entire bean or just a single property. Listing 68 shows a CD class with constraints set on properties, on method parameters and return values.

Listing 68. A Bean with Property and Method Constraints

```java
public class CD {

  @NotNull @Size(min = 4, max = 50)
  public String title;
  @NotNull @Positive
  public Float price;
  @Size(min = 10, max = 5000)
  public String description;
  @Pattern(regexp = "[A-Z][a-z]+")
  public String musicCompany;
  @Max(value = 5)
  public Integer numberOfCDs;
  public Float totalDuration;

  @NotNull @DecimalMin("5.8")
  public Float calculatePrice(@DecimalMin("1.4") Float discountRate) {
    return price * discountRate;
  }

  @DecimalMin("9.99")
  public Float calculateVAT() {
    return price * 0.196f;
  }
}
```

To validate all the bean properties, we just need to create an instance of CD and call the Validator.validate() method (see Listing 69). If the instance is valid, then an empty set of ConstraintViolation is returned. The following code validates a CD instance which has a valid title and price. The code then checks that the set of constraint violations is empty.

Listing 69. Validating a Valid Bean

```java
CD cd = new CD().title("Kind of Blue").price(12.5f);

Set<ConstraintViolation<CD>> violations = validator.validate(cd);
assertEquals(0, violations.size());
```

On the other hand, the code in Listing 70 will return two ConstraintViolation objects - one for the title and another one for the price (both violating @NotNull):

Listing 70. Validating an Invalid Bean

```java
CD cd = new CD();

Set<ConstraintViolation<CD>> violations = validator.validate(cd);
assertEquals(2, violations.size());
```

In Listing 71, we create a CD with a negative price. You can see how we use the ConstraintViolation API. When testing the values of our CD, we can check the error message, the message template, the invalid value, or the property.

Listing 71. Checking the ConstraintViolation API

```
CD cd = new CD().title("Kind of Blue").price(-10f);

Set<ConstraintViolation<CD>> violations = validator.validate(cd);
assertEquals(1, violations.size());
ConstraintViolation<CD> violation = violations.iterator().next();

assertEquals("must be greater than 0", violation.getMessage());
assertEquals("{javax.validation.constraints.Positive.message}", violation
.getMessageTemplate());
assertEquals(-10f, violation.getInvalidValue());
assertEquals("price", violation.getPropertyPath().toString());
assertEquals(CD.class, violation.getRootBeanClass());
assertTrue(violation.getConstraintDescriptor().getAnnotation() instanceof javax
.validation.constraints.Positive);
assertEquals("Kind of Blue", violation.getRootBean().title);
```

Cascading Validation

By default, if one bean (e.g. Order) has a reference to another bean (e.g. Address), or to a list of beans (e.g. List<OrderLine>), the validation is not transitive to nested beans. In addition to supporting instance validation, validation of graphs of objects is also supported. In other words, validating one bean is a good start, but often, beans are nested one into another. To validate a graph of beans in one go, we can apply cascading validation with the @Valid annotation. @Valid marks a property, method parameter or method return type to be included for cascading validation. This feature is also referred to as object graph validation.

In Listing 72, the Order bean uses a few Bean Validation annotations: order identifier must not be null, delivery address must be valid, and the list of ordered items must be valid too.

Listing 72. Order Cascading Validation to Its Order Lines

```
public class Order {

  @NotNull
  public Long id;
  public Double totalAmount;

  @NotNull @Valid
  public Address deliveryAddress;

  public List<@Valid OrderLine> orderLines;

}
```

In Listing 72, the @Valid constraint will instruct Bean Validator to delve into the Address and OrderLine, and validate all constraints found there. This means that each order line must have a positive unitPrice and a positive quantity (see Listing 73).

Listing 73. OrderLine Has Its Own Constraints

```
public class OrderLine {

    public  String item;
    @NotNull @PositiveOrZero
    public  Double unitPrice;
    @NotNull @Positive
    public  Integer quantity;

}
```

To be valid, an address has a mandatory street, city and zipcode (see Listing 74).

Listing 74. Address Has Its Own Constraints

```
public class Address {

    @NotNull
    public String street;
    @NotNull
    public String city;
    @NotNull @Size(max = 5)
    public String zipcode;

}
```

Listing 75 shows how to validate an order. As you can see, there is nothing special to be done here. We just create the object graph with one purchase order containing two order lines, and use the validator.validate(order) method as usual. Bean Validation will automatically cascade the validation to the delivery address and the two order lines.

Listing 75. Validating an Order with Valid OrderLines

```
Order order = new Order().id(1234L).totalAmount(40.5);
order.deliveryAddress = new Address().street("Ritherdon Rd").zipcode("SE123").city(
"London");
order.add(new OrderLine().item("Help").quantity(1).unitPrice(10.5));
order.add(new OrderLine().item("Sergeant Pepper").quantity(2).unitPrice(15d));

Set<ConstraintViolation<Order>> violations = validator.validate(order);

assertEquals(0, violations.size());
```

In Listing 76, we are purposely supplying an invalid value to the OrderLine (quantity(null)) to see the `@Valid` annotation in action. Notice how we use the `getRootBean()` and `getLeafBean()` methods. They respectively give us access to the `Order` bean (the root) and the `OrderLine` bean (the leaf). The method `getPropertyPath()` gives us the exact location of the constraint violation: the attribute `quantity` of the first order line in the array (`orderLines[0].quantity`).

Listing 76. First OrderLine Has Null Quantity Therefore Order Is Invalid

```
Order order = new Order().id(1234L).totalAmount(40.5);
order.deliveryAddress = new Address().street("Ritherdon Rd").zipcode("SE123").city(
"London");
order.add(new OrderLine().item("Help").quantity(null).unitPrice(10.5));
order.add(new OrderLine().item("Sergeant Pepper").quantity(2).unitPrice(15d));

Set<ConstraintViolation<Order>> violations = validator.validate(order);
assertEquals(1, violations.size());
ConstraintViolation<Order> violation = violations.iterator().next();

assertEquals("orderLines[0].quantity", violation.getPropertyPath().toString());
assertEquals(Order.class, violation.getRootBean().getClass());
assertEquals(OrderLine.class, violation.getLeafBean().getClass());
```

If we remove the `@Valid` annotation from the `orderLines` attributes in Listing 72, then the code in Listing 76 will not validate the null value on `quantity`; no constraint will be violated, therefore the `order` bean will be considered valid.

But `@Valid` can be used in other different ways. The example below will first cascade the validation on `Order` and will only invoke the `sendPurchaseOrder()` method if the order is valid.

```
public String sendPurchaseOrder(@Valid Order order)
```

As you will see in future chapters, Bean Validation is well integrated with other technologies such as JPA or JAX-RS. That means that, in most cases, you don't have to validate programmatically. Validation will happen automatically in JPA entities before insert, update or delete, and in JAX-RS endpoints when a request is received. You will see this automatic validation working in Chapter 12, *Putting It All Together*.

5.1.4. Configuring Hibernate Validator

And if you need to tweak validation, you can configure Hibernate Validator using the namespace[144] `quarkus.hibernate-validator`. Table 22 lists the most common configuration properties.

Table 22. Some Quarkus Bean Validation Configuration Properties

Property	Default
`quarkus.hibernate-validator.fail-fast` When fail fast is enabled, the validation will stop on the first constraint violation detected	`false`

Property	Default
`quarkus.hibernate-validator.method-validation.allow-overriding-parameter-constraints` Define whether overriding methods that override constraints should throw a `ConstraintDefinitionException`	false
`quarkus.hibernate-validator.method-validation.allow-parameter-constraints-on-parallel-methods` Define whether parallel methods that define constraints should throw a `ConstraintDefinitionException`	false
`quarkus.hibernate-validator.method-validation.allow-multiple-cascaded-validation-on-return-values` Define whether more than one constraint on a return value may be marked for cascading validation	false

5.2. Java Persistence API

The JPA implementation used by Quarkus is Hibernate ORM[160]. *Java Persistence API*[161] (JPA) is a Java specification that manages objects stored in a relational database. JPA gives the developer an object-oriented view in order to transparently use entities instead of tables. It also comes with a query language (*Java Persistence Query Language*, or JPQL), allowing complex queries over objects.

The Java Persistence API APIs are all defined under the `javax.persistence` package. Table 23 lists the main subpackages defined in JPA 2.2 (under the root `javax.persistence` package[162]).

Table 23. Main javax.persistence Subpackages

Subpackage	Description
root	Root package of the JPA APIs
`criteria`	Java Persistence Criteria API, allowing the writing of queries in an object-oriented way
`metamodel`	Java Persistence Metamodel API, bringing type safety to the queries
`spi`	Internal SPIs (*Service Provider Interfaces*) implemented by the provider

In these packages you will find many APIs and annotations. Table 24 shows the main APIs that we will be using.

Table 24. Main JPA APIs

API	Description
`EntityManager`	This is the primary JPA interface used by applications to manage persistent objects
`Query` and `TypedQuery`	Set of interfaces allowing the querying of persistent objects that meet certain criteria
`PersistenceException`	Thrown by the persistence provider when a problem occurs

Along with APIs, JPA comes with a set of annotations. Table 25 lists a subset of the most commonly used annotations.

Table 25. Main JPA Annotations

Annotation	Description
@Entity	POJOs become persistent objects when annotated with @Entity
@Column	Specifies the mapped column for a persistent property (name, length, unique, etc.)
@GeneratedValue	Defines the value generation policy of primary keys
@Id	Specifies the primary key of an entity
@Table	Specifies the primary table for the annotated entity
@Transient	Specifies that the property is not persistent
@OneToOne, @OneToMany, @ManyToOne, @ManyToMany	Relation multiplicity

 If you like the format of this fascicle and are interested in Java Persistence API, check out the references for my *Understanding JPA 2.2* fascicle in Appendix F.

To be able to use all the Java Persistence API APIs and annotations, you need to add the Quarkus extension described in Listing 77 to your pom.xml.

Listing 77. JPA Extension

```
<dependency>
  <groupId>io.quarkus</groupId>
  <artifactId>quarkus-hibernate-orm</artifactId>
</dependency>
```

5.2.1. Understanding Object-Relational Mapping

Relational databases store data in tables made of rows and columns. Data is identified by primary keys, which are special columns (or a combination of columns) designated to uniquely identify each table record. The relationships between tables are based on foreign keys and join tables with integrity constraints.

All this vocabulary is completely unknown in an object-oriented language such as Java. In Java, we manipulate objects that are instances of classes. Objects inherit from others, have references to collections of other objects, and sometimes recursively point to themselves. We have concrete classes, abstract classes, interfaces, enumerations, annotations, methods, attributes, and so on.

As seen in Figure 27, the principle of *Object-Relational Mapping*[163] (ORM) is to bring the world of relational databases and objects together. ORMs are external tools that give an object-oriented view of relational data, and vice versa.

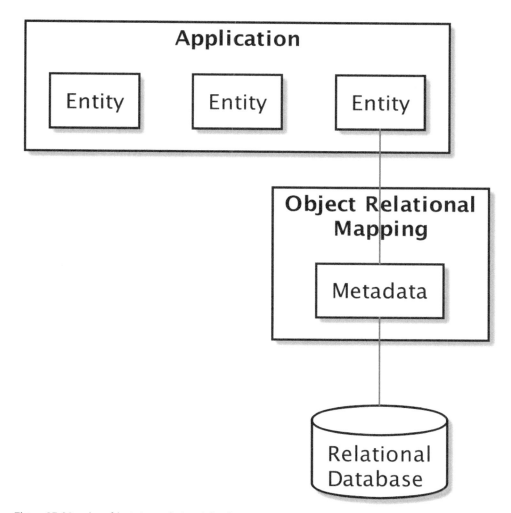

Figure 27. Mapping objects to a relational database

Relational Databases

The relational model organises data into one or more tables made of columns and rows, with a unique key identifying each row. Rows are also called records or tuples. Generally, each table represents one entity type (such as a book, author or purchase order). The rows represent instances of that type of entity (such as the book "*H2G2*" or "*Design Patterns*") with the columns representing values attributed to that instance (such as the title of the book or the price).

How would you store data representing a book in a relational database? Listing 78 shows an SQL script that creates such a table.

Listing 78. SQL Script Creating a BOOK Table Structure

```
CREATE TABLE BOOK
(
    ID              BIGINT NOT NULL,
    DESCRIPTION     VARCHAR(255),
    ILLUSTRATIONS   BOOLEAN,
    ISBN            VARCHAR(255),
    NBOFPAGES       INTEGER,
    PRICE           FLOAT,
    TITLE           VARCHAR(255),
    PRIMARY KEY (ID)
)
```

A *Data Definition Language* (DDL, or data description language) uses a syntax for defining database structures. The table BOOK is where we will find all the books of our application. Each book is identified by a unique primary key column (PRIMARY KEY (ID)) and each attribute is stored in a column (e.g. TITLE, PRICE, ISBN etc.). A column in a table has a type (e.g. VARCHAR, INTEGER, BOOLEAN etc.) and can accept null values or not (NOT NULL).

Entities

When talking about mapping objects to a relational database, persisting objects, or querying objects, the term *entity* should be used rather than *object*. Objects are instances that just live in memory. Entities are objects that live for a short time in memory and persistently in a relational database. They have the ability to be mapped to a database; they can be concrete or abstract; and they support inheritance, relationships, and so on.

In the JPA persistence model, an entity is a *Plain Old Java Object* (POJO). This means an entity is declared, instantiated and used just like any other Java class. An entity usually has attributes (its state), can have business methods (its behaviour), constructors, getters and setters. Listing 79 shows a simple entity.

Listing 79. Simple Example of a Book Entity

```
@Entity
public class Book {

  @Id
  @GeneratedValue
  private Long id;
  private String title;
  private Float price;
  private String description;
  private String isbn;
  private Integer nbOfPages;
  private Boolean illustrations;

  // Constructors, getters, setters
}
```

The example in Listing 79 represents a Book entity from which I've omitted the getters and the setters for clarity. As you can see, except for some annotations, this entity looks exactly like any Java class: it has several attributes (id, title, price etc.) of different types (Long, String, Float, Integer, and Boolean), a default constructor, and getters and setters for each attribute. So how does this map to a table? The answer is: thanks to mapping.

5.2.2. Mapping Entities

The principle of *Object-Relational Mapping* (ORM) is to delegate the task of creating a correspondence between objects and tables, to external tools or frameworks (in our case, JPA). The world of classes, objects, and attributes can then be mapped to relational databases which are made up of tables containing rows and columns. Mapping gives an object-oriented view to developers who can transparently use entities instead of tables. And how does JPA map objects to a database? This is done through *metadata*.

Associated with every entity are metadata that describe the mapping. The metadata enable the persistence provider to recognise an entity and to interpret the mapping. The metadata can be written in two different formats:

- *Annotations*: The code of the entity is directly annotated with all sorts of annotations.

- *XML descriptors*: Instead of (or in addition to) annotations, we can use XML descriptors. The mapping is defined in an external XML file that will be deployed with the entities.

These entities, once mapped, can be managed by JPA. You can persist an entity in the database, remove it, and query it. An ORM lets you manipulate entities while, under the covers, the database is being accessed.

The Book entity (shown in Listing 79) uses JPA annotations so the persistence provider can synchronise the data between the attributes of the Book entity and the columns of the BOOK table. Therefore, if the attribute isbn is updated by the application, the ISBN column will be synchronised (see Figure 28).

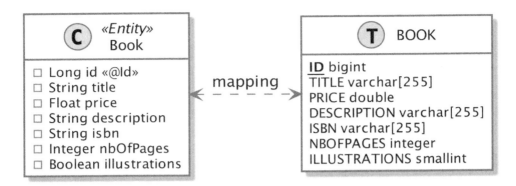

Figure 28. Data synchronisation between the entity and the table

As shown in the DDL in Listing 78, the Book entity is mapped to a BOOK table, and each column is named after the attribute of the class (e.g. the isbn attribute of type String is mapped to a column named ISBN of type VARCHAR).

 In this fascicle, I use CamelCase for Java code (e.g. Book entity, isbn attribute) and UpperCase for SQL script (e.g. BOOK table, ISBN column). But you need to be careful when picking up a specific case as some databases are case-sensitive.

Without JPA and metadata, the Book entity in Listing 79 would be treated just like a POJO. If you manually tried to map a POJO with JPA, then it would be ignored by JPA which would throw an exception. So you need to tell JPA that it deals with an *entity*, not an object, by using the @Entity annotation. It is the same for the identifier. You need a way to tell the persistence provider that the id attribute has to be mapped to a primary key, so you annotate it with @Id. The value of this identifier is automatically generated by the persistence provider, using the optional @GeneratedValue annotation. This type of decision characterises the configuration by exception approach (a.k.a. *configuring a component is the exception*), in which annotations are not required for the more common cases and are only used as metadata to be understood by an external provider.

Customising Mappings

@Entity and @Id are the only two required annotations to map an entity to a relational database. Then, Hibernate ORM applies the mapping rules, also known as *configuration by exception*. This allows you to write the minimum amount of code to get your application running, relying on the provider's defaults. For example, the entity name is mapped to a relational table name (e.g. the Book entity is mapped to a BOOK table). Attribute names are mapped to a column name (e.g. the id attribute, or the getId() method, is mapped to an ID column). If you don't want the provider to apply the default rules, you can customise the mapping to your own needs using metadata as shown in Listing 80.

Listing 80. Book Entity with Mapping Annotations

```
@Entity
@Table(name = "t_book")
public class Book {

  @Id
  @GeneratedValue
  private Long id;
  @NotNull
  @Column(name = "book_title", nullable = false, updatable = false)
  private String title;
  @Min(1)
  private Float price;
  @Column(length = 2000)
  private String description;
  private String isbn;
  @Column(name = "nb_of_pages", nullable = false)
  private Integer nbOfPages;
  private Boolean illustrations;
  @Transient
  private Instant creationDate;

  // Constructors, getters, setters
}
```

Notice in Listing 80 that the entity is also annotated with Bean Validation built-in constraints. Here we tell the Bean Validation runtime to make sure the book title is not null (@NotNull) and the minimum price is $1 (@Min(1)). Bean Validation and JPA integrate well. When JPA entities include Bean Validation constraints, they are automatically validated. In fact, validation is performed automatically as JPA delegates entity validation to Bean Validation before insert or update.

In Listing 80 several annotations are used to declare the object-relational mapping which should be applied to the class and attributes of a Book class:

- The @javax.persistence.Table annotation changes the default mapping values related to the table. So, instead of mapping the Book entity to the default BOOK table, the @Table annotation changes the name to T_BOOK.

- The book attribute id is mapped to the primary key column of the T_BOOK table and its value is automatically generated by the JPA provider Hibernate.

- The book title is mapped to a column called book_title, cannot be null and cannot be updated.

- The price property has no mapping annotation (so the default mapping will be used).

- The description can be null, but if it's not, its size must be less than 2000 characters long.

- The date of creation is not mapped to the table as it is transient.

All in all, the Book entity defined in Listing 80 will be mapped to a table structure shown in Listing

81.

Listing 81. SQL Script Creating a Customised BOOK Table Structure

```
CREATE TABLE T_BOOK
(
    ID              BIGINT      NOT NULL,
    DESCRIPTION     VARCHAR(2000),
    ILLUSTRATIONS   BOOLEAN,
    ISBN            VARCHAR(255),
    NB_OF_PAGES     INTEGER     NOT NULL,
    PRICE           FLOAT,
    BOOK_TITLE      VARCHAR(255) NOT NULL,
    PRIMARY KEY (ID)
)
```

 Here I just show you a very small subset of mapping annotations. JPA is a rich specification allowing you to map simple data structures as well as very complex ones. If you want to know more, I encourage you to check out Chapter 11 of the JPA 2.2 specification[164] where every annotation is explained. I have also published an entire fascicle on JPA called *Understanding JPA 2.2* (see Appendix F for more details).

Advanced Mapping

The world of object-oriented programming abounds with classes and associations between classes. These associations are structural in that they link objects of one kind to objects of another. Several types of relations can exist between classes:

- *Associations*: An association has a *direction* and a *multiplicity* (or *cardinality*). It can be *unidirectional* (i.e. one object can navigate towards another) or *bidirectional* (i.e. one object can navigate towards another and vice versa). It can be a one-to-one or a one-to-many cardinality.

- *Inheritance*: Object-oriented languages such as Java support inheritance. This paradigm is where a child class reuses code by inheriting the attributes and behaviour of parent classes.

Figure 29 shows a class diagram with classes, an abstract class and an enumeration. These classes inherit from each other (e.g. Author extends Artist) and are associated with each other (e.g. one Musician appears on many CD or a Book is published by one Publisher).

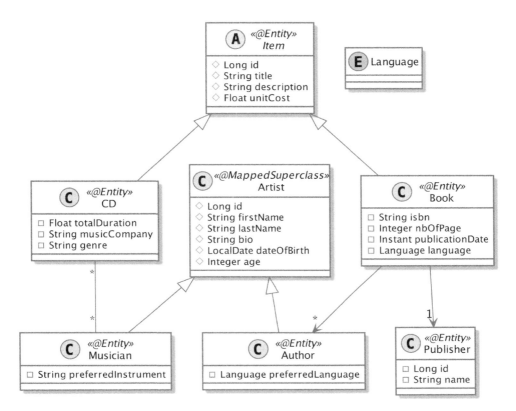

Figure 29. Entity class diagram

JPA can map such a complex class diagram to several datatables thanks to default mapping and annotations. For example, in Listing 82, we can see that a book is written by several authors. This is represented by a one-to-many relationship (@OneToMany annotation) and mapped to a join table called book_author. Thanks to the joinColumns and inverseJoinColumns members, we can map the book and author identifiers to the book_fk and author_fk foreign keys. Also notice that the Book entity extends the Item entity (see Listing 83).

Listing 82. Child Entity with Relationship Annotations

```java
@Entity
public class Book extends Item {

    @Column(length = 15)
    private String isbn;

    @Column(name = "nb_of_pages")
    private Integer nbOfPage;

    @Column(name = "publication_date")
    private Instant publicationDate;

    @Enumerated(EnumType.STRING)
    private Language language;

    @OneToMany
    @JoinTable(name = "book_author",
        joinColumns = @JoinColumn(name = "book_fk"),
        inverseJoinColumns = @JoinColumn(name = "author_fk")
    )
    private Set<Author> authors = new HashSet<>();

    @ManyToOne
    @JoinColumn(name = "publisher_pk")
    private Publisher publisher;

    // Constructors, getters, setters
}
```

The Item entity in Listing 83 uses the @Inheritance annotation to specify the inheritance strategy. Because databases do not support table inheritance, JPA has three different inheritance mapping strategies you can choose from.

- *A single-table-per-class hierarchy strategy*: The sum of the attributes of the entire entity hierarchy is flattened down to a single table (this is the default strategy). For instance, the ITEM table will have all the attributes of Book, Item and CD in a single table and an extra discriminator column to differentiate which type each row is.

- *A joined-subclass strategy*: In this approach, each entity in the hierarchy, concrete or abstract, is mapped to its own dedicated table. So Book, Item and CD will have their own tables, each with its own attributes and will be linked together by having the same identifier.

- *A table-per-concrete-class strategy*: This strategy maps each concrete entity class to its own separate table. For instance, the BOOK table will contain all the Book and Item attributes, and the CD table will contain all the CD and Item attributes.

Listing 83 shows the parent entity Item, with Book and CD extending it. Item specifies the single-table-per-class strategy with the @Inheritance annotation. So in this case, all the sub-classes of Item, Book and CD, will get mapped into the single table ITEM.

Listing 83. Parent Entity with Inheritance Annotations

```java
@Entity
@Inheritance(strategy = InheritanceType.SINGLE_TABLE)
public abstract class Item {

    @Id
    @GeneratedValue(strategy = GenerationType.AUTO)
    protected Long id;

    @Column(length = 100)
    protected String title;

    @Column(length = 3000)
    protected String description;

    @Column(name = "unit_cost")
    protected Float unitCost;

    // Constructors, getters, setters
}
```

I will end this section on mapping entities to relational databases. JPA can map most of the edge case scenarios and requires an entire book to master it, but you don't need to master it for the most common use-cases. I just wanted to show you some basics as it will be useful in understanding how to manage and query entities with JPA. Later in this chapter, you will see how Hibernate ORM with Panache is based on JPA and how it simplifies the developer's life.

5.2.3. Managing Entities

JPA allows us to map entities to a table and also to query them using different criteria. JPA's power is that it offers the ability to query entities and their relationships in an object-oriented way without the developer having to use the foreign keys or columns of the underlying database. The central piece of the API responsible for orchestrating entities is the javax.persistence.EntityManager. Its role is to manage entities, read from and write to a given database, and allow simple CRUD (create, read, update, and delete) operations on entities as well as complex queries using JPQL (*Java Persistence Query Language*). In a technical sense, the entity manager is just an interface whose implementation is done by the persistence provider. At its core, the entity manager delegates all the low-level calls to JDBC bringing the developer a higher-level of abstraction.

In Figure 30, you can see how the EntityManager interface can be used by a class (here Main) to manipulate entities (in this case, Book). With methods such as persist() and find(), the entity manager hides the JDBC calls to the database as well as the INSERT or SELECT SQL (*Structured Query Language*) statements.

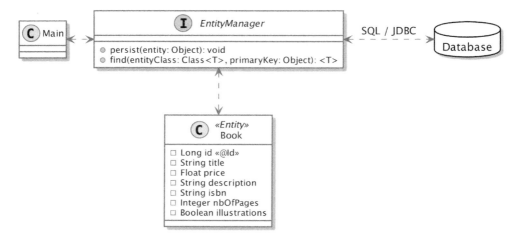

Figure 30. The entity manager interacts with the entity and the underlying database

The way to acquire an entity manager is through injection. With a simple @Inject, Quarkus will be responsible for managing the life cycle of the entity manager (creating and closing the entity manager) and injecting an instance of it.

```
@Inject
EntityManager em;
```

Being the central piece of JPA, we use the entity manager for both simple entity manipulation and complex JPQL query execution. When manipulating single entities, the EntityManager interface can be seen as a generic *Data Access Object*[165] (DAO), which allows CRUD operations on any entity.

To help you gain a better understanding of these methods, I use a simple example of a one-way, one-to-one relationship between a Customer and an Address. Both entities have automatically generated identifiers (thanks to the @GeneratedValue annotation), and Customer (see Listing 84) has a link to Address (see Listing 85).

Listing 84. The Customer Entity with a One-way, One-to-one Address

```
@Entity
public class Customer {

  @Id
  @GeneratedValue
  private Long id;
  private String firstName;
  private String lastName;
  private String email;
  @OneToOne
  @JoinColumn(name = "address_fk")
  private Address address;

  // Constructors, getters, setters
}
```

Listing 85. The Address Entity

```
@Entity
public class Address {

  @Id
  @GeneratedValue
  private Long id;
  private String street1;
  private String city;
  private String zipcode;
  private String country;

  // Constructors, getters, setters
}
```

These two entities will get mapped into the database structure shown in Figure 31. Note the ADDRESS_FK column is the foreign key to ADDRESS.

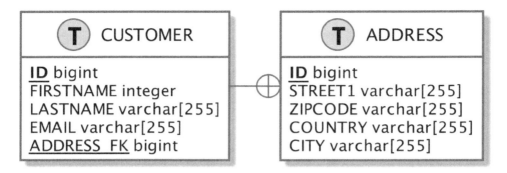

Figure 31. CUSTOMER and ADDRESS tables

For better readability, the fragments of code used in the upcoming sections assume that the `em` attribute is of type `EntityManager`.

Persisting an Entity

Persisting an entity means inserting data into the database when the data doesn't already exist. To do so, it's necessary to create a new entity instance using the `new` operator, set the values of the attributes, bind one entity to another when there are associations (`customer.setAddress(address)`), and finally call the `EntityManager.persist()` method as shown in the JUnit test case in Listing 86.

Listing 86. Persisting a Customer with an Address

```
Customer customer = new Customer("Anthony", "Balla", "aballa@mail.com");
Address address = new Address("Ritherdon Rd", "London", "8QE", "UK");
customer.setAddress(address);

// Persists the object
em.persist(customer);
em.persist(address);

assertNotNull(customer.getId());
assertNotNull(address.getId());
```

In Listing 86, `customer` and `address` are just two objects that reside in the JVM memory. Both become managed entities when the entity manager (variable `em`) takes them into account by persisting them (`em.persist()`). At this time, both objects become eligible for insertion in the database. When the transaction is committed, the data is flushed to the database, an address row is inserted into the `ADDRESS` table, and a customer row is inserted into the `CUSTOMER` table. As the `Customer` is the owner of the relationship, its table holds the foreign key to `ADDRESS`. The `assertNotNull` expressions check that both entities have received a generated identifier (thanks to the persistence provider and the `@Id` and `@GeneratedValue` annotations).

Note the ordering of the `persist()` methods: a customer is persisted and then an address. If it were the other way round, the result would be the same. Until the transaction is committed, the data stays in memory and there is no access to the database. The entity manager caches data and, when the transaction is committed, flushes the data in the order that the underlying database is expecting (respecting integrity constraints). Because of the foreign key in the CUSTOMER table, the insert statement for ADDRESS will be executed first, followed by that for CUSTOMER.

Finding by Id

To find an entity by its identifier, you can use two different methods. The first is the EntityManager.find() method, which has two parameters: the entity class and the unique identifier (see Listing 87). If the entity is found, it is returned; if it is not found, a null value is returned.

Listing 87. Finding a Customer by Id

```
Customer customer = em.find(Customer.class, id);
if (customer != null) {
  // Process the object
}
```

The second method is getReference() (see Listing 88). It is very similar to the find operation, as it has the same parameters, but it retrieves a reference to an entity (via its primary key) but does not retrieve its data. Think of it as a proxy to an entity, not the entity itself. It is intended for situations where a managed entity instance is needed, but no data, other than potentially the entity's primary key, being accessed. With getReference(), the state data is fetched lazily, which means that if you don't access state before the entity is detached, the data might not be there. If the entity is not found, an EntityNotFoundException is thrown.

Listing 88. Finding a Customer by Reference

```
try {
  Customer customer = em.getReference(Customer.class, id);
  // Process the object
  assertNotNull(customer);
} catch (
  EntityNotFoundException ex) {
  // Entity not found
}
```

Removing an Entity

An entity can be removed with the EntityManager.remove() method. Once removed, the entity is deleted from the database, is detached from the entity manager, and cannot be synchronised with the database anymore. In terms of Java objects, the entity is still accessible until it goes out of scope and the garbage collector cleans it up. The code in Listing 89 shows how to remove an object after it has been created.

Listing 89. Creating and Removing Customer and Address Entities

```
Customer customer = new Customer("Anthony", "Balla", "aballa@mail.com");
Address address = new Address("Ritherdon Rd", "London", "8QE", "UK");
customer.setAddress(address);

// Persists the object
em.persist(customer);
em.persist(address);

assertNotNull(customer.getId());
assertNotNull(address.getId());

// Removes the object from the database
em.remove(customer);
em.remove(address);

// The entities are not in the database
assertNull(em.find(Customer.class, customer.getId()));
assertNull(em.find(Address.class, address.getId()));
```

5.2.4. Querying Entities

The relational database world relies on *Structured Query Language*[166], or SQL. This programming language is designed for managing relational data (retrieval, insertion, updating and deletion), and its syntax is table oriented. You can select columns from tables made of rows, join tables together, combine the results of two SQL queries through unions, and so on. There are no objects here, only rows, columns, and tables. In the Java world, where we manipulate objects, a language made for tables (SQL) has to be tweaked to suit a language made of objects (Java). This is where Java Persistence Query Language comes into play.

JPQL (*Java Persistence Query Language*[167]) is the language defined in JPA to query entities stored in a relational database. JPQL syntax resembles SQL but operates against entity objects rather than directly working with database tables. JPQL does not see the underlying database structure or deal with tables or columns but rather objects and attributes. And, for that, it uses the dot (.) notation that Java developers are familiar with.

Java Persistence Query Language

You just saw how to manipulate entities individually with the EntityManager API. You know how to find an entity by Id, persist it, remove it, and so on. But finding an entity by Id is quite limiting, as you only retrieve a single entity using its unique identifier. In practice, you may need to retrieve an entity by criteria other than the Id (by name, ISBN etc.) or retrieve a set of entities based on some other criteria (e.g. all customers living in the United States). This possibility is inherent to relational databases, and JPA has a language that allows this interaction: *Java Persistence Query Language* (JPQL).

JPQL is used to define searches for persistent entities independent of the underlying database. JPQL is a query language that takes its roots in the syntax of SQL, which is the standard language for database interrogation. But the main difference is that, in SQL, the results obtained are in the form of rows and columns (tables), whereas JPQL results will yield an entity or a collection of entities. JPQL syntax is object oriented and therefore more easily understood by developers who are familiar with object-oriented languages. Developers manage their entity domain model, not a table structure, by using the dot notation (e.g. myClass.myAttribute).

Under the hood, JPQL uses the mapping mechanism in order to transform a JPQL query into language comprehensible by an SQL database. The query is executed on the underlying database with SQL and JDBC calls, and then entity instances have their attributes set and are returned to the application - all in a very simple and powerful manner, using a rich query syntax.

Here we have the simplest JPQL query that selects all the instances of a single entity.

```
SELECT b
FROM Book b
```

If you know SQL, this should look familiar to you. Instead of selecting from a table, JPQL selects entities, here Book. The FROM clause is also used to give an alias to the entity: b is an alias for Book. The SELECT clause of the query indicates that the result type of the query is the b entity (the Book). Executing this statement will result in a list of zero or more b (Book instances).

To restrict the result you just add a search criteria using the WHERE clause as follows:

```
SELECT b
FROM Book b
WHERE b.title = 'H2G2'
```

The alias is used to navigate across entity attributes through the dot operator. Since the Book entity has a persistent attribute named title of type String, b.title refers to the title attribute of the Book entity. Executing this statement will result in a list of zero or more Book instances that have a title equal to 'H2G2'.

The simplest select query consists of two mandatory parts: the SELECT and the FROM clause. SELECT defines the format of the query results. The FROM clause defines the entity or entities from which the results will be obtained, and the optional WHERE, ORDER BY, GROUP BY, and HAVING clauses can be used to restrict or order the result of a query. Listing 90 outlines a simplified syntax of a JPQL statement.

Listing 90. Simplified JPQL Statement Syntax

```
SELECT <select clause>
FROM <from clause>
[WHERE <where clause>]
[ORDER BY <order by clause>]
[GROUP BY <group by clause>]
[HAVING <having clause>]
```

Listing 90 defines a SELECT statement but DELETE and UPDATE statements can also be used to perform delete and update operations across multiple instances of a specific entity class.

Dynamic Queries

You've just seen the JPQL syntax and how to describe statements using different clauses (SELECT, FROM, WHERE etc.). But how do you integrate a JPQL statement in your application? Through queries. JPA has different types of queries that can be used in code, each for a different purpose (*Named queries*, *Criteria API*, etc.). But, in this fascicle, I'll focus on *Dynamic queries*. It is the simplest form of query, consisting of nothing more than a JPQL query string, dynamically specified at runtime.

The central point for choosing from these types of queries is the EntityManager interface, which has several factory methods returning either a Query or a TypedQuery. The Query interface is used in cases when the result type is Object, and TypedQuery is used when a typed result is preferred. The methods that are mostly used in this API are ones that execute the query itself. To execute a SELECT query, you have to choose between three methods, depending on the required result.

- The getResultList() method executes the query and returns a list of results (entities, attributes, expressions etc.).

- The getResultStream() method executes the query and returns the query results as a java.util.stream.Stream.

- The getSingleResult() method executes the query and returns a single result (throws a NonUniqueResultException if more than one result is found).

Dynamic queries are defined on the fly as needed by the application. To create a dynamic query, we use the EntityManager.createQuery() method, which takes a String as a parameter that represents a JPQL query. It's called *dynamic* because the query string can be dynamically created by the application, which can then specify a complex query at runtime not known ahead-of-time. String concatenation can be used to construct the query dynamically, depending on the criteria. The following query retrieves customers named 'Mike' depending on certain criteria. That's why the query cannot be predicted: if the boolean is true, the query will have a WHERE clause, if it's false, it won't.

```
String jpqlQuery = "SELECT c FROM Customer c";
if (someCriteria)
    jpqlQuery += " WHERE c.firstName = 'Mike'";

TypedQuery<Customer> typedQuery = em.createQuery(jpqlQuery, Customer.class);
List<Customer> customers = typedQuery.getResultList();
```

When concatenating strings, you can end-up passing an unchecked value to the database. This can raise security concerns because it can be easily hacked by SQL injection. You have to avoid the above code and use parameter binding instead. For that, there are two possible choices for passing a parameter: using names or positions. In the following example, I use a named parameter called :fname (note the : symbol) in the query and bind it with the setParameter() method:

```
TypedQuery<Customer> typedQuery = em.createQuery(
  "SELECT c FROM Customer c WHERE c.firstName = :fname", Customer.class);
typedQuery.setParameter("fname", "Mike");
List<Customer> customers = typedQuery.getResultList();
```

Note that the parameter name fname does not include the colon used in the query. You can also use positional parameters. It is *1-based* meaning that the first parameter is number *1*, the second parameter number *2*, and so on. The equivalent code would look like the following:

```
TypedQuery<Customer> typedQuery = em.createQuery(
  "SELECT c FROM Customer c WHERE c.firstName = ?1", Customer.class);
typedQuery.setParameter(1, "Mike");
List<Customer> customers = typedQuery.getResultList();
```

If you need to use pagination to display the list of customers in chunks of five, you can use the setMaxResults() method as follows:

```
TypedQuery<Customer> typedQuery = em.createQuery(
  "SELECT c FROM Customer c ORDER BY c.age", Customer.class);
typedQuery.setMaxResults(5);
List<Customer> customers = typedQuery.getResultList();
```

And if you need to set the position of the first result to retrieve, then you can use the setFirstResult() method:

```
TypedQuery<Customer> typedQuery = em.createQuery(
  "SELECT c FROM Customer c ORDER BY c.age", Customer.class);
typedQuery.setFirstResult(3);
typedQuery.setMaxResults(10);
List<Customer> customers = typedQuery.getResultList();
```

An issue to consider with dynamic queries is the cost of translating the JPQL string into an SQL statement at runtime. Because the query is dynamically created and cannot be predicted, the persistence provider has to parse the JPQL string, get the ORM metadata, and generate the equivalent SQL. The performance cost of processing each of these dynamic queries can be an issue. If you have static queries that are unchangeable and want to avoid this overhead, then you can use named queries instead.

This was a short overview of JPQL queries as you can have much more complex ones using joins, unions, exclusions, etc. But this overview has set the basis for JPQL and you will see how it differs from the Hibernate ORM with Panache Queries you will later see in this chapter.

5.2.5. Configuring Hibernate ORM

Like most extensions in Quarkus, object-relational mapping can also be configured. For that, it's just a matter of using the `quarkus.hibernate-orm.` namespace[144].

Table 26. Some Quarkus Hibernate Configuration Properties

Property	Default
`quarkus.hibernate-orm.dialect` Class name of the Hibernate ORM dialect (e.g. PostgreSQL, MariaDB, Microsoft SQL Server and H2)	
`quarkus.hibernate-orm.mapping-files` XML files to configure the entity mapping, e.g. `META-INF/my-orm.xml`. Pass no-file to force Hibernate ORM to ignore `META-INF/orm.xml`.	`META-INF/orm.xml` if it exists
`quarkus.hibernate-orm.sql-load-script` Name of the file containing the SQL statements to execute when Hibernate ORM starts.	`import.sql`
`quarkus.hibernate-orm.metrics.enabled` Whether or not metrics are published in case the `smallrye-metrics` extension is present	`false`
`quarkus.hibernate-orm.database.generation` Select whether the database schema is generated or not (`none`, `create`, `drop-and-create`, `drop`, `update`)	`none`
`quarkus.hibernate-orm.scripts.generation` Select whether the database schema DDL files are generated or not. Accepted values: `none`, `create`, `drop-and-create`, `drop`, `update`, `validate`.	`none`
`quarkus.hibernate-orm.log.sql` Show SQL logs and format them nicely	`false`
`quarkus.hibernate-orm.log.bind-parameters` Logs SQL bind parameters. Setting it to true is obviously not recommended in production.	`false`
`quarkus.hibernate-orm.log.format-sql` Format the SQL logs if SQL log is enabled	`true`
`quarkus.hibernate-orm.log.queries-slower-than-ms` If set, Hibernate will log queries that took more than specified number of milliseconds to execute.	

5.3. Java Transaction API

JPA is about mapping entities to tables, managing, and querying them. And JTA is about managing entities in a transactional way. In Java, transaction management is done through the *Java Transaction API* (JTA) specified by JSR 907[168]. JTA defines a set of interfaces for the application or the container in order to demarcate transaction boundaries, and it also defines APIs to deal with the transaction manager.

The Java Transaction API APIs are all defined under the `javax.transaction` package. Table 27 lists the main subpackages defined in JTA 1.2 (under the root `javax.transaction` package[169]).

Table 27. Main javax.transaction Subpackages

Subpackage	Description
root	Root package of the JTA APIs
xa	Interfaces and classes to accomplish distributed XA transactions[170]

In this root package, you'll find all the APIs and annotations. Table 28 shows the main JTA APIs.

Table 28. Main JTA APIs

API	Description
Transaction	Allows operations to be performed against a transaction
UserTransaction	Defines the methods that allow an application to explicitly manage transaction boundaries
RollbackException	Thrown when the transaction has been marked for rollback

Along with APIs, JTA comes with a set of annotations. Table 29 lists a subset of the most commonly used annotations.

Table 29. Main JTA Annotations

Annotation	Description
@Transactional	Gives the ability to declaratively control transaction boundaries
@TransactionScoped	Provides the ability to define bean instances whose life cycle is scoped to the currently active transaction

To use transactions, you need the Java Transaction API APIs and annotations. This is done by adding the Narayana extension to your pom.xml (see Listing 91).

Listing 91. JTA Extension

```
<dependency>
  <groupId>io.quarkus</groupId>
  <artifactId>quarkus-narayana-jta</artifactId>
</dependency>
```

5.3.1. Understanding Transactions

Transaction management is an important matter for enterprises. It allows applications to have consistent data and to process that data in a reliable manner. Transaction management is a low-level concern that a business developer shouldn't have to code. That's why JTA (*Java Transaction API*) provides these services in a very simple way: either programmatically with a high level of abstraction or declaratively using metadata.

A *transaction* is used to ensure that the data is kept in a consistent state. It represents a logical group of operations that must be performed as a single unit, also known as a *unit of work*. These operations can involve persisting data in one or several databases, sending messages to a MOM (*Message-Oriented Middleware*), or invoking web services. Companies rely on transactions every day for their banking and e-commerce applications or business-to-business interactions with partners.

These indivisible business operations are performed either sequentially or in parallel over a relatively short period of time. Every operation must succeed for the transaction to succeed (we say that the transaction is *committed*). If one of the operations fails, the transaction fails as well (the transaction is rolled back).

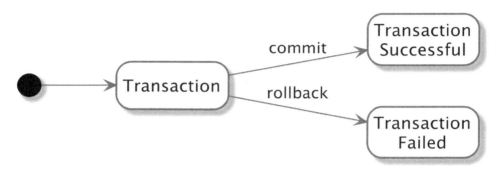

Figure 32. Transaction Management

Transactions must guarantee a degree of reliability and robustness and follow the ACID[171] properties. ACID refers to the four properties that define a reliable transaction: *Atomicity, Consistency, Isolation,* and *Durability* (described in Table 30).

Table 30. ACID Properties

Property	Description
Atomicity	A transaction is composed of one or more operations grouped in a unit of work. At the conclusion of the transaction, either these operations are all performed successfully (a commit) or none of them is performed at all (a rollback) if something unexpected or irrecoverable happens.
Consistency	At the end of the transaction, the data are left in a consistent state.
Isolation	The intermediate state of a transaction is not visible to external applications.
Durability	Once the transaction is committed, the changes made to the data are visible to other applications.

To explain these properties, I'll take the classic example of a bank transfer: you need to debit your savings account to credit your current account.

When you transfer money from one account to the other, you can imagine a sequence of database accesses: the savings account is debited using an SQL update statement, the current account is credited using a different update statement, and a log is created in a different table to keep track of the transfer. These operations have to be done in the same unit of work (*Atomicity*) because you don't want the debit to occur but not the credit. From the perspective of an external application querying the accounts, only when both operations have been successfully performed are they visible (*Isolation*). With isolation, the external application cannot see the interim state when one account has been debited and the other is still not credited (if it could, it would think the customer has less money than they really do). *Consistency* is when transaction operations (either with a commit or a rollback) are performed within the constraints of the database (such as primary keys, relationships, or fields). Once the transfer is completed, the data can be accessed from other applications (*Durability*).

5.3.2. Declarative Transaction Management

When managing transactions declaratively, you delegate the demarcation policy to the container. You don't have to explicitly use the JTA transaction management to explicitly start or commit a transaction; you can leave the container to demarcate transaction boundaries by automatically beginning and committing transactions based on annotations.

Listing 93 shows a transactional service. You know this service is transactional thanks to the `javax.transaction.Transactional` annotation. This annotation will cause every method invocation to be intercepted and start a transaction if needed.

Listing 92. A Transactional Service

```java
@ApplicationScoped
@Transactional
public class ItemService {

  @Inject
  EntityManager em;

  @Inject
  StatisticsService statistics;

  public List<Book> findBooks() {
    return em.createQuery("SELECT b FROM Book b", Book.class).getResultList();
  }

  public Book createBook(Book book) {
    em.persist(book);
    statistics.addNew(book);
    return book;
  }
}
```

You might ask how does the code in Listing 92 work? The answer is that the container is intercepting the method invocation and managing the transaction. Figure 33 shows what happens when a client invokes the `ItemService.createBook()` method. The client call is intercepted by the container, which checks immediately before invoking the method whether a transaction context is associated with the call. By default, if no transaction context is available, the container begins a new transaction before entering the method and then invokes the `createBook()` method. Once the method exits, the container automatically commits the transaction or rolls it back (if a particular type of exception is thrown).

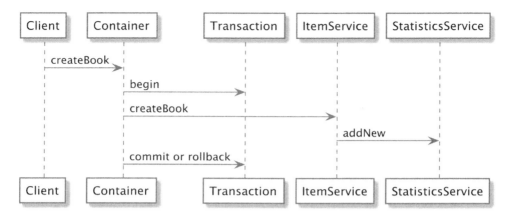

Figure 33. The container handles the transaction

The default transactional behaviour is that whatever transaction context is used for `createBook()` (from the client or created by the container), it is applied to `addItem()`. The final commit happens if both methods have returned successfully. This behaviour can be changed using metadata. Depending on the transaction attribute you choose (`REQUIRED`, `REQUIRES_NEW`, `SUPPORTS`, `MANDATORY`, `NOT_SUPPORTED`, or `NEVER`), you can affect the way the container demarcates transactions: on a client invocation of a transactional method, the container uses the client's transaction, runs the method in a new transaction, runs the method with no transaction, or throws an exception. Table 31 defines the transaction attributes of the `@Transactional` annotation.

Table 31. Transaction Types

Attribute	Description
REQUIRED	This attribute (default value) means that a method must always be invoked within a transaction. The container creates a new transaction if the method is invoked from a non-transactional client. If the client (caller) has a transaction context, the business method runs within the client's transaction. You should use REQUIRED if you are making calls that should be managed in a transaction, but you can't assume that the client is calling the method from a transaction context.
REQUIRES_NEW	The container always creates a new transaction before executing a method, regardless of whether the client is executed within a transaction. If the client is running within a transaction, the container suspends that transaction temporarily, creates a second one, commits or rolls it back, and then resumes the first transaction. This means that the success or failure of the second transaction has no effect on the existing client transaction. You should use REQUIRES_NEW when you don't want a rollback to affect the client.
SUPPORTS	The transactional method inherits the client's transaction context. If a transaction context is available, it is used by the method; if not, the container invokes the method with no transaction context. You should use SUPPORTS when you have read-only access to the database table.

Attribute	Description
MANDATORY	The container requires a transaction before invoking the business method but should not create a new one. If the client has a transaction context, it is propagated; if not, a javax.transaction.TransactionalException is thrown.
NOT_SUPPORTED	The transactional method cannot be invoked in a transaction context. If the client has no transaction context, nothing happens; if it does, the container suspends the client's transaction, invokes the method, and then resumes the transaction when the method returns.
NEVER	The transactional method must not be invoked from a transactional client. If the client is running within a transaction context, the container throws a javax.transaction.TransactionalException.

To apply one of these six demarcation attributes to your service, you have to use the @Transactional annotation. This annotation can be applied either to individual methods or to the entire bean. If applied at the bean level, all business methods will inherit the bean's transaction attribute value. Listing 93 shows how the PublisherService uses a SUPPORT transaction demarcation policy and overrides the update() method with REQUIRED.

Listing 93. A Custom Transactional Service

```
@ApplicationScoped
@Transactional(SUPPORTS)
public class PublisherService {

  @Inject
  EntityManager em;

  public List<Publisher> findAll() {
    return em.createQuery("SELECT p FROM Publisher p", Publisher.class).getResultList
();
  }

  public Optional<Publisher> findByIdOptional(Long id) {
    Publisher publisher = em.find(Publisher.class, id);
    return publisher != null ? Optional.of(publisher) : Optional.empty();
  }

  @Transactional(REQUIRED)
  public Publisher update(Publisher publisher) {
    return em.merge(publisher);
  }

}
```

So if you look at the PublisherService in Listing 93, then you'll understand that the update() method is transactional. If the caller hasn't created a transaction, then the container will create one. On the other hand, when the find methods are invoked, if it hasn't been invoked in a transactional context, then the container will not create a new one.

Exceptions and Transactions

Exception handling in Java has been confusing since the creation of the language (as it involves both checked exceptions and unchecked exceptions). Associating transactions and exceptions is also quite intricate. Before going any further, I just want to say that throwing an exception in a business method will not always mark the transaction for rollback. It depends on the type of exception or the metadata defining the exception.

- *Application exceptions*: Exceptions related to business logic. For example, an application exception might be raised if invalid arguments are passed to a method, the inventory level is too low, or the credit card number is invalid. Throwing an application exception does not automatically result in marking the transaction for rollback. That's because by default the container doesn't roll back when checked exceptions (which extend java.lang.Exception) are thrown, but it does for unchecked exceptions (which extend RuntimeException).

- *System exceptions*: Exceptions caused by system-level faults, such as JVM errors, failure to acquire a database connection, and so on. A system exception must be a subclass of a RuntimeException. Throwing a system exception results in marking the transaction for rollback.

With this definition, we know now that if the container detects a system exception, such as an ArithmeticException, ClassCastException, IllegalArgumentException, or NullPointerException, it will rollback the transaction. But this default behaviour can be overridden in the @Transactional annotation using the rollbackOn and dontRollbackOn attributes. As shown in Listing 94, the persist() method will rollback if the StatisticsService throws a StatisticsException.

Listing 94. Transaction Rollbacks on Exception

```
@ApplicationScoped
public class PublisherService {

    @Inject
    EntityManager em;

    @Inject
    StatisticsService statistics;

    @Transactional(value = REQUIRED, rollbackOn = StatisticsException.class)
    public Publisher persist(Publisher publisher) throws Exception {
        em.persist(publisher);
        statistics.addNew(publisher);
        return publisher;
    }

}
```

To override the default behaviour and cause transactions to be marked for rollback for all application exceptions, you need to write the following:

```
@Transactional(rollbackOn = Exception.class)
```

On the other hand, if you want to prevent transactions from being marked for rollback by the interceptor when an IllegalStateException (unchecked exception) or any of its subclasses is caught, you can use the dontRollbackOn as follows:

```
@Transactional(dontRollbackOn = IllegalStateException.class)
```

You can use both attributes to refine the transactional behaviour. Each attribute takes an array of classes and can be used as follows:

```
@Transactional(rollbackOn = SQLException.class,
            dontRollbackOn = {SQLWarning.class, ArrayIndexOutOfBoundsException.class})
```

5.3.3. Programmatic Transaction Management

With @Transactional, you leave the container to do the transaction demarcation just by specifying a transaction attribute and the exceptions to mark a transaction for rollback or not. In some cases, transaction demarcation may not provide the granularity that you require (e.g. a method cannot generate more than one transaction). To address this issue, JTA offers a programmatic way to explicitly manage transaction boundaries (begin, commit, rollback).

The main interface used to explicitly manage a transaction is javax.transaction.UserTransaction. It allows the bean to demarcate a transaction, get its status, set a timeout, and so on.

Listing 95 shows how to manage a transaction. First of all, we get a reference to the UserTransaction using injection. The oneItemSold() method begins the transaction, does some business processing, and then, depending on some business logic, commits or rolls back the transaction. Notice also that the transaction is marked for rollback in the catch block (I've simplified exception handling for better readability).

Listing 95. Programmatically Managing Transactions

```
@ApplicationScoped
public class InventoryService {

  @Inject
  UserTransaction tx;

  @Inject
  InventoryRepository repository;

  public void oneItemSold(Item item) throws Exception {
    try {
      tx.begin();
      repository.add(item);
      repository.decreaseAvailableStock(item);
      sendShippingMessage();

      if (inventoryLevel(item) == 0)
        tx.rollback();
      else
        tx.commit();
    } catch (InventoryException e) {
      tx.rollback();
    }
  }
}
```

5.3.4. Configuring Transactions

In Quarkus, you can configure transaction management. But be careful as transactions are low-level concerns that sometimes depend on the database you are using. For example, you can configure the default transaction timeout configuration property or the isolation level[172]. More on transaction configuration properties[144] can be found on the Quarkus website.

Table 32. Some Quarkus Transaction Configuration Properties

Property	Default
quarkus.datasource.jdbc.transactions Whether we want to use regular JDBC transactions, XA, or disable all transactional capabilities (enabled, xa, disabled)	enabled
quarkus.datasource.jdbc.transaction-isolation-level The transaction isolation level (undefined, none, read-uncommitted, read-committed, repeatable-read, serializable)	
quarkus.transaction-manager.default-transaction-timeout The default transaction timeout	60

5.4. DataSource

We've seen how to map and query entities, and how to access them in a transactional way. But there is still one piece of the puzzle missing: a relational database. The usual way of obtaining connections to a database is to use a *datasource*[173] and configure a JDBC driver.

In Quarkus, the datasource and connection pooling implementation is called Agroal. *Agroal*[174] is a modern, lightweight connection pool implementation designed for very high performance and scalability, and features first-class integration with the other components in Quarkus, such as security, transaction management components and health metrics. To configure the datasource, you just have to configure it in the application.properties, for example:

```
quarkus.datasource.db-kind=h2
quarkus.datasource.jdbc.driver=org.h2.Driver
quarkus.datasource.jdbc.url=jdbc:h2:mem:vintageStoreDB
```

The database kind (property db-kind) defines which type of database you will connect to. Currently Quarkus supports these built-in database kinds:

- Apache Derby[175]: derby
- H2[176]: h2
- MariaDB[177]: mariadb
- Microsoft SQL Server[178]: mssql
- MySQL[179]: mysql
- DB2[180]: db2
- PostgreSQL[181]: postgresql, pgsql or pg

By installing a JDBC driver in your dependencies (e.g. for PostgreSQL by adding the quarkus-jdbc-postgresql dependency in the pom.xml) and setting the kind in the configuration, Quarkus resolves the JDBC driver automatically, so you don't need to configure it yourself. So the following datasource configuration is the same as the previous one, we just skip the JDBC driver:

```
quarkus.datasource.db-kind=h2
quarkus.datasource.jdbc.url=jdbc:h2:mem:vintageStoreDB
```

And because there is a good chance you will need to define some credentials to access your database, you can use the following configuration:

```
quarkus.datasource.db-kind=h2
quarkus.datasource.jdbc.url=jdbc:h2:mem:vintageStoreDB
quarkus.datasource.username=app
quarkus.datasource.password=app
```

5.4.1. Dev Services

Sometimes you just want to quickly develop a new feature and don't want to configure a datasource and install a database. That's when Dev Services can be very handy. Quarkus supports the automatic provisioning of unconfigured services in development and test mode. It is called *Dev Services*[182]. This means that if an extension is not configured, then Quarkus will automatically start the relevant service (using TestContainers), configure it with default properties and wire it up to the application. Dev Services works with external resources such as databases, but also with Kafka, Keycloak or Redis.

For example, if you quickly want to use a PostgreSQL database, you just need to add the extension to the pom.xml and all the magic is done: the datasource is configured will all the defaults, a PostgreSQL database is downloaded (thanks to TestContainers) and started, so the application can use it. That's all! No need to add configuration to the application.properties file.

```xml
<dependency>
  <groupId>io.quarkus</groupId>
  <artifactId>quarkus-jdbc-postgresql</artifactId>
</dependency>
```

5.4.2. Configuring DataSources

Dev Services is perfect for development and testing, but in real life we need to configure the database carefully. Configuring a datasource can affect performance. If you have many concurrent users accessing your database, you might want to set its minimum and maximum pool size, for example. Or you might want to generate metrics so you can visualise them and take action. If you look for the quarkus.datasource. namespace on the Quarkus website, you will find all the datasource configurations[144]. Table 33 shows a subset of these configuration properties.

Table 33. Some Quarkus Datasource Configuration Properties

Property	Default
quarkus.datasource.db-kind The kind of database we will connect to (e.g. h2, PostgreSQL…)	
quarkus.datasource.username The datasource username	
quarkus.datasource.password The datasource password	
quarkus.datasource.jdbc If we create a JDBC datasource for this datasource	true
quarkus.datasource.jdbc.driver The datasource driver class name	
quarkus.datasource.jdbc.enable-metrics Enable datasource metrics collection (enabled by default if the smallrye-metrics extension is active)	

Property	Default
`quarkus.datasource.jdbc.url` The datasource URL	
`quarkus.datasource.jdbc.initial-size` The initial size of the pool	
`quarkus.datasource.jdbc.min-size` The datasource pool minimum size	0
`quarkus.datasource.jdbc.max-size` The datasource pool maximum size	20

5.5. Hibernate ORM with Panache

As you've just seen, Quarkus supports JPA and JTA. That means you can use these two APIs. But if you want to ease your development life, you can also use *Hibernate ORM with Panache*. Hibernate ORM is the Quarkus JPA implementation and offers you the full breadth of a JPA object-relational mapper. It makes complex mappings and queries possible, but it does not make simple and common mappings trivial. Hibernate ORM with Panache (pronounced *pa·nash*) focuses on simplifying your JPA entities as well as your repositories.

 Panache is about more than just making JPA easier. In fact, there is also a MongoDB with Panache extension and an experimental RESTful web service with Panache extension. MongoDB with Panache provides active record style entities (and repositories) and focuses on making entities trivial to map to a MongoDB database. To differentiate both technologies, we use the terms *Hibernate ORM with Panache* and *MongoDB with Panache*.

The Hibernate ORM with Panache APIs are all defined under the `io.quarkus.hibernate.orm.panache` package. Table 34 lists the main subpackages under the root `io.quarkus.hibernate.orm.panache` package.

Table 34. Main Hibernate ORM with Panache Subpackages

Subpackage	Description
root	Root package of the Hibernate ORM with Panache APIs
`runtime`	Contains the APIs to interact with the JPA runtime

The main APIs of Hibernate ORM with Panache are listed in Table 35.

Table 35. Main Hibernate ORM with Panache APIs

API	Description
`Panache`	Utility class for Panache
`PanacheEntityBase`	Represents an entity
`PanacheEntity`	Represents an entity with a generated ID of type `Long`

API	Description
PanacheQuery	Represents a query, which abstracts the use of paging, number of results, and operating on lists or streams
PanacheRepositoryBase	Represents a repository for a PanacheEntityBase
PanacheRepository	Represents a repository for an entity with an ID of type Long

Panache depends on Hibernate ORM. So to use the Panache and JPA APIs and annotations, one single extension is needed. Add the Panache extension to your pom.xml as shown in Listing 96 and you will get the Hibernate ORM provider as well.

Listing 96. Panache Extension

```
<dependency>
  <groupId>io.quarkus</groupId>
  <artifactId>quarkus-hibernate-orm-panache</artifactId>
</dependency>
```

5.5.1. Panache Entities

Hibernate ORM with Panache provides an *active record*[183] pattern implementation for JPA. In the active record pattern, the entity is an object that wraps a row in a database table (or view), encapsulates the database access, but also adds domain logic on that data. So the entity carries both data and behaviour. Listing 97 shows a *Panache entity* carrying data and behaviour.

Listing 97. A Panache Entity

```
@Entity
public class Publisher extends PanacheEntity {

  @Column(length = 30)
  public String name;

  public static Optional<Publisher> findByName(String name) {
    return find("name", name).firstResultOptional();
  }

  public static long deleteByName(String name) {
    return delete("name", name);
  }
}
```

If you compare the Panache entity in Listing 97 with its JPA counterpart, you will notice a few differences:

- Public attributes with no getters and setters (here name): Since Java lacks support for properties in the language, we have to create fields, then generate getters and setters for those fields. With Hibernate ORM with Panache you don't have to.

- Identifier logic in the parent class: Entities need a technical identifier to be able to map to a primary key column in the database. Being a technical id, it's usually not relevant to our model and can be inherited from a parent class (the id attribute is declared in the PanacheEntity class).

- State and behaviour in the same class (name attribute and findByName() method): Traditional patterns advise to split entity definition (the model) from the operations you can do on them (using DAOs or Repositories). You don't have to with Panache Entities, but if you really want to, you can also have repositories in Hibernate ORM with Panache (see below).

- Simplified queries: JPQL is a very rich and powerful query language. But it's also very verbose for common operations, requiring you to write queries even when you don't need all the statements.

Hibernate ORM with Panache takes an opinionated approach to tackle all these problems and makes your code as concise as possible. For that, you need to follow certain rules:

- Make your entities extend PanacheEntity: It has an identifier field that is auto-generated. If you require a custom ID strategy, you can extend PanacheEntityBase instead and handle the ID yourself (see class diagram in Figure 34).

- Use public fields: Get rid of boilerplate getter and setters: under the hood, Hibernate ORM with Panache generates all getters and setters that are missing, and rewrite every access to these fields to use the accessor methods. This way you can still write useful accessors when you need them, which will be used even though you use field accesses.

- Use the active record pattern: Put all your entity logic in static methods in your entity class. The PanacheEntityBase superclass already comes with lots of useful static methods, and you can add your own in your entity class.

Figure 34 shows the class diagram of the entity hierarchy. To be a Panache entity, your entity needs to extend from the PanacheEntity mapped superclass that gives you an identifier. PanacheEntity extends from the abstract class PanacheEntityBase that gives you most of the common CRUD operations, plus a few queries.

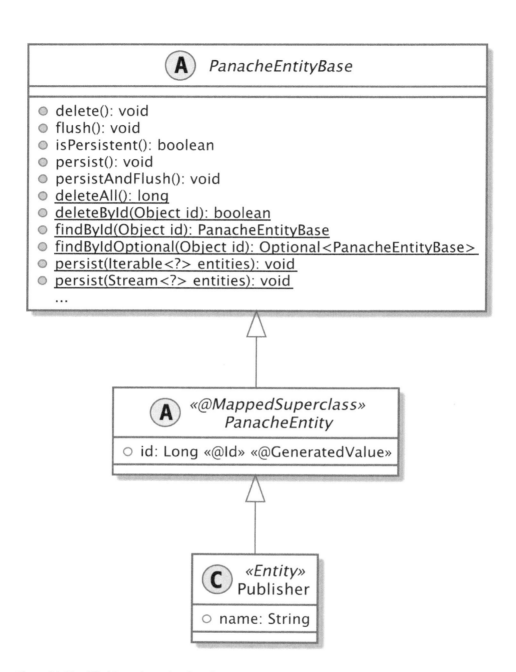

Figure 34. Simplified Panache entity class diagram

Mapping Panache Entities

To be a JPA entity, a class needs at least to be annotated with `@Entity` and have an identifier annotated with `@Id`. If you want to use Hibernate ORM with Panache, you still need to annotate the class with @Entity but you also need to extend PanacheEntity (so you get an autogenerated identifier) or from PanacheEntityBase (if you want to manage your own identifier). Then, map your Panache entity as you would have done with JPA. Listing 98 shows a Publisher Panache entity with a name attribute. Thanks to the JPA @Column annotation, the column in the database would be 30 characters long.

Listing 98. Simple Panache Entity Mapping

```
@Entity
public class Publisher extends PanacheEntity {

  @Column(length = 30)
  public String name;
}
```

Panache entities can benefit from the powerful object-relational mapping annotations of JPA: from simple mapping to more complex ones. For example, Listing 99 shows the Item parent entity annotated by @Inheritance. This annotation instructs JPA to map all the fields from the parent entity (Item), as well as the child entities (CD, Book), in a single table. Notice that Item is the parent entity, but it still extends PanacheEntity.

Listing 99. Parent Panache Entity

```
@Entity
@Inheritance(strategy = InheritanceType.SINGLE_TABLE)
public class Item extends PanacheEntity {

  @Column(length = 100)
  public String title;

  @Column(length = 3000)
  public String description;

  @Column(name = "unit_cost")
  public Float unitCost;
}
```

The child entity CD in Listing 100 extends Item (which extends PanacheEntity, so CD is a Panache entity). CD uses the @ManyToMany and @JoinTable JPA annotations to customise the relationship mapping with the Musician Panache entity, like any other plain JPA entity. One big difference though, is that the JPA annotations are set on the public fields of the Panache entity (not private fields as we are used to). So reading the title attribute of a CD is as simple as reading the cd.title attribute (instead of using a getter: cd.getTitle()).

Listing 100. Child Panache Entity

```java
@Entity
public class CD extends Item {

  @Column(name = "total_duration")
  public Float totalDuration;

  @Column(name = "music_company")
  public String musicCompany;

  public String genre;

  @ManyToMany
  @JoinTable(name = "cd_musician",
    joinColumns = @JoinColumn(name = "cd_fk"),
    inverseJoinColumns = @JoinColumn(name = "musician_fk")
  )
  public Set<Musician> musicians = new HashSet<>();
}
```

Managing Panache Entities

In JPA, we use the `EntityManager` interface to interact with entities. We use the `EntityManager` to persist, delete or find an entity, as well as create and execute a query. Thanks to the `PanacheEntityBase` parent class (see the class diagram in Figure 34), we get most of the CRUD operations on the Panache entity itself. Listing 101 shows some operations you can do on a Panache entity.

Listing 101. Operations on a Panache Entity

```java
// Creates a publisher
Publisher publisher = new Publisher();
publisher.name = "AGoncal Fascicle";

// Persists it
publisher.persist();

// Gets a list of all publisher entities
List<Publisher> allPublishers = Publisher.listAll();

// Finds a specific publisher by ID
publisher = Publisher.findById(publisherId);

// Finds a specific publisher by ID via an Optional
Optional<Publisher> optional = Publisher.findByIdOptional(publisherId);
publisher = optional.orElseThrow(EntityNotFoundException::new);

// Counts all publishers
long countAll = Publisher.count();

// Checks if it's persistent
if (publisher.isPersistent()) {
  // Deletes it
  publisher.delete();
}

// Deletes by id
boolean deleted = Publisher.deleteById(publisherId);

// Deletes all publishers
Publisher.deleteAll();
```

But always remember that Panache is based on JPA. So, if you need to use the `EntityManager` directly, it's very easy. It's just a matter of invoking the `getEntityManager()` method from a Panache entity as shown in Listing 102.

Listing 102. Using the EntityManager

```java
Publisher publisher = new Publisher();
publisher.name = "AGoncal Fascicle";

// Persists an entity with Panache
publisher.persist();

// Finds an entity with the entity manager
publisher = Publisher.getEntityManager().find(Publisher.class, publisherId);
```

But you can also inject it with a `@Inject` annotation (see Listing 103) and combine entity manager and Panache operations.

Listing 103. Injecting the EntityManager

```
// Injects the entity manager
@Inject
EntityManager em;

Publisher publisher = new Publisher();
publisher.name = "AGoncal Fascicle";

// Persists an entity with Panache
publisher.persist();

// Finds an entity with the injected entity manager
publisher = em.find(Publisher.class, publisherId);
```

Querying Panache Entities

One strength of JPA is its query language (*Java Persistence Query Language*). You can do all sorts of simple as well as complex queries on entities. As you can see in Listing 104, Panache gives you the possibility to write a full JPQL query as you would write in JPA, but you can also simplify it. The list() method can take a fragment of a JPQL query and contextualise the rest. So you don't have to write the SELECT and FROM clause and just focus on the WHERE clause (even omitting the WHERE keyword). That makes for very concise yet readable code.

Listing 104. Simplified JPQL Queries

```
// Full JPQL query
books = Book.list("SELECT b FROM Book b WHERE b.nbOfPage > 100 ORDER BY b.title");

// Simplified JPQL query
books = Book.list("FROM Book b WHERE b.nbOfPage > 100 ORDER BY b.title");

// Very simplified JPQL query
books = Book.list("nbOfPage > 100 ORDER BY title");
```

A Panache entity extends from PanacheEntityBase. As you can see in the class diagram in Figure 35, PanacheEntityBase has several methods to handle queries (find(), list(), stream(), etc.). These methods return a PanacheQuery that takes parameters (the Parameter class) and can be grouped within a page (the Page class). Also notice the Sort class allowing you to easily sort data in ascending or descending order.

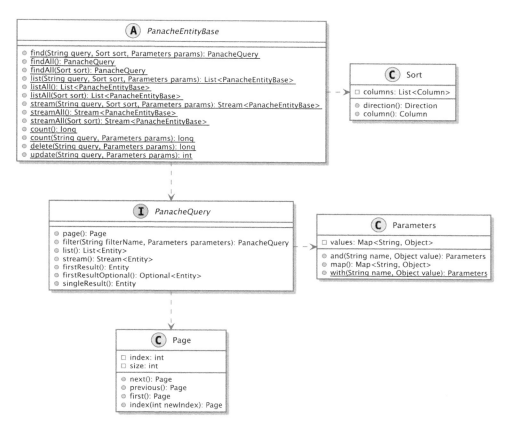

Figure 35. Panache query class diagram

As you can see in Listing 105, the find() method takes a simplified JPQL query and returns a PanacheQuery. With this PanacheQuery you can execute it and get the list of books (invoking the list() method), the number of books (via the count() method) or the first result of the query. Notice that the list() method is a shortcut of find().list(). In fact, simple use-cases will use list(), while find() will allow you more options such as paging or locking.

Listing 105. Panache Queries

```
// Find returns a PanacheQuery
PanacheQuery<Book> bookQuery = Book.find("nbOfPage > 100 ORDER BY title");
List<Book> books       = bookQuery.list();
Long nbBooks           = bookQuery.count();
Book firstBook         = bookQuery.firstResult();
Optional<Book> oBook = bookQuery.firstResultOptional();

// list() is a shortcut to find().list()
books = Book.find("nbOfPage > 100 ORDER BY title").list();
books = Book.list("nbOfPage > 100 ORDER BY title");
```

Passing Parameters

Hibernate ORM with Panache is based on JPA which is based on JDBC[184] (*Java DataBase Connectivity*). So in Panache you can pass parameters to a query either using positional parameters (e.g. ?1, ?2, etc.), name parameters (e.g. :min, : max) or the Panache Parameters class. Listing 106 shows how to pass parameters to a query using these different techniques.

Listing 106. Query Parameters

```
// Hard coded parameters
cheapBooks = Book.list("unitCost between 0 and 30");

// Positional parameters
cheapBooks = Book.list("unitCost between ?1 and ?2", min, max);

// Named parameters
Map<String, Object> params = Map.of("min", min, "max", max);
cheapBooks = Book.list("unitCost between :min and :max", params);

// Using the Parameters class
cheapBooks = Book.list("unitCost between :min and :max",
        Parameters.with("min", min).and("max", max));

// Passing an enumeration
List<Book> englishBooks = Book.list("language", Language.ENGLISH);
```

Paging

When you invoke the method list() it returns the entire list of entities that have met the query. This list can be large and difficult to display on a user interface. You might want to retrieve only a portion of it, of a certain size, and maybe iterate the following or previous portion. This is called *paging* (a.k.a *pagination*).

The PanacheQuery has several methods that deal with paging using the Page class. Page represents the paging information on which you can iterate (using next() and previous() methods) or go straight to a position (first() or index()). Listing 107 shows how to return the entire list of musicians from the database, and iterate pages of size five.

Listing 107. Paging Through Panache Entities

```
// Create a query for all musicians
PanacheQuery<Musician> musicianQuery = Musician.findAll();

// Make it use pages of 5 entries at a time
musicianQuery.page(Page.ofSize(5));

// Get the first page
List<Musician> firstPage = musicianQuery.list();

// Get the second page
List<Musician> secondPage = musicianQuery.nextPage().list();

// Get the third page
List<Musician> lastPage = musicianQuery.nextPage().list();

// Get page 3 using index
List<Musician> page3 = musicianQuery.page(Page.of(2, 5)).list();

// Get the number of pages
int numberOfPages = musicianQuery.pageCount();
```

Sorting

In JPQL, you can order a query using the ORDER BY clause. Remember that Panache queries can take a full JPQL query, so you can still use ORDER BY if you want to. But Panache makes it easier by using the Sort class (see the class diagram in Figure 35). Most Panache query methods accept an optional Sort parameter, which allows you to configure your sorting. The Sort class has a few methods for adding columns and specifying sort direction as you can see in Listing 108.

Listing 108. Sorting Panache Entities

```
// Sorts by first name ascending
authors = Author.listAll(Sort.by("firstName"));

// Sorts by first name descending
authors = Author.listAll(Sort.by("firstName", Descending));

// Sorts by first name ascending and last name descending
authors = Author.listAll(Sort.by("firstName").and("lastName", Descending));
```

State and Behaviour on Panache Entities

A typical JPA entity has private attributes with getters and setters, and sometimes a few business methods (e.g. a method that calculates the customer age based on his/her date of birth). But that's it. We don't encapsulate JPQL queries or CRUD operations on a JPA entity.

On the contrary, once you have written your Panache entities with public attributes with the required JPA mapping annotations, why not add some business logic to them? That's the purpose of the active record design pattern. By extending `PanacheEntity` you already get so many methods, why not add custom queries on your entities inside the entities themselves? That way, developers can easily find them, and queries are co-located with the object they operate on. Adding them as static methods in your entity class is the active record pattern way.

Listing 109 shows a `Book` Panache entity (extending from `Item` which inherits from `PanacheEntity`). As you can see, it uses JPA annotations to customise the mapping and declares queries in the entity itself.

Listing 109. State and Behaviour in a Panache Entity

```java
@Entity
public class Book extends Item {

  @Column(length = 15)
  public String isbn;

  @Column(name = "nb_of_pages")
  public Integer nbOfPage;

  @Column(name = "publication_date")
  public Instant publicationDate;

  @Enumerated(EnumType.STRING)
  public Language language;

  @OneToMany
  @JoinTable(name = "book_author",
    joinColumns = @JoinColumn(name = "book_fk"),
    inverseJoinColumns = @JoinColumn(name = "author_fk")
  )
  public Set<Author> authors = new HashSet<>();

  @ManyToOne
  @JoinColumn(name = "publisher_pk")
  public Publisher publisher;

  public static List<Book> findEnglishBooks() {
    return list("language", Language.ENGLISH);
  }

  public static long countEnglishBooks() {
    return count("language", Language.ENGLISH);
  }

  public static List<Book> findBetweenPrices(Float min, Float max) {
    return list("unitCost between :min and :max",
                Parameters.with("min", min).and("max", max));
  }

  public static List<Book> findAllOrderByTitle() {
    return listAll(Sort.by("title").and("publicationDate"));
  }
}
```

5.5.2. Panache Repositories

What was described above is essentially the active record pattern, sometimes just called the entity pattern. But Panache also allows you to use the more classical *Data Access Object*[185] (DAO, a.k.a.

Repository) pattern. This basically means that you use the entities only to handle the state and the mapping, and the repository handles the database access. This separation of concerns can be handy in some cases.

As you can see in Listing 110, the repository does not have any attributes (they are in the entity), but only methods querying the database. Notice that Publisher can be a Panache entity as well as a JPA entity. This can be handy if you have legacy JPA entities and want to benefit from the Panache repositories.

Listing 110. A Panache Repository

```
@ApplicationScoped
public class PublisherRepository implements PanacheRepository<Publisher> {

  public Optional<Publisher> findByName(String name) {
    return find("name", name).firstResultOptional();
  }

  public long deleteByName(String name) {
    return delete("name", name);
  }
}
```

As shown in Figure 36, a Panache repository implements the PanacheRepository interface which extends PanacheRepositoryBase . When using repositories, you get the exact same convenient methods as with the active record pattern, by making them implement PanacheRepository.

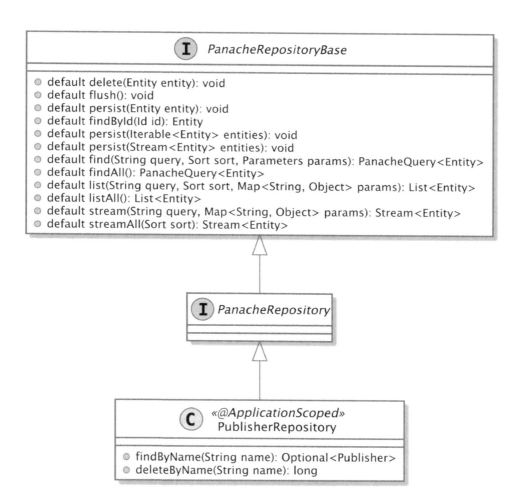

Figure 36. Panache repository class diagram

Listing 111 shows some operations that are available on your repository. As you can see, you can use it in exactly the same way as with the active record pattern.

Listing 111. Operations on a Panache Repository

```
@Inject
PublisherRepository publisherRepository;

void shouldManagePublishers() {

  // Creates a publisher
  Publisher publisher = new Publisher();
  publisher.name = "AGoncal Fascicle";

  // Persists it
  publisherRepository.persist(publisher);

  // Gets a list of all publisher entities
  List<Publisher> allPublishers = publisherRepository.listAll();

  // Finds a specific publisher by ID
  publisher = publisherRepository.findById(publisherId);

  // Finds a specific publisher by ID via an Optional
  Optional<Publisher> optional = publisherRepository.findByIdOptional(publisherId);
  publisher = optional.orElseThrow(EntityNotFoundException::new);

  // Counts all publishers
  long countAll = publisherRepository.count();

  // Checks if it's persistent
  if (publisherRepository.isPersistent(publisher)) {
    // delete it
    publisherRepository.delete(publisher);
  }

  // Deletes by id
  boolean deleted = publisherRepository.deleteById(publisherId);

  // Deletes all publishers
  publisherRepository.deleteAll();
}
```

And, as shown in Listing 112, if you need to use the EntityManager from a Panache repository, you can either inject it, or directly get him from the repository itself (thanks to the getEntityManager() method).

Listing 112. Using the EntityManager

```
Publisher publisher = new Publisher();
publisher.name = "AGoncal Fascicle";

// Persists an entity with the Panache repository
publisherRepository.persist(publisher);

// Finds an entity with the entity manager
publisher = publisherRepository.getEntityManager().find(Publisher.class, publisherId);
```

And of course, as shown in Listing 113, a repository can also use simplified JPQL queries, and query parameters, sorting or paging, the same way a Panache entity would do.

Listing 113. Queries using a Panache Repository

```
// Simplified JPQL query
books = repository.list("nbOfPage > 100 ORDER BY title");

// Positional parameters
cheapBooks = repository.list("unitCost between ?1 and ?2", min, max);

// Using the Parameters class
cheapBooks = repository.list("unitCost between :min and :max",
             Parameters.with("min", min).and("max", max));
```

5.5.3. Transactions

Panache entities and repositories allow you to easily map attributes to a relational database, and access them through queries. But what about transactions? What about persisting or removing data in a transactional way? For that, we just need to use transactional boundaries (eg. a service or a REST endpoint) using JTA. These transactional boundaries can either directly use the Panache entities, or inject the repositories.

Using Panache Entities

Listing 114 shows a transactional service that persists, deletes and retrieves publisher entities in a transactional way. For that, it marks methods with the JTA declarative transaction management annotation @Transactional. Then, it directly uses the Panache entity methods (e.g. invoking Publisher.persist() to persist a publisher).

168

Listing 114. Transactional Service Using Panache Entities

```java
@ApplicationScoped
@Transactional(SUPPORTS)
public class PublisherService {

  @Transactional(REQUIRED)
  public Publisher persist(Publisher publisher) {
    Publisher.persist(publisher);
    return publisher;
  }

  public List<Publisher> findAll() {
    return Publisher.listAll();
  }

  public Optional<Publisher> findByIdOptional(Long id) {
    return Publisher.findByIdOptional(id);
  }

  @Transactional(REQUIRED)
  public void deleteById(Long id) {
    Publisher.deleteById(id);
  }
}
```

Using Panache Repositories

But if you have chosen to have a repository layer instead of using the active record pattern, then, you follow the same principles, but instead of using the Panache entity directly, you inject the Panache repository. Listing 115 shows the same transactional service as Listing 114. The only difference is that it injects the repository.

Listing 115. Transactional Service Using Panache Repositories

```java
@ApplicationScoped
@Transactional(SUPPORTS)
public class PublisherService {

  @Inject
  PublisherRepository repository;

  @Transactional(REQUIRED)
  public Publisher persist(Publisher publisher) {
    repository.persist(publisher);
    return publisher;
  }

  public List<Publisher> findAll() {
    return repository.listAll();
  }

  public Optional<Publisher> findByIdOptional(Long id) {
    return repository.findByIdOptional(id);
  }

  @Transactional(REQUIRED)
  public void deleteById(Long id) {
    repository.deleteById(id);
  }
}
```

5.6. Summary

This chapter was all about how to handle data with Quarkus. Quarkus doesn't do anything special per-se, instead, it delegates data validation to Hibernate Validator, object-relational mapping to Hibernate ORM, transaction management to Narayana[186] and uses the datasource connection pool Agroal.

First, we saw how to validate data so that we make sure the data is valid before persisting or updating it into a database. Bean Validation has a very comprehensive approach to validation problems and solves most of the use cases by validating properties or methods in any application layer. It also comes with already built-in constraints handling common use-cases (@NotNull, @Size, @Email).

In the previous chapter we saw that CDI objects were usually called *beans*. When it comes to being persistent, an object is usually called an *entity*. The Java Persistence API is all about mapping entities to relational databases. It handles common mappings (e.g. mapping an attribute to a column), but also complex ones (e.g. relationships or inheritance). Thanks to the entity manager API and the JPQL syntax, we can easily manage and query JPA entities.

In this chapter, we've seen how to handle transactions. We can define transaction management either decoratively or programmatically. Transactions allow the business tier to keep the data in an accurate state even when accessed concurrently by several applications.

Then, we ended this chapter by having aan in-depth look at Panache. Hibernate ORM with Panache is a way to easily map and access entities based on JPA. It gives us either an active record pattern where we can add simplified queries to our entities, or repositories that follow the DAO pattern.

The next chapter is about *HTTP Microservices*. You will learn how to expose and document a REST endpoint that consumes and produces JSON.

[156] **Bean Validation** https://jcp.org/en/jsr/detail?id=380

[157] **Bean Validation GitHub** https://github.com/eclipse-ee4j/beanvalidation-api

[158] **Java Beans** http://download.oracle.com/otndocs/jcp/7224-javabeans-1.01-fr-spec-oth-JSpec

[159] **Programming by Contract** https://en.wikipedia.org/wiki/Design_by_contract

[160] **Hibernate** https://hibernate.org

[161] **JPA** https://jcp.org/en/jsr/detail?id=338

[162] **JPA GitHub** https://github.com/eclipse-ee4j/jpa-api

[163] **ORM** https://en.wikipedia.org/wiki/Object%E2%80%93relational_mapping

[164] **JPA Specification** https://jcp.org/en/jsr/detail?id=338

[165] **DAO** https://en.wikipedia.org/wiki/Data_access_object

[166] **SQLz** https://en.wikipedia.org/wiki/SQL

[167] **JPQL** https://en.wikipedia.org/wiki/Jakarta_Persistence_Query_Language

[168] **JTA** https://jcp.org/en/jsr/detail?id=907

[169] **JTA GitHub** https://github.com/eclipse-ee4j/jta-api

[170] **Open XA** https://en.wikipedia.org/wiki/X/Open_XA

[171] **ACID** https://en.wikipedia.org/wiki/ACID

[172] **Isolation Levels** https://en.wikipedia.org/wiki/Isolation_(database_systems)

[173] **DataSource** https://docs.oracle.com/en/java/javase/11/docs/api/java.sql/javax/sql/DataSource.html

[174] **Agroal** https://agroal.github.io

[175] **Apache Derby** http://db.apache.org/derby

[176] **H2** https://www.h2database.com

[177] **MariaDB** https://mariadb.org

[178] **Microsoft SQL Server** https://www.microsoft.com/en-us/sql-server/sql-server-downloads

[179] **MySQL** https://www.mysql.com

[180] **DB2** https://www.ibm.com/products/db2-database

[181] **PostgreSQL** http://db.apache.org/derby

[182] **Dev Services** https://quarkus.io/guides/dev-services

[183] **Active Record Pattern** https://en.wikipedia.org/wiki/Active_record_pattern

[184] **JDBC** https://en.wikipedia.org/wiki/Java_Database_Connectivity

[185] **DAO** https://en.wikipedia.org/wiki/Data_access_object

[186] **Narayana** https://github.com/jbosstm/narayana

Chapter 6. HTTP Microservices

As we've seen in the previous *Data, Transactions and ORM* chapter, Quarkus is not only about microservices. It has deep core functionalities such as injection or configuration, and a set of extensions to deal with validating or mapping data into relational databases. Thanks to Hibernate ORM with Panache you can easily leverage JPA and JTA to access data in a transactional manner.

Quarkus is *not only* about microservices but it has been strongly influenced by microservices. When it comes to microservices, we can distinguish between HTTP and reactive microservices (see Chapter 8 for reactive microservices). This chapter focuses on RESTful microservices which are based on HTTP. To expose REST endpoints, Quarkus relies on the *JAX-RS* specification which goes hand in hand with *JSON Binding* and *JSON Processing*. There is another specification when it comes to document a REST endpoint, and that's OpenAPI v3. As you will see, Quarkus transparently enables REST documentation with *Eclipse MicroProfile OpenAPI*.

 The code in this chapter can be found at https://github.com/agoncal/agoncal-fascicle-quarkus/tree/2.0/http

6.1. Java API for RESTful Web Services

Let's start from the beginning. In Java, RESTful web services can be implemented using different frameworks or APIs. MicroProfile has chosen JAX-RS as it has a long history of exposing web services within the Jakarta EE platform. Quarkus implements JAX-RS through the RESTEasy implementation.

Representational State Transfer[187] (REST) is an architectural style based on how the Web works. Applied to services, it tries to put the Web back into web services. To design a RESTful web service, you need to know *Hypertext Transfer Protocol*[188] (HTTP) and *Uniform Resource Identifiers* (URIs), and to observe a few design principles. This basically means that each unique URI is a representation of a resource. You can then interact with that resource using an HTTP GET (to get its content), DELETE (to delete it), POST (to create it), or PUT (to update the content).

RESTful architectures quickly became popular because they rely on a very robust transport protocol: *HTTP*. RESTful web services reduce the client/server coupling, making it much easier to evolve a REST interface over time without breaking existing clients. Like the protocol they are based on, RESTful web services are stateless and can make use of HTTP cache and proxy servers to help you handle high load and scale much better. Furthermore, they are easy to build as no special toolkit is required.

Java API for RESTful Web Services[189] (JAX-RS) is a specification that provides support for creating web services according to the Representational State Transfer (REST) architectural style. JAX-RS provides a set of annotations and classes/interfaces to simplify the development and deployment of REST endpoints. It also brings a client API to programmatically invoke REST endpoints.

The Java API for RESTful Web Services APIs and annotations are all defined under the javax.ws.rs. Table 36 lists the main subpackages defined in JAX-RS 2.1 (under the root javax.ws.rs package[190]).

Table 36. Main javax.ws.rs Subpackages

Subpackage	Description
root	Root package of the CDI APIs
client	Classes and interfaces of the new JAX-RS client API
container	Container-specific JAX-RS API
core	Low-level interfaces and annotations used to create RESTful web resources
ext	APIs that provide extensions to the types supported by the JAX-RS API

In these packages, you'll find all the APIs and annotations. Table 37 shows a few JAX-RS APIs.

Table 37. Main JAX-RS APIs

API	Description
Response	Returns a body and metadata
MediaType	Represents a media type
UriBuilder	Utility class for building URIs from their components
UriInfo	Provides access to application and request URI information

Along with APIs, JAX-RS comes with a set of annotations. Table 38 lists a subset of the most commonly used annotations.

Table 38. Main JAX-RS Annotations

Annotation	Description
@GET, @POST, @PUT, @DELETE	Indicates that the annotated method responds to HTTP GET, POST, PUT or DELETE requests
@Path	Identifies the URI path that a resource class or class method will serve requests for
@PathParam	Binds the value of a URI template parameter or a path segment
@QueryParam	Binds the value(s) of an HTTP query parameter to a resource method parameter
@Produces, @Consumes	Defines the media types that the methods of a resource can produce or accept
@Context	Injects information into a field, a property or a method parameter

The JAX-RS extension shown in Listing 116 is the default extension that is added to a pom.xml when generating a new Quarkus application. RESTeasy is the Java API for RESTful Web Services implementation used by Quarkus.

Listing 116. JAX-RS Extension

```
<dependency>
  <groupId>io.quarkus</groupId>
  <artifactId>quarkus-resteasy</artifactId>
</dependency>
```

6.1.1. Understanding RESTful Web Services

RESTful web services are HTTP-centric and make the most of this very rich protocol. In the REST architectural style, every piece of information is a resource, and these resources are addressed using *Uniform Resource Identifiers*[101] (URIs), typically links on the Web. The resources are acted on by using a set of simple, well-defined operations. The REST client-server architectural style is designed to exchange representations of these resources using a defined interface and protocol (see Figure 37). These principles encourage RESTful applications to be simple and lightweight, and to have high performance.

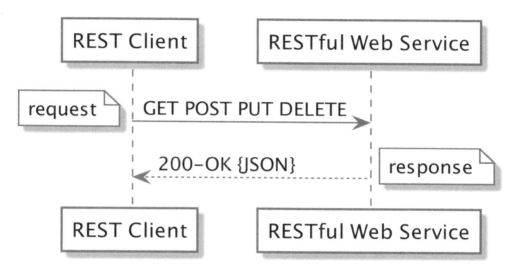

Figure 37. RESTful web services

6.1.2. Exposing RESTful Web Services

Some of the low-level concepts (such as the HTTP protocol) might have you wondering how the code would look when developing a RESTful web service. The good news is that you don't have to write *plumbing* code to digest HTTP requests, nor create HTTP responses by hand. JAX-RS is a very elegant API allowing you to describe a RESTful web service with only a few annotations. RESTful web services are POJOs that have at least one method annotated with `@javax.ws.rs.Path` and an HTTP method annotation (e.g `@GET`, `@POST`, etc.). Listing 117 shows a typical resource.

Listing 117. A Simple Book RESTful Web Service

```
@Path("/book")
public class BookResource {

  @GET
  @Produces("text/plain")
  public String getBookTitle() {
    return "H2G2";
  }
}
```

The `BookResource` is a Java class annotated with `@Path`, indicating that the resource will be hosted at the URI path `/book`. The `getBookTitle()` method is marked to process HTTP `GET` requests (using `@GET` annotation) and produces text (the content type is identified by the MIME Media `text/plain`; we could have also used the constant `MediaType.TEXT_PLAIN` which is less error prone). To access this resource, you need an HTTP client such as a browser to point to the URL http://www.vintage-store.com/book.

JAX-RS is HTTP-centric by nature and has a set of clearly defined classes and annotations to deal with HTTP and URIs. A resource can have several representations, so the API provides support for a variety of content types.

HTTP Method Matching

You've seen how the HTTP protocol works with its requests, responses, and action methods (`GET`, `POST`, `PUT` etc.). JAX-RS defines these common HTTP methods using annotations: `@GET`, `@POST`, `@PUT`, `@DELETE`, `@HEAD`, and `@OPTIONS`. Only public methods may be exposed as resource methods. Listing 118 shows a customer RESTful web service exposing CRUD methods: `@GET` methods to retrieve resources, `@POST` methods to create a new resource, `@PUT` methods to update an existing resource, and `@DELETE` methods to delete a resource.

```java
@Path("/customers")
public class CustomerResource {

  @GET
  public Response getCustomers() {
    // ...
    return Response.ok(customers).build();
  }

  @GET
  @Path("{customerId}")
  public Response getCustomer(@PathParam("customerId") String customerId) {
    // ...
    return Response.ok(customer).build();
  }

  @POST
  public Response createCustomer(Customer customer) {
    // ...
    return Response.created(createdCustomerURI).build();
  }

  @PUT
  public Response updateCustomer(Customer customer) {
    // ...
    return Response.ok(customer).build();
  }

  @DELETE
  @Path("{customerId}")
  public Response deleteCustomer(@PathParam("customerId") String customerId) {
    // ...
    return Response.noContent().build();
  }
}
```

The HTTP specification defines what HTTP response codes should be on a successful request. You can expect JAX-RS to return the same default response codes:

- GET methods retrieve whatever information (in the form of an entity) is identified by the requested URI. GET should return 200-OK.

- The PUT method refers to an already existing resource that needs to be updated. If an existing resource is modified, either the 200-OK or 204-No Content response should be sent to indicate successful completion of the request.

- The POST method is used to create a new resource identified by the request URI. The response should return 201-CREATED with the URI of this new resource (in the Location header) or 204-No Content if it does not result in a resource that can be identified by a URI.

- The DELETE method requests that the server deletes the resource identified by the requested URI. A successful response should be 200-OK if the response includes an entity, 202-Accepted if the action has not yet been enacted, or 204-No Content if the action has been enacted but the response does not include an entity.

URI Definition and Binding URIs

The @Path annotation represents a relative URI. It can annotate a class or a method. When used on classes, it is referred to as the *root resource*, providing the root of the resource tree and giving access to subresources. Each class should use a different root resource so each resource can be uniquely identified. Listing 119 shows a REST service that can be accessed at http://www.vintage-store.com/items/toprated. All the methods of this service will have /items/toprated as root.

Listing 119. Root Path to an Item Resource

```
@Path("/items/toprated")
public class ItemResource {

  @GET
  public List<Item> getItems() {
    // ...
  }
}
```

Once we have a root path (e.g. /items), you can then add subpaths to your methods, which can be useful to group together common functionalities for several resources as shown in Listing 120.

Listing 120. Several Subpaths in the ItemResource

```java
@Path("/items")
public class ItemResource {

  @GET
  public List<Item> getItems() {
    // URI : /items
  }

  @GET
  @Path("/cds")
  public List<CD> getCDs() {
    // URI : /items/cds
  }

  @GET
  @Path("/books")
  public List<Book> getBooks() {
    // URI : /items/books
  }

  @POST
  @Path("/books")
  public Response createBook(Book book) throws URISyntaxException {
    // URI : /items/book
  }
}
```

Listing 120 represents a RESTful web service that will give you methods to get all the items (CDs and books) from the Vintage Store application. When requesting the root resource /items, the only method without sub @Path will be selected (getItems()). Then, when @Path exists on both the class and method, the relative path to the method is a concatenation of both. For example, to get all the CDs, the path will be /items/cds. When requesting /items/books, the getBooks() method will be invoked. To create a new book you need to point at /items/books.

If @Path("/items") only existed on the class, and not on any methods, the path to access each method would be the same. The only way to differentiate them would be the HTTP verb (GET, PUT etc.) and the content negotiation (text, XML etc.), as you'll later see.

Extracting Parameters

Having nice URIs by concatenating paths to access your resource is very important in REST. But paths and subpaths are not enough: you also need to pass parameters to your RESTful web services and extract and process them at runtime. JAX-RS provides a rich set of annotations to extract the different parameters that a request could send (@PathParam, @QueryParam, @MatrixParam, @CookieParam, @HeaderParam, and @FormParam).

Listing 121 shows how the @PathParam annotation is used to extract the value of a URI template parameter. A parameter has a name (eg. text) and is represented by a variable between curly braces (e.g. {text}). This variable can accept any String (e.g. the searchCustomers method) or can follow a regular expression such as in the getCustomerByLogin method that only allows lowercase/uppercase alphabetical letters ([a-zA-Z]*) and getCustomerById only digits (\\d+).

Listing 121. Extracting Path Parameters and Regular Expressions

```
@Path("/customers")
public class CustomerResource {

  @GET
  @Path("search/{text}")
  public List<Customer> searchCustomers(@PathParam("text") String textToSearch) {
    // URI : /customers/search/smith
  }

  @GET
  @Path("{login: [a-zA-Z]*}")
  public Customer getCustomerByLogin(@PathParam("login") String login) {
    // URI : /customers/foobarsmith
  }

  @GET
  @Path("{customerId : \\d+}")
  public Customer getCustomerById(@PathParam("customerId") Long id) {
    // URI : /customers/12345
  }
}
```

The @QueryParam annotation extracts the value of a URI query parameter. Query parameters are key/value pairs separated by an & symbol such as http://www.vintage-store.com/customer?zip=75012&city=Paris. The @MatrixParam annotation acts like @QueryParam, except it extracts the value of a URI matrix parameter (; is used as a delimiter instead of ?). Listing 122 shows how to extract both query and matrix parameters from URIs.

Listing 122. Extracting Query and Matrix Parameters

```
@Path("/customers")
public class CustomerResource {

  @GET
  public List<Customer> getByZipCodeCity(@QueryParam("zip") Long zip,
                                         @QueryParam("city") String city) {
    // URI : /customer?zip=75012&city=Paris
  }

  @GET
  @Path("search")
  public List<Customer> getByName(@MatrixParam("firstname") String firstname,
                                  @MatrixParam("surname") String surname) {
    // URI : /customer/search;firstname=Antonio;surname=Goncalves
  }
}
```

Consuming and Producing Content Types

With REST, the same resource can have several representations; a book can be represented as a web page, a PDF, or an image showing the book cover. JAX-RS specifies a number of Java types that can represent a resource such as String, OutputStream or a bean. The @javax.ws.rs.Consumes and @javax.ws.rs.Produces annotations may be applied to a resource where several representations are possible. It defines the media types of the representation exchanged between the client and the server. JAX-RS has a javax.ws.rs.core.MediaType class that acts as an abstraction for a *MIME type*[192]. It has several methods and defines the constants listed in Table 39.

Table 39. MIME Types Defined in MediaType

Constant name	MIME type
APPLICATION_ATOM_XML	application/atom+xml
APPLICATION_FORM_URLENCODED	application/x-www-form-urlencoded
APPLICATION_JSON	application/json
APPLICATION_OCTET_STREAM	application/octet-stream
APPLICATION_SVG_XML	application/svg+xml
APPLICATION_XHTML_XML	application/xhtml+xml
APPLICATION_XML	application/xml
MULTIPART_FORM_DATA	multipart/form-data
TEXT_HTML	text/html
TEXT_PLAIN	text/plain
TEXT_XML	text/xml
WILDCARD	*/*

Using the @Consumes and @Produces annotations on a method overrides any annotations on the resource class for a method argument or return type. In the absence of either of these annotations, support for any media type (*/*) is assumed. By default, CustomerResource produces plain text representations that are overridden in some methods (see Listing 123). Note that the getAsJsonAndXML produces an array of representations (XML or JSON).

Listing 123. A Customer Resource with Several Representations

```
@Path("/api/customers")
public class CustomerResource {

  @GET
  @Produces(MediaType.TEXT_PLAIN)
  public Response getAsPlainText() {
    // ...
  }

  @GET
  @Produces(MediaType.TEXT_HTML)
  public Response getAsHtml() {
    // ...
  }

  @GET
  @Produces({MediaType.APPLICATION_JSON, MediaType.APPLICATION_XML})
  public Response getAsJsonAndXML() {
    // ...
  }

  @PUT
  @Consumes(MediaType.TEXT_PLAIN)
  public void putName(String customer) {
    // ...
  }
}
```

If a RESTful web service is capable of producing more than one media type, the targeted method will correspond to the most acceptable media type, as declared by the client in the Accept header of the HTTP request. For example, if the Accept header is Accept: text/plain and the URI is /api/customers, the getAsPlainText() method will be invoked.

Returned Types

So far you've seen mostly how to invoke a method (using parameters, media type, HTTP methods etc.) without caring about the returned type. What can a RESTful web service return? Like any Java class, a method can return any standard Java type, a bean or any other object as long as it has a textual representation that can be transported over HTTP. In this case, the runtime determines the MIME type of the object being returned and invokes the appropriate *Entity Provider*[193] to get its representation. The runtime also determines the appropriate HTTP return code to send to the consumer (204-No Content if the resource method's return type is void or null; 200-OK if the returned value is not null). But sometimes you want finer control of what you are returning: the response body (a.k.a. an entity) of course, but also the response code and/or response headers or cookies. That's when you return a Response object. It is good practice to return a javax.ws.rs.core.Response with an entity since it would guarantee a return content type. Listing 124 shows you different return types.

Listing 124. A Customer Service Returning Data Types, a Bean, and a Response

```java
@Path("/customer")
public class CustomerResource {

  @GET
  public String getAsPlainText() {
    return new Customer("John", "Smith").toString();
  }

  @GET
  @Path("max")
  public Integer getMaximumAge() {
    return 42;
  }

  @GET
  @Produces(MediaType.APPLICATION_XML)
  public Customer getAsXML() {
    Customer customer = new Customer("John", "Smith");
    return customer;
  }

  @GET
  @Produces(MediaType.APPLICATION_JSON)
  public Response getAsJson() {
    Customer customer = new Customer("John", "Smith");
    return Response.ok(customer).encoding("utf-8").build();
  }
}
```

The getAsPlainText() method returns a String representation of a customer and the getMaximumAge() returns a numerical constant. The defaults will apply so the return HTTP status on both methods will be 200-OK (if no exception occurs). The getAsXML() returns a Customer object that the runtime will marshal into XML.

The getAsJson() method doesn't return an entity but instead a javax.ws.rs.core.Response object. A Response wraps the entity that is returned to the consumer and it's instantiated using the ResponseBuilder class as a factory. In this example, we still want to return an object (the Customer) with a 200-OK status code (the ok() method), but we also want to specify the encoding to be UTF-8. Calling the ResponseBuilder.build() method creates the final Response instance.

Table 40 shows a subset of the Response API.

Table 40. The Response API

Method	Description
accepted()	Creates a new ResponseBuilder with a 202-Accepted status
created()	New ResponseBuilder for a 201-Created resource (with its URI)
noContent()	New ResponseBuilder for an empty response (204-No Content)
notModified()	New ResponseBuilder with a 304-Not Modified status
ok()	New ResponseBuilder with a 200-OK status
serverError()	New ResponseBuilder with a 500-Internal Server Error status
status()	New ResponseBuilder with the supplied status
temporaryRedirect()	Temporary redirection (307- Temporary Redirect)
getCookies()	Gets the cookies from the response message
getHeaders()	Gets the headers from the response message
getLinks()	Gets the links attached to the message as a header
getStatus()	Gets the status code associated with the response
readEntity()	Reads the message entity

The Response and ResponseBuilder follow the fluent API design pattern. Meaning you can easily write a response by concatenating methods. This also makes the code more readable. Here are some examples of what you can write with this API:

```
Response.ok().build();
Response.ok().cookie(new NewCookie("SessionID", "5G79GDIFY09")).build();
Response.ok("Plain Text").expires(new Date()).build();
Response.ok(new Customer("Ennio", "Smith"), APPLICATION_JSON).build();
Response.noContent().build();
Response.accepted(new Customer("Ligia", "Smith")).build();
Response.notModified().header("User-Agent", "Mozilla").build();
```

6.1.3. Invoking RESTful Web Services

JAX-RS has a client API so that you can make HTTP requests to your remote RESTful web services easily (despite all the low-level details of the HTTP protocol). It is a fluent request building API (i.e. using the Builder design pattern) that uses a small number of classes and interfaces (see Table 41 to have an overview of the javax.ws.rs.client package[194]). Very often, you will come across three main classes: Client, WebTarget, and Response. The Client interface (obtained with the ClientBuilder) is a builder of WebTarget instances. A WebTarget represents a distinct URI from which you can invoke requests on to obtain a Response. From this Response you can check HTTP status, length or cookies but more importantly, you can get its content (a.k.a. entity, message body or payload) through the Entity class.

Table 41. Main Classes and Interfaces of the javax.ws.rs.client Package

Class/Interface	Description
Client	Main entry point to the fluent API used to build and execute client requests in order to consume responses returned
ClientBuilder	Entry point to the client API used to bootstrap Client instances
Configurable	Client side configuration from Client, WebTarget, and Invocation
Entity	Encapsulates message entity including the associated variant information
Invocation	A request that has been prepared and is ready for execution
Invocation.Builder	A client request invocation builder
WebTarget	A resource target identified by the resource URI

 In Chapter 7, you will see how an HTTP microservice invokes another one. Basically, it uses the Eclipse MicroProfile REST Client which is part of MicroProfile. Eclipse MicroProfile REST Client is based on the JAX-RS 2.1 client API, so it's important that you know the basis before diving into REST Client.

Bootstrapping the Client

The main entry point for the API is the Client interface. The Client interface manages and configures HTTP connections. It is also a factory for WebTargets and has a set of methods for creating resource links and invocations. The Client instances are created using one of the static methods of the ClientBuilder class:

```
Client client = ClientBuilder.newClient();
```

Targets and Invocations

Once you have a Client you can now target a RESTful web service URI and invoke some HTTP methods on it. That's what the WebTarget and Invocation interfaces allow you to do. The Client.target() methods are factories for web targets that represent a specific URI. You build and execute requests from a WebTarget instance. You can create a WebTarget with the String representation of a URI:

```
WebTarget target = client.target("http://localhost:8081/customers");
```

You can also obtain a WebTarget from a java.net.URI, javax.ws.rs.core.UriBuilder or javax.ws.rs.core.Link:

```
URI uri = new URI("http://localhost:8081/customers");
WebTarget target = client.target(uri);
```

Now that you have a URI to target, you need to build your HTTP request. The WebTarget allows you to do that by using the Invocation.Builder. To build a simple HTTP GET on a URI just write:

```
Invocation invocation = target.request().buildGet();
```

Invocation.Builder allows you to build a GET method as well as POST, PUT and DELETE methods. You can also build a request for different MIME types and even add path, query and matrix parameters. For PUT and POST methods you need to pass an Entity, which represents the payload to send to your RESTful web service:

```
target.request().buildDelete();
target.queryParam("author", "Eloise").request().buildGet();
target.path(bookId).request().buildGet();
target.request(MediaType.APPLICATION_XML).buildGet();
target.request(MediaType.APPLICATION_XML).acceptLanguage("pt").buildGet();
target.request().buildPost(Entity.entity(new Book()));
```

The code below just builds an Invocation. You then need to call the invoke() method to actually invoke your remote RESTful web service and get a Response object back. The Response is what defines the contract with the returned instance and is what you will consume:

```
Response response = invocation.invoke();
```

So if you put everything together, these are the lines of code to invoke a GET method on a remote RESTful web service located at http://localhost:8081/customers and return a text/plain value:

```
Client client = ClientBuilder.newClient();
WebTarget target = client.target("http://localhost:8081/customers");
Invocation invocation = target.request(MediaType.TEXT_PLAIN).buildGet();
Response response = invocation.invoke();
```

Thanks to the builder API and some shortcuts, you can write the same behaviour in a single line of code:

```
Response response = ClientBuilder
  .newClient()
  .target("http://localhost:8081/customers")
  .request(MediaType.TEXT_PLAIN)
  .get();
```

6.1.4. Configuring RESTEasy

As usual with Quarkus, if you need to configure an extension, you just add a few properties to the application.properties file. For configuring RESTful web services, you can look for the quarkus.resteasy namespace for the configuration keys[144].

Table 42. Some Quarkus RESTEasy Configuration Properties

Property	Default
`quarkus.resteasy.gzip.enabled` If gzip is enabled	false
`quarkus.resteasy.gzip.max-input` Maximum deflated file bytes size (if the limit is exceeded, a `413-Payload Too Large` is returned)	10M
`quarkus.resteasy.singleton-resources` If true then JAX-RS will use only a single instance of a resource, if false then it will create a new instance of the resource per request	true
`quarkus.resteasy.path` Overrides the default path for JAX-RS resources if there are no annotated application classes	/
`quarkus.resteasy.metrics.enabled` Whether or not JAX-RS metrics should be enabled if the Metrics capability is present	false

6.2. Eclipse MicroProfile OpenAPI

JAX-RS lets you consume and expose REST APIs. But it doesn't help you in documenting your APIs, you need to use external tools. That's what Quarkus allows you to do. By default, a Quarkus application exposes its API description through an *OpenAPI* specification. It can even let you test it via a user-friendly UI named *Swagger UI*.

Exposing RESTful APIs has become an essential part of all modern applications. From the microservices developer's point of view, it is important to understand how to interact with these APIs and how to test that they are still valid and backward compatible. For that, there needs to be a clear and complete contract. Therefore a standard API documentation mechanism is required and can also be used for API testing. That's when *OpenAPI*[195] comes along.

Eclipse MicroProfile OpenAPI[196] provides a Java API for the OpenAPI v3 specification that all application developers can use to expose their API documentation. It aims to provide a set of Java interfaces and programming models which allow Java developers to natively produce OpenAPI v3 documents from their JAX-RS endpoints.

The Eclipse MicroProfile OpenAPI APIs and annotations are all defined under the main `org.eclipse.microprofile.openapi` package, either at the root, or under the other subpackages. Table 43 lists the main subpackages defined in Eclipse MicroProfile OpenAPI version 2.0 (under the root `org.eclipse.microprofile.openapi` package[197]).

Table 43. Main org.eclipse.microprofile.openapi Subpackages

Subpackage	Description
root	Root package of the OpenAPI APIs
`annotations`	Set of annotations to produce a valid OpenAPI document
`models`	Interfaces to define OpenAPI document programmatically
`spi`	Internal SPIs (*Service Provider Interfaces*) implemented by the provider

In these packages, you'll find all the APIs and annotations. Table 44 shows a few OpenAPI APIs.

Table 44. Main OpenAPI APIs

API	Description
OASConfig	Configurable properties in MicroProfile OpenAPI
OASFactory	Allows developers to build new OpenAPI model elements
OASFilter	Allows to filter different parts of the OpenAPI model tree
OASModelReader	Allows to programmatically contribute an OpenAPI model tree

Along with APIs, OpenAPI comes with a set of annotations. Table 45 lists a subset of the most commonly used annotations.

Table 45. Main OpenAPI Annotations

Annotation	Description
@APIResponse	Describes the endpoint's response (response code, data structure, types, etc.)
@Operation	Describes a single API operation on a path
@OpenAPIDefinition	Root document object of the OpenAPI document
@Parameter	The name of the method parameter
@RequestBody	A brief description of the request body
@Schema	Allows the definition of input and output data types
@Tag	Used to add tags to the REST endpoint contract to provide more description

The Eclipse MicroProfile OpenAPI extension shown in Listing 125 is one of these extensions that, once added to your pom.xml brings you new functionalities without having to invoke any APIs. Add this extension, and Quarkus will automatically generate an OpenAPI v3 documentation for your REST endpoints.

Listing 125. OpenAPI Extension

```
<dependency>
  <groupId>io.quarkus</groupId>
  <artifactId>quarkus-smallrye-openapi</artifactId>
</dependency>
```

Before digging more into OpenAPI, we need to define some terminology, such as the *OpenAPI v3 Specification*.

Swagger

The term *Swagger UI* takes its roots from *Swagger*. Let's explain it. At first, there was no specific way to describe a RESTful service. Some developers were not even documenting their APIs or would be using an in-house proprietary format. That's when Swagger came into play.

Swagger[198] is an open source software framework created in 2011 that helps developers design, build, document, and consume RESTful web services. RESTful APIs typically did not have a machine-readable description mechanism at that time, so Swagger became very popular among developers and also companies (Apigee, Intuit, Microsoft, IBM, etc.). Shortly after Swagger was created, alternative structures for describing RESTful APIs were introduced, the most popular being API Blueprint and RAML[199]. In 2015, under the sponsorship of the Linux Foundation, Swagger was donated to the *OpenAPI Initiative*[200]. In 2016, the Swagger specification was renamed *OpenAPI Specification*.

6.2.1. Understanding OpenAPI v3 Specification

OpenAPI specification[201] (formerly known as the *Swagger Specification*) is an API description format for REST APIs. It is a specification for machine-readable interface files for describing, producing, consuming, and visualising RESTful web services. An OpenAPI file allows you to describe your entire API, including:

- Available endpoints (/authors) and operations on each endpoint (GET, POST, etc.),
- Input and output parameters for each operation,
- Authentication methods,
- Contact information, license, terms of use and other information.

The specifications can be written in YAML or JSON. The format is easy to learn and readable to both humans and machines.

Every API definition must include the version of the OpenAPI Specification that this definition is based on:

```
openapi: 3.0.3
```

The info section contains API information:

- title is the API name.
- description (optional) is extended information about the API. It can be multiline and supports CommonMark[202] and HTML syntax for rich text representation.
- version is an arbitrary string that specifies the version of the API.

```
info:
  title: open-api-v3spec API
  version: "1.0"
tags:
  - name: Author Endpoint
```

The `paths` section defines individual endpoints (or *paths*) of the API, and the HTTP methods (or *operations*) supported by these endpoints (GET, POST, PUT, DELETE, etc.). For example, *return a specific author* can be described as an HTTP `GET` operation on the `/authors/{index}` path:

```
paths:
  /authors/{index}:
    get:
      summary: Returns an author for a given index
```

Operations can have parameters passed via URL path (`/authors/{index}`), query string (`/authors?name=Adams`), headers (`X-CustomHeader: Value`) or cookies (`Cookie: debug=0`). You can define the parameter data types, format, whether they are required or optional, and other details:

```
parameters:
  - name: index
    in: path
    description: Author index
    required: true
    schema:
      format: int32
      type: integer
```

For each operation, you can define possible status codes, such as `200-OK` or `404-Not Found`, and the response body schema. Schemas can be defined inline or referenced via `$ref`. You can also provide example responses for different content types:

```
responses:
  "200":
    description: OK
    content:
      text/plain: {}
  "204":
    description: The author is not found for a given index
```

6.2.2. Exposing OpenAPI Contracts

Eclipse MicroProfile OpenAPI integrates with Java API for RESTful Web Services. That means that OpenAPI processes all the relevant JAX-RS annotations (such as `@Path`, `@Consumes`, etc.) as well as Java objects used as input or output to JAX-RS operations. Without any additional annotation or configuration, you get your API documentation out-of-the-box. The JAX-RS classes and annotations are scanned so that a default documentation is generated. The RESTful web service described in Listing 126 only has JAX-RS annotations.

Listing 126. Author Endpoint with no OpenAPI Annotations

```
@Path("/authors")
@Produces(MediaType.TEXT_PLAIN)
public class AuthorResource {

  String[] scifiAuthors = {"Isaac Asimov", "Nora Jemisin", "Douglas Adams"};

  @GET
  @Path("/{index}")
  public String getScifiAuthor(@PathParam("index") int index) {
    return scifiAuthors[index];
  }
}
```

Thanks to the integration of JAX-RS, Eclipse MicroProfile OpenAPI is capable of generating a default contract as described in Listing 127.

Listing 127. Default Generated OpenAPI Contract

```
openapi: 3.0.3
info:
  title: open-api-default API
  version: "1.0"
paths:
  /authors/{index}:
    get:
      parameters:
      - name: index
        in: path
        required: true
        schema:
          format: int32
          type: integer
      responses:
        "200":
          description: OK
          content:
            text/plain:
              schema:
                type: string
```

The default contract described in Listing 127 is comprehensive enough, but it lacks documentation. We could give some description of the API, or an example on how to use it and you could say if the index parameter is required or not, etc. The Eclipse MicroProfile OpenAPI allows you to customise several aspects of your REST endpoints thanks to annotations.

When you expose RESTful web services with Quarkus, you can get the OpenAPI contract under the URL /q/openapi. You can either access it with your browser, or you can use cURL. With cURL, by changing the HTTP header, you can retrieve the OpenAPI document in several formats:

- YAML: curl http://localhost:8080/q/openapi
- JSON: curl -H "Accept: application/json" http://localhost:8080/q/openapi

Customising OpenAPI Contracts

Relying on the default JAX-RS mapping is usually not enough. You want to really document your APIs, and for that, Eclipse MicroProfile OpenAPI has a set of annotations. For example, in Listing 128 we add extra information to the JAX-RS annotations. On the getScifiAuthor() method we add an @Operation annotation so we can give a summary to the endpoint. This is very useful for a third-party partner to understand what your API does. The @APIResponse gives some information about the response returned by the API. Here, we express that the API can return a 200-OK and a 204-No Content.

Listing 128. Author Endpoint with OpenAPI Annotations

```
@Path("/authors")
@Produces(MediaType.TEXT_PLAIN)
public class AuthorResource {

    String[] scifiAuthors = {"Isaac Asimov", "Nora Jemisin", "Douglas Adams"};

    @GET
    @Path("/{index}")
    @Operation(summary = "Returns an author for a given index")
    @APIResponse(responseCode = "204", description = "Author not found")
    @APIResponse(responseCode = "200",
                 description = "Author returned for a given index")
    public String getScifiAuthor(@PathParam("index") int index) {
        return scifiAuthors[index];
    }
}
```

As you can see below, the summary of the @Operation annotation is reflected into the OpenAPI v3 contract.

```
# Without annotation
paths:
  /authors/{index}:
    get:

# With the @Operation annotation
paths:
  /authors/{index}:
    get:
      summary: Returns an author for a given index
```

Adding the @APIResponse annotations to the code also makes the contract clearer so all the returned status codes are listed and documented.

```
# Without annotation
  "200":
    description: OK
    content:
      text/plain:
        schema:
          type: string

# With the @APIResponse annotations
responses:
  "204":
    description: Author not found
  "200":
    description: Author returned for a given index
    content:
      text/plain:
        schema:
          type: string
```

Advanced Customisation

If you have external clients accessing your endpoints, you want to add further information for them to understand what each endpoint is about. Not just about the operations and return code, but parameters, returned values, general documentation, etc. Fortunately, OpenAPI defines a rich set of annotations you can use to customise the API documentation.

Figure 38 shows a BookResource REST endpoint that consumes and produces a Book class. Notice the BookApplication which is a general class and not an endpoint. We annotate this class using Open API to provide some application level documentation. In fact, OpenAPI lets you document the entire application: from the BookApplication, BookResource to the Book itself.

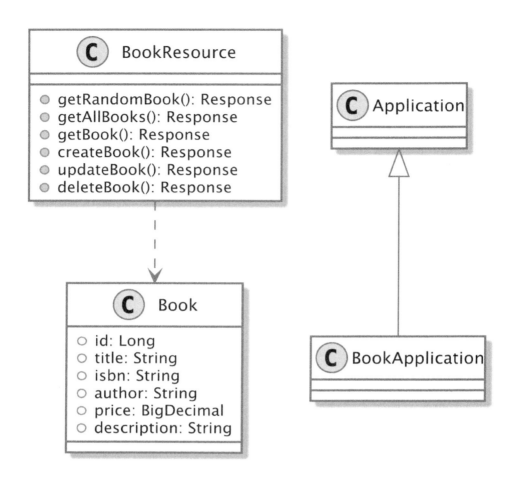

Figure 38. REST application

Documenting Applications

Having a documented contract for a given REST endpoint is not enough. It is also important to document the entire application. The difference is that OpenAPI annotations are not just on the endpoint itself, but instead on another Java class configuring the entire application (see the `BookApplication` in Listing 129). To define a class that globally defines a JAX-RS application, the `BookApplication` needs to extend the JAX-RS `javax.ws.rs.core.Application` class. This allows the application and supplies additional meta-data. For example, the `@OpenAPIDefinition` annotation. This annotation is used to add extra information to the root document of the contract. It contains several fields such as the description of the application, its version, the team to contact or the license used.

Listing 129. Application Information

```
@OpenAPIDefinition(
  info = @Info(
    title = "Book API",
    description = "This API allows CRUD operations on books",
    version = "1.0",
    contact = @Contact(name = "@agoncal", url = "https://twitter.com/agoncal"),
    license = @License(
      name = "MIT",
      url = "https://opensource.org/licenses/MIT")),
  externalDocs = @ExternalDocumentation(url = "https://github.com/agoncal/agoncal-
fascicle-quarkus", description = "All the Quarkus fascicle code"),
  tags = {
    @Tag(name = "api", description = "Public API that can be used by anybody"),
    @Tag(name = "books", description = "Anybody interested in books")
  }
)
public class BookApplication extends Application {
}
```

The result is that the root of the OpenAPI v3 contract is now fully documented (see Listing 130). The documentation is not about an endpoint per-se, but the entire application.

Listing 130. Root of the OpenAPI v3 Contract

```
openapi: 3.0.3
info:
  title: Book API
  description: This API allows CRUD operations on books
  contact:
    name: '@agoncal'
    url: https://twitter.com/agoncal
  license:
    name: MIT
    url: https://opensource.org/licenses/MIT
  version: "1.0"
externalDocs:
  description: All the Quarkus fascicle code
  url: https://github.com/agoncal/agoncal-fascicle-quarkus
```

A tag is extra information you can use to help organise your API endpoints. The array of @Tag annotations can be applied at the method or class level (see Listing 131).

Listing 131. Tags in the Root of the Contract

```
tags:
  - name: api
    description: Public API that can be used by anybody
  - name: books
    description: Anybody interested in books
```

On the `BookApplication` you can also add information about the servers where the APIs can be accessed. For example, in Listing 132 we use the `server` attribute to list the server, host and port. Thanks to `@ServerVariable`, the host and port can be variables and can have default values.

Listing 132. Servers Information

```
servers = @Server(
  description = "Vintage Store server 1",
  url = "http://{host}.vintage-store/{port}",
  variables = {
    @ServerVariable(name = "host",
      description = "Vintage Store main server",
      defaultValue = "localhost"),
    @ServerVariable(name = "port",
      description = "Vintage Store listening port",
      defaultValue = "80")
  }
)
)
public class BookApplication extends Application {
}
```

The result is that the contract will have an extra `servers` section (see Listing 133).

Listing 133. Servers in the Root of the Contract

```
servers:
  - url: "http://{host}.vintage-store/{port}"
    description: Vintage Store server 1
    variables:
      host:
        default: localhost
        description: Vintage Store main server
      port:
        default: "80"
        description: Vintage Store listening port
```

Documenting Parameters

There are several ways to pass parameters to an endpoint operation. For example, JAX-RS uses the `@PathParam` annotation to pass parameters to the URL path, or passes data straight into the request body. Thanks to the OpenAPI @Parameter annotation in Listing 134, you can add a description to the parameter to tell the client what this parameter is about.

Listing 134. Operation with Parameters

```
@GET
@Path("/{id}")
public Response getBook(@Parameter(description = "Book identifier", required = true)
                        @PathParam("id") Long id) {
```

As shown in Listing 135, thanks to @Parameter, the contract is enriched with a description and expresses the fact that a parameter can be required or not.

Listing 135. Contract Describing Operation Parameters

```
/api/books/{id}:
  get:
    summary: Returns a book for a given identifier
    parameters:
      - name: id
        in: path
        description: Book identifier
        required: true
        schema:
          format: int64
          type: integer
```

For POST or PUT operations, Eclipse MicroProfile OpenAPI has a @RequestBody annotation to document the data passed in the body (see Listing 136). In fact, like the @Parameter annotation, @RequestBody takes a @Content that describes the content passed in or out. So it specifies the formats passed in the body (here JSON) but also the type of the structure.

Listing 136. Operation with Request Body Reference

```
@POST
public Response createBook(@RequestBody(
                               required = true,
                               content = @Content(mediaType = APPLICATION_JSON,
                                 schema = @Schema(implementation = Book.class)))
                               Book book, @Context UriInfo uriInfo) {
```

Thanks to @Schema, the contract has a reference (the keyword ref) to #/components/schemas/Book. In fact, the Book structure being a reference, it is used in Listing 137 as an input parameter to the createBook() method as well as in Listing 139.

Listing 137. Operation with Request Body

```
post:
  summary: Creates a book
  requestBody:
    content:
      application/json:
        schema:
          $ref: '#/components/schemas/Book'
    required: true
```

 When the same annotation is used on a class and on a method, the values from the method instance will take precedence for that particular method. This commonly occurs with the @Server and @Tag annotations, for example.

Documenting Responses

A REST endpoint can return a datatype (e.g. String, int, Book, etc.) or a Response. In that case, if we don't specify the type of the response, the contract is unclear. @Schema can also be used on a response, as seen in Listing 138. As the response may contain several books, schema type is set to an array.

Listing 138. Operation Returning an Array

```
@GET
@Operation(summary = "Returns all the books from the database")
@APIResponse(responseCode = "200",
             content = @Content(mediaType = APPLICATION_JSON,
               schema = @Schema(implementation = Book.class, type = SchemaType.ARRAY)))
@APIResponse(responseCode = "204", description = "No books")
public Response getAllBooks() {
```

The result is that, now, the type of the response is a reference to Book (see Listing 139). Being of type array and of media type application/json, the consumer of this API now knows what to expect when invoking getAllBooks().

Listing 139. Array of References to Book

```yaml
paths:
  /api/books:
    get:
      summary: Returns all the books from the database
      responses:
        "200":
          description: OK
          content:
            application/json:
              schema:
                type: array
                items:
                  $ref: '#/components/schemas/Book'
        "204":
          description: No books
```

Within the @Schema annotation, we can reference the response or parameter objects with the schema type. This can point to a *Data Transfer Object* (DTO), for example. Listing 140 represents the Book class that is passed as a request body to the createBook() method (Listing 136) or as the response of getAllBooks() (see Listing 138). As you can see, Book can also use the @Schema annotation to add a description, or to specify which field is required and what the example values are.

Listing 140. Operation with Request Body

```java
@Schema(name = "Book", description = "Book representation")
public class Book {

  @Schema(required = true, readOnly = true)
  public Long id;
  @Schema(required = true)
  public String title;
  @Schema(required = true, example = "9798629562115")
  public String isbn;
  public String author;
  public BigDecimal price;
  public String description;
}
```

The Book class is then described in the schemas section of the OpenAPI v3 contract as shown in Listing 141.

Listing 141. Book Reference Described in the Contract

```
components:
  schemas:
    Book:
      description: Book representation
      required:
        - id
        - title
        - isbn
      type: object
      properties:
        id:
          format: int64
          type: integer
          readOnly: true
        title:
          type: string
        isbn:
          type: string
          example: "9798629562115"
        author:
          type: string
        price:
          type: number
        description:
          type: string
```

As you can see, Eclipse MicroProfile OpenAPI comes with a set of APIs and annotations to document REST endpoints. Quarkus can generate this documentation either in YAML or JSON. These two formats are human-readable and can also be used by external tools to generate stubs or proxies such as *Swagger Codegen*[203], for example. But if the application is made of several endpoints and each endpoint exposes many APIs, then the OpenAPI contract can be huge and difficult to read. Having a user interface instead could be very helpful. Quarkus solves this problem by integrating Swagger UI.

6.2.3. Swagger UI

When building APIs, developers want to analyse them quickly. *Swagger UI*[204] is a great tool that permits you to visualise and interact with your APIs. It's automatically generated from the OpenAPI contract, with the visual documentation making it easy for back end implementation and client side consumption.

The Quarkus `smallrye-openapi` extension comes with a Swagger UI extension embedding a properly configured Swagger UI page. By default, Swagger UI is accessible at /q/swagger-ui (the OpenAPI contract being accessible on /q/openapi). So, once an application is started, you can go to http://localhost:8080/q/swagger-ui and play with the APIs. As shown in Figure 39, Swagger UI lets you visualise the operations and schemas of the APIs, as well as interact with them.

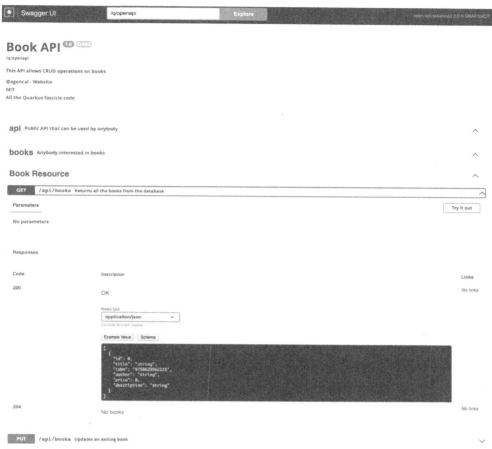

Figure 39. Swagger UI

6.2.4. Configuring SmallRye OpenAPI

By default, Quarkus scans all the classes of all the packages of your application to discover JAX-RS endpoints and OpenAPI annotations. Eclipse MicroProfile OpenAPI comes with a set of properties so you can include or exclude a list of packages to scan, as well as excluding classes. This can be useful if you want to generate a contract only for certain REST endpoints. Table 46 is a subset of standard configuration properties that every vendor must support.

Table 46. MicroProfile OpenAPI Configuration Properties

Property	Description
mp.openapi.scan.disable	Disables annotation scanning (default value is `false`)
mp.openapi.scan.packages	List of packages to scan
mp.openapi.scan.classes	List of classes to scan
mp.openapi.scan.exclude.packages	List of packages to exclude from scans

Property	Description
mp.openapi.scan.exclude.classes	List of classes to exclude from scans
mp.openapi.servers	List of global servers that provide connectivity information

On top of the standard properties listed in Table 46, Quarkus adds a set of configuration properties listed in Table 47. These properties let you change the default paths for the OpenAPI contract or Swagger, as well as enabling Swagger in production, for example.

Table 47. Some Quarkus OpenAPI Configuration Properties

Property	Default
quarkus.smallrye-openapi.path The path at which to register the OpenAPI Servlet	/openapi
quarkus.swagger-ui.path The path where Swagger UI is available (/ is not allowed as it blocks the application from serving anything else)	/swagger-ui
quarkus.swagger-ui.always-include If Swagger UI should be included every time (by default it's only included in dev mode)	false
quarkus.swagger-ui.enable If Swagger UI should be enabled	true
quarkus.smallrye-openapi.info-title Set the title in Info tag in the Schema document	
quarkus.smallrye-openapi.info-version Set the version in Info tag in the Schema document	
quarkus.smallrye-openapi.info-description Set the description in Info tag in the Schema document	
quarkus.smallrye-openapi.info-terms-of-service Set the terms of the service in Info tag in the Schema document	
quarkus.smallrye-openapi.info-contact-email Set the contact email in Info tag in the Schema document	
quarkus.smallrye-openapi.info-contact-name Set the contact name in Info tag in the Schema document	
quarkus.smallrye-openapi.info-contact-url Set the contact url in Info tag in the Schema document	
quarkus.smallrye-openapi.info-license-name Set the license name in Info tag in the Schema document	
quarkus.smallrye-openapi.info-license-url Set the license url in Info tag in the Schema document	

6.3. JSON Binding

Most of the examples of REST endpoints examples that you've seen so far, consume or produce JSON. In fact, a REST endpoint can consume or produce any kind of media type: from plain text, to XML, images or PDFs. But JSON has become a common data format exchanged between microservices. That's why Quarkus implements the two MicroProfile specifications dealing with JSON: JSON Binding and JSON Processing.

JSON Binding[205] (JSON-B) is a standard binding layer for converting Java objects to/from JSON documents. It defines a default mapping algorithm for converting existing Java classes to JSON while enabling developers to customise the mapping process through the use of Java annotations.

The JSON Binding APIs are all defined under the `javax.json.bind` package. Table 48 lists the main subpackages defined in JSON-B 1.0 (under the root `javax.json.bind` package[206]).

Table 48. Main javax.json.bind Subpackages

Subpackage	Description
root	Root package of the JSON-B APIs
adapter	APIs to define a custom mapping for a given Java type
annotation	JSON-B mapping annotations
config	Classes and interfaces to configure the mapping provider
serializer	JSON-B internals for custom serialisers
spi	Internal SPIs (*Service Provider Interfaces*) implemented by the provider

Along with APIs, JSON-B comes with a set of annotations. Table 49 lists a subset of the most commonly used annotations.

Table 49. Main JSON-B Annotations

Annotation	Description
@JsonbDateFormat	Customises the date format of a field
@JsonbProperty	Allows customisation of a field name
@JsonbNumberFormat	Customises the number format of a field
@JsonbTransient	Prevents mapping of a field

To be able to bind JSON objects, you need JSON Binding. JSON-B comes with the RESTeasy extension shown in Listing 142.

Listing 142. JSON-B Extension

```
<dependency>
  <groupId>io.quarkus</groupId>
  <artifactId>quarkus-resteasy-jsonb</artifactId>
</dependency>
```

Jackson and QSON

Maybe you don't know JSON-B but instead have heard of, or used, Jackson. Inspired by the quality and variety of XML tooling, *Jackson*[207] was created back in 2009 as a multi-purpose Java library for processing JSON. It is a high-performance JSON processor including the streaming JSON parser / generator library and matching data-binding library (POJOs to and from JSON).

QSON[208] is another object to json mapper. It does bytecode generation of deserializer and serializer classes. While Jackson or JSON-B are more mature json mappers, QSON aims for better integration with Quarkus and GraalVM. The primary goals of QSON are speed, both boot and runtime, limited heap allocations, a small set of classes (metaspace size), low memory footprint, and zero reflection at runtime.

JSON-B is analogous to Jackson or QSON, and in fact, Quarkus comes with all of them as extensions. This fascicle uses JSON-B instead because JSON-B is part of Eclipse MicroProfile. Just make sure not to mix Jackson, Qson and JSON-B in the same project, since this might introduce some unwanted bugs.

6.3.1. Understanding Binding

As shown in Figure 40, data binding is the process of defining the representation of a JSON document into an object instance, and vice versa. So, *deserialisation* is the process of reading a JSON document and constructing a tree of content objects, where each object corresponds to a part of the JSON document. Thus the content tree reflects the document's content. The inverse process to deserialisation is *serialisation*. This is when the content of the object tree is written to a JSON document that reflects the tree's content.

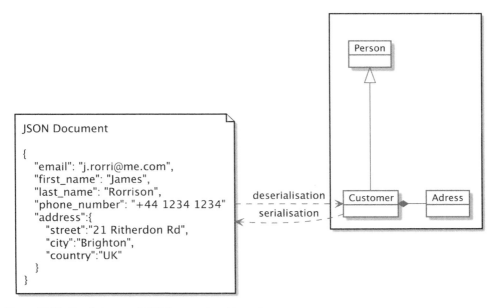

Figure 40. Binding between a JSON document and Java classes

6.3.2. Binding POJOs

So far you've seen how JPA maps objects to a relational database: it uses a default mapping mechanism (a.k.a. *programming by exception* or *convention over configuration*) and gives you a set of annotations to customise the default behaviour. OpenAPI works the same way: an OpenAPI v3 contract is generated based on default endpoint annotations, but Eclipse MicroProfile OpenAPI gives you a set of annotations to add extra information to the contract if needed. The same occurs with JSON-B.

Default Binding

Default mapping is a set of rules used by JSON-B to map default objects without any annotations or any configuration. For JSON-B, the default mapping rules are simple:

- Attribute names are bound to the same JSON key name (e.g. the `title` attribute is bound to the `title` key).
- All the basic Java types (`String`, `Integer`, `int`, etc.), standard Java types (`BigDecimal`, `URL`, `Optional`, etc.) or dates have their value bound to the JSON value. These values have to follow the RFC 7159[209] standard (the *JSON Data Interchange Format*) and be encoded in UTF-8.

So let's have a look at the default binding in a simple example. Listing 143 represents a `Book` object from which I've omitted the getters and the setters for clarity. As you can see, this object has several attributes (`title`, `price` etc.) of different types (`String`, `Float`, `Integer`, and `Boolean`), a default constructor, and getters and setters for each attribute.

Listing 143. Simple Book Class

```java
public class Book {

    private String title;
    private Float price;
    private String isbn;
    private Integer nbOfPages;
    private Boolean illustrations;
    private String description;
    private LocalDate publicationDate;

    // Constructors, getters, setters
}
```

So how does this map to JSON? The answer is: thanks to default binding, the JSON-B runtime serialises the Book instances into the JSON document shown in Listing 144.

Listing 144. Default JSON Representation of a Book Object

```json
{
    "title": "H2G2",
    "price": 12.5,
    "isbn": "1-84023-742-2",
    "nbOfPages": 354,
    "illustrations": false,
    "description": "Best Sci-fi book ever",
    "publicationDate": "1999-04-28"
}
```

Customising Binding

Like what we saw previously with JPA or OpenAPI, if you need to customise the default binding, you use annotations. In JSON-B, you can add a binding annotation either on a field, getter or setter. If the annotation is specified on a field, the binding is used both for serialisation and deserialisation. If it annotates a getter, it is used only for serialisation, and used only for deserialization if specified on a setter.

Listing 145 uses several JSON-B annotations on fields:

- @JsonbProperty is used to change the name of a particular property (e.g. book_title instead of the default title). The nillable attribute switches on and off the serialisation of null values.

- By default, JSON-B uses ISO formats to serialise and deserialise dates and numbers. But sometimes it's required to override these settings. This can be done using @JsonbDateFormat and @JsonbNumberFormat annotations. These two annotations take a parameter following the java.time.format.DateTimeFormatter and java.text.DecimalFormat patterns.

- Also notice that the property description is annotated with @JsonbTransient, therefore, it will be ignored by the JSON binding engine.

Listing 145. Customised Book Class

```java
public class Book {

    @JsonbProperty(value = "book_title", nillable = false)
    private String title;
    @JsonbNumberFormat("#0.00")
    private Float price;
    private String isbn;
    @JsonbProperty(value = "nb_of_pages", nillable = true)
    private Integer nbOfPages;
    private Boolean illustrations;
    @JsonbTransient
    private String description;
    @JsonbDateFormat("dd/MM/yyyy")
    private LocalDate publicationDate;

    // Constructors, getters, setters
}
```

When the Book object in Listing 145 is serialised into a JSON document it looks like the JSON in Listing 146: the title has been renamed, the price and publication date have been formatted, and the description does not appear in the document.

Listing 146. Custom JSON Representation of a Book

```json
{
    "book_title": "H2G2",
    "price": "12.50",
    "isbn": "1-84023-742-2",
    "nb_of_pages": 354,
    "illustrations": false,
    "publicationDate": "28/04/1999"
}
```

Advanced Customisation

JSON-B also supports binding collections as well as inheritance. As you can see in Figure 41, the class diagram represents a purchase order that has several relationships: a one-to-one relationship between credit card and customer, as well as a one-to-many order lines. Customer inherits from the abstract class Person.

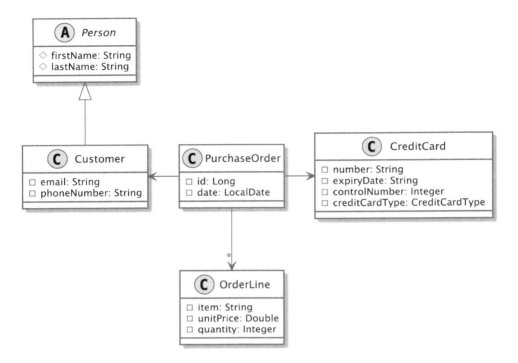

Figure 41. Binding complex object graphs

As complex as this class diagram looks, JSON-B will apply the same binding mechanisms to all the classes. It will also cascade the serialisation/deserialisation from the root class to the child classes. JSON-B supports binding arrays, as well as Java collections (e.g. Collection, Map, Set, etc.). Listing 147 represents the root class PurchaseOrder with all its relationships.

Listing 147. Purchase Order with Relationships

```
public class PurchaseOrder {

    private Long id;
    private LocalDate date;
    @JsonbProperty("purchase_order_content")
    private List<OrderLine> orderLines;
    @JsonbProperty("credit_card")
    private CreditCard creditCard;
    private Customer customer;

    // Constructors, getters, setters
}
```

Serialising a purchase order results in a more complex JSON document (see Listing 148). As you can see, the purchase_order_content is an array of order lines. credit_card and customer are nodes in the JSON document representing the Customer and CreditCard one-to-one relationships. And the `customer` node inherits from the attributes of `Person` (`firstName` and `lastName`).

Listing 148. JSON Representation of a Purchase Order

```
{
  "id": 1234,
  "date": "2019-12-07",
  "purchase_order_content": [
    {
      "item": "H2G2",
      "quantity": 1,
      "unit_price": 23.5
    },
    {
      "item": "Harry Potter",
      "quantity": 2,
      "unit_price": 34.99
    }
  ],
  "credit_card": {
    "control_number": 372,
    "expiry_date": "10/23",
    "number": "2156 7655 1234 9876",
    "type": "VISA"
  },
  "customer": {
    "email": "j.rorri@me.com",
    "first_name": "James",
    "last_name": "Rorrison",
    "phone_number": "+44 1234 1234"
  }
}
```

JAX-B

There is also an XML equivalent called JAX-B (*Java Architecture for XML Binding*) that does the binding between a Java object and an XML document. To have XML binding in Quarkus, you first need to add the `quarkus-resteasy-jaxb` Maven dependency. Then, you need to annotate your POJOs with JAX-B annotations such as:

```
@XmlRootElement
public class CD {
}
```

And if you need your RESTful web service to produce XML, then it's just a matter of using the appropriate media type:

```
@GET
@Produces(MediaType.APPLICATION_XML)
public CD getRandomCD() {
    return service.findRandomBook();
}
```

6.3.3. Serialising and Deserialising

Serialisation is when the content of an object tree is written to a JSON document, and deserialisation is the inverse, the process of reading a JSON document and constructing an object tree. JSON-B has an API to programmatically serialise and deserialise content. But the beauty of it is the integration with other technologies, such as JAX-RS, which makes serialisation and deserialisation transparent.

Programmatic Serialisation and Deserialisation

The main entry point in JSON-B is the `javax.json.bind.Jsonb` API. It provides a façade over the JSON Binding operations. As seen in Listing 149, an instance of `Jsonb` is created using a `JsonbBuilder`. It provides a `toJson()` method to serialise Java objects to a String and deserialises them back with the `fromJson()` method.

Listing 149. Serialising and Deserialising JSON using an API

```java
// Creates a book instance
Book book = new Book().title("H2G2").price(12.5F).isbn("1-84023-742-2");

// Creates Jsonb using a builder
Jsonb jsonb = JsonbBuilder.create();

// Serialises
String json = jsonb.toJson(book);

// Deserialises back
book = jsonb.fromJson("{\"isbn\":\"1-84023-742-2\",\"price\":12.5,\"title\":\"H2G2\"}
", Book.class);
```

In Listing 149, the toJson() method serialises a Book object to a String. If you want to return this String from a JAX-RS REST endpoint, you have two possibilities as shown in Listing 150: you either return a String (getBookAsString()) or return a Response and embed the String to it (getBookAsResponseString()).

Listing 150. Serialising JSON in a REST Endpoint

```java
@GET
@Produces(APPLICATION_JSON)
public String getBookAsString() {

  Book book = new Book().title("H2G2").price(12.5F).isbn("1-84023-742-2");
  Jsonb jsonb = JsonbBuilder.create();
  String json = jsonb.toJson(book);

  return json;
}

@GET
@Produces(APPLICATION_JSON)
public Response getBookAsResponseString() {

  Book book = new Book().title("H2G2").price(12.5F).isbn("1-84023-742-2");
  Jsonb jsonb = JsonbBuilder.create();
  String json = jsonb.toJson(book);

  return Response.ok(json).build();
}
```

Automatic Serialisation and Deserialisation

JSON-B is nicely integrated with JAX-RS. If a REST endpoint produces JSON (MediaType.APPLICATION_JSON) and returns an object, this object is automatically serialised to JSON. If this object is annotated with JSON-B annotations, then the binding is done transparently, no need to use the Jsonb API. As you can see in Listing 151, the method getBook() returns a Book object. The method getBookAsResponse() embeds the Response. In terms of output, both methods are similar: they both return a JSON representation of a Book object.

Listing 151. Automatic Serialisation and Deserialisation in JAX-RS

```
@GET
@Produces(APPLICATION_JSON)
public Book getBook() {

   Book book = new Book().title("H2G2").price(12.5F).isbn("1-84023-742-2");

   return book;
}

@GET
@Produces(APPLICATION_JSON)
public Response getBookAsResponse() {

   Book book = new Book().title("H2G2").price(12.5F).isbn("1-84023-742-2");

   return Response.ok(book).build();
}
```

Creating an instance of Jsonb with a builder on each request is very expensive. It's better to obtain an instance of Jsonb through CDI injection as seen in Listing 152.

Listing 152. Injecting the Jsonb Entry Point

```
@Path("/api/vinyl")
public class VinylResource {

   @Inject
   Jsonb jsonb;

   @GET
   @Produces(APPLICATION_JSON)
   public String getVinyl() {

      Vinyl vinyl = new Vinyl().title("Horses").artist("Patti Smith")
                                     .musicCompany("Arista Records");
      return jsonb.toJson(vinyl);
   }
}
```

6.4. JSON Processing

JSON-B allows you to convert JSON from and to Java objects. Thanks to annotations you can even customise the binding and produce or consume JSON that can be slightly different from the object structure. But sometimes you need to generate, build, read and write JSON that has nothing to do with a Java object. That's when JSON-P comes along. Like JSON-B, JSON-P is part of MicroProfile and therefore included in Quarkus.

JSON Processing[210] (JSON-P), is a specification that allows JSON processing in Java. The processing includes mechanisms to parse, generate, transform, and query JSON data. JSON-P provides a standard to build a Java object in JSON using an API similar to DOM for XML. At the same time, it provides a mechanism to produce and consume JSON by streaming in a manner similar to StAX[211] (*Streaming API for XML*) for XML.

The JSON Processing APIs are all defined under the main `javax.json` package, either at the root, or under the other subpackages. Table 50 lists the main subpackages defined in JSON-P 1.1 (under the root `javax.json` package[212]).

Table 50. Main javax.json Subpackages

Subpackage	Description
root	Root package of the JSON-P APIs
stream	Provides a streaming API to parse and generate JSON
spi	Internal SPIs (*Service Provider Interfaces*) implemented by the provider

JSON-P has a main `javax.json.Json` API, which is a class for creating JSON processing objects. These APIs are listed in Table 51.

Table 51. Main JSON-P APIs

API	Description
Json	Façade for creating JSON processing objects
JsonObject	Represents an immutable JSON object value
JsonArray	Represents an immutable JSON array (an ordered sequence of zero or more values)
JsonWriter	Writes a JSON object or array structure to an output source
JsonReader	Reads a JSON object or an array structure from an input source
JsonParser	Provides forward, read-only access to JSON data in a streaming way
JsonGenerator	Writes JSON data to an output source in a streaming way

JSON-P and JSON-B share the same extension. So with the extension shown in Listing 153 you can do bind and process JSON.

Listing 153. JSON-P Extension

```
<dependency>
  <groupId>io.quarkus</groupId>
  <artifactId>quarkus-resteasy-jsonb</artifactId>
</dependency>
```

6.4.1. Understanding Processing

JSON-P provides two different programming models to process JSON documents: the *Object Model* API, and the *Streaming* API.

Similar to the DOM API for XML, the Object Model API provides classes to model JSON objects and arrays (using the JsonObject and JsonArray APIs) in a treelike structure that represents JSON data in memory. As with the DOM API, the Object Model API provides flexible navigation and queries to the whole content of the tree. It also allows you to read and write JSON files thanks to the JsonReader and JsonWriter APIs.

The streaming API (under the stream package) is a low-level API designed to process large amounts of JSON data efficiently. The Streaming API is much like the StAX API for XML. It provides a way to stream JSON without maintaining the whole document in memory. The streaming API provides an event-based parser based on a pull parsing streaming model (JsonParser), enabling the user to process or discard the parser event, and ask for the next event (pull the event). Thanks to the JsonGenerator, you can also generate and write JSON by streaming.

6.4.2. Building JSON

The object and array structures in JSON are represented by the javax.json.JsonObject and javax.json.JsonArray classes. The API lets you navigate and query the tree structure of data.

JsonObject provides a Map view to access the unordered collection of zero or more name/value pairs. Similarly, JsonArray provides a list view to access the ordered sequence of zero or more values. The API uses the builder patterns to create the tree representation of JsonObject and JsonArray through the javax.json.JsonObjectBuilder and javax.json.JsonArrayBuilder interfaces.

Listing 154 shows how to build a JSON object representing a customer. As you can see, the Json class is the façade used to create a JsonObjectBuilder object that will end up building a JsonObject (using the final build() method). JsonObject provides a map view to the JSON object name/value mappings. Therefore, invoking the add() method will add a name/value to the JSON object.

Listing 154. Building a JSON Object

```
@GET
@Produces(APPLICATION_JSON)
public JsonObject getCustomer() {
  JsonObject customer = Json.createObjectBuilder()
    .add("firstName", "Antonio")
    .add("lastName", "Goncalves")
    .add("email", "agoncal.fascicle@gmail.com")
    .build();
  return customer;
}
```

Notice that the REST endpoint in Listing 154 returns the JsonObject. In fact, if you print this JSON object you get a valid JSON document, so you can return it straight from a JAX-RS endpoint or use it as an HTTP request body:

```
{
    "firstName": "Antonio",
    "lastName": "Goncalves",
    "email": "agoncal.fascicle@gmail.com"
}
```

The same logic applies to an array. In Listing 155, we build an array of phone numbers and send them back. Again, we use the Json class to create a JsonArrayBuilder object so we can build a JsonArray.

Listing 155. Building a JSON Array

```
@GET
@Produces(APPLICATION_JSON)
public JsonArray getPhones() {
    JsonArray phones = Json.createArrayBuilder()
        .add(Json.createObjectBuilder()
            .add("type", "mobile")
            .add("number", "+33 123 456"))
        .add(Json.createObjectBuilder()
            .add("type", "home")
            .add("number", "+33 646 555"))
        .build();
    return phones;
}
```

The result is a JSON array with two phone numbers which looks like the following JSON document:

```
[
    {
        "type": "mobile",
        "number": "+33 123 456"
    },
    {
        "type": "home",
        "number": "+33 646 555"
    }
]
```

And of course, you can then mix JSON objects and JSON arrays. Listing 156 shows how you can build a more complex JSON document with nodes and arrays.

Listing 156. Building a Complex JSON Object

```
@GET
@Produces(APPLICATION_JSON)
public JsonObject getCustomerDetails() {
  JsonObject customer = Json.createObjectBuilder()
    .add("firstName", "Antonio")
    .add("lastName", "Goncalves")
    .add("email", "agoncal.fascicle@gmail.com")
    .add("address", Json.createObjectBuilder()
      .add("street", "21 Ritherdon Rd")
      .add("city", "Brighton")
      .add("country", "UK"))
    .add("phoneNumbers", Json.createArrayBuilder()
      .add(Json.createObjectBuilder()
        .add("type", "mobile")
        .add("number", "+33 123 456"))
      .add(Json.createObjectBuilder()
        .add("type", "home")
        .add("number", "+33 646 555")))
    .build();
  return customer;
}
```

If you look carefully at Listing 156, you'll understand the pattern used. You always start with the Json façade to either create an `ObjectBuilder` or `ArrayBuilder`. You then add some key/values to the `JsonObject` or `JsonArray` (using the `add()` method), and you then build the entire document (invoking the `build()` method). Listing 157 shows the end result of the JSON document built in Listing 156.

Listing 157. Complex JSON Object

```
{
  "firstName": "Antonio",
  "lastName": "Goncalves",
  "email": "agoncal.fascicle@gmail.com",
  "address": {
    "street": "21 Ritherdon Rd",
    "city": "Brighton",
    "country": "UK"
  },
  "phoneNumbers": [
    {
      "type": "mobile",
      "number": "+33 123 456"
    },
    {
      "type": "home",
      "number": "+33 646 555"
    }
  ]
}
```

6.4.3. Reading and Writing JSON

A JsonObject can also be created from an input source (such as an InputStream or a Reader) using the interface javax.json.JsonReader. The code in Listing 158 shows how to read and create a JsonObject from a String and a file using the interface JsonReader. JsonReader provides the general read() method to read any javax.json.JsonStructure subtype (e.g. JsonObject or JsonArray).

Listing 158. Reading JSON from a File

```
StringReader string = new StringReader("{\"hello\":\"world\"}");
JsonReader reader = Json.createReader(string);

FileReader file = new FileReader("src/main/resources/customer.json");
JsonReader reader = Json.createReader(file);
JsonObject jsonObject = reader.readObject();
```

Once the getJsonObject() method is called, it returns a JsonObject. Then, you can navigate in this JsonObject to get any value, any JSON array, or, any other embedded JSON object. For example, the code in Listing 159 gets the String value of firstName, the object address or the array of phone numbers. Notice that when you get the String value of a JSON key, the API returns a JsonString. Depending on the datatype, it can also return a JsonNumber if the value is a number.

Listing 159. Navigating the JSON Object

```
JsonString firstName = jsonObject.getJsonString("firstName");
JsonObject address = jsonObject.getJsonObject("address");
JsonArray phones = jsonObject.getJsonArray("phoneNumbers");

// Getting the value of a JsonString
String firstName = jsonObject.getJsonString("firstName").getString();
```

Similarly, JsonObject and JsonArray can be written to an output source (such as OutputStream or Writer) using the class javax.json.JsonWriter. The builder method Json.createWriter() can create a JsonWriter for different outputs. In Listing 160, the customer JSON object is written to a file.

Listing 160. Writing a JSON Object to a File

```
File file = new File("src/main/resources/customer.json");
try (OutputStream outputStream = new FileOutputStream(file);
     JsonWriter jsonWriter = Json.createWriter(outputStream)) {

  jsonWriter.write(customer);
}
```

Json.createWriter() is a simple way to have a writer. But if you need to configure a writer, you can instead use the Json.createWriterFactory() passing a configuration as a parameter, and then obtain a JsonWriter. As an example, Listing 161 configures the writer so it can write a JSON object to a file in pretty-print.

Listing 161. Writing a Formatted JSON Object to a File

```
Map<String, Boolean> config = new HashMap<>();
config.put(JsonGenerator.PRETTY_PRINTING, true);
JsonWriterFactory writerFactory = Json.createWriterFactory(config);

File file = new File("src/main/resources/customer.json");
try (OutputStream outputStream = new FileOutputStream(file);
     JsonWriter jsonWriter = writerFactory.createWriter(outputStream)) {

  jsonWriter.write(customer);
}
```

6.4.4. Parsing and Generating JSON

The *Object Model* API that we just saw, keeps the JSON structure in memory. So, if your use case is to process big JSON objects (which might not fit into memory), you should have a look at the *Streaming* API. Streaming works for both parsing (JsonParser) and generating (JsonGenerator) JSON objects.

The Streaming API (package javax.json.stream) facilitates parsing JSON via streaming with forward and read-only access. It provides the javax.json.stream.JsonParser interface to parse a JSON document. The entry point is the `javax.json.Json` factory class, which provides a `createParser()` method that returns a `javax.json.stream.JsonParser` from a specified input source (such as a `Reader` or an `InputStream`). Listing 162 shows how to create a JSON parser without any configuration, or, by passing properties to the `createParserFactory()` method.

Listing 162. Getting a JSON Parser

```
StringReader string = new StringReader("{\"hello\":\"world\"}");
JsonParser parser = Json.createParser(string);

// Configuring the parsing factory
StringReader string = new StringReader("{\"hello\":\"world\"}");
JsonParserFactory factory = Json.createParserFactory(config);
JsonParser parser = factory.createParser(string);
```

The `JsonParser` offers a rather low-level access to the JSON object based on a pull parsing streaming model. Meaning that the parser generates events when a JSON name/value is reached or the beginning/end of an object/array is read. Table 52 lists all of the events triggered by the parser.

Table 52. JSON Parsing Events

Event	Description
START_OBJECT	Event for start of a JSON object (fired when { is reached)
END_OBJECT	Event for end of an object (fired when } is reached)
START_ARRAY	Event for start of a JSON array (fired when [is reached)
END_ARRAY	Event for end of an array (fired when] is reached)
KEY_NAME	Event for a name in name(key)/value pair of a JSON object
VALUE_STRING	Event for a string value
VALUE_NUMBER	Event for a number value
VALUE_TRUE	Event for a true value
VALUE_FALSE	Event for a false value
VALUE_NULL	Event for a null value

Let's first take a simple example to explain how events work. The code in Listing 163 creates a parser based on a very simple JSON document that contains only one key `hello` and one value `world`. Then, the parser loops (`parser.hasNext()`) until reaching the last event of the document (`END_OBJECT`). It displays the start and the end of the JSON object, the keys and the values.

Listing 163. Getting a JSON Parser

```
StringReader string = new StringReader("{\"hello\":\"world\"}");
JsonParser parser = Json.createParser(string);

while (parser.hasNext()) {
  JsonParser.Event event = parser.next();
  switch (event) {
    case START_OBJECT:
    case END_OBJECT:
      System.out.println(event);
      break;
    case KEY_NAME:
      System.out.print("KEY_NAME " + parser.getString() + " - ");
      break;
    case VALUE_STRING:
      System.out.println("VALUE_STRING " + parser.getString());
      break;
  }
}
```

The result of the code in Listing 163 is displayed below. A START_OBJECT event is sent when the root object is detected. Then, the KEY_NAME event with the value hello is followed by the VALUE_STRING event world. Finally, the END_OBJECT is thrown once the parser has reached the end of the JSON document.

```
START_OBJECT
KEY_NAME hello - VALUE_STRING world
END_OBJECT
```

This technique of listening to events is very low-level, but it allows you to parse huge JSON documents without filling the memory. For example, the class in Listing 164 parses a JSON file and extracts the customers' email. The parser moves forward until it encounters the email key (event KEY_NAME).

Listing 164. Parsing Emails

```java
FileReader file = new FileReader("src/main/resources/customer.json");
JsonParser parser = Json.createParser(file);

while (parser.hasNext()) {
  JsonParser.Event event = parser.next();
  switch (event) {
    case KEY_NAME:
      if (parser.getString().equals("email")) {
        parser.next();
        System.out.println("Email: " + parser.getString());
      }
      break;
  }
}
```

By using a switch, you can determine the type of event you want (KEY_NAME in Listing 164) and process the JSON based on the event. While the JsonParser streams the JSON, you can use the getString() method to get a String representation for each name (key) and value depending on the state of the parser.

The JsonParser parses a JSON object via streaming, whereas the javax.json.stream.JsonGenerator allows the writing of JSON to a stream by writing one event at a time. The class in Listing 165 uses the createGenerator() method from the main javax.json.Json factory to get a JsonGenerator to generate some JSON. The generator writes name/value pairs in JSON objects and JSON arrays.

Listing 165. Generating a Customer

```
StringWriter writer = new StringWriter();
JsonGenerator generator = Json.createGenerator(writer);
generator
  .writeStartObject()
  .write("firstName", "Antonio")
  .write("lastName", "Goncalves")
  .write("email", "agoncal.fascicle@gmail.com")
    .writeStartObject("address")
      .write("street", "21 Ritherdon Rd")
      .write("city", "Brighton")
      .write("country", "UK")
    .writeEnd()
    .writeStartArray("phoneNumbers")
      .writeStartObject()
        .write("type", "mobile")
        .write("number", "+33 123 456")
      .writeEnd()
      .writeStartObject()
        .write("type", "home")
        .write("number", "+33 646 555")
      .writeEnd()
    .writeEnd()
  .writeEnd()
.close();
```

While the writeStartObject() method writes a JSON start object character ({), the writeStartArray() method is used to write a JSON start array character ([). Each opened context must be terminated using the writeEnd() method. After writing the end of the current context, the parent context becomes the new current context.

The writeStartObject() method is used to start a new child object context and the writeStartArray() method starts a new child array context. Both methods can be used only in an array context or when a context is not yet started and both can only be called when no context is started. A context is started when one of these methods is used. The JsonGenerator class provides other methods, such as write(), to write a JSON name/value pair in the current object context or to write a value in the current array context. The close() method closes the generator and frees any associated resources.

6.5. Summary

This chapter was about the HTTP microservices. We first looked at Java API for RESTful Web Services which allows us to expose and consume RESTful web services. JAX-RS has an easy API to expose endpoints mostly based on annotations: @Path to define URIs, @Consumes and @Produces to pick up the right media type and @GET, @POST, @PUT, @DELETE to interact with the resource. JAX-RS also comes with a *Client API* to consume RESTful web services. This *Client API* is used under the hood in the Eclipse MicroProfile REST Client that you will see in next chapter.

When exposing web services, you usually need to document them: what the available endpoints are, which URIs are accessible, which methods are supported, what the returned status codes are, and so on. Eclipse MicroProfile OpenAPI is part of MicroProfile and integrates with JAX-RS to generate some basic documentation. Thanks to the OpenAPI, with only a small set of annotations (@Operation, @APIResponse, @Schema, etc.) you can add extra information to your OpenAPI v3 contract.

And because JSON is such a common data format, MicroProfile includes two specifications to handle it. JSON Binding can serialise an object tree into JSON and deserialise it back with no effort. Thanks to a few annotations (@JsonbProperty, @JsonbDateFormat, @JsonbTransient, etc.), you can customise the binding so you get the JSON you really need. And because binding is not always enough, JSON-P gives us some APIs to build, read, write and stream JSON.

Now that we know how to build and expose HTTP microservices, the next chapter, *Communication and Fault Tolerance*, will focus on how microservices can communicate with each other. One thing is invoking a microservice with the Eclipse MicroProfile REST Client, and the other thing is dealing with communication failure thanks to Eclipse MicroProfile Fault Tolerance.

[187] REST https://www.ics.uci.edu/~fielding/pubs/dissertation/rest_arch_style.htm

[188] HTTP https://www.w3.org/Protocols

[189] JAX-RS https://jcp.org/en/jsr/detail?id=370

[190] JAX-RS GitHub https://github.com/eclipse-ee4j/jaxrs-api

[191] URI https://www.w3.org/Addressing/URL/uri-spec.html

[192] MIME Type https://en.wikipedia.org/wiki/Media_type

[193] Entity Provider https://eclipse-ee4j.github.io/jersey.github.io/documentation/latest/message-body-workers.html

[194] JAX-RS GitHub https://github.com/eclipse-ee4j/jaxrs-api

[195] OpenAPI Specification https://github.com/OAI/OpenAPI-Specification

[196] OpenAPI https://microprofile.io/project/eclipse/microprofile-open-api

[197] OpenAPI GitHub https://github.com/eclipse/microprofile-open-api

[198] Swagger https://en.wikipedia.org/wiki/Swagger_(software)

[199] RAML https://en.wikipedia.org/wiki/RAML_(software)

[200] OpenAPI Initiative https://www.openapis.org

[201] OpenAPI Specification https://github.com/OAI/OpenAPI-Specification

[202] CommonMark https://commonmark.org

[203] Swagger-Codegen https://github.com/swagger-api/swagger-codegen

[204] Swagger UI https://swagger.io/tools/swagger-ui

[205] JSON-B https://jcp.org/en/jsr/detail?id=367

[206] JSON-B GitHub https://github.com/eclipse-ee4j/jsonb-api

[207] Jackson https://github.com/FasterXML/jackson

[208] QSON https://github.com/quarkusio/qson

[209] RFC 7159 https://tools.ietf.org/html/rfc7159

[210] JSON-P https://jcp.org/en/jsr/detail?id=374

[211] StAX https://en.wikipedia.org/wiki/StAX

[212] JSON-P GitHub https://github.com/eclipse-ee4j/jsonp

Chapter 7. Communication and Fault Tolerance

The previous chapter presented the technologies around *HTTP Microservices*. The main one is Java API for RESTful Web Services which allows us to expose and invoke REST endpoints. Often those endpoints produce and/or consume JSON. For that, Quarkus integrates with JSON Binding and JSON Processing. Eclipse MicroProfile OpenAPI is used to document an endpoint so external clients know how to invoke it.

But in a microservice architecture, there is not one microservice but several, and they need to talk to each other. They can use messaging (as you will see in Chapter 8) or HTTP. When we need an HTTP microservice to invoke another one, we can use *Eclipse MicroProfile REST Client*. It is based on the JAX-RS Client API and simplifies HTTP invocations. But when this invocation is synchronous, we quickly realise that our microservices need to handle communication failure. That's when *Eclipse MicroProfile Fault Tolerance* becomes very useful. Microservices can also be accessed by user interfaces, browsers, mobile devices, etc. In this case, we need to deal with CORS issues. And once again, Quarkus is here to help.

 The code in this chapter can be found at https://github.com/agoncal/agoncal-fascicle-quarkus/tree/2.0/communication

7.1. CORS

In a microservice architecture, you easily end-up with several REST endpoints interacting with each other, crossing different servers, different domains. And you usually want to have a graphical interface so your users can interact with the system. That's when you will hit CORS! *Cross-origin Resource Sharing*[213] (CORS) is a mechanism that allows restricted resources on a web page to be requested from another domain outside the domain from which the first resource was served.

7.1.1. Understanding CORS

In a nutshell, CORS allows web clients to make HTTP requests to servers hosted on different origins. By origin, we mean a combination of the URI scheme, hostname, and port number. It is a mechanism that uses additional HTTP headers to tell browsers to give a web application running at one origin, access to selected resources from a different origin. For example, if the front-end JavaScript code in Figure 42 is served from https://domain-a.com and makes a request on https://domain-b.com, then the browsers restrict the access. For security reasons, a web application can only request resources from the same origin the application was loaded from, unless the response from other origins includes the right CORS headers. CORS defines a way in which a browser and server can interact to determine whether it is safe to allow the cross-origin request.

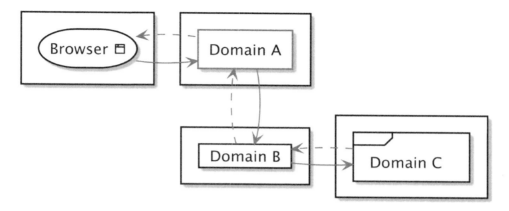

Figure 42. Crossing origins

The specification for CORS is included as part of the WHATWG's Fetch Living Standard (*Web Hypertext Application Technology Working Group*[214]). This specification describes how CORS is currently implemented in browsers.

7.1.2. Configuring CORS

To solve this CORS issue, Quarkus comes with a CORS filter which intercepts all incoming HTTP requests. It can be enabled in the Quarkus configuration file, `src/main/resources/application.properties`. If enabled and an HTTP request is identified as cross-origin, the CORS policy and headers will be applied before passing the request on to its actual target.

```
quarkus.http.cors=true
```

If you need to be more precise in terms of controlling the origin access, Quarkus comes with a few extra configuration properties (see Table 53).

Table 53. Some Quarkus CORS Configuration Properties

Property	Default
`quarkus.http.cors.origins` Comma-separated list of origins allowed for CORS. The filter allows any origin if this is not set.	
`quarkus.http.cors.methods` Comma-separated list of HTTP methods allowed for CORS. The filter allows any method if this is not set.	
`quarkus.http.cors.headers` Comma-separated list of HTTP headers allowed for CORS. The filter allows any header if this is not set.	

Property	Default

`quarkus.http.cors.exposed-headers`
Comma-separated list of HTTP headers exposed in CORS.

`quarkus.http.cors.access-control-max-age`
The duration that indicates how long the results of a preflight request can be cached.
This value will be returned in an `Access-Control-Max-Age` response header.

The following is a configuration that allows CORS for all domains, all HTTP methods, and all common headers:

```
quarkus.http.cors.origins=*
quarkus.http.cors.methods=GET,PUT,POST,DELETE
quarkus.http.cors.headers=accept, authorization, content-type
```

But you might want to be more specific and set the list of allowed origins to the domain asking to connect remotely:

```
quarkus.http.cors.origins=https://domain-b.com
```

7.2. Eclipse MicroProfile REST Client

In the previous chapter, you saw that JAX-RS comes along with a *Client API,* meaning that JAX-RS has all the required APIs to expose and consume RESTful web services. *Eclipse MicroProfile REST Client*[215] provides a type safe approach using proxies and annotations for invoking RESTful services over HTTP. The Eclipse MicroProfile REST Client builds upon the JAX-RS 2.1 APIs for consistency and ease-of-use.

The Eclipse MicroProfile REST Client APIs and annotations are all defined under the main `org.eclipse.microprofile.rest.client` package, either at the root, or under the other subpackages. Table 54 lists the main subpackages defined in Eclipse MicroProfile REST Client version 2.0 (under the root `org.eclipse.microprofile.rest.client` package[216]).

Table 54. Main org.eclipse.microprofile.rest.client Subpackages

Subpackage	Description
root	Root package of the REST Client APIs
annotation	APIs for annotating client interfaces
ext	APIs for extending REST Client functionality
inject	APIs to aid in CDI-based injection
spi	Internal SPIs (*Service Provider Interfaces*) implemented by the provider

In these packages, you'll find all the APIs and annotations. Table 55 shows a few REST Client APIs.

Table 55. Main REST Client APIs

API	Description
RestClientBuilder	Main entry point for creating a Type Safe Rest Client

Along with APIs, REST Client comes with a set of annotations. Table 56 lists a subset of the most commonly used annotations.

Table 56. Main REST Client Annotations

Annotation	Description
@RegisterRestClient	A marker annotation to register a rest client at runtime
@RestClient	CDI qualifier used to indicate that this injection point is meant to use an instance of a type safe REST Client

To be able to invoke a remote REST endpoint you need to add the REST Client extension to your pom.xml as shown in Listing 166.

Listing 166. REST Client Extension

```xml
<dependency>
    <groupId>io.quarkus</groupId>
    <artifactId>quarkus-rest-client</artifactId>
</dependency>
```

7.2.1. Understanding RESTful Web Services Invocation

One microservice does not make a microservice architecture. A microservice architecture is about several microservices talking to each other (see Figure 43). For that, the client of an HTTP microservice needs to handle the HTTP communication. That means, opening a connection to the remote service, sending an HTTP request and processing the response.

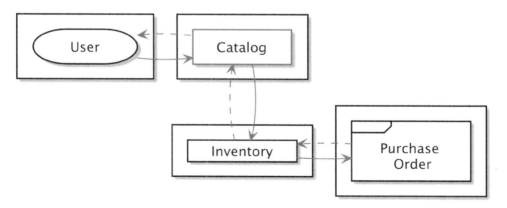

Figure 43. Microservices invoking each other

7.2.2. Invoking RESTful Web Services

The Eclipse MicroProfile REST Client builds on JAX-RS 2.1 client APIs to provide a type safe approach for invoking RESTful services. This means writing client applications with more model-centric code and less HTTP *plumbing*.

Client Proxies

One of the central ideas in Eclipse MicroProfile REST Client is the good-old distributed object communication that we find implemented in Java RMI, for example. To invoke a remote object, we use a proxy. Consider the RESTful endpoint in Listing 167. As you can see, this is a simple JAX-RS web service that generates ISBN numbers. There is only one method, accessible through an HTTP GET, and returns an IsbnNumber object (made up of a GS1 code and an ISBN 13 number).

Listing 167. Endpoint Taking a Query Parameter and Returning an Object

```
@Path("/api/isbn")
@Produces(MediaType.APPLICATION_JSON)
@ApplicationScoped
public class IsbnResource {

  @GET
  public IsbnNumber generateIsbn(
                      @DefaultValue("true")
                      @QueryParam("separator") boolean separator) {
    IsbnNumber isbnNumber = new IsbnNumber();
    isbnNumber.isbn13 = new Faker().code().isbn13(separator);
    isbnNumber.gs1 = new Faker().code().isbnGs1();
    return isbnNumber;
  }
}

public class IsbnNumber {
  public String gs1;
  public String isbn13;
}
```

Reading Listing 167, you might wonder what Faker is. The *Java Faker*[217] library is a port of Ruby's faker[218] gem that generates fake data. It's useful when you're developing a project and need some pretty data for a showcase. Here, we use it to generate some random data.

This web service takes a query parameter. So, depending if you pass true or false in the query, you get an ISBN number with or without separators. Below you can see both cURL invocations:

```
$ curl 'http://localhost:9081/api/isbn?separator=true'
{"gs1":"979","isbn13":"978-0-9883021-6-7"}

$ curl 'http://localhost:9081/api/isbn?separator=false'
{"gs1":"979","isbn13":"9791935525065"}
```

How can a third-party microservice invoke such an endpoint? Well, using an OpenAPI v3 contract. As you saw in Chapter 6, Eclipse MicroProfile OpenAPI is integrated with JAX-RS. So OpenAPI can generate the contract defined in Listing 168 just by scanning the JAX-RS annotations.

Listing 168. OpenAPI Contract

```
openapi: 3.0.3
info:
  title: Generated API
  version: "1.0"
paths:
  /api/isbn:
    get:
      parameters:
        - name: separator
          in: query
          schema:
            default: true
            type: boolean
      responses:
        "200":
          description: OK
          content:
            application/json:
              schema:
                $ref: '#/components/schemas/IsbnNumber'
components:
  schemas:
    IsbnNumber:
      type: object
      properties:
        gs1:
          type: string
        isbn13:
          type: string
```

With the OpenAPI contract in Listing 168, the built-in JAX-RS Client API and the JSON-P integration, you can easily access the IsbnResource with the few lines of code in Listing 169.

Listing 169. OpenAPI Contract

```
JsonObject isbnNumber = ClientBuilder
  .newClient()
  .target("http://localhost:9081/api/isbn?separator=true")
  .request()
  .get(JsonObject.class);

String gs1 = isbnNumber.getString("gs1");
String isbn13 = isbnNumber.getString("isbn13");
```

The call in Listing 169 is not particularly onerous, but it lacks a more strongly-typed syntax. And that's where Eclipse MicroProfile REST Client can help. Instead of using an OpenAPI v3 contract or parsing the JSON response with JSON-B, Eclipse MicroProfile REST Client lets you define a contract as Java interfaces. Using the Eclipse MicroProfile REST Client is as simple as creating an interface using the proper JAX-RS and MicroProfile annotations.

First, we start off with an interface that proxies calls to the remote service. The methods of the interface should match the RESTful APIs of the endpoint (annotations, return type, list of arguments and exception declarations). In fact, the client interface is so similar to the web service itself that you can basically copy/paste the resource and make it an interface. So if we want to access the endpoint in Listing 167, we create an interface that looks like Listing 170.

Listing 170. Client Interface

```
@Path("/api/isbn")
@Produces(MediaType.APPLICATION_JSON)
@RegisterRestClient
public interface IsbnProxy {

  @GET
  IsbnNumber generateIsbn(@QueryParam("separator") boolean separator);
}
```

The purpose of the annotations in Listing 170 is the following:

- @RegisterRestClient allows Quarkus to know that this interface is meant to be available for CDI injection as a REST Client.

- @Path, @GET and @QueryParam are the standard JAX-RS annotations used to define how to access the service.

- @Produces defines the expected content-type. While @Consumes and @Produces are optional as auto-negotiation is supported, it is recommended to annotate your interface with them to define precisely the expected content-types.

By using a Java interface as the contract, you will be able to have direct access to the methods within the client and issues with type or mistakes not following the contract won't happen anymore. Eclipse MicroProfile REST Client automatically generates a client instance based on what is defined in the interface. The sequence of invocation is better described in the diagram shown in

Figure 44. The client (here `BookResource`) invokes a method on the Java interface `IsbnProxy` and Eclipse MicroProfile REST Client does the work of sending an HTTP request to the remote endpoint `IsbnResource`. It will handle all the networking and marshalling, leaving our code clean of such technical details.

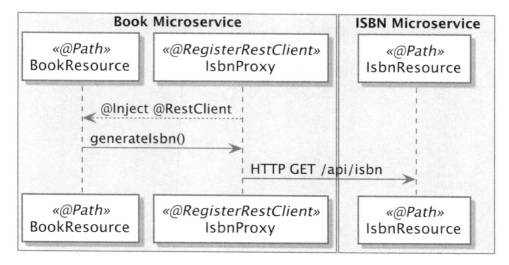

Figure 44. Microservices invoking another one

Now that we have the interface, we just need to build the implementation and then invoke it. There are two ways to build the implementation: programmatically using the `RestClientBuilder` API or declaratively using CDI and Eclipse MicroProfile Configuration.

Programmatic Invocation

Let's start with the `org.eclipse.microprofile.rest.client.RestClientBuilder`. It is a little more verbose but can come in handy in environments where CDI is not available. As shown in Listing 171, to create a new instance of the `RestClientBuilder` we first specify the `baseUrl` value for the remote endpoint. Then we build the client, passing in the interface class. After that, we can invoke methods on the client like it was any other Java object.

Listing 171. Programmatic HTTP Invocation

```
IsbnProxy isbnProxy = RestClientBuilder.newBuilder()
  .baseUri(new URI("http://localhost:9081"))
  .build(IsbnProxy.class);

IsbnNumber isbnNumber = isbnProxy.generateIsbn(false);
```

Declarative Invocation

In addition to programmatic invocation, it is also possible to register the Java interface declaratively with annotations. In fact, thanks to the `@RegisterRestClient` annotation on the interface, it makes the client usable through CDI.

As you can see in Listing 172, the BookResource needs to invoke two external microservices: one returning an ISBN book number (using the IsbnProxy interface), and another one an ISSN number (the IssnProxy in Listing 173). These two interfaces are injected using the MicroProfile @RestClient annotation. By injecting the interfaces as @RestClient, we will be able to proxy the remote REST endpoint.

Listing 172. REST Endpoint Injecting Client Proxy Interfaces

```
@Path("/books")
@Produces(MediaType.APPLICATION_JSON)
@ApplicationScoped
public class BookResource {

    @RestClient
    IsbnProxy isbnProxy;

    @RestClient
    IssnProxy issnProxy;

    @GET
    @Path("/numbers")
    public JsonObject generateBookNumbers() {

        IsbnNumber isbnNumber = isbnProxy.generateIsbn(true);
        String isbn13 = isbnNumber.isbn13;

        JsonObject issnJsonObject = issnProxy.generateIssn();
        String issn = issnJsonObject.getJsonString("issn").getString();

        return Json.createObjectBuilder()
          .add("isbn13", isbn13)
          .add("isbn10", issn)
          .build();
    }
}
```

The implementation of the interface will include the qualifier @RestClient to differentiate the use of an API call against any other beans registered of the same type. But remember that the interface is a *Bean* and therefore can use other CDI goodies. If greater discrimination is needed at injection, the interface and the injection point can be annotated with extra qualifiers:

```
@Inject @RestClient @ISBN
NumberProxy isbnProxy;

@Inject @RestClient @ISSN
NumberProxy issnProxy;
```

As seen in Listing 172, injecting an interface is less verbose than invoking it programmatically with the RestClientBuilder API. But something is missing: the base URI of the remote endpoint. There are two ways to define the URI. As you can see in Listing 173, a baseUri value can be set in the @RegisterRestClient annotation. Eclipse MicroProfile REST Client then concatenates the @Path annotations to this URI to invoke the remote endpoint (here at http://localhost:9082/api/issn).

Listing 173. Client Interface with Base URI

```
@Path("/api/issn")
@Produces(MediaType.APPLICATION_JSON)
@RegisterRestClient(baseUri = "http://localhost:9082")
public interface IssnProxy {

  @GET
  JsonObject generateIssn();
}
```

However, this value can be configured (or overridden) by a base URI property defined in a configuration file. For that, we use the Eclipse MicroProfile Configuration. The configuration property to use is the fully qualified interface name with the url. In the example below, the IsbnProxy is configured to the default http://localhost:9081 URL. This configuration is automatically picked up by the Eclipse MicroProfile Configuration API.

```
quarkus.rest-
client."org.agoncal.fascicle.quarkus.restclient.book.IsbnProxy".url=http://localhost:9
081
quarkus.rest-
client."org.agoncal.fascicle.quarkus.restclient.book.IsbnProxy".scope=javax.inject.Sin
gleton
```

Having this configuration means that all requests performed using IsbnProxy will use http://localhost:9081 as the base URL. So, calling the generateIsbn() method of IsbnProxy with a value true for the separator, would result in an HTTP GET request being made to http://localhost:9081/api/isbn?separator=true. The configuration also defines the scope of IsbnProxy to be @Singleton. Supported scopes are @Singleton, @Dependent, @ApplicationScoped and @RequestScoped. The default scope is @Dependent. The default scope can also be defined on the interface. CDI scopes were explained in Chapter 4. Make sure to select the right scope to avoid concurrency issues between different calls.

7.2.3. Configuring RestEasy Client Microprofile

Table 57 lists some Eclipse MicroProfile REST Client configuration properties[144] which are provided via MicroProfile Config.

Table 57. Some REST Client Configuration Properties

Property	Default
`quarkus.rest-client."<myclass>".url` Base URL to use for this service	
`quarkus.rest-client."<myclass>".uri` Base URI to use for this service (will override any `baseUri` value specified in the `@RegisterRestClient` annotation)	
`quarkus.rest-client."<myclass>".scope` CDI scope to use for injection	`@Dependent`
`quarkus.rest-client."<myclass>".providers` Provider classnames to include in the client (equivalent of the register method or the `@RegisterProvider` annotation)	
`quarkus.rest-client."<myclass>".connectTimeout` Timeout specified in milliseconds to wait to connect to the remote endpoint	
`quarkus.rest-client."<myclass>".readTimeout` Timeout specified in milliseconds to wait for a response from the remote endpoint	

7.3. Eclipse MicroProfile Fault Tolerance

CORS is about allowing, or blocking, client invocations to cross different origins. But once all the invocations start to go through, you'll need to handle communication failure and make resilient applications. For that, Quarkus contains an implementation of the Eclipse MicroProfile Fault Tolerance specification. As the number of services grows, the odds of any service failing also grows. If one of the involved services does not respond as expected, e.g. because of fragile network communication, we have to compensate for this exceptional situation. *Eclipse MicroProfile Fault Tolerance*[219] allows us to build up our microservice architecture to be resilient and fault tolerant by design. This means we must not only be able to detect any issue but also to handle it automatically.

The Eclipse MicroProfile Fault Tolerance APIs and annotations are all defined under the main `org.eclipse.microprofile.faulttolerance` package, either at the root, or under the other subpackages. Table 58 lists the main subpackages defined in Eclipse MicroProfile Fault Tolerance version 3.0 (under the root `org.eclipse.microprofile.faulttolerance` package[220]).

Table 58. Main org.eclipse.microprofile.faulttolerance Subpackages

Subpackage	Description
root	Root package of the Fault Tolerance APIs
exceptions	Exceptions for Fault Tolerance

Along with APIs, Fault Tolerance comes with a set of annotations. Table 59 lists a subset of the most commonly used annotations.

Table 59. Main Fault Tolerance Annotations

Annotation	Description
@Timeout	Defines a duration for timeout
@Retry	Defines a criteria on when to retry
@Fallback	Provides an alternative solution for a failed execution
@Bulkhead	Isolates failures in part of the system while the rest of the system can still function
@CircuitBreaker	Offers a way to fail fast by automatically failing the execution to prevent the system overloading and an indefinite wait or timeout by the clients
@Asynchronous	Invokes the operation asynchronously

You get fault-tolerance just by adding the extension in Listing 174 to your pom.xml.

Listing 174. Fault Tolerance Extension

```
<dependency>
    <groupId>io.quarkus</groupId>
    <artifactId>quarkus-smallrye-fault-tolerance</artifactId>
</dependency>
```

7.3.1. Understanding Fault Tolerance

Microservices helps to break down problems into pieces, which helps for easy maintenance and testability. But the problem with an architecture using dozens of interdependent microservices, is that there is a high chance of network, hardware, database or application issues (see Figure 45). This will lead to the temporary unavailability of a component. To avoid or minimise this kind of outage, we have to build resilient microservices. This means that instead of throwing the problem at the user, we need to recover from failures and remain functional. For that, there are a few resiliency patterns that we can use, such as timeout, retry, circuit breaker, fail-fast, bulkhead, load balancing or failover. And some of these patterns are implemented by Eclipse MicroProfile Fault Tolerance.

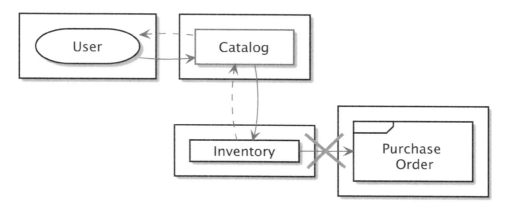

Figure 45. Microservices invocation failing

Network Fallacies

When talking about network issues, it's always interesting to refer to the network fallacies. The *fallacies of distributed computing*[221] are a set of false assumptions that programmers new to distributed applications invariably make. The fallacies are:

- The network is reliable;
- Latency is zero;
- Bandwidth is infinite;
- The network is secure;
- Topology doesn't change;
- There is one administrator;
- Transport cost is zero;
- The network is homogeneous.

7.3.2. Falling Back

If a service A calls a service B, what happens when service B is down? What is the fallback plan in such a scenario? A fallback is an alternative plan that may be used in case part of the system is unavailable.

To illustrate fallbacks, let's have a look at the `BookResource` in Listing 175. This REST endpoint has a method to generate book numbers (ISBN and ISSN) on the `/books/numbers` path. Thanks to the `@RestClient` annotation from Eclipse MicroProfile REST Client, the `BookResource` delegates the number generation to the `NumberProxy` which ends-up invoking the remote `NumberResource` microservice. And what if `NumberResource` is not available? What should we do? Throw an exception or hang until the microservice becomes available again?

Instead let's provide a fallback way for generating book numbers in case of failure. For that, we add one fallback method to the `BookResource` called `fallbackGenerateBookNumbers` and a `@Fallback` annotation to the `generateBookNumbers()` method (see Listing 175).

Listing 175. Falling Back on Generating Book Numbers

```java
@Path("/books")
@Produces(MediaType.APPLICATION_JSON)
@ApplicationScoped
public class BookResource {

  @RestClient
  NumberProxy numberProxy;

  @GET
  @Path("/numbers")
  @Fallback(fallbackMethod = "fallbackGenerateBookNumbers")
  public JsonObject generateBookNumbers() {

    // Invoking microservices
    IsbnNumber isbnNumber = numberProxy.generateIsbn(true);
    JsonObject issnNumber = numberProxy.generateIssn();

    return Json.createObjectBuilder()
      .add("isbn13", isbnNumber.isbn13)
      .add("gs1", isbnNumber.gs1)
      .add("isbn10", issnNumber.getJsonString("isbn10").getString())
      .build();
  }

  private JsonObject fallbackGenerateBookNumbers() {
    return Json.createObjectBuilder()
      .add("isbn13", "dummy isbn")
      .add("gs1", "dummy gs1")
      .add("isbn10", "dummy issn")
      .build();
  }
}
```

The fallbackGenerateBookNumbers() method must have the same method signature as generateBookNumbers() (in our case ,it takes no parameters and returns a JsonObject object). As shown in Figure 46, in case the *Book* microservice cannot invoke the *Number* microservice, the fallbackGenerateBookNumbers() is invoked and the JSON representation of temporary book numbers is sent back.

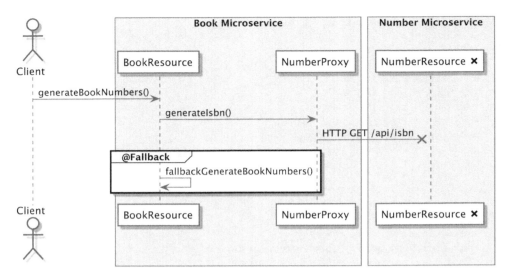

Figure 46. HTTP request falling back

There are two ways to specify a fallback: we can specify a method name in the `fallbackMethod` attribute as we did in Listing 175, or we can specify an external class that implements the `FallbackHandler` interface:

```
// Method in the same class
@Fallback(fallbackMethod = "fallbackGenerateBookNumbers")
public JsonObject generateBookNumbers() { ... }

// Different class implementing FallbackHandler
@Fallback(CallNumberBackupService.class)
public JsonObject generateBookNumbers() { ... }
```

ISBN and ISSN

ISBN and ISSN are referred to very often in this fascicle. Here is a quick reminder on terminology:

- ISBN (*International Standard Book Number*[222]): Thirteen-digit book identifier which is intended to be unique.
- ISSN (*International Standard Serial Number*[223]): Eight-digit serial number used to uniquely identify a serial publication.

7.3.3. Timing Out

Fallbacks are good when the remote microservice is not available at all. But what if it's there but is taking too long due to being overloaded or due to network latency?

Let's say that to create a book we need to invoke a remote microservice to get an ISSN. Getting ISSN numbers can actually take longer than expected. What happens to the *Book* microservice invoking a long-running *Number* microservice to get the ISSN numbers? It hangs too, and we don't want that to happen, we would rather time it out. For that, we add the @Timeout annotation to the method createBook() method (see Listing 176). @Timeout takes the number of milliseconds it has to wait before timing out.

Listing 176. Timing out if the Invocation Takes Long

```java
@Path("/books")
@Produces(MediaType.APPLICATION_JSON)
@ApplicationScoped
public class BookResource {

  @RestClient
  NumberProxy numberProxy;

  @POST
  @Timeout(250)
  @Fallback(fallbackMethod = "fallbackCreateBook")
  public Book createBook() {

    // Invoking microservice
    JsonObject issnNumber = numberProxy.generateIssn();

    Book book = new Book();
    book.title = faker.book().title();
    book.issn = issnNumber.getString("isbn10");
    book.generatedAt = Instant.now();

    return book;
  }

  private Book fallbackCreateBook() {
    Book book = new Book();
    book.title = "dummy title";
    book.issn = "dummy issn";
    book.generatedAt = Instant.now();
    return book;
  }
}
```

Note that the timeout is configured to 250ms. If the createBook() method in Listing 176 was annotated with just @Timeout (and no @Fallback) and invoking the *Number* microservice takes longer than 250ms, then the request is interrupted with a TimeoutException:

```
ERROR [QuarkusErrorHandler] HTTP Request to /books failed
  org.jboss.resteasy.spi.UnhandledException: org.eclipse.microprofile.faulttolerance
.exceptions.TimeoutException:
  Timeout[org.agoncal.fascicle.quarkus.faulttolerance.book.BookResource#createBook]
timed out
```

By default, if the execution takes longer than the specified timeout, the TimeoutException will be thrown and the execution result will be discarded. That's it if you only have a @Timeout annotation. That's what's shown in the sequence diagram in Figure 47. But you might want to add an extra @Fallback annotation to the method (like in Listing 176). In this case, if the TimeoutException exception is caught, the fallback method is automatically invoked.

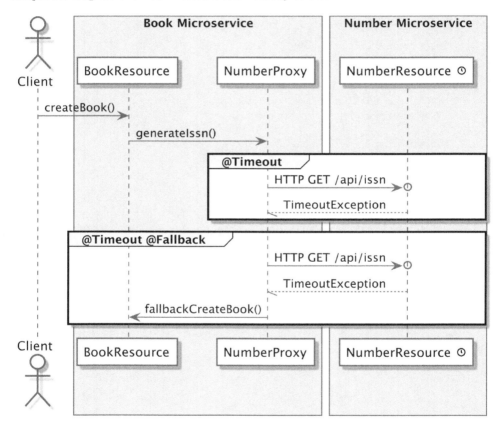

Figure 47. HTTP request timing out

 @Timeout, @Fallback, etc. annotations can be bound at the class level or method level. If the annotation is bound to the class level, it applies to all the methods of the class.

7.3.4. Circuit Breaker

Having fallback and timeout is a good start. But it doesn't solve the problem that the client could still be doing HTTP requests on a resource. Invocations will timeout and fall back, but the client could just keep sending load in the network and hammering the resource which could be already overloaded. A *circuit breaker*[224] is useful for stopping sending load to the system, when part of the system becomes temporarily unstable.

A circuit breaker prevents repeated failures, so that dysfunctional services or APIs fail fast. As shown in Figure 48, a circuit breaker is similar to an electrical circuit breaker since it has the following states:

- *Closed*: A closed-circuit represents a functional system available to its clients. When some failures are detected, the state changes to half-open.

- *Half-open*: In this state, it checks whether the failed component is restored. If so, it closes back the circuit. Otherwise, it moves to an open state.

- *Open*: An open state means the service is temporarily disabled. After checks have been made, it verifies whether it's safe to switch to a half-open state.

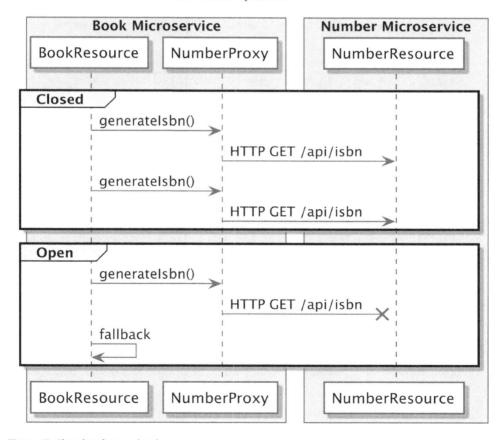

Figure 48. Closed and open circuit

As you can see in Listing 177, the Eclipse MicroProfile Fault Tolerance API uses the @CircuitBreaker annotation to control incoming requests. This annotation records successful and failed invocations of the createLegacyBook() method, and when the ratio of failed invocations reaches the specified threshold, the circuit breaker opens and blocks all further invocations of that method for a given time. In closed state, the requestVolumeThreshold and failureRatio parameters may be configured in order to specify the conditions under which the breaker will transition the circuit to open.

Listing 177. Circuit Breaker on the Book Resource

```java
@Path("/books")
@Produces(MediaType.APPLICATION_JSON)
@ApplicationScoped
public class BookResource {

    @RestClient
    NumberProxy numberProxy;

    @POST
    @Fallback(fallbackMethod = "fallbackCreateLegacyBook")
    @CircuitBreaker(requestVolumeThreshold = 4, failureRatio = 0.5,
                    delay = 2000, successThreshold = 2)
    public Book createLegacyBook() {

        // Invoking microservice
        JsonObject issnNumber = numberProxy.generateIssn();

        Book book = new Book();
        book.title = faker.book().title();
        book.issn = issnNumber.getString("isbn10");
        book.generatedAt = Instant.now();

        return book;
    }

    private Book fallbackCreateLegacyBook() {
        Book book = new Book();
        book.title = "dummy legacy title";
        book.issn = "dummy legacy issn";
        book.generatedAt = Instant.now();
        return book;
    }
}
```

In Listing 177, if, within the last four invocations (requestVolumeThreshold), 50% failed (failureRatio), then the circuit transits to an open state. The circuit will stay open for 2,000 ms (delay). After 2 consecutive successful invocations (successThreshold), the circuit will be back to close again.

If you want to test the circuit breaker code, and see it opening and closing, you need to add some load. One easy way is to loop through a cURL command. On bash, you could write the following:

```
$ while true; do sleep 1; curl -X POST http://localhost:9080/books;
echo; done
```

7.4. Summary

By design, in a microservice architecture, microservices have to talk to each other. Being RESTful web services, they use the HTTP protocol to target specific URLs, with given parameters, verbs and passing payloads following different formats (a.k.a. media types or mime types) and dealing with headers, requests and responses. Consuming HTTP can be cumbersome, that's why JAX-RS comes with a client API. But Eclipse MicroProfile REST Client goes further and simplifies the consumption of a remote microservice response. By using interfaces as proxies, the client code invokes a method on an interface without worrying about the underlying complexity.

In this chapter, we also looked at Cross-Origin Resource Sharing (CORS). It is a way to prevent browsers' requests from crossing different domains. Quarkus allows us to configure CORS so requests can be accepted or not, depending on the level of security you need.

But once requests start to flow from domain to domain, from microservice to microservice, failures start to appear. Eclipse MicroProfile Fault Tolerance allows us to improve the resiliency of our applications, without having an impact on the complexity of our business logic. Fault tolerance is about leveraging different strategies to guide the execution and result of some logic. Fallbacks, timeouts and circuit breakers are popular patterns in this area of distributed systems.

Even if REST is a very common architectural style when it comes to microservices, it's not the only one. In the next chapter, *Event-Driven Microservices*, you will see how reactive programming and reactive messaging can be used to decouple microservices.

[213] CORS https://en.wikipedia.org/wiki/Cross-origin_resource_sharing

[214] WHATWG https://fetch.spec.whatwg.org

[215] REST Client https://microprofile.io/project/eclipse/microprofile-rest-client

[216] REST Client GitHub https://github.com/eclipse/microprofile-rest-client

[217] Java Faker https://github.com/DiUS/java-faker

[218] Ruby faker https://github.com/faker-ruby

[219] Fault Tolerance https://microprofile.io/project/eclipse/microprofile-fault-tolerance

[220] Fault Tolerance GitHub https://github.com/eclipse/microprofile-fault-tolerance

[221] Fallacies of distributed computing https://en.wikipedia.org/wiki/Fallacies_of_distributed_computing

[222] ISBN https://www.isbn-international.org

[223] ISSN https://www.issn.org

[224] Circuit Breaker https://microservices.io/patterns/reliability/circuit-breaker.html

Chapter 8. Event-Driven Microservices

The theory of microservices is simple and we've seen it in the previous chapters: break a monolith into small, purpose-specific microservices (Chapter 2, *Understanding Quarkus*), and have them communicate through HTTP (Chapter 6, *HTTP Microservices*). But in practice, with the network being unreliable and the microservices having to be up and running, we need to deal with fault-tolerance (Chapter 7, *Communication and Fault Tolerance*).

Event-driven architecture (also called reactive architecture or reactive systems) is another way of having our microservices talking to each other. It is about microservices sending events (a.k.a. messages or records) between them. This decouples microservices and brings reliability: events are sent to the eventing/messaging platform (e.g. a JMS or a Kafka broker) which distributes them to the microservices. So, instead of thinking "*which microservice should I invoke?*", you should think of "*what events should my microservice process?*" and "*what events will my microservice emit?*".

In this chapter, you will see two major technologies used for event-driven microservices in Quarkus. *Reactive Programming* (with Mutiny) allows your code to react to events using a nice fluent API. As for *Reactive Messaging*, it allows microservices to interact through messages in a very easy way.

Make sure your development environment is set up to execute the code in this chapter. You can go to Appendix A to check that you have all the required tools installed, in particular Kafka. The code in this chapter can be found at https://github.com/agoncal/agoncal-fascicle-quarkus/tree/2.0/reactive

8.1. Reactive Programming

Java is not a "*reactive language*" in the sense that it doesn't support it natively. There are other languages on the JVM (Scala and Clojure) that support reactive models more natively, but Java itself does not until version 9 with the Flow API[225]. For that, several Java frameworks have emerged throughout the years to allow reactive programming: RxJava[226] or Reactor[227]. Mutiny is a new reactive programming library designed after having experienced difficulties with these libraries.

Eclipse Mutiny[228] is a reactive programming library. Mutiny provides a guided API, making reactive programming easy. It avoids having classes with hundreds of methods that are not always very explicit (e.g. map() or flatmap() on other reactive frameworks). But Mutiny has several converters from and to other reactive programming libraries, so you can always pivot and use the map() method if you really wish.

Mutiny was designed years after existing reactive programming libraries. It is based on the experience of many developers, lost in an endless sequence of map and flatMap operators. Mutiny does not provide as many operators as the other reactive libraries, focusing instead on the most used operators. Furthermore, it helps developers by providing a more guided API, which avoids having classes with hundreds of methods to choose from.

The Eclipse Mutiny APIs and annotations are all defined under the main io.smallrye.mutiny package, either at the root, or under the other subpackages. Table 60 lists the main subpackages defined in Eclipse Mutiny version 0.7 (under the root io.smallrye.mutiny package[229]).

Table 60. Main io.smallrye.mutiny Subpackages

Subpackage	Description
root	Root package of the Mutiny APIs
converters	Converters Uni and Multi from/to several formats
operators	Operations that can be done on Uni and Multi

Table 61. Main Mutiny APIs

API	Description
Uni	Lazy asynchronous action that follows the subscription pattern: the action is only triggered once a subscriber subscribes to it
Multi	Publishes an unlimited number of sequenced elements according to the demand received from its subscriber(s)

Because Quarkus brings imperative and reactive programming together transparently, the Mutiny extension is often used by several extensions and you don't have to declare it explicitly. But if you want to use it in a standalone application, you will have to add the Mutiny extension as seen in Listing 178.

Listing 178. Mutiny Extension

```
<dependency>
    <groupId>io.quarkus</groupId>
    <artifactId>quarkus-mutiny</artifactId>
</dependency>
```

8.1.1. Uni and Multi

Mutiny provides two types that are used everywhere: a Uni and a Multi. Both Uni and Multi are asynchronous types. They receive events and fire events, at any time. You can see this as:

- A Uni handles a stream of 0..1 item;
- A Multi handles a stream of 0..* items (potentially unlimited). You can think of a Multi as being a *publisher*.

To understand the difference between these two types, let's go on and create them. On both Uni and Multi, Mutiny comes with a set of createFrom() methods allowing you to create these types based on items, an array of items, a range, etc. Listing 179 shows how to create a Uni based on a single item of type String. You will soon see how this code really works, but let's say for now that this item of type String is transformed to upper case and displayed on the console.

Listing 179. Creating a Uni From an Item

```
Uni.createFrom().item("Terri Lyne Carrington")
    .onItem().transform(s -> s.toUpperCase() + " ")
    .subscribe().with(System.out::println);
```

Both `Uni` and `Multi` are said to be lazy meaning that you can define the pipeline but the events are not passed until there is an actual subscriber. The code in Listing 180 constructs a pipeline of actions (i.e. transforming a String to uppercase), but it's not until the `subscribe()` method is invoked that the pipeline is actually executed.

Listing 180. Lazily Creating a Uni From an Item

```
// Lazily creates a Uni
Uni<String> uni = Uni.createFrom().item("Terri Lyne Carrington")
  .onItem().transform(s -> s.toUpperCase() + " ");

// Subscribes to it
uni.subscribe().with(System.out::println);
```

The `Uni` handles a stream of one item, and the `Multi` handles more than one. You can see how you can create a `Multi` out of a stream of several Strings in Listing 181. We have an array of items, and for each item, we execute the pipeline of actions.

Listing 181. Creates a Multi From Several Items

```
Multi.createFrom().items("Carla Bley", "John Coltrane", "Juliette Gréco")
  .onItem().transform(String::toUpperCase)
  .subscribe().with(System.out::println);
```

Notice in Listing 181 that the `with()` method takes only one callback (here a `System.out.println`) which is invoked when the item is received. But in this case, the method does not handle failure. In Listing 182, the `with()` takes two callbacks: one callback invoked when the item is received successfully, and a second callback invoked when a failure event is received.

Listing 182. Creates a Uni Handling Success and Failure

```
Uni.createFrom().item("Terri Lyne Carrington")
  .onItem().transform(s -> s.toUpperCase() + " ")
  .subscribe().with(
    item -> System.out.println("Received: " + item),
    failure -> System.out.println("Failed with " + failure.getMessage())
);
```

You can convert Unis to Multis and vice-versa. In Listing 183, we create a `Multi` made of three items, but because we convert it to a `Uni` (with the `toUni()` method), only the first item is processed (in our case, only the String "Carla Bley" will be transformed to uppercase).

Listing 183. Transforms a Multi to a Uni

```
Multi.createFrom().items("Carla Bley", "John Coltrane", "Juliette Gréco")
  .onItem().transform(String::toUpperCase)
  .toUni()
  .subscribe().with(System.out::println);
```

So far we've created Unis and Multis out of *items*. But you can also create Unis from Unis, or Multis from Multis. In Listing 184, we first create a Multi called ticks. Notice that we do not invoke the subscribe() method, so nothing will happen. What we do at this stage is creating a pipeline that will send ticks every second when subscribed.

With this first Multi, we create a second one that will take the first three ticks and display them. Only at this stage, it is when the method subscribe() is invoked, the entire pipeline, composed of two Multis, will be executed ((taking the first three ticks each at every one second).

Listing 184. Creates a Multi From Another Multi

```
Multi<Long> ticks = Multi.createFrom().ticks().every(Duration.ofSeconds(1));

Multi.createFrom().publisher(ticks)
  .select().first(3)
  .subscribe().with(System.out::println);
```

8.1.2. Events

Creating Unis and Multis is just the first step in creating the pipeline. Once created, these asynchronous types react to different kinds of events. Four types of events can flow:

- onItem: This event is triggered once per item. It contains the item itself.

- onCompletion: This event is triggered only once when no more items are emitted.

- onFailure: This event happens zero or once. If there is a failure, a no onCompletion event is sent indicating that a failure has been encountered.

- subscribe: Indicates that the upstream has taken the subscription into account.

Notice that failure and completion are terminal events. Once they are emitted, no more items are emitted.

Let's see how these events work. In Listing 185, we create a Multi with three items of type String. Then, on each event display a message (Received when onItem is triggered, Completed when onCompletion is triggered, and so on).

Listing 185. Multi Reacting to Events

```
Multi.createFrom().items("Carla Bley", "John Coltrane", "Juliette Gréco")
  .onItem().invoke(item -> System.out.println("Received   " + item))
  .onCompletion().invoke(() -> System.out.println("Completed"))
  .onFailure().invoke(failure -> System.out.println("Failed " + failure.getMessage()))
  .subscribe().with(item -> System.out.println("Subscriber " + item));
```

The result below shows what happens. Each item triggers an onItem and subscribe event. In the end, the onCompletion event is triggered only once. In case of failure, we would have received an onFailure event instead:

```
Received    Carla Bley
Subscriber  Carla Bley
Received    John Coltrane
Subscriber  John Coltrane
Received    Juliette Gréco
Subscriber  Juliette Gréco
Completed
```

Listing 186 shows the same kind of code but for a `Uni` instead of a `Multi`. One difference with the code in Listing 185 is that the `Uni` does not need the complete ceremony as there is only one item that needs to be processed.

Listing 186. Uni with No Completion

```
Uni.createFrom().item("Carla Bley")
    .onItem().invoke(item -> System.out.println("Received    " + item))
    .onFailure().invoke(failure -> System.out.println("Failed " + failure.getMessage()))
    .subscribe().with(item -> System.out.println("Subscriber " + item));
```

Below are the events that are triggered when a `Uni` is executed:

```
Received    Carla Bley
Subscriber  Carla Bley
```

So far we know how Reactive Programing allows us to react to events. Talking about Microservices, now is the time to see how messaging should be handled between Microservices in the reactive world.

8.2. Reactive Messaging

In Chapter 2, *Understanding Quarkus*, you saw that one of the goals of Quarkus is to unify imperative and reactive programming. So Mutiny is heavily used under the hood without you noticing or having to deal with Unis and Multis if you don't need to. This is true also for Reactive Messaging which is based on Mutiny.

Eclipse Reactive Messaging[230] is made for building event-driven, data streaming, and event-sourcing applications. It lets your application interact with various messaging technologies such as Apache Kafka, AMQP or MQTT. The framework provides a flexible programming model bridging CDI and event-driven APIs.

The Eclipse Reactive Messaging APIs and annotations are all defined under the main `org.eclipse.microprofile.reactive.messaging` package, either at the root, or under the other subpackages. Table 62 lists the main subpackages defined in Eclipse Reactive Messaging version 1.1 (under the root `org.eclipse.microprofile.reactive.messaging` package[231]).

Table 62. Main org.eclipse.microprofile.reactive.messaging Subpackages

Subpackage	Description
root	Root package of the Reactive Messaging APIs
spi	Internal SPIs (*Service Provider Interfaces*) implemented by the provider

Table 63 lists a few Reactive Messaging APIs that are used to emit messages to channels. Messages have an optional set of metadata.

Table 63. Main Reactive Messaging APIs

API	Description
Emitter	It acts as a message producer and feeds a channel from imperative code
Message	Contains a payload, a set of metadata, and an acknowledgement function
Metadata	Stores message metadata that can be related to the transport layer or to the business / application

Along with APIs, Reactive Messaging comes with a set of annotations. Table 64 lists a subset of the most commonly used annotations.

Table 64. Main Reactive Messaging Annotations

Annotation	Description
@Outgoing	Used by publishers to send messages
@Incoming	Used to notify a subscriber of incoming messages
@Acknowledgment	Configures the acknowledgement policy for the given @Incoming (MANUAL, PRE_PROCESSING, POST_PROCESSING, NONE)
@Broadcast	Used by publishers to dispatch messages to several subscribers
@Channel	CDI qualifier to indicate which channel should be injected
@OnOverflow	Configures the back pressure policy on an injected Emitter

To integrate Reactive Messaging into your Quarkus application, you need the extension defined in Listing 187. This extension uses reactive programming under the hood, and therefore, depends on Mutiny.

Listing 187. Reactive Messaging Extension

```
<dependency>
  <groupId>io.quarkus</groupId>
  <artifactId>quarkus-smallrye-reactive-messaging</artifactId>
</dependency>
```

8.2.1. Understanding Messaging

Before digging into messaging, let's have a quick look at the difference between synchronous and asynchronous programming.

Synchronous Programming

Basically, *synchronous* means that you can only execute one thing at a time. The code in Listing 188, is what we usually do while programming in Java. In this code, we wait for each method to finish before invoking another method.

Listing 188. Synchronous Code

```java
public PurchaseOrder create(PurchaseOrder po) {

  bankService.validate(po);

  if (po.creditCard.status == VALID) {
    po.status = VALID;

    inventoryService.prepareItems(po);

    shippingService.prepareShipping(po);
  } else {
    invalidate(po);
  }

  return po;
}
```

If you translate the code in Listing 188 to the sequence diagram in Figure 49, it's easier to see the time dependency between components. To create a purchase order, several components are invoked to validate the credit card details and prepare the items to be shipped. And all these components depend on each other's execution. For example, if the InventoryService takes too long, the ShippingService will have to wait until the other task has completed.

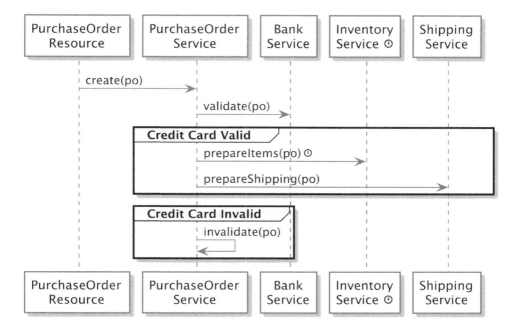

Figure 49. Synchronous method invocation

Asynchronous Programming using Messages

Asynchronous means that you can execute multiple things at a time and you don't have to finish executing the current thing in order to move on to the next one. In Java, asynchronous programming can be done at a very low-level, such as manipulating threads, or through higher-level Java APIs (e.g. `CompletableFuture` or `CompletionStage`). But you can also use messaging.

Sending messages asynchronously allows temporal decoupling between components so the system can do several tasks in parallel. In the diagram in Figure 50, we send messages back and forth between components. So if we take back our example where one component takes too long to complete, this is what happens now. Once the `BankService` validates the credit card, a message `po-validated` is sent to several subscribers. These subscribers then execute their own task at their own pace, not depending on the execution of other components. If the `InventoryService` takes too long, the `ShippingService` does not have to wait for its completion and can prepare the shipping.

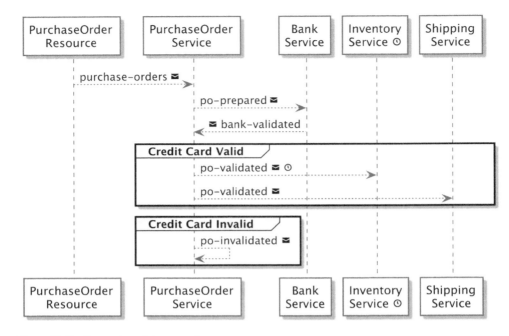

Figure 50. Sending and receiving asynchronous messages

Broker Architecture

A *Broker* is a software that enables the exchange of messages asynchronously between heterogeneous systems. It can be seen as a buffer between systems that produce and consume messages at their own pace (e.g. one system is 24/7, the other runs only at night). It is inherently loosely coupled, as producers don't know who is at the other end of the communication channel to consume the message and perform actions. The producer and the consumer do not have to be available at the same time in order to communicate. In fact, they do not even know about each other, as they use an intermediate buffer. In this respect, a broker differs completely from synchronous technologies which require an application to know the signature of a remote application's methods.

A broker (a.k.a. *message provider* or *provider*) uses a special vocabulary. The message sender is called a *producer* (or an *emitter*), and the location where the message is sent is called a *topic* (or a *channel* or *destination*). The component receiving the message is called a *consumer* (or a *subscriber*). What's exchanged between the producer and the consumer is called a *message*, an *event*, or a *record*. A message is an envelope wrapping a payload. A message is sent to a specific topic and, when received and processed successfully, acknowledged. Figure 51 illustrates these concepts.

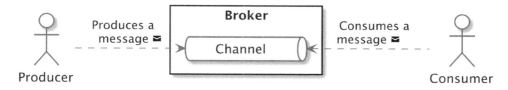

Figure 51. The broker architecture

In a microservice architecture, messages can be exchanged within the microservice itself, or, between remote microservices (see Figure 52). Having local exchanges allows components to use reactive programming to react to messages. While remote exchanges allow us to decouple microservices.

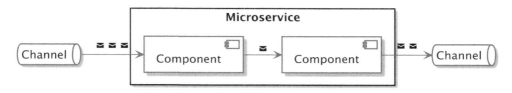

Figure 52. Local and remote message exchanges

There are several frameworks and APIs used to send and receive messages: Quarkus uses Eclipse Reactive Messaging. There are also several brokers and, as of today, Quarkus interacts with Kafka, AMQP and MQTT through connectors (more on *connectors* in the Kafka section below).

8.2.2. Sending Messages

There are two ways of sending messages with Eclipse Reactive Messaging. One is using the @Outgoing annotation and another one is by programmatically emitting messages into a channel.

The @Outgoing annotation is used to annotate a method to indicate that the method publishes messages to a specified channel. Inside the application, messages transit on channels that are identified by a name. So in Listing 189, the message containing a conversion rate of type Float is sent to a channel called euro-rate. Somewhere, a subscriber listening to the channel will receive the rate asynchronously.

Listing 189. Sending a Message with @Outgoing

```
@Outgoing("euro-rate")
public Message<Float> sendEuroRate() {
  return Message.of(euroRate);
}
```

To communicate, publishers and subscribers exchange messages. They can either be *messages* that are represented by the Message interface, or just the content of the message (a.k.a. *payload*). This Message interface is kept minimal so that connectors can provide their own implementations with additional metadata that is relevant to that connector. For instance, a KafkaRecord implements the Message interface and provides access to Kafka specific information (such as the topic or the partition).

Below we see some examples of code manipulating this Message interface. Plain messages are created using the of() method which wraps a given payload with optional metadata (withMedata() method). The getPayload() method retrieves the wrapped payload while ack() acknowledges the message.

```
// Creating messages with different datatypes
Message<Integer> msg = Message.of(1);
Message<String> msg = Message.of("Janis Joplin tape sold");
Message<CreditCard> msg = Message.of(new CreditCard("1234 5678", AMERICAN_EXPRESS));

// Getting the payload
Message<String> msg = Message.of("Euro rate: 1.345");
assertEquals("Euro rate: 1.345", msg.getPayload());

// Creating messages with metadata
Metadata metadata = Metadata.of(LocalDate.now());
Message<String> msg = Message.of("Jimi Hendrix vinyl sold", metadata);
Message<String> msg = Message.of("Jimi Hendrix vinyl sold").withMetadata(metadata);

// Acknowledging a message
Message<String> msg = Message.of("Ella vinyl sold");
msg.ack();
```

Manipulating messages can be cumbersome if you don't use metadata or programmatic acknowledgement. If you are only interested in the payload, you can just pass it to the channel (Float instead of Message<Float>). So, the code in Listing 190 is equivalent to the one in Listing 189.

Listing 190. Sending a Payload

```
@Outgoing("pound-rate")
public Float sendPoundRate() {
    return poundRate;
}
```

In a single application it is not rare to combine imperative parts (JAX-RS, CDI beans) and reactive parts (beans with @Incoming and @Outgoing annotations). And sometimes you need to send messages from the imperative part to the reactive part. In this scenario, you can't use the @Outgoing annotation on the imperative code but instead use the Emitter class and @Channel annotation.

As shown in Listing 191, the REST endpoint is invoked through an HTTP POST request, not a message (so @Incoming cannot be used). To be able to send a message, it injects an Emitter which is used to send a message to a specific channel (thanks to the @Channel annotation). Then, it's just a matter of invoking the send() method passing a message, and this message is sent to the channel.

Listing 191. REST Endpoint Sending a Message

```java
@Path("/pomsg")
@Consumes(MediaType.APPLICATION_JSON)
@ApplicationScoped
public class PurchaseOrderMessageResource {

  @Inject
  @Channel("purchase-orders-msg")
  Emitter<Message<PurchaseOrder>> emitter;

  @POST
  public Response create(PurchaseOrder po) {

    emitter.send(Message.of(po));

    URI temporaryPO = UriBuilder.fromResource(PurchaseOrderMessageResource.class)
                                .path(tmpId).build();
    return Response.temporaryRedirect(temporaryPO).build();
  }
}
```

But the Emitter API can also be used in the reactive world. The code in Listing 192 needs to validate a purchase order depending on a previous message sent by the bank. If the credit card used to pay this purchase order is valid, then the purchase order is valid and a message can be sent to the channel po-validated. If not, the same message is sent to a different channel called po-invalidated. In this case, we inject two different emitters so we can choose which channel to send the message to. Notice that here, we are just interested in the payload (not the metadata). So the purchase order is directly sent instead of a Message<PurchaseOrder> as in Listing 191.

Listing 192. Sending Messages to Different Topics

```java
@ApplicationScoped
public class PurchaseOrderService {

    @Inject
    @Channel("po-validated")
    Emitter<PurchaseOrder> emitterForValidPO;

    @Inject
    @Channel("po-invalidated")
    Emitter<PurchaseOrder> emitterForInvalidPO;

    @Incoming("bank-validated")
    public void validate(PurchaseOrder po) {

        if (po.creditCard.status == VALID) {
            po.status = VALID;
            emitterForValidPO.send(po);
        } else {
            po.status = INVALID;
            emitterForInvalidPO.send(po);
        }
    }
}
```

8.2.3. Receiving Messages

Once a message is sent to a channel, it can be consumed by another component (or remote microservice as we'll later see). If the @Outgoing annotation indicates the name of the channel to send messages to, its counterpart @Incoming indicates the name of the channel to consume messages from. The method in Listing 193 subscribes to the channel purchase-orders-ms. Each time a message is received, this method is invoked. Notice that this method programmatically acknowledges the message by invoking the ack() method.

Listing 193. Receiving a Message

```java
@Incoming("purchase-orders-msg")
public CompletionStage<Void> create(Message<PurchaseOrder> msg) {

    PurchaseOrder po = msg.getPayload();
    persist(po);

    return msg.ack();
}
```

Again, if you are only interested in the payload and want to rely on automatic acknowledgement, then you can follow the code in Listing 194: The method takes a PurchaseOrder object as a parameter instead of a Message<PurchaseOrder>.

Listing 194. Receiving a Payload

```
@Incoming("po-validated")
public void prepareShipping(PurchaseOrder po) {

  for (OrderLine orderLine : po.orderLines) {
    orderLine.status = Status.SHIPPING;
  }

  shipItems(po);
}
```

Then, you can use in-memory message exchanges by using @Incoming to produce data and @Outgoing to consume data. In fact, a method can combine the @Incoming and @Outgoing annotations to act as a reactive streams processor. As shown in Listing 195, matching @Outgoing to @Incoming annotation forms a chain. When a message arrives in the channel po-prepared it is processed and then sent to the bank-validated channel and ends in the bank-authorised channel.

Listing 195. Receiving and Sending Messages

```
@Incoming("po-prepared")
@Outgoing("bank-validated")
public PurchaseOrder validate(PurchaseOrder po) {

  if (complexValidationLogic(po)) {
    po.creditCard.status = VALID;
  } else {
    po.creditCard.status = INVALID;
  }
  return po;
}

@Incoming("bank-validated")
@Outgoing("bank-authorised")
public PurchaseOrder authorise(PurchaseOrder po) {
  po.creditCard.status = AUTHORISED;
  return po;
}

@Incoming("bank-authorised")
public void pay(PurchaseOrder po) {
  makePayment(po);
}
```

These methods annotated with @Incoming or @Outgoing don't have to be in the same bean. They can be distributed among several beans, or, several microservices. In this case, you need remote interactions, and for that, you need *connectors* to connect to remote brokers, such as Kafka.

You should not programmatically call methods annotated with `@Incoming` and/or `@Outgoing` directly from your code. They are invoked by the framework. Having user code invoking them would have an unexpected outcome.

8.2.4. Connectors

So far we've seen that Reactive Messaging can handle messages generated from within the application. In this case, everything happens *in-memory*, and the streams are created by chaining methods all together. Each chain is still a reactive stream and enforces the backpressure protocol. But if you need to send messages to distant microservices, you need a message broker such as Kafka, AMQP or MQTT. For that, Reactive Messaging uses connectors. A connector is an extension managing the communication (between microservices in this context) with a specific transport technology:

- It receives messages from the broker and propagates them to the application;
- It sends messages provided by the application to the broker.

From a developer's point of view, whether the messages come from co-located beans or from a remote message broker, is transparent. The only thing we need is to add a Quarkus extension depending on the connector's technology. Let's see an example with Kafka.

Kafka[232] (or *Apache Kafka*) is an open source distributed event streaming platform. It provides a unified, high-throughput, low-latency platform for handling real-time data feeds thanks to its optimised binary TCP-based protocol. To be able to connect to Kafka, we need to add the Kafka extension described in Listing 196.

Listing 196. Reactive Messaging and Kafka Extensions

```
<dependency>
  <groupId>io.quarkus</groupId>
  <artifactId>quarkus-smallrye-reactive-messaging-kafka</artifactId>
</dependency>
```

Quarkus comes with connectors other than Kafka, such as AMQP or MQTT. Each connector has its own dedicated extension targeting a specific technology.

AMQP[233] (or *Advanced Message Queuing Protocol*) is an open standard application layer protocol for message-oriented middleware. The defining features of AMQP are message orientation, queuing, routing (including point-to-point and publish-and-subscribe), reliability and security.

MQTT[234] (or *Message Queuing Telemetry Transport*) is the standard messaging protocol for the Internet of Things (IoT). It is designed as an extremely lightweight publish/subscribe messaging transport that is ideal for connecting remote devices with a small code footprint and minimal network bandwidth.

Let's take our previous example of a REST endpoint sending a message to a remote Kafka broker. As you can see in Listing 197, the code is identical to what we've seen before: the `Emitter` sends a

PurchaseOrder to a channel called po-write.

Listing 197. REST Endpoint Sending a Message to a Kafka Topic

```
@Path("/po")
@Consumes(MediaType.APPLICATION_JSON)
@ApplicationScoped
public class PurchaseOrderResource {

  @Inject @Channel("po-write")
  Emitter<PurchaseOrder> emitter;

  @POST
  public Response create(PurchaseOrder po) {

    emitter.send(po);

    URI temporaryPO = UriBuilder.fromResource(PurchaseOrderResource.class)
                                .path(tmpId).build();
    return Response.temporaryRedirect(temporaryPO).build();
  }
}
```

The difference comes from the configuration. Eclipse Reactive Messaging determines the connector and configuration for each channel. The syntax is:

```
mp.messaging.[outgoing|incoming].{channel-name}.<property>=<value>.
```

In the application.properties file, to specify that the channel po-write uses a Kafka connector, we need to set the connector's type to smallrye-kafka. And because we are sending a JSON representation of a purchase order over the network, we also need to specify the serializer.

```
mp.messaging.outgoing.po-write.connector=smallrye-kafka
mp.messaging.outgoing.po-
write.value.serializer=io.quarkus.kafka.client.serialization.JsonbSerializer
```

On the other side of the Kafka topic, the microservice in Listing 198 listens to messages arriving in the channel called po-read.

Listing 198. Remote Service Receiving a Message from a Kafka Topic

```
@Incoming("po-read")
public PurchaseOrder create(PurchaseOrder po) {

  // Create a PO
  return po;
}
```

Notice that the channel used to send a message to (po-write) and the channel used to receive the message from (po-read) have different names. That's because we need to map a specific channel to a remote topic for both the publisher and subscriber sides. This is done through the configuration defined in Listing 199: the po-read channel listens to the topic called po-write.

Listing 199. Configuring Kafka Topics

```
mp.messaging.outgoing.po-write.connector=smallrye-kafka
mp.messaging.outgoing.po-
write.value.serializer=io.quarkus.kafka.client.serialization.JsonbSerializer

mp.messaging.incoming.po-read.connector=smallrye-kafka
mp.messaging.incoming.po-read.topic=po-write
mp.messaging.incoming.po-
read.value.deserializer=org.agoncal.fascicle.quarkus.PurchaseOrderDeserializer
```

Because the purchase order is serialised to JSON, the po-read channel needs to deserialise the JSON to a PurchaseOrder object. This is done using the JSON-B serialise/deserialise objects. To deserialise we need to create our own deserialiser and provide a type as shown in Listing 200.

Listing 200. Purchase Order JSON Deserialiser

```
public class PurchaseOrderDeserializer extends JsonbDeserializer<PurchaseOrder> {
    public PurchaseOrderDeserializer() {
        super(PurchaseOrder.class);
    }
}
```

When starting, Quarkus needs to connect to Kafka. If Kafka is not up and running, this is the kind of warning messages that you will get in the console:

```
[WARN] [NetworkClient] Connection to node -1 (localhost:9092) could not
be established. Broker may not be available.
[WARN] [NetworkClient] Bootstrap broker localhost:9092 disconnected
```

Make sure to read Appendix A so you know how to start and stop a Kafka broker.

8.2.5. Configuring Reactive Messages

Table 65. Some Reactive Messaging and Kafka Configuration Properties

Property	Default
quarkus.reactive-messaging.health.enabled Whether or not a health check is published in case the smallrye-health extension is present	true

Property	Default
`quarkus.reactive-messaging.metrics.enabled` Whether or not Reactive Messaging metrics are published in case the smallrye-metrics extension is present	false
`quarkus.kafka.health.enabled` Whether or not a health check is published in case the Kafka extension is present	false

8.3. Summary

While event-driven microservices may seem difficult initially, they are the future of most microservices and IT strategies. So, as seen in this chapter, Quarkus is not limited to HTTP microservices, but also fits perfectly in this event-driven architecture. Why? Because as explained in Chapter 2, *Understanding Quarkus*, behind the scenes, Quarkus uses a single reactive engine for both imperative and reactive code, without you noticing.

There are a number of Reactive libraries or frameworks for the JVM, all under active development. To a large extent they provide similar features, but increasingly, thanks to Reactive Streams, they are interoperable. That's what Eclipse Mutiny is all about. Mutiny is a new reactive framework, implementing the Reactive Streams, and it is heavily used in Quarkus internals. In this chapter, you saw how to programmatically use Mutiny APIs (with its `Uni` and `Multi`) and its operators (`onItem()`, `onFailure()`, `invoke()`, etc.).

Mutiny is also hidden behind Eclipse Reactive Messaging. So you don't have to directly use it for simple use cases such as receiving or sending simple messages. You just use a few annotations (`@Channel`, `@Outgoing`, `@Incoming`) and you are ready to process messages within your microservice, or, thanks to some configuration, use a remote broker such as Kafka.

But reactive microservices can also fail, consume too many resources, or behave incorrectly. Reactive and HTTP microservices need to be monitored. In the next chapter *Observability* you will see how Quarkus helps in checking the health of your microservices and getting some metrics.

[225] Flow API https://docs.oracle.com/en/java/javase/11/docs/api/java.base/java/util/concurrent/Flow.html

[226] RxJava https://github.com/ReactiveX/RxJava

[227] Reactor https://projectreactor.io

[228] Mutiny https://github.com/smallrye/smallrye-mutiny

[229] Mutiny GitHub https://github.com/smallrye/smallrye-mutiny

[230] Reactive Messaging https://github.com/eclipse/microprofile-reactive-messaging

[231] Reactive Messaging GitHub https://microprofile.io/project/eclipse/microprofile-reactive-messaging

[232] Kafka https://kafka.apache.org

[233] AMQP https://www.amqp.org

[234] MQTT https://mqtt.org

Chapter 9. Observability

As you've seen in the previous chapters, your architecture can easily mix *HTTP Microservices* and *Event-Driven Microservices*. When it comes to HTTP microservices, the chapter *Communication and Fault Tolerance* showed that synchronous communication is not reliable, that's why we need Eclipse MicroProfile Fault Tolerance to have fallbacks or circuit breakers.

With all these microservices interacting with each other, over HTTP or messages, it is essential to allow each microservice to report and publish its health status. This information can then be collected by a service orchestrator which can take decisions based on the health of the system. Reporting health status can be achieved with *Eclipse MicroProfile Health*.

Knowing the health of our microservices is the first step. But that doesn't tell us if they are processing correctly in a correct amount of time or with good throughput. *Eclipse MicroProfile Metrics* brings a unified way of exporting statistics indicators, such as the number of times and the rate at which a service has been requested, the duration of each request, and so on.

 The code in this chapter can be found at https://github.com/agoncal/agoncal-fascicle-quarkus/tree/2.0/observability

9.1. Eclipse MicroProfile Health

Eclipse MicroProfile Health[235] provides the ability to probe the state of a computing node from another machine. The Eclipse MicroProfile Health APIs allow applications to provide information about their state to external viewers which is typically useful in cloud environments where automated processes must be able to determine whether the application should be discarded or restarted. Quarkus implements the Eclipse MicroProfile Health specification through the SmallRye Health extension.

The Eclipse MicroProfile Health APIs and annotations are all defined under the org.eclipse.microprofile.health package. Table 66 lists the main subpackages defined in Eclipse MicroProfile Health version 3.1 (under the root org.eclipse.microprofile.health package[236]).

Table 66. Main org.eclipse.microprofile.health Subpackages

Subpackage	Description
root	Root package of the Health APIs
spi	Internal SPIs (*Service Provider Interfaces*) implemented by the provider

In these packages, you'll find all the APIs and annotations. Table 67 shows a few Health APIs.

Table 67. Main Health APIs

API	Description
HealthCheck	Used by the runtime hosting the application to verify the healthiness of the computing node
HealthCheckResponse	Signals the health status to a consuming end

API	Description
HealthCheckResponseBuilder	A builder to construct a health check response

Along with APIs, Health comes with a set of annotations. Table 68 lists a subset of the most commonly used annotations.

Table 68. Main Health Annotations

Annotation	Description
@Startup	Defines a Startup Health Check procedure mapped to the Startup Kubernetes
@Liveness	Used to define a liveness health check procedure
@Readiness	Used to define a readiness health check procedure

When you add the Health extension in your pom.xml (see Listing 201), then some Quarkus components can automatically expose their health. That's the case for datasources or reactive messaging.

Listing 201. Health Extension

```
<dependency>
    <groupId>io.quarkus</groupId>
    <artifactId>quarkus-smallrye-health</artifactId>
</dependency>
```

9.1.1. Understanding Health Checks

In a microservice architecture, we quickly end-up having hundreds or thousands of processes running on several servers. If we use a hybrid cloud, we might have a few microservices in-house and others in different clouds and different datacentre locations. It is important to know the health of the entire system as well as each individual microservice as shown in Figure 53. It may seem obvious, but a microservice must report its health so it can be collected by a service orchestrator, which can then use the health status to make decisions. For that, there's a need for standardisation in how to log health events that ultimately end up being collected for querying and viewing.

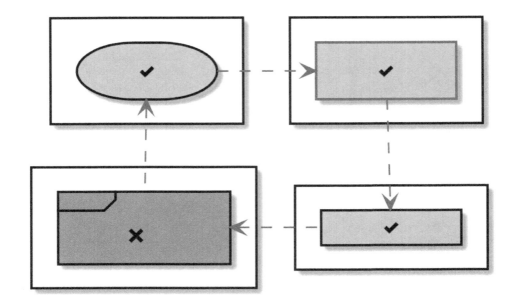

Figure 53. Microservices up and down

9.1.2. Checks

A service checks its own health by performing necessary self-checks. A self-check can be a check on anything that the service needs: enough disk space, a successful database connection, a system property, etc. A service reports UP if it is available and reports DOWN if it is unavailable. Although a service might currently be unhealthy, the service might still be operational. Therefore, Eclipse MicroProfile Health handles several types of checks (the difference between them is only semantic):

- *Startup*: Initial verification of the application before the liveness takes over.
- *Liveness*: Is the application running? Checks if the microservice is alive.
- *Readiness*: Is the application ready to process requests or not? Checks if the microservice is able to accept requests and respond (e.g. by checking external dependencies such as the database, the message broker, etc.) so the microservice can do what it's supposed to do.

Eclipse MicroProfile Health allows services to report their health, and it publishes the overall health status to defined endpoints:

- /health/started: Returns the result of all startup checks and determines whether or not your application is started.
- /health/live: Returns the result of all liveness checks and determines whether or not your application is up and running.
- /health/ready: Returns the result of all readiness checks and determines whether or not your application can process requests.
- /health: Accumulates the result of all health check types.

These endpoints are linked to health check procedures annotated respectively with `@Startup`, `@Liveness` and `@Readiness` annotations.

Liveness Checks

A liveness check determines if the microservice is running. This means that if this procedure fails, the microservice can be discarded and restarted. For example, in Listing 202, to check that our *Number* endpoint is live, we make sure it can generate ISSN numbers (by invoking the `generateIssn()` method and making sure it doesn't throw an exception). For that, the health check procedure has to implement the `HealthCheck` interface and be annotated with the CDI qualifier `@Liveness`.

Listing 202. Liveness Check

```java
@Liveness
@ApplicationScoped
public class NumberResourceCheck implements HealthCheck {

  @Inject
  NumberResource numberResource;

  @Override
  public HealthCheckResponse call() {
    numberResource.generateIssn();
    return HealthCheckResponse.named("Ping Number REST Endpoint").up().build();
  }
}
```

`HealthCheck` is a functional interface whose single method `call` returns a `HealthCheckResponse` object which can be easily constructed by the fluent builder API. The `call()` method is used to return the health status of a particular service. So, in Listing 202, we invoke the `generateIssn()` method. If it throws an exception, the response will be `DOWN`. If it succeeds, the response will be `UP`. As you can add multiple checks, you need to give every check a dedicated name. The `HealthCheckResponse.named()` method is used to indicate what service the health check is done for.

The liveness check is accessible at `/q/health/live`. Access this URL (by browser or cURL) and you should see a JSON output similar to Listing 203.

Listing 203. Liveness Check Result in JSON

```json
{
  "status": "UP",
  "checks": [
    {
      "name": "Ping Number REST Endpoint",
      "status": "UP"
    }
  ]
}
```

Readiness Checks

Once we know that a microservice is alive, we need to know if it is actually ready to process requests. Generally, the liveness procedures determine whether the microservice should be restarted, while readiness procedures determine whether it makes sense to contact the microservice with requests. As shown in Listing 204, a readiness check is very similar to a liveness check. You need a Java class that implements HealthCheck and is annotated with @Readiness. Here, the call() method checks that the environment variable server.name is set. If not, the service is down and is not ready to process requests.

Listing 204. Readiness Check

```
@Readiness
@ApplicationScoped
public class ServerVariableCheck implements HealthCheck {

  @Override
  public HealthCheckResponse call() {
    if (System.getProperty("server.name") == null) {
      return HealthCheckResponse.named("System Variable Check").down().build();
    } else {
      return HealthCheckResponse.named("System Variable Check").up().build();
    }
  }
}
```

When the ServerVariableCheck class in Listing 204 is deployed with the microservice, you can access the health/ready endpoint. You will get the health checks defined with the @Readiness qualifier (see Listing 205).

Listing 205. Readiness Check Result in JSON

```
{
  "status": "DOWN",
  "checks": [
    {
      "name": "System Variable Check",
      "status": "DOWN"
    }
  ]
}
```

If you access the health endpoint, you will get back both liveness and readiness checks as shown in Listing 206.

Listing 206. Liveness and Readiness Checks

```
{
  "status": "DOWN",
  "checks": [
    {
      "name": "Ping Number REST Endpoint",
      "status": "UP"
    },
    {
      "name": "System Variable Check",
      "status": "DOWN"
    }
  ]
}
```

All of the health REST endpoints return a simple JSON object with two fields:

- status: The general status of the health check is computed as a logical AND of all the declared health check procedures.

- checks: An array of individual checks.

Combining Checks

A health check implementation may be annotated with multiple kinds of checks. The procedure will be used to resolve every kind of health check for which it is annotated. For instance, the code in Listing 207 resolves both startup and liveness health check by annotating the class with both @Startup and @Liveness annotations.

Listing 207. Combining Checks

```
@Startup
@Liveness
@ApplicationScoped
public class NumberResourceCheck implements HealthCheck {

  @Inject
  NumberResource numberResource;

  @Override
  public HealthCheckResponse call() {
    numberResource.generateRandom();
    return HealthCheckResponse.named("Invoke Number REST Endpoint").up().build();
  }
}
```

When you combine checks, you can see the output either on the /q/health/started or /q/health/live endpoints. The JSON output is the same for both cases (see Listing 208).

Listing 208. Startup Check Result in JSON

```json
{
    "status": "UP",
    "checks": [
        {
            "name": "Invoke Number REST Endpoint",
            "status": "UP"
        }
    ]
}
```

Built-In Quarkus Checks

The Eclipse MicroProfile Health specification does not implement any health checks, it just gives you the APIs to implement your own. But SmallRye comes with some already implemented health checks for checking common services (all under the io.smallrye.health.checks package):

- HeapMemoryHealthCheck: Checks heap memory usage against available heap memory.
- InetAddressHealthCheck: Checks if the host is reachable using *InetAddress.isReachable*[237] method.
- NonHeapMemoryHealthCheck: Checks memory usage against available memory.
- SocketHealthCheck: Checks if the host is reachable using a socket.
- SystemLoadHealthCheck: Checks average load usage against max load.
- ThreadHealthCheck: Checks the number of threads.
- UrlHealthCheck: Checks if the host is reachable using an HTTP URL connection.

Listing 209 uses the UrlHealthCheck to check that a URL is pingable or not.

Listing 209. Checking a URL

```java
@ApplicationScoped
public class BlogCheck {

    @Liveness
    HealthCheck checkURL() {
        return new UrlHealthCheck("https://antoniogoncalves.org").name("Blog Check");
    }
}
```

9.1.3. Constructing a Response

Liveness and readiness health checks implement the call() method that returns a HealthCheckResponse. Up to now, we've seen that a response contains a name to identify a check from other checks and a UP or DOWN flag, to indicate the state. But there is more to it. HealthCheckResponse also provides a way for the applications to supply arbitrary data in the form of key-value pairs sent to the consuming end. This can be done by using the `withData(key, value)` method shown in Listing 210. Instead of using the `up()` and `down()` method, we can calculate the state with the `state()` method. In Listing 210, we check for free disk space as the service might rely on storage to persist files. If there is more than 100Mb of free space, then a status of UP is returned.

Listing 210. Response with Data and State

```java
@Readiness
@ApplicationScoped
public class DiskCheck implements HealthCheck {

  @Override
  public HealthCheckResponse call() {

    File file = new File("/");
    long totalSpace = file.getTotalSpace() / 1024 / 1024;
    long freeSpace = file.getFreeSpace() / 1024 / 1024;

    return HealthCheckResponse
      .named(DiskCheck.class.getSimpleName() + "Readiness")
      .withData("totalSpace", totalSpace)
      .withData("remainingSpace", freeSpace)
      .status(freeSpace > 100)
      .build();
  }
}
```

The JSON result of the health check in Listing 210 is shown in Listing 211. As you can see, the `data` node is an array of key/value pairs containing the metadata of our response.

Listing 211. Readiness Check with Array of Data

```json
{
  "status": "UP",
  "checks": [
    {
      "name": "DiskCheckReadiness",
      "status": "UP",
      "data": {
        "remainingSpace": 1897665,
        "totalSpace": 1908108
      }
    }
  ]
}
```

The `HealthCheckResponse` can be easily constructed by the fluent builder API `HealthCheckResponseBuilder`. In Listing 212, we get a builder, and depending on whether or not the system variable `server.name` is declared, we gather different data and take different actions (up or down).

Listing 212. Building a Response

```java
@Liveness
@ApplicationScoped
public class ServerVariableCheck implements HealthCheck {

  @Override
  public HealthCheckResponse call() {

    HealthCheckResponseBuilder builder = HealthCheckResponse
      .named(ServerVariableCheck.class.getSimpleName() + "Liveness")
      .withData("variable", "server.name");

    if (System.getProperty("server.name") == null) {
      return builder
        .withData("server", "not available")
        .down()
        .build();
    } else {
      return builder
        .withData("server", "available")
        .up()
        .build();
    }
  }
}
```

No matter which health endpoint you target, Eclipse MicroProfile Health will return the same status codes:

- `200-OK` for a health check with a positive status (UP).

- `503-Service Unavailable` in case the overall status is negative (DOWN).

- `500-Internal Server Error` in case the producer wasn't able to process the health check request (i.e. error in procedure).

9.1.4. Visualising Health Checks with Health-UI

Getting health checks in JSON format is fine for tooling, but can be cumbersome for a human to read if there are many checks. Quarkus has a web interface that nicely displays the JSON output. It is called *Health UI*[238] and it is accessible at `/q/health-ui/`. Figure 54 shows what Health UI looks like and how it displays the list of checks with their status up or down.

Figure 54. Health UI

9.1.5. Configuring SmallRye Health

As usual, Quarkus comes with a set of properties to configure SmallRye Health, the implementation of Eclipse MicroProfile Health. These properties have the `quarkus.smallrye-health.` namespace[144].

Table 69. Some Quarkus Health Configuration Properties

Property	Default
`quarkus.smallrye-health.root-path` Root path for health-checking endpoints	`/health`
`quarkus.smallrye-health.liveness-path` The relative path of the liveness health-checking endpoint	`/live`
`quarkus.smallrye-health.readiness-path` The relative path of the readiness health-checking endpoint	`/ready`
`quarkus.smallrye-health.startup-path` The relative path of the startup health-checking endpoint	`/started`
`quarkus.smallrye-health.ui.enable` If Health UI should be enabled	`true`
`quarkus.smallrye-health.ui.root-path` The path where Health UI is available	`/health-ui`

9.2. Eclipse MicroProfile Metrics

Knowing the health of a single microservice or the entire system is crucial. But it doesn't tell you if one component is slowing down or not responding quickly as it should. For that, you need to gather metrics. *Eclipse MicroProfile Metrics*[239] provides a unified way for MicroProfile servers to export monitoring data to management agents. Metrics will also provide a common Java API for exposing their telemetry data. MicroProfile Metrics allows applications to gather various metrics and statistics that provide insights into what is happening inside the application. The metrics can be read remotely using a JSON or OpenMetrics format to be processed by additional tools such as Prometheus, and stored for analysis and visualisation. Quarkus implements the Eclipse MicroProfile Metrics specification through the SmallRye Metrics extension.

The Eclipse MicroProfile Metrics APIs and annotations are all defined under the main `org.eclipse.microprofile.metrics` package, either at the root, or under the other subpackages. Table

70 lists the main subpackages defined in Eclipse MicroProfile Metrics version 3.0 (under the root `org.eclipse.microprofile.metrics` package[240]).

Table 70. Main org.eclipse.microprofile.metrics Subpackages

Subpackage	Description
root	Root package of the Metrics APIs
`annotation`	APIs for annotating methods and classes to get metrics from

In these packages, you'll find all the APIs and annotations. Table 71 shows a few Metrics APIs.

Table 71. Main Metrics APIs

API	Description
`Counter`	An incrementing counter metric
`Gauge`	Instantaneous reading of a particular value (e.g. instrumenting a queue's depth)
`Histogram`	Metric which calculates the distribution of a value
`Meter`	Metric which measures mean throughput and one-, five-, and fifteen-minute exponentially-weighted moving average throughputs
`Timer`	Metric which aggregates timing durations and provides duration statistics, plus throughput statistics

Along with APIs, Metrics comes with a set of annotations. Table 72 lists a subset of the most commonly used annotations.

Table 72. Main Metrics Annotations

Annotation	Description
`@Counted`	Marks a method, constructor, or class invocation as counted
`@Gauge`	Simplest metric type that just returns a value
`@Metered`	Measures the rate at which a set of events occur
`@Timed`	Aggregates timing durations and provides duration statistics, plus throughput statistics
`@SimplyTimed`	Tracks elapsed time duration and count

Like for Health, when you add the Metrics extension in your `pom.xml` (see Listing 213), then some Quarkus components start automatically gathering metrics. That's the case, for example, for database connection pools, Hibernate ORM, RESTeasy or reactive messaging.

Listing 213. Metrics Extension

```xml
<dependency>
  <groupId>io.quarkus</groupId>
  <artifactId>quarkus-smallrye-metrics</artifactId>
</dependency>
```

9.2.1. Understanding Measures

In the world of Microservices, knowing how servers, applications, containers, etc. are doing is crucial. You want to be able to query for JVM state, CPU utilisation, GC executions, the container memory, the disk or the network. Also you need to know how many times a service is being called, how long this service took to execute, and several other metrics that help to manage services before they become unavailable.

By themselves, metrics are just an up-to-date snapshot of the platform state (see Figure 55). If you want to analyse them and compare these snapshots over time, metrics should be retrieved at constant periods of time and gathered. Gathering, analysing and displaying metrics will help you for capacity planning, or to decide when to scale a service to run with more or fewer resources.

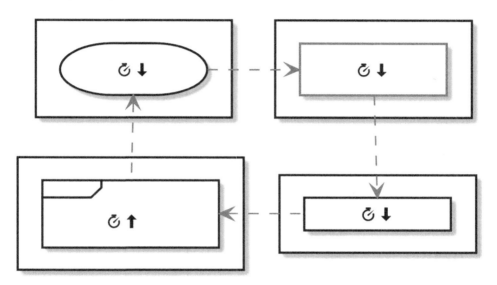

Figure 55. Measuring microservices performances

There is already JMX (*Java Management Extensions*[241]) as a standard to expose metrics, but remote-JMX is not easy to deal with. Eclipse MicroProfile Metrics is specially targeted at exposing remote APIs to collect metrics.

9.2.2. Metrics

Eclipse MicroProfile Metrics handles three types of metrics:

- *Base Metrics*: Metrics that all MicroProfile vendors have to provide.
- *Vendor Metrics*: Vendor specific metrics (optional).
- *Application Metrics*: Application-specific metrics (optional).

Each metric has a different endpoint. The Eclipse MicroProfile Metrics architecture consists of four endpoints:

- /metrics/base: Set of metrics that all MicroProfile-compliant servers have to provide.

- /metrics/vendor: Vendor-specific metrics on top of the basic set of required metrics.

- /metrics/application: Metrics provided by the application at runtime.

- /metrics: Aggregates all the metrics.

Base Metrics

Base metrics is a list of metrics that all vendors need to implement. This scope provides data on, among other things, heap memory, thread count, and available processors. Table 73 gives you a subset of all the required metrics. Each vendor can also implement base metrics that are marked as *optional*[242] by the specification.

Table 73. Subset of Required Base Metrics

Subpackage	Description
Used Heap Memory	Amount of used heap memory in bytes
Committed Heap Memory	Amount of memory committed for the JVM to use
Max Heap Memory	Maximum amount of heap memory that can be used for memory management
Garbage Collection Count	Total number of GC collections that have occurred
Garbage Collection Time	Approximate accumulated GC collection elapsed time
JVM Uptime	Time elapsed since the start of the JVM
Thread Count	Current number of live threads (both daemon and non-daemon threads)
Daemon Thread Count	Current number of live daemon threads
Peak Thread Count	Peak live thread count since the JVM started
Current Loaded Class Count	Number of classes that are currently loaded in the JVM
Total Loaded Class Count	Total number of classes loaded since the JVM has started execution
Total Unloaded Class Count	Total number of classes unloaded since the JVM has started execution
Available Processors	Number of processors available to the JVM

As an example, Listing 214 shows the output in JSON format of what based metrics can look like.

Listing 214. Base Metrics in JSON

```json
{
  "classloader.loadedClasses.count": 6697,
  "classloader.loadedClasses.total": 6697,
  "classloader.unloadedClasses.total": 0,
  "cpu.availableProcessors": 20,
  "cpu.processCpuLoad": 0.00019676867466752725,
  "cpu.systemLoadAverage": 2.38916015625,
  "gc.total;name=G1 Old Generation": 0,
  "gc.total;name=G1 Young Generation": 7,
  "gc.time;name=G1 Old Generation": 0,
  "gc.time;name=G1 Young Generation": 44,
  "jvm.uptime": 95261,
  "memory.committedHeap": 1346371584,
  "memory.maxHeap": 17179869184,
  "memory.usedHeap": 65131392,
  "thread.count": 74,
  "thread.daemon.count": 24,
  "thread.max.count": 74
}
```

Vendor Metrics

Vendor scope exposes vendor-specific information. Each vendor may have different implementations or internal components that can be monitored. On the opposite of base metrics, vendor metrics don't need to be portable between different implementations.

Listing 215 shows metrics that are specific to Quarkus. Different vendors may provide other metrics. Quarkus exposes internal core metrics (such as CPU, memory or memory pool), but each Quarkus extension will have its own built-in metrics exposed. These are described in the guide[243] for each particular extension that supports built-in metrics.

Listing 215. Vendor Metrics in JSON

```
{
  "cpu.processCpuTime": 4913697000,
  "cpu.systemCpuLoad": 0.0,
  "memory.committedNonHeap": 57540608,
  "memory.freePhysicalSize": 1280987136,
  "memory.freeSwapSize": 1283719168,
  "memory.maxNonHeap": -1,
  "memory.usedNonHeap": 54142672,
  "memoryPool.usage.max;name=CodeHeap 'non-nmethods'": 1269248,
  "memoryPool.usage.max;name=CodeHeap 'non-profiled nmethods'": 10081024,
  "memoryPool.usage.max;name=Compressed Class Space": 4532448,
  "memoryPool.usage.max;name=G1 Eden Space": 100663296,
  "memoryPool.usage.max;name=G1 Old Gen": 37993176,
  "memoryPool.usage.max;name=G1 Survivor Space": 12582912,
  "memoryPool.usage.max;name=Metaspace": 38250944,
  "memoryPool.usage;name=CodeHeap 'non-nmethods'": 1269248,
  "memoryPool.usage;name=CodeHeap 'non-profiled nmethods'": 10088832,
  "memoryPool.usage;name=Compressed Class Space": 4532448,
  "memoryPool.usage;name=G1 Eden Space": 0,
  "memoryPool.usage;name=G1 Old Gen": 0,
  "memoryPool.usage;name=G1 Survivor Space": 12582912,
  "memoryPool.usage;name=Metaspace": 38251744
}
```

Application Metrics

Base and vendor metrics give you some statistics about the system, but applications may also want to expose specific information. Application specific metrics need to be provided by the application at runtime. Therefore Eclipse MicroProfile Metrics provides an API supporting *Counters, Gauges, Meters* and *Time*. Let's have a look at these APIs.

Counter

A counter is increased by one each time a request is made. In Listing 216, we want to know how many times the getRandomBook() has been invoked. For that, we just annotate the method with @Counted.

Listing 216. Counting Method Invocations

```
@GET
@Path("/random")
@Counted(name = "countGetRandomBook",
        description = "Counts how many times the createBook method has been invoked")
public Response getRandomBook() {
  Book book = service.findRandomBook();
  return Response.ok(book).build();
}
```

Now, if we target the `/q/metrics/application` endpoint, we will see a counter increasing its value at each call:

```
{
    "BookResource.countGetRandomBook": 274
}
```

Gauge

A gauge is the simplest metric type that just returns a value. Although you could depend on simple counters to describe the state of any given service, with gauge, you can create your own metric. In Listing 217, the method `countAllBooks()` is annotated with `@Gauge` and returns the number of books from a datastore. So, when the value of the gauge is retrieved, the underlying `countAllBooks()` method is called to return the size of the inventory.

Listing 217. Getting Database Rows

```
@GET
@Gauge(name = "gaugeCountAllBooks",
       description = "Instantaneous time of the countAllBooks method",
       unit = "correctness")
public Long countAllBooks() {
    return service.countAllBooks();
}
```

Like the counter, the JSON output of the gauge is just a number and looks like this:

```
{
    "BookResource.gaugeCountAllBooks": 5507847
}
```

Meter

So far we've seen how to count requests, but that doesn't tell us if we are charging the endpoint with requests? Well, we can measure the usage rate with `@Metered`. The meter in Listing 218 measures the rate at which the method `getBook()` is invoked.

Listing 218. Measuring Usage Rate

```
@GET
@Path("/{id}")
@Metered(name = "meteredGetBook",
         description = "Measures throughput of the getBook method")
public Response getBook(@PathParam("id") Long id) {
  Optional<Book> book = service.findBookById(id);
  if (book.isPresent()) {
    return Response.ok(book).build();
  } else {
    return Response.status(NOT_FOUND).build();
  }
}
```

The result is richer than what we've seen so far. The JSON output gives you a detailed report about the invocation rates:

- count: The number of observations.

- meanRate, oneMinRate, fiveMinRate, fifteenMinRate: Mean throughput and one-, five-, and fifteen-minute exponentially-weighted moving average throughput.

```
{
  "BookResource.meteredGetBook": {
    "count": 278,
    "meanRate": 0.657970418481868,
    "oneMinRate": 0.6481905990593267,
    "fiveMinRate": 0.6436398552008425,
    "fifteenMinRate": 0.6214981180132817
  }
}
```

Timed

The @Timed annotation goes further, as it tracks how frequently the method is invoked and how long it takes for each invocation of the method to complete. Listing 219 benchmarks how much time the getRandomBook() method takes. Notice that you can have multiple metrics annotations on a method (here @Counted and @Timed).

Listing 219. Measuring How Long a Method Takes

```
@GET
@Path("/random")
@Counted(name = "countGetRandomBook",
         description = "Counts how many times the createBook method has been invoked")
@Timed(name = "timeGetRandomBook",
       description = "Times how long it takes to invoke the getRandomBook method",
       unit = MetricUnits.MILLISECONDS)
public Response getRandomBook() {
  Book book = service.findRandomBook();
  return Response.ok(book).build();
}
```

This is a timer, therefore a compound metric with all durations expressed in milliseconds. It consists of these values:

- min: The shortest duration it took to perform a request.

- max: The longest duration.

- mean: The mean value of the measured durations.

- stddev: The standard deviation.

- p50, p75, p95, p99, p999: Percentiles of the durations. For example, the value in p95 means that 95% of the measurements were faster than this duration.

```
{
  "BookResource.countGetRandomBook": 274,
  "BookResource.timeGetRandomBook": {
    "p99": 1014.066566,
    "min": 18.458872,
    "max": 1014.28636,
    "mean": 587.7500411272563,
    "p50": 576.884334,
    "p999": 1014.28636,
    "stddev": 285.88828298456485,
    "p95": 994.982235,
    "p98": 1014.066566,
    "p75": 853.727789,
    "count": 274,
    "meanRate": 0.6484994811976507,
    "oneMinRate": 0.6140485447801801,
    "fiveMinRate": 0.6285496448252238,
    "fifteenMinRate": 0.616546519810499
  }
}
```

The count, oneMinRate, fiveMinRate, fifteenMinRate and meanRate are the same as the one described for @Metered.

9.2.3. Metrics Format

So far we've seen metrics representation in JSON. But in fact, data exposed via the REST endpoints under /metrics can be expressed in two different data formats:

- JSON format: Used when the HTTP Accept header matches application/json.

- OpenMetrics format: Used when the HTTP Accept header matches text/plain. If the Accept header is not present, or equally accepts both text/plain and application/json, then this format is returned.

The metrics are exposed either in JSON or *OpenMetrics*[244] format so that they can be processed by additional tools such as Prometheus, and stored for analysis and visualisation.

When using JSON, the REST API will respond to GET requests. You just need to pass the right Accept header:

```
$ curl -X GET -H "Accept: application/json"
http://localhost:8080/q/metrics/application
```

This returns the metrics data:

```
{
  "BookResource.meteredGetBook": {
    "count": 278,
    "meanRate": 0.657970418481868,
    "oneMinRate": 0.6481905990593267,
    "fiveMinRate": 0.6436398552008425,
    "fifteenMinRate": 0.6214981180132817
  }
}
```

But there is also a *shadow tree* that responds to OPTIONS that provides the metadata associated to a metric. The following cURL command changes the GET verb to OPTIONS:

```
$ curl -X OPTIONS -H "Accept: application/json"
http://localhost:8080/q/metrics/application
```

The result is different. The output doesn't give you any measures, but instead, the metadata associated with a metric (here you can see the type of the measure and the description that we've set in our annotation in Listing 218):

```
{
  "BookResource.meteredGetBook": {
    "unit": "per_second",
    "type": "meter",
    "description": "Measures throughput of the getBook method",
    "displayName": "",
    "tags": []
  }
}
```

Data can be exposed in the OpenMetrics text format. If you prefer an OpenMetrics export rather than the JSON format, remove the `-H "Accept: application/json"` argument from the command line:

```
$ curl -X GET http://localhost:8080/q/metrics/application
```

Unlike the JSON format, the OpenMetrics format does not support OPTIONS requests. That's because the metadata is included as part of the OpenMetrics text format.

```
# HELP BookResource_meteredGetBook_total Measures throughput of the getBook method
# TYPE BookResource_meteredGetBook_total counter
BookResource_meteredGetBook_total 278
# TYPE BookResource_meteredGetBook_rate_per_second gauge
BookResource_meteredGetBook_rate_per_second 0.657970418481868
# TYPE BookResource_meteredGetBook_one_min_rate_per_second gauge
BookResource_meteredGetBook_one_min_rate_per_second 0.6481905990593267
# TYPE BookResource_meteredGetBook_five_min_rate_per_second gauge
BookResource_meteredGetBook_five_min_rate_per_second 0.6436398552008425
# TYPE BookResource_meteredGetBook_fifteen_min_rate_per_second gauge
BookResource_meteredGetBook_fifteen_min_rate_per_second 0.6214981180132817
```

9.2.4. Visualising Metrics with Prometheus

Having metrics is one thing but visualising them is another. That's when Prometheus comes into play. *Prometheus*[245] is an open source systems monitoring and alerting toolkit. Out of the box, you get a lot of basic JVM metrics or even metrics of Prometheus itself, which are useful.

Thanks to its admin console, it's really easy to get a graph from our metrics. For example, Figure 56 shows the `one_min_rate_per_second` metric of the `getBook()` method over 30 minutes. As you can see, a tool like Prometheus can store metrics for analysis and visualisation.

Figure 56. Visualising metrics on Prometheus

9.2.5. Configuring SmallRye Metrics

Like most Quarkus extensions, SmallRye Metrics has a few properties[144] that you can find under the `quarkus.smallrye-metrics.` namespace (see Table 74) and configure.

Table 74. Some Quarkus Metrics Configuration Properties

Property	Default
`quarkus.smallrye-metrics.path` The path to the metrics handler	`/metrics`
`quarkus.smallrye-metrics.extensions.enabled` Whether or not metrics published by Quarkus extensions should be enabled	`true`
`quarkus.smallrye-metrics.micrometer.compatibility` Apply Micrometer compatibility mode	`false`
`quarkus.smallrye-metrics.jaxrs.enabled` Whether or not detailed JAX-RS metrics should be enabled. See MicroProfile Metrics: Optional REST metrics.	`false`

9.3. Summary

One of the challenges of distributed architecture is monitoring. You end up with microservices deployed in different locations, they communicate using an unreliable network, the logs are distributed all over and some processes might take longer to accomplish than expected. Without monitoring, you can't easily react to a malfunctioning system.

The first thing to know about a microservice is: "*Is the service running, and how well is it doing?*" To differentiate between these states, the Eclipse MicroProfile Health API has the concept of liveness and readiness. You develop a class that tests the health of your component, service, or runtime, add a simple annotation (`@Liveness` or `@Readiness`) and Quarkus will expose the health of the entire system on a special endpoint.

On the other side, Metrics presents instant or periodical metrics on how services are reacting to consumer requests. Using Eclipse MicroProfile Metrics increases the transparency of your production resulting in higher reliability. Both Health and Metrics are critical for monitoring microservices.

Talking about production, the next chapter is about *Cloud Native*. You will learn how Quarkus can help you to package your microservices into Docker containers and orchestrate them with Kubernetes.

[235] **Health** https://microprofile.io/project/eclipse/microprofile-health

[236] **Health GitHub** https://github.com/eclipse/microprofile-health

[237] **InetAddress** https://docs.oracle.com/en/java/javase/11/docs/api/java.base/java/net/InetAddress.html#isReachable(int)

[238] **Health UI** https://github.com/microprofile-extensions/health-ext/tree/master/health-ui

[239] **Metrics** https://microprofile.io/project/eclipse/microprofile-metrics

[240] **Metrics GitHub** https://github.com/eclipse/microprofile-metrics

[241] **JMX** https://en.wikipedia.org/wiki/Java_Management_Extensions

[242] **Optional and required base metrics** https://download.eclipse.org/microprofile/microprofile-metrics-3.0/microprofile-metrics-spec-3.0.html#required-metrics

[243] **Quarkus Guide** https://quarkus.io/guides

[244] **OpenMetrics** https://openmetrics.io

[245] **Prometheus** https://prometheus.io

Chapter 10. Cloud Native

With Chapter 6, *HTTP Microservices* and Chapter 8, *Event-Driven Microservices*, we now know how to develop microservices. A microservice architecture is made up of several microservices accessing data stores (Chapter 5, *Data, Transactions and ORM*), communicating with each other (Chapter 7, *Communication and Fault Tolerance*) and being monitored (Chapter 9, *Observability*). So far we've executed all these code samples using the development mode (mvn quarkus:dev). That's the easiest way to develop microservices with Quarkus as you can change the code and see your changes live. But when going to production, you need to package your code so it can be executed either on a server, a VM or a container. And that's a different story.

With Quarkus, you can package an application using different formats (a.k.a. *JVM mode* and *Native mode*) depending on your needs. And because Quarkus comes with *Cloud Native* in mind, it has some extensions to easily build a container image and execute it with an orchestrator. The container used in this chapter is *Docker*, and the orchestrator *Kubernetes*.

Make sure your development environment is set up to execute the code in this chapter. You can go to Appendix A to check that you have all the required tools installed, in particular Docker, VirtualBox and Kubernetes. The code in this chapter can be found at https://github.com/agoncal/agoncal-fascicle-quarkus/tree/2.0/cloud

10.1. Packaging Quarkus Applications

Before building a Docker image and executing it with Kubernetes, you need to package the code of your application or microservice. If you come from the Jakarta EE world, you might already be familiar with various packaging formats (all being simple zip files):

- JAR: A *Java ARchive* (.jar extension) is used to package Java code, property files, XML descriptors, etc. that make up a Java application. It requires a JVM to run.

- WAR: A *Web ARchive* (.war extension) packages a web application and requires a Jakarta EE Web Profile application server to run.

- EAR: An *Enterprise ARchive* (.ear extension) packages an enterprise application and requires a full Jakarta EE application server.

Quarkus does not support WAR or EAR packaging, only JARs and native executables: we call that the *JVM mode* and the *Native mode*. The different formats are:

- JVM mode: JAR, Legacy-JAR, Uber-JAR.
- Native mode: Native Executable (OS dependent), Linux Native Executable.

To choose between these packaging formats, it's just a matter of changing the quarkus.package.type configuration property. As usual, you can either change its value in the command line when packaging (mvn package -Dquarkus.package.type=uber-jar) or in the application.properties file:

```
# Possible values are jar, legacy-jar, uber-jar, native and native-sources
quarkus.package.type=jar
```

Let's see all these formats in detail.

10.1.1. JVM Mode

Quarkus is first and foremost a Java framework that lets you package and run classic JAR applications. So in JVM mode, Quarkus generates an executable JAR and you execute it with the `java -jar` command. In this mode, you need a Java runtime environment installed. There are several JAR formats you can choose from depending on your needs. Some are easier to package and distribute, some are better suited for containers, others faster to startup, etc. Let's have a closer look at these JAR formats.

JAR

If you package your code into a JAR format (`mvn package -Dquarkus.package.type=jar`), then Quarkus generates a JAR with a fast startup time. The idea is that, at build time, Quarkus knows all the classes that are used by the application. So it creates an index at build time to know which class is under which JAR. The speedup happens because there is no need to go through each JAR to figure out which contains the class being loaded. The Legacy-JAR (see below) doesn't have this kind of information and therefore needs to iterate over all the jars on the ClassPath using the `URLClassLoader`. As shown in Listing 220, the application and its dependencies are located under the `target/quarkus-app` directory as well as the index (the file `quarkus-application.dat`).

Listing 220. Thin JAR with Dependencies and Index

```
$ mvn package -Dquarkus.package.type=jar
$ tree target/quarkus-app

target/quarkus-app
├── app
│   └── packaging-rest-2.0.0-SNAPSHOT.jar
├── lib
│   ├── boot
│   │   ├── io.quarkus.quarkus-bootstrap-runner-2.5.0.Final.jar
│   │   ├── io.quarkus.quarkus-development-mode-spi-2.5.0.Final.jar
│   │   ├── org.graalvm.sdk.graal-sdk-21.2.0.jar
│   │   ├── org.jboss.logging.jboss-logging-3.4.2.Final.jar
│   │   ...
│   └── main
│       ├── com.fasterxml.jackson.core.jackson-annotations-2.12.5.jar
│       ├── io.netty.netty-common-4.1.68.Final.jar
│       ├── io.quarkus.quarkus-arc-2.5.0.Final.jar
│       ├── io.vertx.vertx-core-4.1.5.jar
│       ├── jakarta.annotation.jakarta.annotation-api-1.3.5.jar
│       ├── org.jboss.resteasy.resteasy-core-spi-4.7.0.Final.jar
│       ├── org.reactivestreams.reactive-streams-1.0.3.jar
│       ...
├── quarkus
│   ├── generated-bytecode.jar
│   ├── quarkus-application.dat
│   └── transformed-bytecode.jar
├── quarkus-app-dependencies.txt
└── quarkus-run.jar
```

If you need to distribute the application, you need the entire content of the target/quarkus-app directory. Then, to execute the application, you need to execute the following command:

```
$ java -jar target/quarkus-app/quarkus-run.jar
```

Legacy-JAR

If you need to stay compatible with older versions of Quarkus, then you can use the Legacy-JAR format. To do so, execute mvn package -Dquarkus.package.type=legacy-jar. Quarkus creates a thin JAR and a separate lib directory with all the dependencies. For example, Listing 221 shows the content of the target directory. At its root, we have the thin JAR (suffixed with -runner.jar extension) and at the same level, a lib directory. This is where Quarkus adds all the dependencies. So depending on the complexity of your application, the lib directory can fluctuate and be larger or smaller.

Listing 221. Thin JAR with Separate Lib Directory

```
$ mvn package -Dquarkus.package.type=legacy-jar
$ tree target

target/
├── lib/
│   ├── com.fasterxml.jackson.core.jackson-annotations-2.12.5.jar
│   ├── io.netty.netty-common-4.1.68.Final.jar
│   ├── io.quarkus.quarkus-arc-2.5.0.Final.jar
│   ├── io.vertx.vertx-core-4.1.5.jar
│   ├── jakarta.annotation.jakarta.annotation-api-1.3.5.jar
│   ├── org.jboss.resteasy.resteasy-core-spi-4.7.0.Final.jar
│   ├── io.quarkus.quarkus-bootstrap-runner-2.5.0.Final.jar
│   ├── io.quarkus.quarkus-core-2.5.0.Final.jar
│   ├── io.quarkus.quarkus-development-mode-spi-2.5.0.Final.jar
│   └── ...
└── packaging-rest-2.0.0-SNAPSHOT-runner.jar
```

If you need to distribute the application, you need the `-runner.jar` file together with `lib` directory. Then, to run the application, it's just a matter of executing:

```
$ java -jar target/packaging-rest-2.0.0-SNAPSHOT-runner.jar
```

JAR and Legacy-JAR are targeted at layered Docker images since it is more frequent to change the code of the application than the libraries it depends on. This way, you build Docker images faster.

 Until Quarkus 1.12, the default JAR format didn't have the class index to speed up boot time. This feature was then introduces experimentally and called *Fast-JAR*. Then, from Quarkus 1.12 onwards, the default JAR format was renamed to *Legacy-JAR* and *Fast-JAR* was renamed to *JAR*. So don't get confused. Today, the default JAR format is the *Fast-JAR*.

Uber-JAR

Uber-JARs are not specific to Quarkus and have existed for quite a long time now. An Uber-JAR is a self-contained executable JAR. Think of it as a JAR containing the classes of the application as well as all the classes of all the other dependencies. This means that the JAR functions as an *all-in-one* distribution of the software, without needing any other Java code. This is why Uber-JARs are often called Fat-JARs (they consist of a single huge JAR file).

The Quarkus Maven plugin supports the generation of Uber-JARs by specifying a `quarkus.package.type=uber-jar` configuration option (either in the `application.properties` file or via the `mvn package -Dquarkus.package.type=uber-jar` command). The original jar will still be present in the `target` directory, but it will be renamed to contain the `.original` suffix:

```
$ mvn package -Dquarkus.package.type=uber-jar
$ tree target

target/
├── packaging-rest-2.0.0-SNAPSHOT-runner.jar
└── packaging-rest-2.0.0-SNAPSHOT.jar.original
```

And if you unzip the Uber -runner.jar, you will see all the Java classes flatten into their package structure as shown in Listing 222.

Listing 222. Exploded Uber-JAR

```
packaging-rest-2.0.0-SNAPSHOT-runner.jar/
├── META-INF
├── application.properties
├── io/
│   ├── quarkus/.../...
│   └── ...
├── javax/
│   ├── inject/
│   ├── transaction/
│   ├── validation/
│   └── ...
├── org/
│   ├── agoncal/fascicle/quarkus/packaging/rest/
│   │   ├── AuthorResource.class
│   │   └── AuthorResource_Bean.class
│   ├── eclipse/
│   └── ...
└── xml-formatter.xsd
```

10.1.2. Native Mode

As we've just seen, in JVM mode, Quarkus lets you package and run executable JARs. But thanks to GraalVM, you can also compile your Java application into machine-specific code (a.k.a. Native mode). Native compilation is a resource-intensive process, so you might not want to use this mode during development. But as you will see, it is an interesting format for production when you want to speed up startup time and improve memory usage. In fact, native executables make Quarkus applications ideal for containers and serverless workloads. It comes in two flavours: native executables that run on your operating system, or native executables that run on Linux (if your operating system is not Linux). This last option is very useful when you deploy your application onto a Linux environment or a container.

Native Executable

To create a native executable that is specific to your operating system, you need GraalVM installed (see Appendix A to make sure GraalVM is correctly set up). Also make sure that your pom.xml has the proper native profile, because creating a native executable can either be done with:

- `mvn package -Dquarkus.package.type=native`: This will create a native executable but will not run the native tests (see Chapter 11 for native tests).

- `mvn package -Pnative`: This is the preferred way as it sets the `quarkus.package.type` to `native` and executes the native tests.

When you execute these commands, the Quarkus Maven plugin will use GraalVM to compile the application. This long process will output logs that look like the following:

```
[packaging-rest-runner:6633]    classlist:  2 946,66 ms,  0,96 GB
[packaging-rest-runner:6633]        (cap):  2 400,01 ms,  0,96 GB
[packaging-rest-runner:6633]     (clinit):    593,34 ms,  3,23 GB
[packaging-rest-runner:6633]    (objects): 10 701,24 ms,  3,23 GB
[packaging-rest-runner:6633]   (features):    432,41 ms,  3,23 GB
[packaging-rest-runner:6633]     analysis: 19 751,35 ms,  3,23 GB
[packaging-rest-runner:6633]     universe:    743,99 ms,  3,23 GB
[packaging-rest-runner:6633]     (inline):  2 137,72 ms,  4,36 GB
[packaging-rest-runner:6633]      compile: 14 151,81 ms,  5,51 GB
[packaging-rest-runner:6633]        image:  2 381,22 ms,  5,51 GB
[packaging-rest-runner:6633]        write:    764,91 ms,  5,51 GB
[packaging-rest-runner:6633]      [total]: 44 611,44 ms,  5,51 GB
```

Then, under the `target` directory, you will have an executable application that contains all the libraries and just what it needs from the JVM to run our application.

```
$ mvn package -Pnative
$ tree target

target/
├── packaging-rest-2.0.0-SNAPSHOT-runner
└── packaging-rest-2.0.0-SNAPSHOT.jar
```

Maven still produces a JAR file, but that's Maven's default behaviour: this JAR file is therefore useless. What you have to look for is the executable: the file that has no extension (here `packaging-rest-2.0.0-SNAPSHOT-runner`).

You can execute it with the following command:

```
$ target/packaging-rest-2.0.0-SNAPSHOT-runner
```

As you can see, we don't need a Java runtime environment to execute the file (we don't need a `java -jar` command). We just run it as any other binary executable file.

The produced executable is specific to your operating system. For example, if you are running on macOS, this executable will only work on macOS, not on Linux nor Windows. This is ok for testing, but for production, you might want to produce a Linux executable to be executed on a Linux box or on a container. Quarkus can help you in generating such executables.

Linux Native Executable

To create an executable that will run on a Linux machine or in a container, you need to set another Quarkus variable when using the `native` profile. So the command would be: `mvn package -Pnative -Dquarkus.native.container-build=true`.

The build process is now slightly different from building a native executable for your operating system as seen above. To produce a 64-bit Linux executable, the build itself needs to run in a Docker container. This means that, by default, the native executable will be generated using the `quay.io/quarkus/ubi-quarkus-native-image:21.3.0-java11` Docker image. So you don't need to have GraalVM installed locally, the Docker image has everything it needs. But you need Docker installed (to download and execute the Docker image).

> If you want to build a native executable with a different Docker image (for instance to use a different GraalVM version), use the `-Dquarkus.native.builder-image=<image name>` property. The list of the available Docker images[246] can be found on quay.io. Be aware that a given Quarkus version might not be compatible with all the images available.

Like before, the 64-bit Linux executable is generated under the `target` directory:

```
$ mvn package -Pnative -Dquarkus.native.container-build=true
$ tree target

target/
├── packaging-rest-2.0.0-SNAPSHOT-runner
└── packaging-rest-2.0.0-SNAPSHOT.jar
```

But, depending on your operating system, it may no longer be runnable. For example, if you are running on macOS and execute this file, you will get the following error:

```
$ target/packaging-rest-2.0.0-SNAPSHOT-runner

Failed to execute process 'target/packaging-rest-2.0.0-SNAPSHOT-runner'.
Reason: Exec format error
The file 'target/packaging-rest-2.0.0-SNAPSHOT-runner' is marked as an executable but
could not be run by the operating system.
```

10.1.3. Performances

Each format has its pros and cons. So let's recap how we build these different executables, how we execute them, but more importantly, which one is the fastest to boot and which one to choose.

Build and Execute

Let's first quickly recap the commands that we've used. Table 75 summarises the Maven commands used to build each executable, while Table 76 shows the command to run the generated executable.

Table 75. Command to Build

Packaging Format	Command
JAR	`mvn package -Dquarkus.package.type=jar`
Legacy-JAR	`mvn package -Dquarkus.package.type=legacy-jar`
Uber-JAR	`mvn package -Dquarkus.package.type=uber-jar`
Native	`mvn package -Pnative`
Linux Native	`mvn package -Pnative -Dquarkus.native.container-build=true`

Table 76. Command to Execute

Packaging Format	Command
JAR	`java -jar target/quarkus-app/quarkus-run.jar`
Legacy-JAR	`java -jar target/quarkus-app/quarkus-run.jar`
Uber-JAR	`java -jar target/<name>-runner.jar`
Native	`target/<name>-runner`
Linux Native	`target/<name>-runner`

Executable Size

One easy metric to get is the size of the executable: you package your application picking up a format, and you get the size in megabytes. Of course, the more complex your application is, the more dependencies it needs and the larger the executable will be. So in order to compare, Table 77 shows the size of the executable for two different types of application:

• A REST application:A simple JSON REST endpoint.

• A complex application: A JSON REST endpoint with validation, Hibernate ORM with Panache, transactions, injection and an H2 database.

Table 77. Executable Size

Packaging Format	REST App	Complex App
JAR (`target/quarkus-app`)	11 Mb	31 Mb
Legacy-JAR (`target/quarkus-app`)	11 Mb	31 Mb
Uber-JAR	10 Mb	30 Mb
Native	27 Mb	69 Mb
Linux Native	27 Mb	69 Mb

On the JVM mode, most JAR formats have the same size (around 10 Mb for a simple REST application, 30 Mb for a complex one). The same happens for Native mode: a Linux executable is more or less the same size as the executable for your operating system. The main difference is the size between JVM and Native modes. The native executables are bigger because they embed the part of the Java runtime environment needed to execute the application. But in all scenarios, the more dependencies an application has (i.e. the complex application) the bigger the executable is.

Time to First Request

Another useful measure to consider is the time to serve the first request. It is more accurate than just measuring the startup time as some frameworks can use aggressive lazy initialisation techniques. Therefore, it is important to measure the time it takes to start the framework plus the time to serve the first request. This is the most accurate way to reflect how long an application actually replies. Table 78 shows, for each executable format, the time, in milliseconds, it took to serve the first request.

Table 78. Time to First Request

Packaging Format	REST App	Complex App
JAR	160 ms	160 ms
Legacy-JAR	165 ms	170 ms
Uber-JAR	185 ms	190 ms
Native	10 ms	25 ms

The startup time includes the time that Quarkus needs to start but also the time to serve the first request. The numbers in Table 78 were made on macOS with a JVM 11 with no optimisation. To get these numbers I followed a recipe described on the Quarkus guide[247]:

- Loop a GET curl command on a REST endpoint;
- Startup the application;
- Start counting when Quarkus starts, finish counting when the first request is served;
- Repeat 10 times and calculate the average time.

Depending on your hardware and JVM version you will get different results. What's important here is to be able to compare startup times depending on the packaging format.

Pros and Cons

So, which format to use? Well, it depends if you want a JVM or Native mode and if you target deploying the executable on a container or not. Table 79 gives you some pros and cons on each format so you can make up your mind.

Table 79. Pros and Cons

Packaging Format	Pros	Cons
JAR	• Fast to start • Dependencies in `/lib` so we reuse the Docker layers when rebuilding an image • Quarkus comes with a Dockerfile for this format	• Not easy to distribute as there are several files and directories
Legacy-JAR	• Quick to build • Dependencies in `/lib` so we reuse the Docker layers when rebuilding an image • Quarkus comes with a Dockerfile for this format	• Not easy to distribute as there are several files and directories • Slightly slower to start than the default JAR due to classpath scanning
Uber-JAR	• Easy to distribute as there is only one single JAR	• Impossible to reuse libraries in Docker layers, takes time to rebuild an image • Quarkus does not come with a Dockerfile for this format (But Jib can handle this)
Native	• Really fast startup • Low memory consumption	• Takes time to build • Only for local operating system • Quarkus does not come with a Dockerfile for this format
Linux Native	• Really fast startup • Portable across Linux OS • Quarkus comes with a Dockerfile for this format	• Takes time to build

10.1.4. Configuring Packaging

The packaging type is not the only thing that can be configured in Quarkus. Table 80 shows a subset of properties dedicated to packaging. You will find these properties[144] under the `quarkus.package.` namespace.

Table 80. Some Quarkus Packaging Configuration Properties

Property	Default
`quarkus.package.type` The requested output type (`jar`, `legacy-jar`, `uber-jar`, `native` and `native-sources`).	`jar`
`quarkus.package.output-directory` The output folder in which to place the output, this is resolved relative to the build systems target directory.	
`quarkus.package.output-name` The name of the final artifact.	
`quarkus.package.user-configured-ignored-entries` Files that should not be copied to the output artifact.	
`quarkus.package.runner-suffix` The suffix that is applied to the runner jar and native images.	`-runner`
`quarkus.package.main-class` The entry point of the application.	

10.2. Docker

Now that you have chosen the way you want to package your application, you might want to distribute it as a container image. Quarkus comes with several artifacts to ease building container images. First of all, when generating a Quarkus application, you get several Dockerfiles to help you build your Docker image: either manually or with a Docker extension. But if you don't want to maintain Dockerfiles, Quarkus lets you build these images without a Docker environment, thanks to its Jib extensions. Let's take a look at these different artifacts.

10.2.1. Dockerfiles

When bootstrapping a Quarkus application (either with the Web Interface[248], IDE plugin or Maven plugin), you get several Dockerfiles into the `src/main/docker` folder. Each of these files targets a specific packaging format (notice that there is no generated Dockerfile for the Uber-JAR packaging):

- JAR: `Dockerfile.jvm`
- Legacy-JAR: `Dockerfile.legacy-jar`
- Linux Native Executable: `Dockerfile.native`
- Distroless container: `Dockerfile.native-distroless`

A Dockerfile is a plain text file that contains a set of commands that assemble an image so that it can be executed by Docker. Each Dockerfile matches with a specific format (JAR, Legacy-JAR, Native) and has a different set of instructions. You can use them as they are or use them as templates and change their content to suit your needs. Table 81 shows a subset of Dockerfile commands that are used in the samples below.

Table 81. Some Docker Commands

Command	Description
ADD	Defines files to copy from the Host file system onto the container
CMD	Command that will run when the container starts
COPY	Copies files or directories from a source to a destination
ENTRYPOINT	Sets the default application used every time a container is created from the image
ENV	Sets/modifies the environment variables within containers created from the image
EXPOSE	Defines which container ports to expose
FROM	Selects the base image to build the new image on top of
USER	Defines the default user all commands will be run as within any container created from your image
RUN	Executes any commands in a new layer on top of the current image and commits the result
WORKDIR	Defines the default working directory for the command defined in the ENTRYPOINT or CMD instructions

JVM Mode

When we use the Quarkus Maven plugin to bootstrap a new application, two Dockerfiles are created for the JVM mode: one for JAR (Dockerfile.jvm) and another one for Legacy-JAR (Dockerfile.legacy-jar). In both scenarios, these Dockerfiles have the same base image in common. UBI, or *Red Hat Universal Base Image*[249], is a subset of the *Red Hat Enterprise Linux* operating system, stripped down to the bare essentials, and is perfect for containers. Meaning that these Dockerfiles use a Linux environment to run your application.

```
FROM registry.access.redhat.com/ubi8/ubi-minimal:8.4
```

In JVM mode, we need a Java runtime environment to execute the application. But because UBI is such a light Linux operating system, it does not contain a JVM. Therefore, both Dockerfile.jvm and Dockerfile.legacy-jar need to install a JVM for a specific version of the JVM:

```
ARG JAVA_PACKAGE=java-11-openjdk-headless

RUN microdnf install curl ca-certificates ${JAVA_PACKAGE} \
    && microdnf update \
    && microdnf clean all \
    && mkdir /deployments \
    && chown 1001 /deployments \
    && chmod "g+rwX" /deployments \
    && chown 1001:root /deployments \
    && curl https://repo1.maven.org/maven2/io/fabric8/run-java-
sh/${RUN_JAVA_VERSION}/run-java-sh-${RUN_JAVA_VERSION}-sh.sh -o /deployments/run-
java.sh \
    && chown 1001 /deployments/run-java.sh \
    && chmod 540 /deployments/run-java.sh \
    && echo "securerandom.source=file:/dev/urandom" >>
/etc/alternatives/jre/conf/security/java.security

ENV JAVA_OPTIONS="-Dquarkus.http.host=0.0.0.0
-Djava.util.logging.manager=org.jboss.logmanager.LogManager"
```

The difference between both Dockerfiles is in the content that they copy from the target folder to get the application up and running. For example, in the Dockerfile.legacy-jar file we copy the content of the target/quarkus-app directory where the entire application, dependencies and index are located:

```
COPY --chown=1001 target/quarkus-app/lib/ /deployments/lib/
COPY --chown=1001 target/quarkus-app/*.jar /deployments/
COPY --chown=1001 target/quarkus-app/app/ /deployments/app/
COPY --chown=1001 target/quarkus-app/quarkus/ /deployments/quarkus/
```

As for the Legacy-JAR (the Dockerfile.legacy file), we copy the thin JAR file (the one with the -runner.jar extension) as well as the /lib directory (the directory containing all the JARs the application depends on):

```
COPY target/lib/* /deployments/lib/
COPY target/*-runner.jar /deployments/app.jar
```

Then, both Dockerfile.jvm and Dockerfile.legacy-jar expose the listening port 8080 and execute the application with a shell script:

```
EXPOSE 8080
USER 1001

ENTRYPOINT [ "/deployments/run-java.sh" ]
```

Linux Native Executable

For the Linux native executable, the `Dockerfile.native` is totally different. First of all, since there is no need to use a Java layer to start the application, the image doesn't need to install a Java runtime environment. The native executable just runs on Linux (on the Red Hat Universal Base Image), no need to have a JVM runtime. So it's just a matter of copying the executable (the `*-runner` file) from the `target` folder and executing it (the `CMD` command):

Listing 223. Dockerfile for the Native Image

```
FROM registry.access.redhat.com/ubi8/ubi-minimal:8.4
WORKDIR /work/
RUN chown 1001 /work \
    && chmod "g+rwX" /work \
    && chown 1001:root /work
COPY --chown=1001:root target/*-runner /work/application

EXPOSE 8080
USER 1001

CMD ["./application", "-Dquarkus.http.host=0.0.0.0"]
```

10.2.2. Building Docker Images

Now that you have packaged your application into the right executable (JAR, Legacy-JAR or Native) and you understand the structure of its Docker file (`Dockerfile.jvm`, `Dockerfile.legacy-jar`, `Dockerfile.native`), you can easily build its Docker image. In fact, if you are confident with Docker commands, you can manually build a Docker image with just the Dockerfile. If instead you don't want to run Docker commands but want to let your build system automatically create the image, Quarkus comes with a Docker extension for Maven (and Gradle). And if you don't want to maintain Dockerfiles, just get rid of them, and rely on the Quarkus Jib extension: a simple Maven command and Jib will automatically create a Docker image without any Dockerfile.

Building Manually with Docker

If you are used to Docker and prefer to type Docker commands, then you can use your expertise to build Docker images. After you generate the right package for your application, depending on the image you want to build, you just execute a `docker image build` command on the appropriate Dockerfile (`Dockerfile.jvm`, `Dockerfile.legacy-jar` or `Dockerfile.native`). Table 82 shows the Docker commands used to build the images. As you can see, all the commands look the same, except for the Dockerfile name.

Table 82. Command to Build the Docker Image

Packaging Format	Command
JAR	`docker image build -f src/main/docker/Dockerfile.jvm -t agoncal/quarkus-jar .`
Legacy-JAR	`docker image build -f src/main/docker/Dockerfile.legacy-jar -t agoncal/quarkus-legacy-jar .`

Packaging Format	Command
Linux Native	`docker image build -f src/main/docker/Dockerfile.native -t agoncal/quarkus-native .`

When you execute one of these commands, you will see output traces similar to the following one:

Listing 224. Output When Manually Building Docker Image

```
Sending build context to Docker daemon

[1/6] FROM registry.access.redhat.com/ubi8/ubi-minimal:8.4
[2/6] RUN microdnf install curl ca-certificates java-11-openjdk-headless  ...
[3/6] COPY --chown=1001 target/quarkus-app/lib/ /deployments/lib/
[4/6] COPY --chown=1001 target/quarkus-app/*.jar /deployments/
[5/6] COPY --chown=1001 target/quarkus-app/app/ /deployments/app/
[6/6] COPY --chown=1001 target/quarkus-app/quarkus/ /deployments/quarkus/

=> writing image sha256:eac666ddcd574730ce807b
=> naming to docker.io/agoncal/quarkus-jar
```

That's it. The Docker image is successfully built and is ready to be run. If you change your Java code, you need to compile your code, package it (`mvn package`) and run the same `docker image build` command again. To avoid typing all the above commands, Quarkus comes with a Docker extension that allows automating this build process.

 In this chapter, the Docker images are all named using the `agoncal` prefix. This prefix is important because it needs to match the username account on the Docker Hub (so images can be pushed). So you should change the `agoncal` prefix to your username. If you need more information on Docker Hub, such as logging into the remote registry or pushing images, check Appendix A.

Building with the Docker Extension

If you want to avoid typing commands to build Docker images and want to have this process integrated in your build system, then you should use the Docker extension. To have Quarkus generate Docker images based on the Dockerfiles located under `src/main/docker`, just add the Maven dependency in Listing 225 to the `pom.xml`.

Listing 225. Docker Extension

```
<dependency>
    <groupId>io.quarkus</groupId>
    <artifactId>quarkus-container-image-docker</artifactId>
</dependency>
```

Once you've added the Docker extension, you execute a Maven command setting the configuration property `quarkus.container-image.build` to `true` (or setting it in the `application.properties` file). Also remember that you can add other properties, such as the build format, if you want to build a

Docker image for a specific packaging format (JAR, Legacy-JAR or Linux Native). Here are some Maven commands you could execute to package the application and build the Docker image in one go:

```
$ mvn package -Dquarkus.container-image.build=true # default to jar

$ mvn package -Dquarkus.container-image.build=true -Dquarkus.package.type=jar
$ mvn package -Dquarkus.container-image.build=true -Dquarkus.package.type=legacy-jar
$ mvn package -Dquarkus.container-image.build=true -Dquarkus.package.type=native
-Dquarkus.native.container-build=true
```

These Maven commands will produce an output similar to Listing 226. In fact, if you look carefully at the outputs in Listing 224 and Listing 226, you realise that they are similar. The Docker extension just executes a `docker image build` command on the appropriate Dockerfile.

Listing 226. Output When Building Docker Image with Docker Extension

```
[INFO] --- quarkus-maven-plugin:build @ container-docker ---

[INFO] Building docker image for jar.
[INFO] Executing the following command to build docker image: 'docker build -f
Dockerfile.jvm -t agoncal/myapp:1.0'

[INFO] #1 load build definition from Dockerfile.jvm
[INFO] #2 load .dockerignore
[INFO] #3 load metadata for registry.access.redhat.com/ubi8/ubi-minimal:8.4
[INFO] #4 [1/6] FROM registry.access.redhat.com/ubi8/ubi-minimal:8.4
[INFO] #5 [2/6] RUN microdnf install curl ca-certificates java-11-openjdk-headless ...
[INFO] #6 load build context
[INFO] #7 [3/6] COPY --chown=1001 target/quarkus-app/lib/ /deployments/lib/
[INFO] #8 [4/6] COPY --chown=1001 target/quarkus-app/*.jar /deployments/
[INFO] #9 [5/6] COPY --chown=1001 target/quarkus-app/app/ /deployments/app/
[INFO] #10 [6/6] COPY --chown=1001 target/quarkus-app/quarkus/ /deployments/quarkus/
[INFO] #11 writing image sha256:d6d6d03a4ac4396b114197dc
[INFO] #11 naming to docker.io/agoncal/myapp:1.0 done
[INFO] #11 DONE 0.2s

[INFO] Built container image agoncal/myapp:1.0

[INFO] --------------------
[INFO] BUILD SUCCESS
[INFO] --------------------
```

For this extension to work, it needs to have Docker installed. If your build environment does not have Docker or if you don't want to maintain any Dockerfiles, then you can use the Jib extension.

Building with the Jib Extension

Jib[250] is an open source Java tool from Google in order to create Docker images in an easy and fast way. No need to create a Dockerfile, no need to install a Docker daemon, Jib just runs out-of-the-box. As usual, what you need is to use the appropriate extension. To build Docker images using Jib, just add the Jib extension dependency shown in Listing 227 to the pom.xml.

Listing 227. Jib Extension

```xml
<dependency>
  <groupId>io.quarkus</groupId>
  <artifactId>quarkus-container-image-jib</artifactId>
</dependency>
```

You use the Jib extension the same way you use the Docker extension: you pass the same required properties to an mvn package command:

```
$ mvn package -Dquarkus.container-image.build=true
```

What differs is the output. As you can see in Listing 228, this time there is no docker image build command, nor any specific Dockerfile.

Listing 228. Output When Building Docker Image with Jib Extension

```
[INFO] --- quarkus-maven-plugin:build @ container-jib ---

[INFO] Starting container image build
[INFO] Base image 'fabric8/java-alpine-openjdk11-jre'
[INFO] The base image requires auth. Trying again for fabric8/java-alpine-openjdk11-
jre...
[INFO] Using base image with digest: sha256:b459cc59d6c7ddc9fd5
[INFO] Container entrypoint set to [java,
-Djava.util.logging.manager=org.jboss.logmanager.LogManager, -jar, quarkus-run.jar]

[INFO] Created container image agoncal/myapp:1.0

[INFO] --------------------
[INFO] BUILD SUCCESS
[INFO] --------------------
```

By default, the Jib extension uses default values, like the FROM or the ENTRYPOINT. As you can see in Listing 228, by default the base image is fabric8/java-alpine-openjdk11-jre. If you want to change it, Quarkus has the property quarkus.jib.base-jvm-image you can use. For example, below we build a Docker image using OpenJDK 8 instead of 11.

```
$ mvn package -Dquarkus.container-image.build -Dquarkus.jib.base-jvm
-image=fabric8/java-alpine-openjdk8-jre
```

10.2.3. Running Docker Images

So far we've built Docker images (either manually with a Dockerfile, with the Docker extension or with the Jib extension). Now it's time to execute them. Once the images are created and registered in the Docker daemon, you can check that they are available in your local Docker repository by executing the `docker image ls` command.

```
$ docker image ls | grep agoncal/

REPOSITORY                      TAG      IMAGE ID       SIZE
agoncal/quarkus-jar             latest   32a3ad8393bd   502MB
agoncal/quarkus-legacy-jar      latest   568a78cd8a29   502MB
agoncal/quarkus-native          latest   0b0fa9ec5b7d   133MB
```

What's interesting to notice in this output is the size of the images. JVM mode (JAR and Legacy-JAR) need to install a JVM to the UBI, so that's why they are way larger than the image using native mode.

Now is the time to execute the image. Table 83 shows the Docker command needed to run the image depending on the image you've built. Despite the Docker image name, they all look the same and use the same options:

- The `-i` flag connects the container to the terminal.
- `--rm` removes the container's file system after the container exits.
- `-p 8082:8080` exposes the port 8082 externally, thus mapping to port 8080 on the host machine (which is the default port Quarkus is listening to).

Table 83. Command to Run the Docker Image

Packaging Format	Command
JAR	`docker container run -i --rm -p 8080:8080 agoncal/quarkus-jar`
Legacy-JAR	`docker container run -i --rm -p 8081:8080 agoncal/quarkus-legacy-jar`
Linux Native	`docker container run -i --rm -p 8082:8080 agoncal/quarkus-native`

Once the container is up and running, you can access your application as you would do if you were not using containers (e.g. cURL a specific REST endpoint at a specific URL). If you want to check which container is running, you can execute a `docker container ls` command:

```
$ docker container ls

CONTAINER ID   IMAGE                        COMMAND               PORTS
98619dcad837   agoncal/quarkus-jar          "/deployments/run-ja…"   8080->8080/tcp
be54f30af529   agoncal/quarkus-legacy-jar   "/deployments/run-ja…"   8081->8080/tcp
5a964dd7e693   agoncal/quarkus-native       "./application -Dqua…"   8082->8080/tcp
```

10.2.4. Pushing Docker Images

Now that we know that our images run as expected, let's make them available to others by pushing them to a remote Docker registry (Docker Hub being the default). *Docker Hub*[251] is a service provided by Docker for finding and sharing container images.

For publishing images on Docker Hub you need to signup, create a free account and login locally (using the `docker login` command). Your image's name also need to be the same as your account. So in the following command you must change `agoncal` with your Docker Hub account. For pushing manually a Docker image to Docker Hub, just use the `docker image push` command:

```
$ docker image push agoncal/quarkus-legacy-jar

The push refers to repository [docker.io/agoncal/quarkus-legacy-jar]
e62721cac2ee: Pushed
latest: digest: sha256:92ae511aeef73f33b0f1e65ef3 size: 1161
```

This command will push each layer of the image to the remote registry. As shown in Figure 57, you can then log on to Docker Hub and check your images.

Figure 57. Docker images available on Docker Hub

The `docker image push` command allows you to manually push a Docker image. But what if we want to integrate this phase to our building system? Well, if you use the Docker or Jib extension, this can be done automatically. It is just a matter of setting the `quarkus.container-image.push` property to `true` (either in the `application.properties` file or on the Maven command). Listing 229 shows the output of a single Maven command that packages the code into a JAR, builds the Docker image based on the Dockerfile `Dockerfile.jvm` and pushes it to a remote registry.

Listing 229. Output When Building and Pushing a Docker Image

```
$ mvn package -Dquarkus.package.type=jar -Dquarkus.container-image.build=true
-Dquarkus.container-image.push=true

[INFO] --- quarkus-maven-plugin:build @ container-docker ---

[INFO] Building docker image for jar.
[INFO] Executing the following command to build docker image: 'docker build -f
Dockerfile.jvm -t agoncal/myapp:1.0'

[INFO] #1 load build definition from Dockerfile.jvm
[INFO] #2 load .dockerignore
[INFO] #3 load metadata for registry.access.redhat.com/ubi8/ubi-minimal:8.4
[INFO] #4 [1/6] FROM registry.access.redhat.com/ubi8/ubi-minimal:8.4
[INFO] #5 [2/6] RUN microdnf install curl ca-certificates java-11-openjdk-headless ...
[INFO] #6 load build context
[INFO] #7 [3/6] COPY --chown=1001 target/quarkus-app/lib/ /deployments/lib/
[INFO] #8 [4/6] COPY --chown=1001 target/quarkus-app/*.jar /deployments/
[INFO] #9 [5/6] COPY --chown=1001 target/quarkus-app/app/ /deployments/app/
[INFO] #10 [6/6] COPY --chown=1001 target/quarkus-app/quarkus/ /deployments/quarkus/
[INFO] #11 writing image sha256:d6d6d03a4ac4396b114197dc
[INFO] #11 naming to docker.io/agoncal/myapp:1.0 done
[INFO] #11 DONE 0.2s

[INFO] Built container image agoncal/myapp:1.0

[INFO] No container image registry was set, so 'docker.io' will be used
[INFO] The push refers to repository [docker.io/agoncal/myapp]
[INFO] 2262a6a8a0e9: Preparing
[INFO] b8d0e430b1ad: Preparing
[INFO] d60a60fdbcec: Preparing
[INFO] d60418694048: Preparing
[INFO] 2262a6a8a0e9: Pushed
[INFO] 1.0: digest: sha256:4668ccb5fb21f81d2b09e3 size: 1371
[INFO] Successfully pushed docker image agoncal/myapp:1.0

[INFO] --------------------
[INFO] BUILD SUCCESS
[INFO] --------------------
```

Now that the Docker images are available on a public repository, they can be pulled by anyone. This also includes orchestrators such as Kubernetes.

10.2.5. Configuring Containers

Table 84 shows a subset of properties that can be used to customise the container image build process. Common properties are defined under the `quarkus.container-image.` namespace, and depending on the container implementation (Docker or Jib), you have specific properties under the `quarkus.docker.` and `quarkus.jib.` namespaces.

Table 84. Some Quarkus Container Configuration Properties

Property	Default
quarkus.native.container-build If the build should be done using a container runtime. If this is set, Docker will be used by default.	false
quarkus.native.container-runtime The container runtime (e.g. docker) that is used to do an image based build.	
quarkus.native.graalvm-home The location of the Graal distribution	${GRAALVM_HOME:}
quarkus.native.java-home The location of the JDK	${java.home}
quarkus.native.debug.enabled If debug is enabled and debug symbols are generated. The symbols will be generated in a separate .debug file.	false
quarkus.container-image.group The group the container image will be part of.	${user.name}
quarkus.container-image.name The name of the container image.	${quarkus.application.name: unset}
quarkus.container-image.tag The tag of the container image.	${quarkus.application.versi on:latest}
quarkus.container-image.build Whether or not an image build will be performed.	false
quarkus.container-image.push Whether or not an image push will be performed.	false
quarkus.docker.dockerfile-jvm-path Path to the JVM Dockerfile.	src/main/docker/Dockerfile. jvm
quarkus.docker.dockerfile-native-path Path to the native Dockerfile.	src/main/docker/Dockerfile. native
quarkus.jib.base-jvm-image The base image to be used when a container image is being produced for the jar build.	fabric8/java-alpine-openjdk11-jre
quarkus.jib.base-native-image The base image to be used when a container image is being produced for the native build.	registry.access.redhat.com/ ubi8/ubi-minimal

10.3. Kubernetes

Now that we have verified how simple it is to run Quarkus applications in a container, we will deploy our application into a Kubernetes-native environment. By adding these dependencies, we enable the generation of Kubernetes manifests.

Kubernetes[252] (a.k.a. K8s) is an orchestrator for containerised applications. It takes its name from a Greek word meaning *helmsman*, or *captain*: if Docker packages applications inside containers, Kubernetes is the captain sailing those containers. Kubernetes can schedule, scale, heal, update, start or stop several containers.

10.3.1. Kubernetes Manifest Files

Deploying a Docker image to a Kubernetes cluster implies several steps. You need to create a *Deployment*, associate it several *Services*, several *Pods* (smallest computing unit deployable in Kubernetes), etc (see Figure 58). All these steps can be done separately using the command line interface kubectl (see Appendix A if you want to know more about creating a deployment on the command line). But this can be cumbersome and error prone. The other way to deploy on Kubernetes is using manifest files.

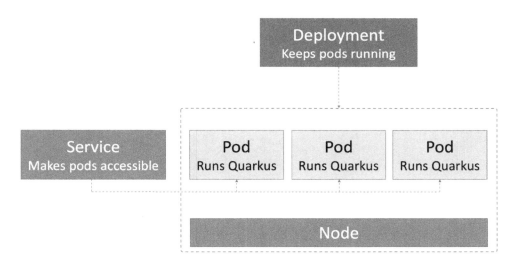

Figure 58. Kubernetes deployment, service and pods

A Kubernetes manifest file describes the desired state of the cluster, not how we want to achieve this state, that is Kubernetes' role. For example, the desired state could be "*I want three instances of Quarkus, so that's 3 pods*". Kubernetes installs the desired state in the actual state. If something goes wrong, and the actual state differs from the desired state (e.g. one instance of Quarkus fails), Kubernetes will do everything to get back the desired state in the actual state. It is very common to define manifests in the form of YAML files and send them to the Kubernetes via commands such as kubectl apply -f vintageStore.yaml or kubectl delete -f vintageStore.yaml. Let's see how to write manifest files to deploy one of the Docker images we've previously built.

Let's start with defining a Deployment, then define a Services and link the service to the Deployment. First, we need to define a deployment as shown in Listing 230. Remember that Kubernetes manages container-based resources. In the case of a *Deployment*, we are creating a set of resources to be managed (in our case, the agoncal/quarkus-jar Docker image). The manifest file starts with the apiVersion. Next, we specify some metadata and give a name to the *Deployment*.

Finally, we get into the spec object where we actually describe the state of the deployment that we expect. We start, in this case, by saying that whatever *Pods* we deploy, we want to have 1 replica (one instance). And then we select (by the selector object) the *Pods* affected by this *Deployment*, the ones that match certain labels (matchLabels) which are defined in the Service definition Listing 231.

Listing 230. Deployment Definition

```
apiVersion: apps/v1
kind: Deployment
metadata:
  labels:
    app.kubernetes.io/name: quarkus-jar
    app.kubernetes.io/version: latest
  name: quarkus-jar
spec:
  replicas: 1
  selector:
    matchLabels:
      app.kubernetes.io/name: quarkus-jar
      app.kubernetes.io/version: latest
  template:
    metadata:
      labels:
        app.kubernetes.io/name: quarkus-jar
        app.kubernetes.io/version: latest
    spec:
      containers:
        - env:
            - name: KUBERNETES_NAMESPACE
              valueFrom:
                fieldRef:
                  fieldPath: metadata.namespace
          image: agoncal/quarkus-jar:latest
          imagePullPolicy: IfNotPresent
          name: quarkus-jar
```

An important thing to note about the *Deployment* is that it uses agoncal/quarkus-jar:latest as the container image of the *Pod*. In Listing 231, we're specifying that we want to create a *Service* (a *Service* is an abstraction which defines a logical set of *Pods*). The spec property includes any containers, network port, or other pieces that Kubernetes needs to know about.

Listing 231. Service Definition

```
apiVersion: v1
kind: Service
metadata:
  labels:
    app.kubernetes.io/name: quarkus-jar
    app.kubernetes.io/version: latest
  name: quarkus-jar
spec:
  ports:
    - name: http
      nodePort: 31826
      port: 80
      targetPort: 8080
  selector:
    app.kubernetes.io/name: quarkus-jar
    app.kubernetes.io/version: latest
  type: NodePort
```

These manifest files can be applied to the cluster using `kubectl`:

```
$ kubectl apply -f vintageStore.yaml
```

Table 85 lists a few objects that you can find in the Kubernetes manifest file.

Table 85. Some Kubernetes Objects

Keyword	Description
apiVersion	Which version of the Kubernetes API you're using to create this object
kind	What kind of object you want to create (Deployment, Service, Pod, etc.)
metadata	Data that helps uniquely identify the object, including a name string, UID, and optional namespace
spec	What state you desire for the object
replicas	Number of pods to create during a deployment
selector	Optional object that tells the Kubernetes deployment controller to only target pods that match the specified labels
ports	Internal and external listening ports
image	Docker image name

10.3.2. Building Kubernetes Manifest Files

Now that we have Docker images deployed on a remote registry and we know how a Kubernetes manifest file works, let's deploy the Docker images we've built to a Kubernetes cluster. As you've just seen, writing a Kubernetes YAML file can be complex and error prone. So why not let Quarkus generate one for us? Like the Jib extension that can create a Docker image, Quarkus comes with several extensions that generate a YAML file based on our application and its configuration (using *Dekorate*[253]). But there is an extra level of complexity: Kubernetes manifest files are not standard. So, depending on the Kubernetes platform you are targeting, the YAML file can be different. For example, a YAML file for OpenShift is not exactly the same as the one for Minikube. That's why Quarkus comes with several Kubernetes extensions targeting specific platforms. Let's have a look at two of them: vanilla Kubernetes and Minikube.

Building with the Kubernetes Extension

To have Quarkus generate Kubernetes deployment descriptors you need the appropriate extension (see Listing 232).

Listing 232. Kubernetes Extension

```
<dependency>
  <groupId>io.quarkus</groupId>
  <artifactId>quarkus-kubernetes</artifactId>
</dependency>
```

Thanks to this extension, a simple `mvn package` command will generate two Kubernetes manifest files (JSON or YAML format) under the `target` directory:

```
target/
└── kubernetes/
    ├── kubernetes.json
    └── kubernetes.yml
```

These manifest files are generated for bare Kubernetes platforms and you usually have to customise them. If you are developing on your laptop, you might have installed Minikube. And if you try to deploy these generated manifest files to a Minikube cluster, you will have a few glitches and will have to slightly change the content of the files. That's why Quarkus comes with a Minikube extension: it allows you to seamlessly deploy onto Minikube without any changes.

Building with the Minikube Extension

Minikube[254] allows you to run Kubernetes locally on a developer's machine. It focuses on making Kubernetes easy to learn and develop by easily setting up and managing a local Kubernetes cluster. Minikube is a single node Kubernetes cluster that runs on a hypervisor on your local machine. To have Quarkus generate Minikube manifest files you need the appropriate extension (see Listing 233).

Listing 233. Minikube Extension

```
<dependency>
  <groupId>io.quarkus</groupId>
  <artifactId>quarkus-minikube</artifactId>
</dependency>
```

This extension will generate vanilla Kubernetes manifest files as well as specific ones for minikube:

```
target/
└── kubernetes/
    ├── kubernetes.json
    ├── kubernetes.yml
    ├── minikube.json
    └── minikube.yml
```

If you look at the differences between `kubernetes.yml` and `minikube.yml` you will notice that they are nearly the same. But if you take other Kubernetes platforms (e.g. OpenShift), then you realise that the YAML files can be very different.

10.3.3. Deploying to a Minikube Cluster

Now that we know how Quarkus generates Kubernetes manifest files, let's deploy them on a Minikube cluster.

For simplicity, I am using the Minikube platform because you can run the same commands on your personal computer. But to interact with Minikube, I am using `kubectl`, which is portable, so you can use the same commands on any Kubernetes platform. The only requirement is that, depending on the platform you want to target (OpenShift, Google, Amazon, Azure, etc.), you will have to change the manifest files accordingly. Remember to check Appendix A if you need more information on how to install Minikube, kubectl and on the different commands.

First, let's check the Kubernetes cluster. If the Minikube cluster is not already started, start it with the following command:

```
$ minikube start
...
Done! kubectl is now configured to use "minikube"
```

At that moment, you should not see any deployment yet.

```
~ $ minikube service list
|-------------|------------|---------------|-----|
|  NAMESPACE  |    NAME    |  TARGET PORT  | URL |
|-------------|------------|---------------|-----|
| default     | kubernetes | No node port  |     |
| kube-system | kube-dns   | No node port  |     |
|-------------|------------|---------------|-----|
```

As you've seen in the previous section, we now need to package a Quarkus application in a native executable or executable JAR and build and push the Docker image to a remote repository so it can be accessible from Minikube. Once these steps are achieved, you'll have a generated `minikube.yml` file that you can manually deploy with the `kubectl apply` command. But Quarkus can help you with a single property. No matter if you have used the Kubernetes, Minikube or OpenShift extension, you can deploy the Docker image with the `quarkus.kubernetes.deploy` property set to `true`. It will automatically build and deploy the Docker image to the targeted platform.

```
$ mvn package -Dquarkus.kubernetes.deploy=true

[INFO] --- quarkus-maven-plugin:build @ orchestrator-minikube ---

[INFO] Deploying target 'minikube'
[INFO] Kubernetes API Server at 'https://192.168.99.127:8443/' successfully contacted.

[INFO] Deploying to minikube server: https://192.168.99.127:8443/ in namespace:
default.
[INFO] Applied: ServiceAccount quarkus-jar.
[INFO] Applied: Service quarkus-jar.
[INFO] Applied: Deployment quarkus-jar.

[INFO] -------------------
[INFO] BUILD SUCCESS
[INFO] -------------------
```

Now you should see the deployment under the Minikube cluster. The command `minikube service list` also gives you the URL and port where the application is accessible:

```
~ $ minikube service list
|-------------|-------------|---------------|----------------------------|
|  NAMESPACE  |    NAME     |  TARGET PORT  |            URL             |
|-------------|-------------|---------------|----------------------------|
| default     | kubernetes  | No node port  |                            |
| default     | quarkus-jar | http/80       | http://192.168.99.127:31826 |
| kube-system | kube-dns    | No node port  |                            |
|-------------|-------------|---------------|----------------------------|
```

So, to execute the `agoncal/quarkus-jar` image it's just a matter of invoking the service's URL. You can now point the browser (or cURL command) to http://192.168.99.127:31826/authors so it invokes the REST endpoint.

Recap

To deploy an image to a Kubernetes cluster, this image has to be built, but also deployed on a remote Docker registry so Kubernetes can pull it and then execute it. So there are several steps involved, and each step has a Quarkus property that has to be set. Table 86 recaps these properties.

Table 86. Quarkus Properties Used for Deployment

Quarkus Property

Description

`quarkus.package.type`

Packages a Quarkus application into a `jar`, `legacy-jar` or `native` executable

`quarkus.container-image.build`

Builds a Docker image either based on a Dockerfile or using the Jib extension

`quarkus.container-image.push`

Pushes the Docker image to a remote registry (default to Docker Hub)

`quarkus.kubernetes.deploy`

Deploys to the Kubernetes cluster

This means that if you check out a project and want to package, build and deploy it to a Kubernetes cluster in a single Maven command, you need to do the following:

```
$ mvn package -Dquarkus.package.type=jar \
              -Dquarkus.container-image.build=true \
              -Dquarkus.container-image.push=true \
              -Dquarkus.kubernetes.deploy=true
```

10.3.4. Configuring Kubernetes

The Quarkus Kubernetes extension is highly configurable. You will find several properties[144] under the `quarkus.kubernetes.` namespace. Table 87 only shows a subset of these properties.

Table 87. Some Quarkus Kubernetes Configuration Properties

Property	Default
`quarkus.kubernetes.name` The name of the application	`${quarkus.container-image.name}`
`quarkus.kubernetes.version` The version of the application	`${quarkus.container-image.tag}`
`quarkus.kubernetes.host` The host under which the application is going to be exposed	
`quarkus.kubernetes.replicas` The number of desired pods	`1`
`quarkus.kubernetes.node-port` The nodePort to set when serviceType is set to node-port	
`quarkus.kubernetes.image-pull-policy` Image pull policy	`always`
`quarkus.kubernetes.labels` Custom labels to add to all resources	

10.4. Summary

Cloud native is all about pushing an application or a microservice to the cloud. Quarkus allows you to very easily package Docker images and deploy them to different Kubernetes platforms. That's what Quarkus means with its tagline "*Cloud Native Ready*". It comes with all the required extensions to make our cloud experience easy.

GraalVM, Docker and Kubernetes are very complex tools. Compiling a Java application by hand with several dependencies on GraalVM is tricky. Writing Dockerfiles can be difficult but nothing compared to writing a set of Kubernetes manifest files. Of course you have different tools to help you, but Quarkus make it easy by integrating them and they ease our pain (such as Dekorate for Kubernetes files).

The next chapter is about *Tests*. If you liked the way Quarkus simplifies deployment, then you will love the way it helps you with testing and mocking.

[246] Quarkus Docker Native Image https://quay.io/repository/quarkus/ubi-quarkus-native-image?tab=tags

[247] Measuring startup time https://quarkus.io/guides/performance-measure#how-do-we-measure-startup-time

[248] Code Quarkus https://code.quarkus.io

[249] UBI https://www.redhat.com/en/blog/introducing-red-hat-universal-base-image

[250] Jib https://github.com/GoogleContainerTools/jib

[251] Docker Hub https://hub.docker.com

[252] Kubernetes https://kubernetes.io

[253] Dekorate https://github.com/dekorateio/dekorate

[254] Minikube https://minikube.sigs.k8s.io

Chapter 11. Tests

The previous chapters focused on presenting different technologies and APIs and how they work together. But what about testing them? If you come from the Jakarta EE world, you might remember how painful it was to test your components running inside an application server. If you come from the Spring world, you know how tests can be executed inside the application context. This takes time but is far more efficient than testing in Jakarta EE. As you've seen up to now, Quarkus has some amazing features (live reload, native compilation, etc.) and testing is one of them.

Quarkus makes testing easy and fast. When a test is executing, the application is started before the test is run. So your tests run with the entire application up and running. And as you know by now, applications tend to start really quickly with Quarkus: so do your tests.

This chapter shows how Quarkus can run tests within the JVM mode as well as the Native mode. It integrates with *JUnit*, but also several frameworks such as *REST Assured, Hamcrest* or *TestContainers*, and offers several mocking capabilities. This allows your tests to be as expressive as possible, easy to write, while being rich, complex and able to interact with several external resources. And if you need to test a microservice that has several external dependencies, Quarkus makes it easy to mock these dependencies by integrating *Mockito*.

 The code in this chapter can be found at https://github.com/agoncal/agoncal-fascicle-quarkus/tree/2.0/testing

11.1. Testing Frameworks

Quarkus integrates with JUnit (more information on JUnit at Appendix A). In fact, Quarkus testing depends on JUnit as tests don't even work with other frameworks (such as TestNG[255], for example). With just one annotation (@QuarkusTest) you get the full power of all the JUnit testing capabilities. But this is just the tip of the iceberg. Quarkus goes way further by integrating several testing frameworks so that tests can be richer and more explicit without too much effort: Hamcrest for having expressive expressions, REST Assured for testing REST endpoints and TestContainers for running Docker images during the test life cycle. Let's have a look at these frameworks and see how Quarkus integrates them.

11.1.1. REST Assured

REST Assured[256] is an open source Java library that provides a *Domain Specific Language* (DSL) for writing powerful and maintainable tests for RESTful APIs. It supports POST, GET, PUT, DELETE, OPTIONS, PATCH and HEAD requests and can be used to validate and verify the response of these requests.

Listing 234 uses REST Assured to execute an HTTP GET on a resource and check that the return code is 200.

Listing 234. Simple HTTP GET Test

```
given().
when()
  .get("/customers").
then()
  .statusCode(200);
```

Listing 235 and Listing 234 are quite similar. Listing 235 uses the REST Assured DSL to pass certain parameters to the HTTP GET such as the ACCEPT header.

Listing 235. HTTP GET Test Given Certain Parameters

```
given()
  .baseUri("http://localhost:8081")
  .header(ACCEPT, APPLICATION_JSON).
when()
  .get("/customers").
then()
  .statusCode(200);
```

As you can see in Listing 236, REST Assured can then help to easily make the GET request and verify the response as well as its content (thanks to the body() method).

Listing 236. HTTP GET Test Checking Response Body

```
given()
  .pathParam("id", 1L).
when()
  .get("/customers/{id}").
then()
  .statusCode(200)
  .contentType(APPLICATION_JSON)
  .body("first-name", is("John"))
  .body("last-name", is("Lennon"));
```

Listing 237 shows how to invoke an HTTP POST passing a Customer object and then check that the response code is a 201 (created).

Listing 237. HTTP POST Test Passing a Body

```
Customer customer = new Customer().firstName("John").lastName("Lennon");

given()
  .body(customer)
  .header(CONTENT_TYPE, APPLICATION_JSON)
  .header(ACCEPT, APPLICATION_JSON).
when()
  .post("/customers").
then()
  .statusCode(201);
```

With Quarkus, when you want to test a REST endpoint, you do it using REST Assured just by adding a dependency to your pom.xml (see Listing 238).

Listing 238. REST Assured Extension

```
<dependency>
  <groupId>io.rest-assured</groupId>
  <artifactId>rest-assured</artifactId>
  <scope>test</scope>
</dependency>
```

Quarkus provides a REST Assured integration that updates the default port used by REST Assured before the tests are run. So in your REST Assured tests, you don't have to specify the default test port 8081 used by Quarkus. But the integration can even go further with the @TestHTTPEndpoint annotation that automatically sets the correct base path URL (i.e. the default URL that serves as the root for every request). This annotation can be applied at the class or method level. Listing 239 tests the ArtistResource endpoint without specifying its URL (.get() instead of .get("/artists). This way, if we ever decide to change the path of the ArtistResource, the test will pick up the correct path without us having to touch it.

Listing 239. Testing REST Endpoint Without a URL

```java
@QuarkusTest
@TestHTTPEndpoint(ArtistResource.class)
public class ArtistHTTPResourceTest {

  @Test
  public void shouldGetAllArtists() {
    given().
    when()
      .get().
    then()
      .statusCode(is(200));
  }

  @Test
  public void shouldGetOneArtist() {
    given()
      .pathParam("id", 1).
    when()
      .get("/{id}").
    then()
      .statusCode(is(200))
      .body("first_name", is("John"))
      .body("last_name", is("Lennon"));
  }
}
```

11.1.2. Hamcrest

Hamcrest[257] is a framework for writing matcher objects allowing "*match*" rules to be defined declaratively. When writing tests it is sometimes difficult to get the balance right between overspecifying the test, and not specifying enough. Hamcrest allows you to pick out precisely the aspect being tested and to describe the values it should have.

Listing 240 shows a very simple JUnit test. Instead of using JUnit's assertEquals() methods, we use Hamcrest's assertThat construct and the standard set of matchers, both of which we statically import.

Listing 240. Simple Hamcrest Assertion

```
class BookTest {

  @Test
  public void shouldTestEquals() {
    Book oneBook = new Book("H2G2");
    Book anotherBook = new Book("H2G2");
    assertThat(oneBook, equalTo(anotherBook));
  }
}
```

The `assertThat()` method is a stylised sentence for making a test assertion. You can write simple assertions that are easy to read such as:

```
assertThat(book.getTitle(), equalTo("H2G2"));
assertThat(book.getYearOfPublication(), equalTo(1979));
assertThat(book, equalTo(anotherBook));
```

If you want to be even more expressive, you can use some sugar syntax. For example, Hamcrest has an `is` matcher that doesn't add any extra behaviour to the underlying matcher. So the following assertions are equivalent to the previous ones:

```
assertThat(book.getTitle(), is(equalTo("H2G2")));
assertThat(book.getYearOfPublication(), is(equalTo(1979)));
assertThat(book, is(anotherBook));
assertThat(book.getTitle(), is(not(nullValue())));
assertThat(book.getIsbn10(), is(nullValue()));
assertThat(book.getNbOfPages(), is(greaterThan(100)));
```

Hamcrest comes with a library of useful matchers. Table 88 shows some of the most important ones.

Table 88. Main Hamcrest Matchers

Matchers	Description
anything	Always matches, useful if you don't care what the object under test is
is	Decorator to improve readability
allOf	Matches if all matchers match (like Java &&)
anyOf	Matches if any matchers match (like Java ||)
not	Matches if the wrapped matcher doesn't match and vice versa
equalTo	Tests object equality using `Object.equals()`
notNullValue, nullValue	Tests for null

Matchers	Description
greaterThan, greaterThanOrEqualTo, lessThan, lessThanOrEqualTo	Tests ordering
equalToIgnoringCase	Tests string equality ignoring case
equalToIgnoringWhiteSpace	Tests string equality ignoring differences in runs of whitespace
containsString, endsWith, startsWith	Tests string matching

When you test your REST endpoints with REST Assured, there is no need to add the Hamcrest dependency to your pom.xml as REST Assured pushes the Hamcrest dependency recursively.

11.2. Quarkus Tests

With all these testing frameworks, Quarkus allows you to execute tests in different modes. Tests can be executed in JVM mode (this is the default), but also in Native mode: it's just a matter of using the appropriate Quarkus JUnit runner.

Quarkus tests come with a set of annotations. Table 89 lists a subset of the most commonly used annotations.

Table 89. Main Quarkus Test Annotations

Annotation	Description
@QuarkusTest	Indicates that a test should be run using the JVM mode of Quarkus
@NativeImageTest	Indicates that a test should be run using a native image, rather than in the JVM
@QuarkusTestProfile	Defines a test profile that has different configuration options to other tests
@Mock	Built-in stereotype intended for use with mock beans injected in tests
@InjectMock	When used on a field of a test class, the field becomes a Mockito mock

11.2.1. JVM Mode Tests

When you develop with Quarkus, you want to have live reload and quick tests: so usually you are in JVM mode. To test your code in JVM mode, it's just a matter of annotating your tests with @QuarkusTest (as shown in Listing 241) and enabling the quarkus-junit5 dependency in your pom.xml. As you can see in Listing 241, the rest of the code uses JUnit with REST Assured as you've seen before. The integration with Quarkus in JVM mode is made through this single annotation: @QuarkusTest.

Listing 241. JVM Mode Test

```java
@QuarkusTest
public class ArtistResourceTest {

  @Test
  public void shouldGetAllArtists() {
    given().
    when()
      .get("/artists").
    then()
      .statusCode(is(200));
  }

  @Test @Disabled("Test is not implemented yet")
  public void shouldCreateAnArtist() {
    // some work to do
  }
}
```

The @QuarkusTest annotation does all the magic: it first starts the Quarkus application and then performs the tests. If you look at the previous logs, you can see this workflow in action:

- Quarkus is started ("*Quarkus on JVM started*") in test profile ("*Profile test activated*");
- Tests are executed ("*Tests run*");
- Quarkus is stopped ("*Quarkus stopped*").

While Quarkus will listen on port 8080 by default, when running tests it defaults to 8081. This allows you to run tests while having the application running in parallel.

11.2.2. Continuous Testing

When you are in JVM mode, Quarkus gives you continuous testing while you develop. Continuous testing means that tests are executed immediately after code changes have been saved. This allows you to get instant feedback on your code changes. Quarkus detects which tests cover which code, and uses this information to only run the relevant tests when code is changed.

When you run Quarkus in development mode (mvn quarkus:dev) you get the following prompt:

```
Tests paused
Press [r] to resume testing, [o] Toggle test output, [h] for more options>
```

If you press r, the tests are automatically executed, and you will get an information that the tests have succeeded or failed:

```
All 2 tests are passing (0 skipped), 2 tests were run in 381ms. Tests completed at
09:29:59 due to changes to ArtistResource.class and 1 other files.
Press [r] to resume testing, [o] Toggle test output, [h] for more options>
```

If you press h, you will get some more help on the commands you can type in the continuous testing
prompt:

```
The following commands are currently available:

== Continuous Testing
[r] - Resume testing
[o] - Toggle test output (disabled)

== HTTP

[w] - Open the application in a browser
[d] - Open the Dev UI in a browser

== System

[s] - Force restart
[i] - Toggle instrumentation based reload (disabled)
[l] - Toggle live reload (enabled)
[j] - Toggle log levels (INFO)
[h] - Shows this help
[q] - Quits the application
```

You get continuous testing automatically when you are in development mode (mvn quarkus:dev) or
you can excceplicitelly invoke it with mvn quarkus:test.

11.2.3. Native Mode Tests

It is also possible to test native executables using a different annotation: @NativeImageTest. The idea
is to run a set of tests against the binary itself instead of the Java code. This can be very handy as
sometimes native code can behave differently (as you'll soon see). Listing 242 shows a native test.
As you can see, it extends the JVM test that we previously saw in Listing 241, and is annotated with
@NativeImageTest instead of @QuarkusTest, that's all. Notice that this class is empty, but it could add
extra methods to test specific native behaviour if needed.

Listing 242. Native Mode Test

```
@NativeImageTest
public class NativeArtistResourceIT extends ArtistResourceTest {

    // Execute the same tests but in native mode.
}
```

To execute tests on the native executable, there is no specific Quarkus extension to add to the pom.xml. The only thing is that the Failsafe plugin has to be properly configured (see Listing 243) under the native profile. Failsafe runs on the verify Maven goal and it sets the native.image.path property to the binary generated under the target directory.

Listing 243. Native Profile

```xml
<profile>
  <id>native</id>
  <activation>
    <property>
      <name>native</name>
    </property>
  </activation>
  <build>
    <plugins>
      <plugin>
        <artifactId>maven-failsafe-plugin</artifactId>
        <executions>
          <execution>
            <goals>
              <goal>integration-test</goal>
              <goal>verify</goal>
            </goals>
            <configuration>
              <systemPropertyVariables>

<native.image.path>${project.build.directory}/${project.build.finalName}-
runner</native.image.path>
                <java.util.logging.manager>
org.jboss.logmanager.LogManager</java.util.logging.manager>
                <maven.home>${maven.home}</maven.home>
              </systemPropertyVariables>
            </configuration>
          </execution>
        </executions>
      </plugin>
    </plugins>
  </build>
  <properties>
    <quarkus.package.type>native</quarkus.package.type>
  </properties>
</profile>
```

To execute the native tests you need to invoke the native profile with the following command:

```
$ mvn verify -Pnative
```

This will execute the JVM mode tests, and then, the native tests. So the workflow is:

- The Surefire plugin executes the JVM mode tests (Quarkus is started in JVM mode);
- GraalVM compiles the code into a binary;
- The Failsafe plugin executes the binary (Quarkus is started in native mode);
- The Failsafe plugin runs the native tests.

But remember that the only thing that runs natively is the Quarkus application, not the test itself. You should see similar traces:

```
[INFO] -----------------------------------------
[INFO] Building Quarkus :: Testing :: Native Mode
[INFO] -----------------------------------------
[INFO]
[INFO] --- maven-surefire-plugin:test
[INFO]
[INFO] ----------
[INFO]  T E S T S
[INFO] ----------
[INFO] Running ArtistResourceTest
[INFO] [io.quarkus] (main) Quarkus on JVM started in 1.169s
[INFO] [io.quarkus] (main) Profile test activated.
[INFO] [io.quarkus] (main) Installed features: [cdi, resteasy, resteasy-jsonb]
[INFO] Tests run: 2, Failures: 0, Errors: 0, Skipped: 1, Time elapsed: 3.827 s
[INFO] [io.quarkus] (main) Quarkus stopped in 0.026s
[INFO]
[INFO] Results:
[INFO]
[INFO] Tests run: 2, Failures: 0, Errors: 0, Skipped: 1
[INFO]
[INFO] --- quarkus-maven-plugin:build
[INFO] Building native image from Code/Agoncal/agoncal-fascicle-qua...
[INFO] Running Quarkus native-image plugin on GraalVM
[INFO] graalvm-ce-java11-20.1.0/Contents/Home/bin/native-i...
[runner]    classlist:   3,010.30 ms,   0.96 GB
[runner]     (clinit):     698.82 ms,   3.24 GB
[runner]     universe:     785.52 ms,   3.24 GB
[runner]      (parse):   2,001.61 ms,   4.20 GB
[runner]        write:     645.63 ms,   5.81 GB
[runner]      [total]:  46,119.87 ms,   5.81 GB
[INFO]
[INFO] --- maven-failsafe-plugin:integration-test
[INFO]
[INFO] ----------
[INFO]  T E S T S
[INFO] ----------
[INFO] Running NativeArtistResourceIT
Executing target/test-jvm-native-mode-2.0.0-SNAPSHOT-runner
[INFO] [io.quarkus] (main) test-jvm-native-mode 2.0.0-SNAPSHOT native
[INFO] [io.quarkus] (main) Profile prod activated.
[INFO] [io.quarkus] (main) Installed features: [cdi, resteasy, resteasy-jsonb]
[INFO]
[INFO] Results:
[INFO]
[INFO] Tests run: 3, Failures: 0, Errors: 0, Skipped: 1
[INFO]
[INFO] -------------
[INFO] BUILD SUCCESS
[INFO] -------------
```

But why would you create tests especially for the native image? Because when building a native executable, GraalVM operates with a closed world assumption. It analyses the call tree and removes all the classes/methods/fields that are not used directly. The elements used via reflection are not part of the call tree so they are dead-code eliminated (if not called directly in other cases). To avoid such code being eliminated by GraalVM, you need to annotate your beans with `@RegisterForReflection`.

For example, Listing 244 shows a bean with JSON-B annotations. JSON libraries use reflection to serialise the objects to JSON. But GraalVM gets rid of reflection. So if we were to use the `Artist` class without the `@RegisterForReflection`, we would get an exception in native mode. To include these elements in your native executable, you need to register them for reflection explicitly. This means that the JVM mode test would succeed, but the native mode test would fail.

Listing 244. Register a Bean for Reflection

```java
@RegisterForReflection
public class Artist {

    private Integer id;
    @JsonbProperty("first_name")
    private String firstName;
    @JsonbProperty("last_name")
    private String lastName;

    // Constructors, getters, setters
}
```

11.2.4. Transactional Tests

In Chapter 5, you saw how you could use Java Persistence API (JPA) and Panache to map entities to a relational database. Thanks to JTA (Java Transaction API) we can insert, update or delete entities in a transactional way. So, if we want to execute tests within a transactional context, we can simply apply the `@Transactional` annotation to the test method (or test class as shown in Listing 245) and the transaction interceptor will handle it.

Listing 245. Transactional Test

```
@QuarkusTest
@Transactional
class MusicianTest {

  @Test
  void shouldPersistAMusician() {
    Musician musician = new Musician();
    musician.firstName = "Janis";
    musician.lastName = "Joplin";
    musician.dateOfBirth = LocalDate.of(1943, 01, 19);
    musician.preferredInstrument = "Voice";

    Musician.persist(musician);

    assertNotNull(musician.id);
  }
}
```

Without this annotation, the test would fail. That's because the persist() method requires running within the context of a transaction. But instead of annotating your test with @Transactional (which will persist the changes), you can annotate your test with @TestTransaction (see Listing 246) and the changes will be automatically rolled back at the end of the test.

Listing 246. Rollbacking Transactional Test

```
@QuarkusTest
@TestTransaction
class MusicianTest {

  @Test
  void shouldPersistAMusician() {
    Musician musician = new Musician();
    musician.firstName = "Janis";
    musician.lastName = "Joplin";
    musician.dateOfBirth = LocalDate.of(1943, 01, 19);
    musician.preferredInstrument = "Voice";

    Musician.persist(musician);

    assertNotNull(musician.id);
  }
}
```

11.2.5. Configuring Quarkus Tests

Some aspects of the JVM and native tests can be configured in Quarkus. One common property that you might find useful to configure is the listening port used during the tests (quarkus.http.test-port property). The default is 8081 but if you set it to 0, it will result in the use of a random port (assigned by the operating system). Table 90 shows other common test properties.

Table 90. Some Quarkus Test Configuration Properties

Property	Default
`quarkus.http.test-port` The HTTP port used to run tests	8081
`quarkus.http.test-ssl-port` The HTTPS port used to run tests	8444
`quarkus.http.test-timeout` The REST Assured client timeout for testing.	30S
`quarkus.test.profile` The profile to use when testing using `@QuarkusTest`	test
`quarkus.test.native-image-profile` The profile to use when testing the native image	prod
`quarkus.test.continuous-testing` If continuous testing is enabled. The default value is `paused`, which will allow you to start testing from the console or the Dev UI, but will not run tests on startup. If this is set to `enabled` then testing will start as soon as the application has started. If this is `disabled` then continuous testing is not enabled, and can't be enabled without restarting the application.	paused
`quarkus.test.type` The type of test to run, this can be either: `quarkus-test` only runs `@QuarkusTest` annotated test classes. `unit` only runs classes that are not annotated with `@QuarkusTest`. `all` Runs both, running the unit tests first. unit, quarkus-test, all	all
`quarkus.native.graalvm-home` The location of the Graal distribution	${GRAALVM_HOME}
`quarkus.native.java-home` The location of the JDK	${java.home}
`quarkus.test.native-image-wait-time` Duration to wait for the native image to be built during testing	PT5M

11.3. Testing with External Resources

A very common need is to start some services on which your application depends, before Quarkus starts for testing. For example, you might want to start a PostgreSQL database, a Kafka broker or an external microservice before executing some integration tests. For such use cases, Quarkus integrates with TestContainers and also provides a few annotations to easily manage external resources during testing.

11.3.1. TestContainers

TestContainers[258] is a Java library that supports JUnit tests, providing lightweight, throwaway instances of common Docker images. It allows us to use Docker containers within our tests. For example, it can use a containerised instance of a PostgreSQL database to test a data access layer but without requiring a complex setup on the developer's machine. The pre-requisites of using TestContainers are to have Docker installed and to use a supported JVM testing framework (such as JUnit or TestNG).

Let's say our application uses PostgreSQL as a relational database and we want to run some tests with a running PostgreSQL. With TestContainers it's easy to make such a test. As you can see in Listing 247, JUnit integration is provided by means of the @org.testcontainers.junit.jupiter.Testcontainers annotation. This JUnit extension finds all fields that are annotated with @Container (PostgreSQLContainer in our example) and calls their container life cycle methods (e.g. start(), stop()). Containers declared as static fields will be shared between test methods. They will be started only once before any test method is executed and stopped after the last test method has executed. Containers declared as instance fields will be started and stopped for every test method.

Listing 247. PostgreSQL TestContainers Test

```
@QuarkusTest
@Testcontainers
public class PingPostgreSQLTest {

  @Container
  public static PostgreSQLContainer pg = new PostgreSQLContainer<>("postgres:14.0")
    .withDatabaseName("vintageStoreDB")
    .withUsername("vintage")
    .withPassword("vintage")
    .withExposedPorts(5432);

  @Test
  public void shouldPingPostgreSQL() throws Exception {
    pg.start();

    try (Connection con = DriverManager.getConnection(pg.getJdbcUrl(), pg.getUsername
(), pg.getPassword());
        Statement st = con.createStatement();
        ResultSet rs = st.executeQuery("SELECT VERSION()")) {

      if (rs.next()) {
        assertTrue(rs.getString(1).contains("PostgreSQL 14"));
      } else {
        throw new Exception();
      }
    }

    pg.stop();
  }
}
```

TestContainers will try to connect to a Docker daemon. So, to execute the test in Listing 247, make sure Docker is up and running. If that's not the case, you will get the following exception:

```
IllegalStateException: Could not find a valid Docker environment.
```

With Docker up and running, TestContainers will first download the PostgreSQL image from Docker Hub[259] if not available locally on your machine. Then, it starts the PostgreSQL container, executes the test, and stops the PostgreSQL container. The output looks like this:

```
INFO --- maven-surefire-plugin:test @ testcontainers ---
--------------------
 T E S T S
--------------------
Running org.agoncal.fascicle.PingPostgreSQLTest

INFO Accessing docker with local Unix socket
INFO Found Docker environment with local Unix socket
INFO Docker host IP address is localhost
INFO Connected to docker:
INFO Checking the system...

INFO [postgres] - Pulling docker image: postgres. Please be patient;
INFO [postgres] - Starting to pull image
INFO [postgres] - Pulling image layers:  0 pending,  0 downloaded,  0 extracted
INFO [postgres] - Pulling image layers: 13 pending,  1 downloaded,  0 extracted
INFO [postgres] - Pulling image layers: 10 pending,  4 downloaded,  0 extracted
INFO [postgres] - Pulling image layers:  7 pending,  7 downloaded,  2 extracted
INFO [postgres] - Pulling image layers:  6 pending,  8 downloaded,  3 extracted

INFO [postgres] - Creating container for image: postgres
INFO [postgres] - Starting container with ID: 77a1669fe4bb3f7f
INFO [postgres] - Container postgres is starting: 77a1669fe4bb3f7f
INFO [postgres] - Container postgres started

Tests run: 1, Failures: 0, Errors: 0, Skipped: 0
INFO --------------------
INFO BUILD SUCCESS
INFO --------------------
```

Quarkus does not have a specific extension for TestContainers. Listing 248 shows the Maven dependencies you need to use in your pom.xml.

Listing 248. TestContainers Dependencies

```xml
<dependency>
  <groupId>org.testcontainers</groupId>
  <artifactId>testcontainers</artifactId>
  <scope>test</scope>
</dependency>
<dependency>
  <groupId>org.testcontainers</groupId>
  <artifactId>junit-jupiter</artifactId>
  <scope>test</scope>
</dependency>
```

11.3.2. Quarkus Test Resource

In some simple scenarios you don't need TestContainers to start and stop a resource before and after the test suite. Some simple hooks can do. To address this need, Quarkus provides the @QuarkusTestResource annotation and a QuarkusTestResourceLifecycleManager interface. The idea is that, you implement QuarkusTestResourceLifecycleManager to start and stop a resource, and you annotate any test with @QuarkusTestResource with the implementation. Quarkus provides a few implementations out of the box to start and stop common resources:

- H2 database: H2DatabaseTestResource

- Derby database: DerbyDatabaseTestResource

- Kubernetes: KubernetesMockServerTestResource

- LDAP server: LdapServerTestResource

For example, the transactional test in Listing 249 uses the @QuarkusTestResource to start and stop an H2 database before and after running the test.

Listing 249. Testing with an H2 Database

```java
@QuarkusTest
@QuarkusTestResource(H2DatabaseTestResource.class)
@Transactional
class MusicianTest {

  @Test
  void shouldPersistAMusician() {
    // ...
  }
}
```

Quarkus has several extensions for testing resources. In fact, as you can see in Listing 250, each resource has its own extension.

Listing 250. Some Dependencies for Testing Resources

```xml
<dependency>
  <groupId>io.quarkus</groupId>
  <artifactId>quarkus-test-h2</artifactId>
  <scope>test</scope>
</dependency>
<dependency>
  <groupId>io.quarkus</groupId>
  <artifactId>quarkus-test-derby</artifactId>
  <scope>test</scope>
</dependency>
<dependency>
  <groupId>io.quarkus</groupId>
  <artifactId>quarkus-test-kubernetes-client</artifactId>
  <scope>test</scope>
</dependency>
<dependency>
  <groupId>io.quarkus</groupId>
  <artifactId>quarkus-test-ldap</artifactId>
  <scope>test</scope>
</dependency>
```

11.3.3. Dev Services

And in some cases, you can even skip writing code. Quarkus supports the automatic provisioning of unconfigured services in development and test mode. It is called *Dev Services*[260]. This means that if an extension is not configured, then Quarkus will automatically start the relevant service (using TestContainers), configure it with default properties and wire it up to the application.

This means that when an external service is supported by Quarkus, you don't have to configure anything, add any code or annotation anywhere. You just add the dependency to your pom.xml and Quarkus downloads the service from the DockerHub (using TestContainers), start it, configure it, and stops it. Here is the list of supported services:

- AMQP
- Apicurio Registry
- Databases
- Kafka
- Keycloak
- MongoDB
- Redis
- Vault

Dev Services is there to help development using default properties so we don't have to worry about configuring a service. But if you need to configure any Dev Service related property, you will have to look for the quarkus.<service>.devservices namespaces[144] depending on the service (<service> being amqp, apicurio-registry, datasource, kafka, keycloak, mongodb, neo4j, redis or vault). Table 91 shows a subset of these configuration properties.

Table 91. Some Dev Services Configuration Properties

Property	Default
quarkus.devservices.enabled Global flag that can be used to disable all Dev Services. If this is set to false then Dev Services will not be used.	true
quarkus.<service>.devservices.enabled Dev Services for a specific type can explicitly enabled or disabled.	true
quarkus.<service>.devservices.port Listening port. If not defined, the port will be chosen randomly.	Randomly chosen
quarkus.<service>.devservices.image-name Docker image of the service to use.	
quarkus.<service>.devservices.shared Indicates if the service managed by Quarkus Dev Services is shared. When shared, Quarkus looks for running containers using label-based service discovery. If a matching container is found, it is used, and so a second one is not started. Otherwise, Dev Services for starts a new container.	true

11.4. Mocking

Mocking is very often used in testing. Let's say you have an object, a microservice or an entire system, that has dependencies on other (complex) objects/microservices/systems. During the test phase, to isolate the behaviour of these dependencies, you might want to replace these dependencies by mocks that simulate their real behaviour. Mocking is a way to only test the functionality of an object/microservice/system and not its dependencies. In Java there are a few mocking frameworks such as: *Mockito*[261], *EasyMock*[262] or *JMockit*[263]. Quarkus integrates with Mockito.

As you've seen in Chapter 7, it's quite easy to have microservices communicating with each other through the Eclipse MicroProfile REST Client. A few annotations (@RestClient, @RegisterRestClient), an interface acting like a proxy (IsbnResourceProxy), some configuration (e.g. the URL of the remote microservice) and you have the BookResource invoking a remote IsbnResource REST endpoint to get an ISBN number.

Listing 251. Book Microservice Invoking the ISBN Microservice

```java
@Path("/api/books")
@Produces(MediaType.APPLICATION_JSON)
public class BookResource {

  @Inject @RestClient
  IsbnResourceProxy isbnService;

  @GET
  public Response getRandomBook() {

    IsbnNumbers isbnNumbers = isbnService.generateIsbnNumbers();
    // ...
  }
}

@Path("/api/numbers")
@RegisterRestClient
public interface IsbnResourceProxy {

  @GET
  IsbnNumbers generateIsbnNumbers();
}
```

But now, with such coupling, we have a problem: to run the tests of the BookResource we need the IsbnResource REST endpoint to be up and running. Of course, if the IsbnResource Docker image is available on a registry, we could use TestContainers to download and run it. But here, we want to avoid this and just test the BookResource in isolation. For this, as seen in Figure 59, we need to mock the IsbnResourceProxy interface.

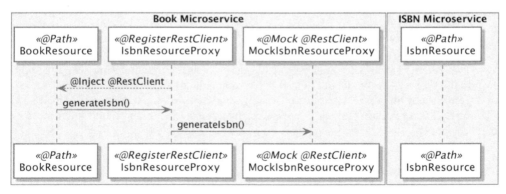

Figure 59. Mocking microservice invocation

Quarkus supports the use of mock objects using the io.quarkus.test.Mock annotation. To use it, you simply override the bean you wish to mock with a class in the src/test/java directory, and annotate it with @Mock. So, to mock the invocation to the remote IsbnResource, we implement the IsbnResourceProxy interface in src/test/java with the class MockIsbnResourceProxy in Listing 252. As you can see, this class implements the generateIsbnNumbers() method and returns fake data. With this fake data, testing the BookResource becomes easier and doesn't depend on any remote microservice.

Listing 252. Mocking ISBN Microservice for Testing

```
@Mock
@ApplicationScoped
@RestClient
public class MockIsbnResourceProxy implements IsbnResourceProxy {

  @Override
  public IsbnNumbers generateIsbnNumbers() {
    IsbnNumbers isbnNumbers = new IsbnNumbers();
    isbnNumbers.setIsbn13("@Mock isbn 13");
    isbnNumbers.setIsbn10("@Mock isbn 10");
    return isbnNumbers;
  }
}
```

If you look under the hood, the @Mock annotation is in fact a CDI alternative (refer back to Chapter 4 if you want to know more about CDI alternatives). So the code in Listing 253 is the same as in Listing 252. We declare the class as being an @Alternative of @Priority(1) and it has the same effect as @Mock.

Listing 253. Mocking with Alternative

```
@Alternative
@Priority(1)
@ApplicationScoped
@RestClient
public class MockIsbnResourceProxy implements IsbnResourceProxy {
  // ...
}
```

This is one way we can provide a global mock that all our Quarkus tests can use. But what if we don't want to have a globally defined mock, but would rather have our mock only within the scope of one test? We can achieve that using @InjectMock. @InjectMock results in a mock implementation available in a test class.

In Listing 254, the BookResourceTest injects a mock implementation of the IsbnResourceProxy thanks to @InjectMock. Then, in the @BeforeEach method we ask Mockito to return fake data when the generateIsbnNumbers() is invoked in tests. This means that when the shouldGetRandomBook test is executed, the BookResource endpoint is invoked and the fake data returned from the mocked IsbnResourceProxy implementation.

Listing 254. Injecting a Mocked Implementation

```java
@QuarkusTest
public class BookResourceTest {

  @InjectMock @RestClient
  IsbnResourceProxy isbnServiceProxy;

  @BeforeEach
  void mockData() {
    Mockito
      .when(isbnServiceProxy.generateIsbnNumbers())
      .thenReturn(new IsbnNumbers("Dummy isbn 10", "Dummy isbn 13"));
  }

  @Test
  void shouldGetRandomBook() {
    given()
      .header(HttpHeaders.ACCEPT, MediaType.APPLICATION_JSON).
    when()
      .get("/api/books").
    then()
      .statusCode(OK.getStatusCode())
      .body("isbn_10", is("Dummy isbn 10"))
      .body("isbn_13", is("Dummy isbn 13"))
      .body("$", hasKey("title"))
      .body("$", hasKey("author"));
  }
}
```

The integration with Mockito is done through an extension (see Listing 255). It also gives you extra annotations such as @InjectMock or @InjectSpy.

Listing 255. Mockito Extension

```xml
<dependency>
  <groupId>io.quarkus</groupId>
  <artifactId>quarkus-junit5-mockito</artifactId>
  <scope>test</scope>
</dependency>
```

11.5. Quarkus Test Profiles

In Chapter 4, *Core Quarkus*, you saw how Quarkus allows having multiple configurations in the same application.properties file and selects between them via a profile name. Quarkus comes with three profiles (prod, dev and test) and you can create your own. So during the test phase, Quarkus automatically activates the test profile. That's why you can read "*Profile test activated*" when Quarkus starts:

```
[INFO] ----------
[INFO]  T E S T S
[INFO] ----------
[INFO] Running org.agoncal.fascicle.InvoiceTest
[INFO] [io.quarkus] (main) Quarkus on JVM started in 0.678s.
[INFO] [io.quarkus] (main) Profile test activated.
[INFO] [io.quarkus] (main) Installed features: [cdi]
[INFO] [io.quarkus] (main) Quarkus stopped in 0.001s
```

Activating the test profile allows us to use the %{profile}.config.key=value syntax to have a different configuration depending on the profile. For example, in the application.properties in Listing 256, we configure the default database to be a PostgreSQL database with a specific JDBC URL. But when testing, and only when testing, we want to use an H2 in-memory database.

Listing 256. Production and Test Properties

```
quarkus.datasource.db-kind=postgresql
quarkus.datasource.jdbc.url=jdbc:postgresql://localhost:5432/vintageStoreDB
quarkus.hibernate-orm.database.generation=update

%test.quarkus.datasource.db-kind=h2
%test.quarkus.datasource.jdbc.url=jdbc:h2:mem:vintageStoreDB
%test.quarkus.hibernate-orm.database.generation=drop-and-create
```

This is a very easy way to configure an entire application depending on the profile. But what if we want to run our tests each in different configurations and not only one? For this, Quarkus offers the concept of a test profile where you can have as many classes as you want, each defining precisely its own configuration (overriding the application.properties file is needed), that you can apply individually on each test case.

Let's say we have a few properties to configure; the vat rate and discount rate of an invoice. By default, the vat rate is set to 10 and the discount is not allowed:

```
org.agoncal.fascicle.Invoice.vatRate=10
org.agoncal.fascicle.Invoice.discount=false
```

As we've just seen, we could change these values for all our test suite by prefixing each property with %test. But that's not what we want. We want to calculate an invoice that is configured differently per country (where each vat rate is different). For that, we start by implementing a QuarkusTestProfile as seen in Listing 257. This interface has several default methods that you can override. For example, here, we configure a specific vat rate for France in the getConfigOverrides() method (another method getEnabledAlternatives() allows you to enable CDI alternatives, for example).

Listing 257. Custom Test Profile

```
public class FrenchTestProfile implements QuarkusTestProfile {
  @Override
  public Map<String, String> getConfigOverrides() {
    return Map.of(
      "org.agoncal.fascicle.Invoice.vatRate", "20",
      "org.agoncal.fascicle.Invoice.discount", "true"
    );
  }
}
```

Finally, with this configuration in place, we can write a test that is specifically configured for French invoices. As we can see in Listing 258, the test is annotated with @TestProfile passing our FrenchTestProfile. It will calculate the vat amount and total amount of the invoice with the custom vatRate and discount properties overridden from the default application.properties, defined in FrenchTestProfile.

Listing 258. Applying a Test Profile

```
@QuarkusTest
@TestProfile(FrenchTestProfile.class)
class FrenchInvoiceTest {

  @Inject
  Invoice invoice;

  @Test
  public void shouldCalculateInvoice() {
    invoice.subtotal = 500f;
    assertEquals(20f, invoice.vatRate);
    assertEquals(100f, invoice.caclculateVatAmount());
    assertEquals(587.5f, invoice.caclculateTotal());
    assertTrue(invoice.discount);
  }
}
```

11.6. Summary

In this chapter, we saw how Quarkus offers excellent support for testing applications. From simple things like dependency management, injection and mocking, to more complex aspects like configuration profiles and native images, Quarkus integrates with many testing and mocking frameworks to create powerful and clean tests.

With just an annotation (@QuarkusTest and @NativeImageTest), Quarkus starts your entire application and runs your test suite, either in JVM or native mode. This makes integration tests very easy. These tests run on top of JUnit, but Quarkus also integrates other popular testing frameworks such as REST Assured, Hamcrest or TestContainers. And when you need to mock external dependencies or remote microservices, Quarkus comes in with the `@Mock` and `@InjectMock` annotations.

In the next chapter, *Putting It All Together*, you will put together some of the concepts that you saw in this fascicle. Get ready for a technical wrap up.

[255] TestNG https://testng.org

[256] REST Assured http://rest-assured.io

[257] Hamcrest http://hamcrest.org/JavaHamcrest

[258] TestContainers https://www.testcontainers.org

[259] Docker Hub https://hub.docker.com

[260] Dev Services https://quarkus.io/guides/dev-services

[261] Mockito https://site.mockito.org

[262] EasyMock https://easymock.org

[263] JMockit https://jmockit.github.io

Chapter 12. Putting It All Together

Now that you've read all the previous chapters on Quarkus, it's time to put some of these concepts all together and write a slightly more complex example. In this chapter, we will write an application made of two microservices that generate random books with ISBN numbers. The architecture diagram in Figure 60 describes the interaction between the two microservices.

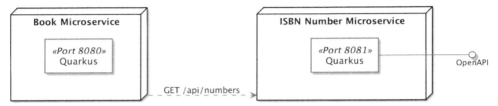

Figure 60. Architecture diagram

Each microservice has a defined business scope:

- The *Isbn Number* microservice has a REST endpoint that returns ISBN numbers. It is used by the *Book* microservice when it needs to return a new book.

- The *Book* microservice has one endpoint that returns a random book.

 Make sure your development environment is set up to execute the code in this chapter. You can go to Appendix A to check that you have all the required tools installed, in particular JDK 11.0.13 or higher, Maven 3.8.3 or higher and GraalVM. The code in this chapter can be found at https://github.com/agoncal/agoncal-fascicle-quarkus/tree/2.0/putting-together

12.1. Developing the REST ISBN Number Microservice

A book has ISBN (*International Standard Book Number*) numbers. To return a random book (with a title, author, genre, etc.), the *Book* microservice needs to interact with the *ISBN Number* microservice. So we need to expose a REST API that generates ISBN numbers of 10 and 13 digits. In this section, we will:

- Bootstrap a Quarkus applications using its Maven plugin,

- Implement a *Number* REST API using JAX-RS,

- Inject external configuration,

- Customise the JSON Output with JSON-B,

- Enable OpenAPI and Swagger UI,

- Check the health of the REST endpoint,

- Configure Quarkus HTTP port listening,

- Test the REST APIs with REST Assured.

12.1.1. Bootstrapping the ISBN Number Microservice

To bootstrap the *ISBN Number* microservice we use the following Maven command:

```
mvn io.quarkus:quarkus-maven-plugin:2.5.0.Final:create \
    -DplatformVersion=2.5.0.Final \
    -DprojectGroupId=org.agoncal.fascicle.quarkus.putting-together \
    -DprojectArtifactId=rest-number \
    -DprojectVersion=2.0.0-SNAPSHOT \
    -DclassName="org.agoncal.fascicle.quarkus.number.NumberResource" \
    -Dpath="/api/numbers" \
    -Dextensions="resteasy-jsonb, smallrye-openapi, smallrye-health"
```

This generates the appropriate directory and package structure with the right Quarkus extensions. Let's have a look at what we got.

12.1.2. Maven Dependencies

First, the generated pom.xml. If you look at the dependencies section in Listing 259, you will see all the required Quarkus extensions used to compile and execute the *ISBN Number* microservice. This section only declares the dependencies, not the versions, as they are defined in the Quarkus BOM (*Bill of Materials*):

- quarkus-resteasy: REST framework implementing JAX-RS.

- quarkus-resteasy-jsonb: JSON-B serialisation support for RESTEasy.

- quarkus-smallrye-openapi: Documents the REST APIs with OpenAPI and comes with Swagger UI.

- quarkus-smallrye-health: MicroProfile Health dependency so we know our microservices are up and running.

- javafaker: This external dependency needs to be added as it helps us in generating fake ISBN numbers.

Listing 259. Maven Dependencies

```xml
<dependency>
  <groupId>io.quarkus</groupId>
  <artifactId>quarkus-smallrye-health</artifactId>
</dependency>
<dependency>
  <groupId>io.quarkus</groupId>
  <artifactId>quarkus-smallrye-openapi</artifactId>
</dependency>
<dependency>
  <groupId>io.quarkus</groupId>
  <artifactId>quarkus-resteasy-jsonb</artifactId>
</dependency>
<dependency>
  <groupId>io.quarkus</groupId>
  <artifactId>quarkus-arc</artifactId>
</dependency>
<dependency>
  <groupId>com.github.javafaker</groupId>
  <artifactId>javafaker</artifactId>
</dependency>
```

12.1.3. Directories and Files

The *ISBN Number* microservice only needs a few Java classes as shown in Figure 61:

- NumberResource: REST endpoint with a single method returning a JSON representation of an ISBN number.

- IsbnNumbers: POJO encapsulating two attributes of an ISBN number (10 and 13 digits).

- NumberApplication: Holds the OpenAPI contract for the microservice.

- NumberResourceHealthCheck: Checks that the NumberResource is up and running.

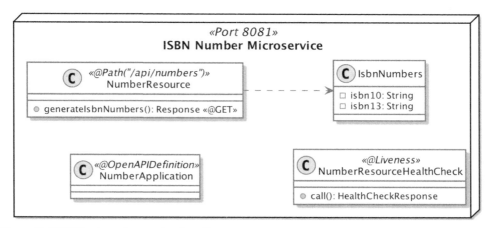

Figure 61. ISBN Number microservice class diagram

The classes and files described in Figure 61 follow the Maven directory structure:

- src/main/java: The directory for the IsbnNumbers, NumberResource, NumberApplication, and NumberResourceHealthCheck classes.

- src/main/resources: The application.properties file to configure the listening port.

- src/test/java: The directory for the test case NumberResourceTest.

- pom.xml: The Maven Project Object Model (POM) describing the project and its dependencies.

12.1.4. ISBN Number REST Endpoint

The NumberResource in Listing 260 uses some JAX-RS annotations. As you can see, NumberResource is a very simple REST endpoint, returning a JSON representation of ISBN numbers on the /api/numbers path. It returns an IsbnNumbers object containing ISBN 10 and ISBN 13 numbers all generated by the Java Faker.

The *Java Faker*[264] library is a port of Ruby's faker[265] gem that generates fake data. It's useful when you're developing a project and need some pretty data for a showcase. Here, we use it to generate some random data.

Listing 260. REST Endpoint Generating ISBN Numbers

```java
@Path("/api/numbers")
@Produces(MediaType.APPLICATION_JSON)
public class NumberResource {

  @Inject
  Logger LOGGER;

  @GET
  public Response generateIsbnNumbers() {
    Faker faker = new Faker();
    IsbnNumbers isbnNumbers = new IsbnNumbers();
    isbnNumbers.setIsbn10(faker.code().isbn10(separator));
    isbnNumbers.setIsbn13(faker.code().isbn13(separator));
    LOGGER.info("ISBN numbers generated " + isbnNumbers);
    return Response.ok(isbnNumbers).build();
  }
}
```

The `NumberResource` returns the `IsbnNumbers` object defined in Listing 261. As you can see, `IsbnNumbers` is just a simple POJO (*Plain Old Java Object*) with attributes, getters and setters. It holds the values of ISBN 10 and 13 numbers.

Listing 261. Java Class Holding ISBN Numbers

```java
public class IsbnNumbers {

  private String isbn10;
  private String isbn13;

  // Getters and setters
}
```

As you can see in Listing 260, the definition for the `separator` attribute (`isbn10(separator)`) is missing. For that reason, the code of the *ISBN Number* REST endpoint does not compile yet, but if it did, you would have the following output:

```
$ curl http://localhost:8080/api/numbers | jq

{
  "isbn10": "1932563601",
  "isbn13": "9791961975483"
}
```

> ℹ️ jq is a nice tool to manipulate JSON in the shell. If you want to know more about jq and install it, see Appendix A.

12.1.5. Injecting Configuration Value

If you look carefully at Listing 260, you'll notice that the generateIsbnNumbers() method of the NumberResource uses a separator variable. separator is a boolean that indicates to Java Faker whether ISBN numbers should be generated with a separator or not. We could easily add a boolean separator attribute and manually set it to true or false depending on our needs. But instead we can use Eclipse MicroProfile Configuration to inject this value. In Listing 262, NumberResource injects a number.separator property.

Listing 262. ISBN Number Endpoint Injecting a Property

```
@Path("/api/numbers")
@Produces(MediaType.APPLICATION_JSON)
public class NumberResource {

  @Inject
  Logger LOGGER;

  @ConfigProperty(name = "number.separator", defaultValue = "false")
  boolean separator;

  @GET
  public Response generateIsbnNumbers() {
    Faker faker = new Faker();
    IsbnNumbers isbnNumbers = new IsbnNumbers();
    isbnNumbers.setIsbn10(faker.code().isbn10(separator));
    isbnNumbers.setIsbn13(faker.code().isbn13(separator));
    LOGGER.info("ISBN numbers generated " + isbnNumbers);
    return Response.ok(isbnNumbers).build();
  }
}
```

If you do not provide a value for a property in the application.properties, the application startup would fail with a javax.enterprise.inject.spi.DeploymentException. That's why we use a default value (using the property defaultValue). If we don't declare a value in the application.properties it would not fail and pick up the defaultValue. Or we can set it up in the application.properties file:

```
number.separator=true
```

Now if you run mvn compile quarkus:dev (under the parent project folder) and curl the URL http://localhost:8080/api/numbers you should see separators on the ISBN numbers.

```
$ curl http://localhost:8080/api/numbers | jq

{
  "isbn10": "1-932563-60-1",
  "isbn13": "979-1-9619754-8-3"
}
```

Alternatively, you can open http://localhost:8080/api/numbers in your browser.

12.1.6. Customising the JSON Output

The JSON output from the *ISBN Number* microservice is not exactly what we want. We would like to change the name of the keys: isbn_13 instead of isbn13 and isbn_10 instead of isbn10. To change the JSON binding, we can use the JSON-B specification.

Listing 263 shows the IsbnNumbers class with some JSON-B mapping annotations. For example, the @JsonbProperty tells the JSON-B provider to change the name isbn10 to isbn_10.

Listing 263. IsbnNumbers with JSON-B Annotations

```
public class IsbnNumbers {

    @JsonbProperty("isbn_10")
    private String isbn10;
    @JsonbProperty("isbn_13")
    private String isbn13;

    // Getters and setters
}
```

Without any other change to the Quarkus runtime or configuration, if you execute mvn quarkus:dev and go back to the same URL, you will see that the JSON has changed and looks like the following:

```
$ curl http://localhost:8080/api/numbers | jq

{
  "isbn_10": "1-383-10381-X",
  "isbn_13": "978-0-929138-68-8"
}
```

12.1.7. OpenAPI

The *ISBN Number* microservice needs to expose an API to be consumed by the *Book* microservice. To document this API, we can use the OpenAPI specification.

Start the application (mvn quarkus:dev) and make a request to the URL http://localhost:8080/q/openapi. As you can see in Listing 264, Quarkus automatically generates the OpenAPI documentation for the *ISBN Number* microservice.

Listing 264. Default OpenAPI YAML Contract

```
openapi: 3.0.3
info:
  title: Generated API
  version: "1.0"
paths:
  /api/numbers:
    get:
      responses:
        "200":
          description: OK
```

You can use cURL to change the HTTP header and to retrieve the OpenAPI document in several formats:

- YAML: curl http://localhost:8080/q/openapi
- JSON: curl -H "Accept: application/json" http://localhost:8080/q/openapi

But this contract lacks documentation. The Eclipse MicroProfile OpenAPI allows us to customise the methods' description of our REST endpoints as well as the entire application itself.

Documenting the Number REST Endpoint

The Eclipse MicroProfile OpenAPI has a set of annotations to customise the REST endpoint class, methods and parameters to make the OpenAPI contract richer and clearer for consumers. Listing 265 shows what the NumberResource endpoint looks like once annotated.

Listing 265. Documenting the REST endpoint

```java
@Path("/api/numbers")
@Produces(MediaType.APPLICATION_JSON)
public class NumberResource {

  @Inject
  Logger LOGGER;

  @ConfigProperty(name = "number.separator", defaultValue = "false")
  boolean separator;

  @GET
  @Operation(
          summary = "Generates ISBN numbers",
      description = "These ISBN numbers have several formats: ISBN 13 and ISBN 10")
  @APIResponse(
      responseCode = "200",
          content = @Content(mediaType = MediaType.APPLICATION_JSON,
            schema = @Schema(implementation = IsbnNumbers.class)))
  public Response generateIsbnNumbers() {
    Faker faker = new Faker();
    IsbnNumbers isbnNumbers = new IsbnNumbers();
    isbnNumbers.setIsbn10(faker.code().isbn10(separator));
    isbnNumbers.setIsbn13(faker.code().isbn13(separator));
    LOGGER.info("ISBN numbers generated " + isbnNumbers);
    return Response.ok(isbnNumbers).build();
  }
}
```

The @Operation annotation describes the method while @APIResponse gives information about the HTTP status code (here, a 200 when the method is invoked successfully) and the content of the Response (which is an IsbnNumbers class).

Documenting the IsbnNumbers POJO

The generateIsbnNumbers() method returns an IsbnNumbers object. As you can see in Listing 266, this object can also be annotated with @Schema to provide more textual description. For example, we can inform the consumers which attributes are required in the JSON document (@Schema(required = true)).

Listing 266. Documenting the IsbnNumbers Class

```
@Schema(description = "Several formats of book ISBN numbers")
public class IsbnNumbers {

  @Schema(required = true)
  @JsonbProperty("isbn_10")
  private String isbn10;
  @Schema(required = true)
  @JsonbProperty("isbn_13")
  private String isbn13;

  // Getters and setters
}
```

Documenting the Application

The previous annotations allow you to customise the contract for a given REST endpoint. But it's also important to customise the contract for the entire microservice. Eclipse MicroProfile OpenAPI also has a set of annotations to serve that purpose. The difference is that these annotations cannot be used on the endpoint itself but, instead, on another Java class which is meant to be configuring the entire application. For this, the NumberApplication described in Listing 267 needs to extend javax.ws.rs.core.Application and be annotated with OpenAPI annotations.

Listing 267. Custom OpenAPI Documentation for the Application

```
@ApplicationPath("/")
@OpenAPIDefinition(
  info = @Info(
         title = "Number API",
    description = "This API allows to generate all sorts of ISBN numbers",
       version = "1.0",
       contact = @Contact(name = "@agoncal", url = "https://twitter.com/agoncal")),
  externalDocs = @ExternalDocumentation(
           url = "https://github.com/agoncal/agoncal-fascicle-quarkus",
   description = "All the Understanding Quarkus code"),
  tags = {
    @Tag(name = "api", description = "Public API that can be used by anybody"),
    @Tag(name = "numbers", description = "Anybody interested in ISBN numbers")
  }
)
public class NumberApplication extends Application {
}
```

The Customised OpenAPI Contract

After applying all the previous modifications to the contract meta-data, go back to the http://localhost:8080/q/openapi endpoint and you will see the customised OpenAPI contract described in Listing 268.

Listing 268. Customised OpenAPI YAML Contract

```yaml
openapi: 3.0.3
info:
  title: Number API
  description: This API allows to generate all sorts of ISBN numbers
  contact:
    name: '@agoncal'
    url: https://twitter.com/agoncal
  version: "1.0"
externalDocs:
  description: All the Understanding Quarkus code
  url: https://github.com/agoncal/agoncal-fascicle-quarkus
tags:
- name: api
  description: Public API that can be used by anybody
- name: numbers
  description: Anybody interested in ISBN numbers
paths:
  /api/numbers:
    get:
      summary: Generates ISBN numbers
      description: "These ISBN numbers have several formats: ISBN 13 and ISBN 10"
      responses:
        "200":
          description: OK
          content:
            application/json:
              schema:
                $ref: '#/components/schemas/IsbnNumbers'
components:
  schemas:
    IsbnNumbers:
      description: Several formats of book ISBN numbers
      required:
      - isbn_10
      - isbn_13
      type: object
      properties:
        isbn_10:
          type: string
        isbn_13:
          type: string
```

The contract in Listing 268 is much richer than the one in Listing 264. There is information about the entire *Number* microservice, as well as all the paths that are accessible through HTTP. In the contract in Listing 268, notice the reference to the IsbnNumbers ($ref: '#/components/schemas/IsbnNumbers) on the generateIsbnNumbers() method. For the consumer of this contract, the returned structure is much clearer than the one defined in Listing 264.

Swagger UI

Visualising an OpenAPI contract in YAML or JSON can be cumbersome if the contract is too large. Instead, we can use Swagger UI.

By default, Swagger UI is accessible at the URL /q/swagger-ui. So, once your application is started, you can go to http://localhost:8080/q/swagger-ui, you will see the contract in a visual format such as Figure 62.

Figure 62. Swagger UI contract of the Number endpoint

You can visualise your API's operations and schemas, but you can also invoke them by simply clicking on the *GET* button and then the *Execute* button as shown in Figure 63.

Figure 63. Invoking the method to generate ISBN numbers

12.1.8. Adding Liveness Health Check

To check that our *Number* microservice is live, we can invoke the `generateIsbnNumbers()` method on the `NumberResource`. For that, we have the `NumberResourceHealthCheck` class as seen in Listing 269. It extends `HealthCheck` and overrides the `call()` method. That's where we invoke the endpoint's `generateIsbnNumbers()` method. If the call succeeds, we return an `up` response (meaning the REST endpoint is live).

Listing 269. Checks the Liveness of the Number Microservice

```java
@Liveness
@ApplicationScoped
public class NumberResourceHealthCheck implements HealthCheck {

  @Inject
  NumberResource numberResource;

  @Override
  public HealthCheckResponse call() {
    numberResource.generateIsbnNumbers();
    return HealthCheckResponse.named("Ping Number REST Endpoint").up().build();
  }
}
```

With Quarkus started in dev mode, you can now invoke the http://localhost:8080/q/health/live url in your browser or by using cURL. Because we defined our health check as a liveness procedure (with `@Liveness` qualifier) the health check procedure is now present in the checks array.

Listing 270. Liveness JSON Result of the Number Microservice

```json
{
  "status": "UP",
  "checks": [
    {
      "name": "Ping Number REST Endpoint",
      "status": "UP"
    }
  ]
}
```

12.1.9. Running the ISBN Number Microservice

By now you've already executed the *Number* microservice by starting Quarkus and invoking some cURL commands. But let's go further with hot reloading the application and configuring it.

Live Reload

With Quarkus running in dev mode (`mvn quarkus:dev`), cURL the following URL http://localhost:8080/api/numbers. You should see something like this:

```json
{
  "isbn_10": "1-383-10381-X",
  "isbn_13": "978-0-929138-68-8"
}
```

Now, update the method `NumberResource.generateIsbnNumbers()` by setting a dummy ISBN number with `isbnNumbers.setIsbn10("dummy")`. Save the `NumberResource` file if your IDE does not do it automatically, and execute the cURL command again. As you can see, the output has changed without you to having to stop and restart Quarkus:

```json
{
  "isbn_10": "dummy",
  "isbn_13": "978-0-929138-68-8"
}
```

You can also change the `application.properties` file by setting the `number.separator` to `false`. Execute the cURL command again, and you will notice that the ISBN numbers do not use separators anymore.

Configuring Quarkus Listening Port

Because we will end-up running several microservices, let's configure Quarkus so it listens to a different port than 8080. This is quite easy as we just need to add one property in the application.properties file:

```
quarkus.http.port=8081
```

Now you need to restart the application to change the port. From now on, check the endpoint at http://localhost:8081/api/numbers instead of http://localhost:8080/api/numbers.

12.1.10. Testing the ISBN Number Microservice

So far so good, but wouldn't it be better with a few tests, just in case? When we bootstrapped the microservice, some extra Maven dependencies were added to the pom.xml file (see Listing 271).

- quarkus-junit5: JUnit 5 support in Quarkus.
- rest-assured: REST Assured to test the REST endpoint.

Listing 271. Maven Test Dependencies

```xml
<dependency>
    <groupId>io.quarkus</groupId>
    <artifactId>quarkus-junit5</artifactId>
    <scope>test</scope>
</dependency>
<dependency>
    <groupId>io.rest-assured</groupId>
    <artifactId>rest-assured</artifactId>
    <scope>test</scope>
</dependency>
```

In Listing 272, the @QuarkusTest runner instructs JUnit to start the application before the tests. Then, the shouldGenerateIsbnNumbers() method checks the HTTP response status code and the JSON content. Notice that these tests use REST Assured[266].

Listing 272. Testing the Generation of ISBN Numbers

```
@QuarkusTest
public class NumberResourceTest {

  @Test
  void shouldGenerateIsbnNumbers() {
    given()
      .header(HttpHeaders.ACCEPT, MediaType.APPLICATION_JSON).
    when()
      .get("/api/numbers").
    then()
      .statusCode(OK.getStatusCode())
      .body("$", hasKey("isbn_10"))
      .body("$", hasKey("isbn_13"));
  }
}
```

 If you like the format of this fascicle and are interested in Quarkus, check out the references for my *Practising Quarkus 2.x* fascicle in Appendix F. In this *Practising* fascicle, you will develop, test, build, package and monitor an entire microservice application.

Now execute the test with mvn test or from your IDE. The test should pass and you should see similar logs to those in Listing 273.

Listing 273. Successful Test Output

```
[INFO] -------------------------------------------------------
[INFO] T E S T S
[INFO] -------------------------------------------------------
[INFO] Running org.agoncal.fascicle.quarkus.number.NumberResourceTest
[INFO] Quarkus started in 0.586s. Listening on: http://0.0.0.0:8081
[INFO] Profile test activated.
[INFO] Installed features: [cdi, resteasy, resteasy-jsonb, smallrye-health, smallrye-
openapi, swagger-ui]
[INFO] ISBN numbers generated BookNumbers{isbn10='1-9635127-0-7', isbn13='978-1-7424-
9845-4'}

[INFO] Quarkus stopped in 0.029s

[INFO] Results:
[INFO] Tests run: 1, Failures: 0, Errors: 0, Skipped: 0
[INFO]
[INFO] -----------------------------------------------
[INFO] BUILD SUCCESS
[INFO] -----------------------------------------------
```

12.2. Developing the REST Book Microservice

Now, it's time to develop a microservice that returns books. The *Book* microservice returns random book data such as the book's title, the author, the genre and the publisher. But the *Book* microservice also needs to interact with the *ISBN Number* microservice to get an ISBN. In this section, we will:

- Bootstrap a Quarkus applications using its Maven plugin,
- Implement a *Book* REST API using JAX-RS,
- Generate the JSON Output with JSON-P,
- Invoke the *ISBN Number* microservice thanks to REST Client,
- Handle fault tolerance,
- Add metrics,
- Test the REST APIs with REST Assured.

12.2.1. Bootstrapping the Book Microservice

To bootstrap the *Book* microservice we use the following Maven command (remember that you can also go to https://code.quarkus.io if you prefer):

Listing 274. Command to Bootstrap the Book Microservice

```
mvn io.quarkus:quarkus-maven-plugin:2.5.0.Final:create \
    -DplatformVersion=2.5.0.Final \
    -DprojectGroupId=org.agoncal.fascicle.quarkus.putting-together \
    -DprojectArtifactId=rest-book \
    -DprojectVersion=2.0.0-SNAPSHOT \
    -DclassName="org.agoncal.fascicle.quarkus.book.BookResource" \
    -Dpath="/api/books" \
    -Dextensions="resteasy-jsonb, rest-client, smallrye-fault-tolerance, smallrye-
metrics"
```

12.2.2. Maven Dependencies

Once the code of the application is generated, you will see all the extensions needed to compile and execute the *Book* microservice in the pom.xml in Listing 275:

- quarkus-resteasy: REST framework implementing JAX-RS.
- quarkus-resteasy-jsonb: JSON-B serialisation support for RESTEasy.
- quarkus-rest-client: REST Client in order to interact with the *ISBN number* microservice.
- quarkus-smallrye-fault-tolerance: The communication with the *ISBN number* microservice being inherently unreliable, we need the Fault Tolerance dependency.
- quarkus-smallrye-metrics: The Fault Tolerance dependency gathers metrics relating to the time it takes to process a request.

- `javafaker`: You need to add this dependency manually so you can generate fake book data.

Listing 275. Maven Dependencies

```xml
<dependency>
    <groupId>io.quarkus</groupId>
    <artifactId>quarkus-smallrye-fault-tolerance</artifactId>
</dependency>
<dependency>
    <groupId>io.quarkus</groupId>
    <artifactId>quarkus-rest-client</artifactId>
</dependency>
<dependency>
    <groupId>io.quarkus</groupId>
    <artifactId>quarkus-resteasy-jsonb</artifactId>
</dependency>
<dependency>
    <groupId>io.quarkus</groupId>
    <artifactId>quarkus-smallrye-metrics</artifactId>
</dependency>
<dependency>
    <groupId>io.quarkus</groupId>
    <artifactId>quarkus-arc</artifactId>
</dependency>
<dependency>
    <groupId>io.quarkus</groupId>
    <artifactId>quarkus-resteasy</artifactId>
</dependency>
<dependency>
    <groupId>com.github.javafaker</groupId>
    <artifactId>javafaker</artifactId>
</dependency>
```

12.2.3. Directories and Files

The *Book* microservice only needs a few Java classes, as shown in Figure 64:

- `BookResource`: REST endpoint returning a JSON representation of a book.

- `IsbnNumbers`: ISBN 10 and 13 numbers obtained by invoking the *ISBN number* microservice.

- `NumberResourceProxy`: REST Client proxy to invoke the *ISBN number* microservice.

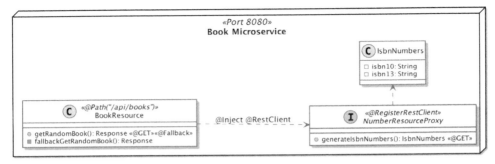

Figure 64. Book microservice class diagram

The classes and files described in Figure 64 follow the Maven directory structure:

- `src/main/java`: The directory for the `BookResource`, `IsbnNumbers` classes and the `NumberResourceProxy` interface.

- `src/main/resources`: The `application.properties` file to configure the microservice invocation.

- `src/test/java`: The directory for the test case `BookResourceTest` and the mock class `MockNumberResourceProxy`.

- `pom.xml`: The Maven Project Object Model (POM) describing the project and its dependencies.

12.2.4. Book REST Endpoint

To expose a REST API to get a random book, we need a REST endpoint using JAX-RS. Listing 276 shows the `BookResource` class. The `@Path` annotation tells us that the API will be accessible through the `/api/books` and will produce JSON. The `getRandomBook()` is accessible through an HTTP GET and returns a random book as a `JsonObject`.

Listing 276. Book REST Endpoint Retrieving a Random Book

```
@Path("/api/books")
@Produces(MediaType.APPLICATION_JSON)
public class BookResource {

  @Inject
  Logger LOGGER;

  @GET
  public Response getRandomBook() {

    IsbnNumbers isbnNumbers = numberResourceProxy.generateIsbnNumbers();

    Faker faker = new Faker();
    JsonObject book = Json.createObjectBuilder()
      .add("isbn_13", isbnNumbers.getIsbn13())
      .add("isbn_10", isbnNumbers.getIsbn10())
      .add("title", faker.book().title())
      .add("author", faker.book().author())
      .add("genre", faker.book().genre())
      .add("publisher", faker.book().publisher())
      .add("timestamp", String.valueOf(LocalDateTime.now()))
      .build();

    LOGGER.info("Random book " + book);
    return Response.ok(book).build();
  }
}
```

Listing 277 shows the code of the IsbnNumbers. It holds two values (the 10 and 13 digits ISBN numbers) and uses JSON-B annotations to bind the JSON result, and Bean Validation annotations to make sure the numbers are not null. Notice that validation happens automatically, you don't have to invoke programmatically the Bean Validation APIs.

Listing 277. POJO with Bean Validation and JSON-B Annotations

```
public class IsbnNumbers {

  @NotNull
  @JsonbProperty("isbn_10")
  private String isbn10;
  @NotNull
  @JsonbProperty("isbn_13")
  private String isbn13;

}
```

12.2.5. Book Microservice Invoking the Number Microservice

In Listing 276, there is something missing. To get the ISBN numbers, the method getRandomBook() invokes a numberResourceProxy. That's when we want the *Book* microservice to invoke the *Number* microservice so that it gets the ISBN numbers.

For that, we use the REST Client API with the @RestClient annotation to inject the NumberResourceProxy interface (see Listing 276). This interface allows us to remotely invoke the *Number* microservice through HTTP to return both ISBN 10 and 13 numbers.

Listing 278. Book REST Endpoint Injecting the Proxy

```
@Path("/api/books")
@Produces(MediaType.APPLICATION_JSON)
public class BookResource {

  @Inject
  Logger LOGGER;

  @Inject
  @RestClient
  NumberResourceProxy numberResourceProxy;

  @GET
  public Response getRandomBook() {

    IsbnNumbers isbnNumbers = numberResourceProxy.generateIsbnNumbers();

    Faker faker = new Faker();
    JsonObject book = Json.createObjectBuilder()
      .add("isbn_13", isbnNumbers.getIsbn13())
      .add("isbn_10", isbnNumbers.getIsbn10())
      .add("title", faker.book().title())
      .add("author", faker.book().author())
      .add("genre", faker.book().genre())
      .add("publisher", faker.book().publisher())
      .add("timestamp", String.valueOf(LocalDateTime.now()))
      .build();

    LOGGER.info("Random book " + book);
    return Response.ok(book).build();
  }
}
```

Using the Eclipse MicroProfile REST Client is as simple as creating a NumberResourceProxy interface using the proper JAX-RS and MicroProfile annotations (see Listing 279):

- @RegisterRestClient allows Quarkus to know that this interface is meant to be available for CDI injection as a REST Client,

- @Path and @GET are the standard JAX-RS annotations used to define how to access the service,

- @Produces defines the expected content-type.

Listing 279. The Proxy Interface

```
@Path("/api/numbers")
@Produces(MediaType.APPLICATION_JSON)
@RegisterRestClient
public interface NumberResourceProxy {

  @GET
  IsbnNumbers generateIsbnNumbers();
}
```

The generateIsbnNumbers() method gives our code the ability to get ISBN numbers from the *Number* microservice. Eclipse MicroProfile REST Client will handle all the networking and marshalling, leaving our code clean of such technical details.

But where is the *Number* microservice located? In order to determine the base URL to which REST calls will be made, the REST Client uses a configuration from the application.properties file. The name of the property needs to follow a certain convention which is displayed in the following code:

```
quarkus.rest-
client."org.agoncal.fascicle.quarkus.book.NumberResourceProxy".url=http://localhost:80
81
quarkus.rest-
client."org.agoncal.fascicle.quarkus.book.NumberResourceProxy".scope=javax.inject.Sing
leton
```

Having this configuration means that all requests performed using the NumberResourceProxy interface will use http://localhost:8081 as the base URL. Using this configuration and the code in Listing 279, calling the generateIsbnNumbers() method of NumberResourceProxy would result in an HTTP GET request being made to http://localhost:8081/api/numbers.

12.2.6. Falling Back

Getting random books works great… until we kill the *Number* microservice. What happens? Well, the *Book* microservice cannot invoke the *Number* microservice anymore and breaks with a ConnectException:

```
ERROR [io.qua.ver.htt.run.QuarkusErrorHandler] HTTP Request to /api/books failed
org.jboss.resteasy.spi.UnhandledException: javax.ws.rs.ProcessingException:
RESTEASY004655: Unable to invoke request: java.net.ConnectException: Connection
refused (Connection refused)
```

One of the challenges brought by the distributed nature of microservices is that communication with external systems is inherently unreliable. Distribution increases the demand for resilient applications. So let's provide a fallback for getting ISBN numbers in case of failure. For example, we could serialise the JSON representation of a book into a file so it can be processed later. Or store a temporary book into a database, or send a message to an event-bus. We will just be sending back dummy data to make it simple.

For that, we add one fallback method to the BookResource called fallbackGetRandomBook and a @Fallback annotation to the getRandomBook() method (see Listing 280).

Listing 280. Falling Back on Getting a Random Book

```java
@Path("/api/books")
@Produces(MediaType.APPLICATION_JSON)
public class BookResource {

  @Inject
  Logger LOGGER;

  @Inject
  @RestClient
  NumberResourceProxy numberResourceProxy;

  @GET
  @Fallback(fallbackMethod = "fallbackGetRandomBook")
  public Response getRandomBook() {

    IsbnNumbers isbnNumbers = numberResourceProxy.generateIsbnNumbers();

    Faker faker = new Faker();
    JsonObject book = Json.createObjectBuilder()
      .add("isbn_13", isbnNumbers.getIsbn13())
      .add("isbn_10", isbnNumbers.getIsbn10())
      .add("title", faker.book().title())
      .add("author", faker.book().author())
      .add("genre", faker.book().genre())
      .add("publisher", faker.book().publisher())
      .add("timestamp", String.valueOf(LocalDateTime.now()))
      .build();

    LOGGER.info("Random book " + book);
    return Response.ok(book).build();
  }

  private Response fallbackGetRandomBook() {
    LOGGER.warn("Falling back on creating a book");
    JsonObject dummyBook = Json.createObjectBuilder()
      .add("title", "Dummy book")
      .add("timestamp", String.valueOf(LocalDateTime.now()))
      .build();
    return Response.ok(dummyBook).build();
  }
}
```

The `fallbackGetRandomBook()` method must have the same method signature as `getRandomBook()` (in our case, it takes no arguments and returns a `Response` object). In case the *Book* microservice cannot invoke the *Number* microservice, the `fallbackGetRandomBook()` is invoked and some dummy data is returned.

12.2.7. Adding Metrics

Before running the application, we would like to add some metrics so we know how many times the `getRandomBook()` method is invoked. For that, we need to annotate the method with `@Counted` as seen in Listing 281.

Listing 281. Metrics on the Method to Get a Random Book

```java
@Path("/api/books")
@Produces(MediaType.APPLICATION_JSON)
public class BookResource {

  @Inject
  Logger LOGGER;

  @GET
  @Counted(name = "getRandomBook",
    description = "Counts how many times the getRandomBook method has been invoked")
  public Response getRandomBook() {

    IsbnNumbers isbnNumbers = numberResourceProxy.generateIsbnNumbers();

    Faker faker = new Faker();
    JsonObject book = Json.createObjectBuilder()
      .add("isbn_13", isbnNumbers.getIsbn13())
      .add("isbn_10", isbnNumbers.getIsbn10())
      .add("title", faker.book().title())
      .add("author", faker.book().author())
      .add("genre", faker.book().genre())
      .add("publisher", faker.book().publisher())
      .add("timestamp", String.valueOf(LocalDateTime.now()))
      .build();

    LOGGER.info("Random book " + book);
    return Response.ok(book).build();
  }
}
```

12.2.8. Running the Book Microservice

Let's see if this code works. For that, it's just a matter of starting both Quarkus instances and executing a few cURL commands. First, start both Quarkus instances, one for the *Book* microservice, and the other one for the *Number* microservice:

```
rest-book$ mvn quarkus:dev
rest-number$ mvn quarkus:dev
```

Then, make sure both microservices are up and running by executing a few HTTP GET cURL commands.

```
$ curl -X GET http://localhost:8081/api/numbers | jq
{
  "isbn_10": "0-06-448352-5",
  "isbn_13": "979-0-09-133656-0"
}

$ curl -X GET http://localhost:8080/api/books | jq
{
  "isbn_13": "978-1-9774472-4-1",
  "isbn_10": "1-911871-53-6",
  "title": "The House of Mirth",
  "author": "Mr. Cindy Lowe",
  "genre": "Narrative nonfiction",
  "publisher": "Ace Books",
  "timestamp": "2020-09-24T14:39:24.278586"
}
```

If the ISBN numbers are set on the book, that means that the *Book* microservice has managed to invoke the *Number* microservices. Now we are ready to test the fallback. For that, kill the *Number* microservice and invoke the *Book* microservice again. You should see the following:

```
$ curl -X GET http://localhost:8080/api/books | jq
{
  "title": "Dummy book",
  "timestamp": "2020-09-24T14:43:15.431364"
}
```

Restart the *Number* microservice and keep on generating new books: the books are returned with their ISBN numbers. At the same time, to view the metrics of the *Book* microservice in JSON format, execute the following command:

```
$ curl -H "Accept: application/json" http://localhost:8080/q/metrics/application

{
  "BookResource.getRandomBook": 13,
  "BookResource.getRandomBook.invocations.total": 13,
  "BookResource.getRandomBook.fallback.calls.total": 1
}
```

12.2.9. Testing the Book Microservice

To test the *Book* microservice, we need the same Maven dependencies as the ones for the *Number* microservice described in Listing 271. Same as before, we annotate our test in Listing 282 with @QuarkusTest. Then, the shouldGetRandomBook() method checks the HTTP response status code as well as the JSON content with REST Assured.

Listing 282. Testing Random Book

```
@QuarkusTest
public class BookResourceTest {

  @Test
  void shouldGetRandomBook() {
    given()
      .header(HttpHeaders.ACCEPT, MediaType.APPLICATION_JSON).
    when()
      .get("/api/books").
    then()
      .statusCode(OK.getStatusCode())
      .body("$", hasKey("isbn_10"))
      .body("$", hasKey("isbn_13"))
      .body("$", hasKey("title"))
      .body("$", hasKey("author"))
      .body("$", hasKey("genre"))
      .body("$", hasKey("publisher"));
  }
}
```

But remember that the *Book* microservice now depends on the *Number* microservice. So now, to test the *Book* microservice we need the *Number* microservice to be up and running. This creates a huge dependency on both microservices, and that's not what we want in our tests. To avoid this, we need to Mock the *Number* REST API interface. For this, we mock the NumberResourceProxy interface with a MockNumberResourceProxy with @Mock as seen in Listing 283.

Listing 283. Class Mocking the Proxy Invocation

```
@Mock
@ApplicationScoped
@RestClient
public class MockNumberResourceProxy implements NumberResourceProxy {

  @Override
  public IsbnNumbers generateIsbnNumbers() {
    IsbnNumbers isbnNumbers = new IsbnNumbers();
    isbnNumbers.setIsbn13("dummy isbn 13");
    isbnNumbers.setIsbn10("dummy isbn 10");
    return isbnNumbers;
  }
}
```

So instead of invoking the `NumberResourceProxy`, the alternative `MockNumberResourceProxy` is automatically called during the test phase. Now if you execute the tests (with `mvn test`) they should pass.

12.3. Summary

In this chapter, you didn't use all the Quarkus APIs, tips and concepts that you previously saw in this fascicle, but you did use some of them. The idea was to put some of these concepts together and develop a more complex example on how to use Quarkus.

You bootstrapped two microservices, thanks to the Quarkus Maven plugin that scaffolds a basic directory structure, Maven dependencies, some code and test classes. The *ISBN Number* microservice generates book numbers and uses injection, JSON binding, OpenAPI and health checks. As for the *Book* microservice, it needs REST Client to invoke the *ISBN Number* microservice remotely. Use fallback if the call fails and expose some metrics so we know how many books have successfully been generated. We ended up testing both microservices and running them.

Time to wrap up. The next chapter will summarise what you've seen in this fascicle. Then, remember to check the Appendix if you want to know more about the releases of Quarkus (Appendix B) or the *Eclipse MicroProfile Specification Versions*.

[264] Java Faker https://github.com/DiUS/java-faker
[265] Ruby faker https://github.com/faker-ruby
[266] REST Assured http://rest-assured.io

Chapter 13. Summary

This fascicle started with some terminology to make sure you would understand all the concepts around Quarkus. Chapter 2, *Understanding Quarkus* defined Microservices, Reactive Systems, MicroProfile, Cloud Native, GraalVM, and briefly presented Quarkus.

Then, thanks to Chapter 3, *Getting Started*, you bootstrapped a simple example and made sure your development environment was up and running: developing, debugging, testing some code, but also using live reload or GraalVM to build native executable and containerising it.

Chapter 4, *Core Quarkus* focused on the fundamentals of Quarkus (injection, configuration, profiles, logging and life cycle). Chapter 5, *Data, Transactions and ORM* uses these fundamentals to add extensions that deal with data validation, object-relational mapping or transactions.

Microservices fail into two main categories: *HTTP Microservices* (Chapter 6) and *Event-Driven Microservices* (Chapter 8). HTTP-related technologies usually use synchronous communication and therefore need to deal with invocation failure (Chapter 7, *Communication and Fault Tolerance*). They can be synchronous or asynchronous, when there are many microservices, observability becomes mandatory as explained in Chapter 9, *Observability*.

Then, comes production time. Today, with all the *Cloud Native* philosophy, we need to package our microservices into containers, deploy them and orchestrate them. Chapter 10 showed you some Quarkus extensions to easily interact with Docker and Kubernetes.

With Chapter 11, *Tests* you saw how easy it is to create JVM and Native tests with Quarkus. That's because Quarkus integrates many testing and mocking frameworks and makes them work with simple code as well as complex microservice architecture.

We finished this fascicle with a final *Putting It All Together* chapter (Chapter 12). We took some of the concepts seen previously, put them together, and built a slightly more complex application.

This is the end of the *Understanding Quarkus 2.x* fascicle. I hope you liked it, learnt a few things, and more importantly, will be able to take this knowledge back to your projects.

Remember that you can find all the code for this fascicle at https://github.com/agoncal/agoncal-fascicle-quarkus/tree/2.0. If some parts were not clear enough, or if you found something missing, a bug, or you just want to leave a note or suggestion, please use the GitHub issue tracker at https://github.com/agoncal/agoncal-fascicle-quarkus/issues.

If you liked the format of this fascicle, you might want to read others that I have written. Check out Appendix F for the full list of fascicles.

Thanks for reading!

Antonio

Appendix A: Setting up the Development Environment on macOS

This appendix focuses on setting up your development environment so you can do some hands-on work by following the code snippets listed in the previous chapters. This fascicle has lots of code samples, and even has a chapter with a *"Putting It All Together"* section. This section provides a step-by-step example showing how to develop, compile, deploy, execute and test the components. To run these examples, you need to install the required software.

Bear in mind that I run all of these tools on macOS. So, this appendix gives you all of the installation guidelines for the macOS operating system. If your machine runs on Linux or Windows, check online to know how to install the following tools on your platform.

A.1. Homebrew

One of the pre-requisites is that you have *Homebrew* installed. *Homebrew*[267] is a package manager for macOS.

A.1.1. A Brief History of Homebrew

The name *Homebrew* is intended to suggest the idea of building software on the Mac depending on the user's taste. It was written by Max Howell in 2009 in Ruby[268]. On September 2016, Homebrew version 1.0.0 was released. In January 2019, Linuxbrew was merged back into Homebrew, adding beta support for Linux and the Windows Subsystem for Linux to Homebrew's feature set.

A.1.2. Installing Homebrew on macOS

To install Homebrew, just execute the following command:

```
$ /bin/bash -c "$(curl -fsSL
https://raw.githubusercontent.com/Homebrew/install/master/install.sh)"
```

You also need *Homebrew Cask*[269] which extends Homebrew and brings installation and management of GUI macOS applications. Install it by running:

```
$ brew tap homebrew/cask
```

A.1.3. Checking for Homebrew Installation

Now you should be able to execute a few Homebrew commands:

```
$ brew --version

Homebrew 3.3.2
Homebrew/homebrew-core
Homebrew/homebrew-cask
```

A.1.4. Some Homebrew Commands

- `brew commands`: Lists the built-in and external commands.

- `brew help`: Displays help.

- `brew doctor`: Checks for potential problems.

- `brew install`: Installs a formula.

- `brew uninstall`: Uninstalls a formula.

- `brew list`: Lists all installed formulae.

- `brew upgrade`: Upgrades outdated casks and formulae.

- `brew update`: Fetches the newest version of Homebrew.

- `brew cask help`: Displays Homebrew Cask help.

- `brew cask install`: Installs a cask.

- `brew cask uninstall`: Uninstalls a cask.

- `brew cask list`: Lists installed casks.

- `brew cask upgrade`: Upgrades all outdated casks (or the specified casks).

A.2. Java 11

Essential for the development and execution of the examples in the fascicle is the *Java Development Kit*[270] (JDK). The JDK includes several tools such as a compiler (`javac`), a virtual machine, a documentation generator (`javadoc`), monitoring tools (Visual VM[271]) and so on. The code in this fascicle uses Java 11 (JDK 11.0.13).

A.2.1. Architecture

One design goal of Java is portability, which means that programs written for the Java platform must run similarly on any combination of hardware and operating system with adequate runtime support. This is achieved by compiling the Java language code to an intermediate representation called *bytecode*, instead of directly to a specific machine code. This bytecode is then analysed, interpreted and executed on the *Java Virtual Machine* (JVM).

The *Interpreter* is the one interpreting the bytecode. It does it quickly, but executes slowly. The disadvantage of the interpreter is that, when one method is called multiple times, a new interpretation is required every time. That's when the *Just In Time* (JIT) compiler kicks in. JIT is basically the component that translates the JVM bytecode (generated by your `javac` command) into machine code which is the language that your underlying execution environment (i.e. your processor) can understand—and all that happens dynamically at runtime! When the JIT finds repeated code, it compiles the bytecode and changes it to native code. This native code will then be used directly for repeated method calls, which improves the performance of the system. This JIT is also called the *Java HotSpot*[272] (a.k.a. Java HotSpot Performance Engine, or HotSpot VM). Then, the *Garbage Collector* will collect and remove unreferenced objects.

When using GraalVM you have the choice of doing just-in-time or ahead-of-time compilation. GraalVM includes a high performance Java compiler, itself called Graal, which can be used in the HotSpot VM.

A.2.2. A Brief History of Java

James Gosling, Mike Sheridan, and Patrick Naughton initiated the Java language project in June 1991. Java was originally designed for interactive television, but it was too advanced for the digital cable television industry at the time. The language was initially called Oak after an oak tree that stood outside Gosling's office. Later, the project went by the name Green and was finally renamed Java, from Java coffee. Gosling designed Java with a C/C++-style syntax that system and application programmers would find familiar. Sun Microsystems released the first public implementation as Java 1.0 in 1996. Following Oracle Corporation's acquisition of Sun Microsystems in 2009–10, Oracle has described itself as the "*steward of Java technology*" since then[273].

A.2.3. Installing the JDK on macOS

To install the JDK 11.0.13, go to the official website, select the appropriate platform and language, and download[274] the distribution. For example, on macOS, download the file jdk-11.0.13_osx-x64_bin.dmg shown in Figure 65 (you should check out the *Accept License Agreement* check box before hitting the download link to let the download start). If you are not on Mac, the download steps are still pretty similar.

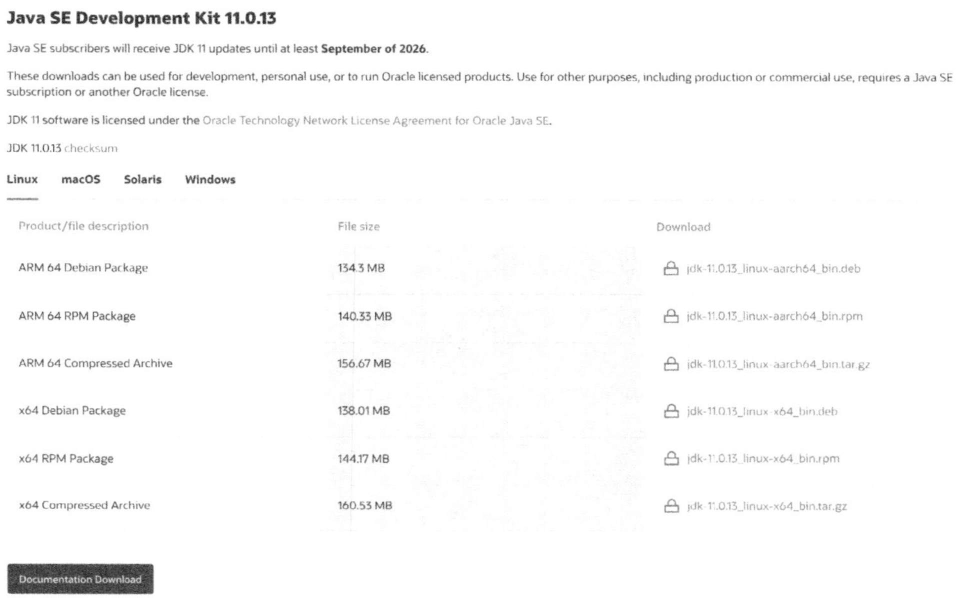

Java SE Development Kit 11.0.13

Java SE subscribers will receive JDK 11 updates until at least **September of 2026**.

These downloads can be used for development, personal use, or to run Oracle licensed products. Use for other purposes, including production or commercial use, requires a Java SE subscription or another Oracle license.

JDK 11 software is licensed under the Oracle Technology Network License Agreement for Oracle Java SE.

JDK 11.0.13 checksum

| Linux | macOS | Solaris | Windows |

Product/file description	File size	Download
ARM 64 Debian Package	134.3 MB	🔒 jdk-11.0.13_linux-aarch64_bin.deb
ARM 64 RPM Package	140.33 MB	🔒 jdk-11.0.13_linux-aarch64_bin.rpm
ARM 64 Compressed Archive	156.67 MB	🔒 jdk-11.0.13_linux-aarch64_bin.tar.gz
x64 Debian Package	138.01 MB	🔒 jdk-11.0.13_linux-x64_bin.deb
x64 RPM Package	144.17 MB	🔒 jdk-11.0.13_linux-x64_bin.rpm
x64 Compressed Archive	160.53 MB	🔒 jdk-11.0.13_linux-x64_bin.tar.gz

Documentation Download

Figure 65. Downloading the JDK distribution

Double-click on the file `jdk-11.0.13_osx-x64_bin.dmg`. This will bring up a pop-up screen (see Figure 66), asking you to start the installation.

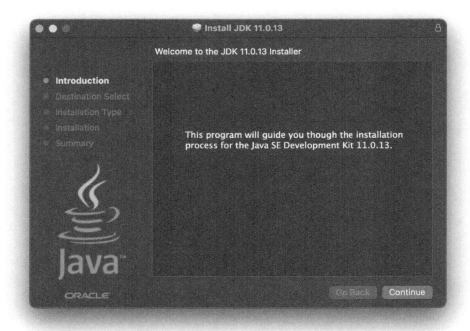

Figure 66. Installation pop-up screen

The wizard invites you to accept the licence for the software and install the JDK successfully (see Figure 67).

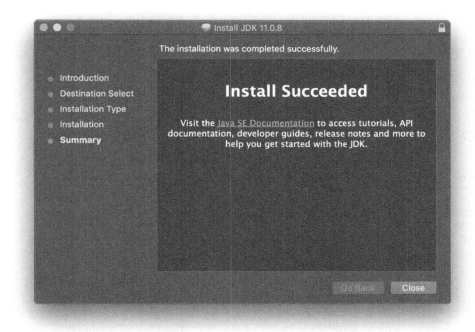

Figure 67. Successful JDK installation

There is also an easier way to install Java using Homebrew. First of all, check if you already have the Java formula installed on your machine:

```
$ brew cask list java11
Error: Cask 'java11' is not installed.
```

If the Java formula is not installed, execute the following Homebrew commands to install it:

```
$ brew tap homebrew/cask-versions
$ brew cask install java11
...
java11 was successfully installed!
```

A.2.4. Checking for Java Installation

Once the installation is complete, it is necessary to set the `JAVA_HOME` variable and the `$JAVA_HOME/bin` directory to the `PATH` variable. Check that your system recognises Java by entering `java -version` as well as the Java compiler with `javac -version`.

```
$ java -version
java version "11.0.13" LTS
Java(TM) SE Runtime Environment 18.9 (build 11.0.13-LTS)
Java HotSpot(TM) 64-Bit Server VM 18.9 (build 11.0.13-LTS, mixed mode)

$ javac -version
javac 11.0.13
```

Notice that, in the previous output, the HotSpot build is displayed. This is one easy way to know that you are using the HotSpot VM instead of the Graal VM.

A.3. GraalVM 21.3.0

GraalVM[275] is an extension of the *Java Virtual Machine* (JVM) to support more languages and several execution modes. It is itself implemented in Java. GraalVM supports a large set of languages: Java, of course, other JVM-based languages (such as Groovy, Kotlin etc.) but also JavaScript, Ruby, Python, R and C/C++.

But it also includes a new high performance Java compiler, itself called *Graal*. Running your application inside a JVM comes with startup and footprint costs. GraalVM has a feature to create *native images* for existing JVM-based applications. The image generation process employs static analysis to find any code reachable from the main Java method and then performs full *Ahead-Of-Time* (AOT) compilation on the *Substrate VM*[276]. The resulting native binary contains the whole program in machine code form for its immediate execution. This improves the performance of Java to match the performance of native languages for fast startup and low memory footprint.

A.3.1. Installing GraalVM on macOS

GraalVM can be installed from the GraalVM web site[277]. As shown in Figure 68, it shows two versions of GraalVM:

- *Community Edition*: Available for free for any use and built from the GraalVM sources available on GitHub.

- *Enterprise Edition*: Provides additional performance, security, and scalability relevant for running applications in production.

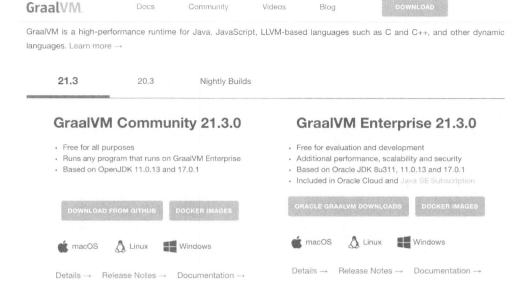

Figure 68. Community and enterprise edition of GraalVM

Using the community edition is enough. So you will be redirected to the GitHub account of GraalVM [278] (see Figure 69) where you can download the latest versions. Make sure you pick up version 21.3.0 and download the GraalVM file specific to your OS platform. For example, on macOS, download the file `graalvm-ce-java11-darwin-amd64-21.3.0.tar.gz` shown in Figure 69. If you are not on Mac, the download steps are still pretty similar.

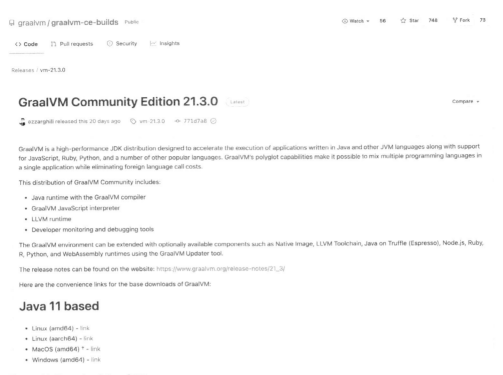

Releases / vm-21.3.0

GraalVM Community Edition 21.3.0 (Latest)

Compare ▾

🧑 ezzarghili released this 20 days ago   ♢ vm-21.3.0   -○- 771d7a8 ⊘

GraalVM is a high-performance JDK distribution designed to accelerate the execution of applications written in Java and other JVM languages along with support for JavaScript, Ruby, Python, and a number of other popular languages. GraalVM's polyglot capabilities make it possible to mix multiple programming languages in a single application while eliminating foreign language call costs.

This distribution of GraalVM Community includes:

- Java runtime with the GraalVM compiler
- GraalVM JavaScript interpreter
- LLVM runtime
- Developer monitoring and debugging tools

The GraalVM environment can be extended with optionally available components such as Native Image, LLVM Toolchain, Java on Truffle (Espresso), Node.js, Ruby, R, Python, and WebAssembly runtimes using the GraalVM Updater tool.

The release notes can be found on the website: https://www.graalvm.org/release-notes/21_3/

Here are the convenience links for the base downloads of GraalVM:

Java 11 based

- Linux (amd64) - link
- Linux (aarch64) - link
- MacOS (amd64) † - link
- Windows (amd64) - link

Figure 69. Download GraalVM

Double-click on the file `graalvm-ce-java11-darwin-amd64-21.3.0.tar.gz` and this will install GraalVM. Once installed, configure the `GRAALVM_HOME` environment variable to point to the directory where GraalVM is installed (e.g. on macOS it will be `/Library/Java/JavaVirtualMachines/graalvm-ce-java11-21.3.0/Contents/Home`).

A.3.2. Installing the Native Image Generator

The *Native Image Generator*[279], or `native-image`, is a utility that processes all the classes of your application and their dependencies, including those from the JDK. It statically analyses these classes to determine which classes and methods are reachable and used during application execution (a.k.a. *closed-world*). Then it passes all this reachable code as the input to the GraalVM compiler which ahead-of-time compiles it to the native binary.

So we need to install the `native-image` tool. This can be done by running the following command from your GraalVM directory (inside the `bin` directory).

```
$GRAALVM_HOME/bin $ ./gu install native-image
```

When installing Native Image, if you have a popup showing an error message such as "*21.3.0 is damaged and can't be opened. You should move it to the Bin.*", then you can get around this by executing:

```
$ xattr -d com.apple.quarantine /Library/Java/JavaVirtualMachines/graalvm-ce-java11-
21.3.0
```

A.3.3. Checking for GraalVM Installation

Once installed and setup, you should be able to run the following command and get the following output.

```
$ $GRAALVM_HOME/bin/native-image --version
GraalVM 21.3.0 Java 11 CE (Java Version 11.0.13)
```

A.4. Maven 3.8.x

All the examples of this fascicle are built and tested using Maven[280]. Maven offers a building solution, shared libraries, and a plugin platform for your projects, allowing you to do quality control, documentation, teamwork and so forth. Based on the *"convention over configuration"* principle, Maven brings a standard project description and a number of conventions such as a standard directory structure. With an extensible architecture based on plugins, Maven can offer many different services.

A.4.1. A Brief History of Maven

Maven, created by Jason van Zyl, began as a subproject of Apache Turbine in 2002. In 2003, it was voted on and accepted as a top-level Apache Software Foundation project. In July 2004, Maven's release was the critical first milestone, v1.0. Maven 2 was declared v2.0 in October 2005 after about six months in beta cycles. Maven 3.0 was released in October 2010, being mostly backwards compatible with Maven 2[281].

A.4.2. Project Descriptor

Maven is based on the fact that a majority of Java projects face similar requirements when building applications. A Maven project needs to follow some standards as well as define specific features in a project descriptor, or *Project Object Model* (POM). The POM is an XML file (pom.xml) placed at the root of the project and contains all the metadata of the project. As shown in Listing 284, the minimum required information to describe the identity of a project is the groupId, the artifactId, the version, and the packaging type.

Listing 284. Header of a Maven Project Descriptor

```xml
<?xml version="1.0" encoding="UTF-8"?>
<project xmlns:xsi="http://www.w3.org/2001/XMLSchema-instance"
         xmlns="http://maven.apache.org/POM/4.0.0"
         xsi:schemaLocation="http://maven.apache.org/POM/4.0.0
http://maven.apache.org/xsd/maven-4.0.0.xsd">

  <modelVersion>4.0.0</modelVersion>
  <groupId>org.agoncal.fascicle</groupId>
  <artifactId>chapter01</artifactId>
  <version>1.0-SNAPSHOT</version>
  <packaging>jar</packaging>
</project>
```

A project is often divided into different artifacts. These artifacts are then grouped under the same groupId (similar to packages in Java) and uniquely identified by the artifactId. Packaging allows Maven to produce each artifact following a standard format (jar, war, ear etc.). Finally, the version allows the identifying of an artifact during its lifetime (version 1.1, 1.2, 1.2.1 etc.). Maven imposes versioning so that a team can manage the life of its project development. Maven also introduces the concept of SNAPSHOT versions (the version number ends with the string -SNAPSHOT) to identify an artifact that is being developed and is not released yet.

The POM defines much more information about your project. Some aspects are purely descriptive (name, description etc.), while others concern the application execution such as the list of external libraries used, and so on. Moreover, the pom.xml defines environmental information to build the project (versioning tool, continuous integration server, artifact repositories), and any other specific process to build your project.

A.4.3. Managing Artifacts

Maven goes beyond building artifacts; it also offers a genuine approach to archive and share these artifacts. Maven uses a local repository on your hard drive (by default in ~/.m2/repository) where it stores all the artifacts that the project's descriptor references. The local repository is filled either by the local developer's artifacts (e.g. myProject-1.1.jar) or by external ones (e.g. javax.annotation-api-1.2.jar) that Maven downloads from remote repositories.

A Maven project can reference a specific artifact including the artifact's dependencies in the POM using groupId, artifactId, version and scope in a declarative way as shown in Listing 285. If necessary, Maven will download them to the local repository from remote repositories. Moreover, using the POM descriptors of these external artifacts, Maven will also download the artifacts they need (so-called "*transitive dependencies*"). Therefore, the development team doesn't have to manually add the project dependencies to the classpath. Maven automatically adds the necessary libraries.

Listing 285. Maven Dependencies

```xml
<dependencies>
  <dependency>
    <groupId>org.eclipse.persistence</groupId>
    <artifactId>javax.persistence</artifactId>
    <version>2.1</version>
    <scope>provided</scope>
  </dependency>
  <dependency>
    <groupId>org.glassfish</groupId>
    <artifactId>javax.ejb</artifactId>
    <version>3.2</version>
    <scope>provided</scope>
  </dependency>
</dependencies>
```

Dependencies may have limited visibility (called scope):

- `test`: The library is used to compile and run test classes but is not packaged in the produced artifact (e.g. war file).

- `provided`: The library is provided by the environment (persistence provider, application server etc.) and is only used to compile the code.

- `compile`: The library is necessary for compilation and execution. Therefore, it will be packaged as part of the produced artifact too.

- `runtime`: The library is only required for execution but is excluded from the compilation (e.g. Servlets).

A.4.4. Installing Maven on macOS

The examples of this fascicle have been developed with Apache Maven 3.8.3. Once you have installed the JDK 11.0.13, make sure the JAVA_HOME environment variable is set. Then, check if you already have the Maven formula installed on your machine:

```
$ brew list maven
Error: No such keg: /usr/local/Cellar/maven
```

If the Maven formula is not installed, execute the following Homebrew command to install it:

```
$ brew install maven
...
maven was successfully installed!
```

You should now see the Maven formula in Homebrew:

```
$ brew list maven
/usr/local/Cellar/maven/3.8.3/bin/mvn
/usr/local/Cellar/maven/3.8.3/bin/mvnDebug
/usr/local/Cellar/maven/3.8.3/bin/mvnyjp
```

A.4.5. Checking for Maven Installation

Once you've got Maven installed, open a command line and enter mvn -version to validate your installation. Maven should print its version and the JDK version it uses (which is handy as you might have different JDK versions installed on the same machine).

```
$ mvn -version

Apache Maven 3.8.3
Maven home: /usr/local/Cellar/maven/3.8.3/libexec
```

Be aware that Maven needs Internet access so it can download plugins and project dependencies from the Maven Central[282] and/or other remote repositories. If you are behind a proxy, see the documentation to configure your settings.

A.4.6. Some Maven Commands

Maven is a command line utility where you can use several parameters and options to build, test or package your code. To get some help on the commands you can type, use the following command:

```
$ mvn --help

usage: mvn [options] [<goal(s)>] [<phase(s)>]
```

Here are some commands that you will be using to run the examples in the fascicle. Each invokes a different phase of the project life cycle (clean, compile, install etc.) and uses the pom.xml to download libraries, customise the compilation, or extend some behaviours using plugins:

- mvn clean: Deletes all generated files (compiled classes, generated code, artifacts etc.).

- mvn compile: Compiles the main Java classes.

- mvn test-compile: Compiles the test classes.

- mvn test: Compiles the main Java classes as well as the test classes and executes the tests.

- mvn package: Compiles, executes the tests and packages the code into an archive (e.g. a war file).

- mvn install: Builds and installs the artifacts in your local repository.

- mvn clean install: Cleans and installs (note that you can add several commands separated by spaces, like mvn clean compile test).

Maven allows you to compile, run, and package the examples of this fascicle. It decouples the fact that you need to write your code (within an IDE) and build it. To develop you need an *Integrated Development Environment* (IDE). I use IntelliJ IDEA from JetBrains, but you can use any IDE you like because this fascicle only relies on Maven and not on specific IntelliJ IDEA features.

A.5. Testing Frameworks

A.5.1. JUnit 5.x

All the examples of this fascicle are tested using JUnit 5.x. JUnit[283] is an open source framework to write and run repeatable tests. JUnit features include: assertions for testing expected results, fixtures for sharing common test data, and runners for running tests.

JUnit is the de facto standard testing library for the Java language, and it stands in a single jar file that you can download from https://junit.org/junit5 (or use Maven dependency management, which we do in this fascicle). The library contains a complete API to help you write your unit tests and execute them. Unit and integration tests help your code to be more robust, bug free, and reliable. Coming up, we will go through the above features with some examples but before that, let's have a quick overview of JUnit's history.

The code in this appendix can be found at https://github.com/agoncal/agoncal-fascicle-commons/tree/master/junit

A Brief History of JUnit

JUnit was originally written by Erich Gamma and Kent Beck in 1998. It was inspired by Smalltalk's SUnit test framework, also written by Kent Beck. It quickly became one of the most popular frameworks in the Java world. JUnit took an important step in achieving test-driven development (TDD). Let's see some of the JUnit features through a simple example.

Writing Tests

Listing 286 represents a `Customer` POJO. It has some attributes, including a date of birth, constructors, getters and setters. It also provides two utility methods to clear the date of birth and to calculate the age of the customer (`calculateAge()`).

Listing 286. A Customer Class

```java
public class Customer {

  private String firstName;
  private String lastName;
  private LocalDate dateOfBirth;
  private Integer age;

  public void calculateAge() {
    if (dateOfBirth == null) {
      age = null;
      return;
    }

    age = Period.between(dateOfBirth, LocalDate.now()).getYears();
  }

  public void clear() {
    this.dateOfBirth = null;
  }

  // Constructors, getters, setters
}
```

The `calculateAge()` method uses the `dateOfBirth` attribute to set the customer's age. It has some business logic and we want to make sure the algorithm calculates the age accurately. We want to test this business logic. For that, we need a test class with some JUnit test methods and assertions.

Test Class

In JUnit, test classes do not have to extend anything. To be executed as a test case, a JUnit test class needs at least one method annotated with `@Test`. If you write a class without at least one `@Test` method, you will get an error when trying to execute it (`java.lang.Exception: No runnable methods`). Listing 287 shows the `CustomerTest` class that initialises the `Customer` object.

Listing 287. A Unit Test Class for Customer

```java
public class CustomerTest {

  private Customer customer = new Customer();
```

Fixtures

Fixtures are methods to initialise and release any common object during tests. JUnit uses `@BeforeEach` and `@AfterEach` annotations to execute code before or after each test. These methods can be given any name (`clearCustomer()` in Listing 288), and you can have multiple methods in one test class. JUnit uses `@BeforeAll` and `@AfterAll` annotations to execute specific code only once, before or after the test suite is executed (`CustomerTest` in this case). These methods must be unique and static. @BeforeAll and @AfterAll can be very useful if you need to allocate and release expensive resources.

Listing 288. Fixture Executed Before Each Test

```
@BeforeEach
public void clearCustomer() {
  customer.clear();
}
```

Test Methods

A test method must use the @Test annotation, return void, and take no parameters. This is controlled at runtime and throws an exception if not respected. In Listing 289, the test method ageShouldBeGreaterThanZero creates a new Customer and sets a specific date of birth. Then, using the assertion mechanism of JUnit (explained in the next section), it checks that the calculated age is greater than zero.

Listing 289. Method Testing Age Calculation

```
@Test
public void ageShouldBeGreaterThanZero() {
  customer = new Customer("Rita", "Navalhas");
  customer.setDateOfBirth(LocalDate.of(1975, 5, 27));

  customer.calculateAge();

  assertTrue(customer.getAge() >= 0);
}
```

JUnit also allows us to check for exceptions. In Listing 290, we are trying to calculate the age of a null customer object so the call to the calculateAge() method should throw a NullPointerException. If it does, then the test succeeds. If it doesn't, or if it throws a different type of exception than the one declared, the test fails.

Listing 290. Method Testing Nullity

```
@Test
public void shouldThrowAnExceptionCauseDateOfBirtheIsNull() {

  customer = null;
  assertThrows(NullPointerException.class, () -> customer.calculateAge());
}
```

Listing 291 does not implement the shouldCalculateOldAge() method. However, you don't want the test to fail; you just want to ignore it. You can add the @Disable annotation next to the @Test annotation. JUnit will report the number of disabled tests, along with the number of tests that succeeded and failed. Note that @Disable takes an optional parameter (a String) in case you want to record why a test is being disabled.

Listing 291. Disabling a Method for Testing

```
@Test @Disabled("Test is not implemented yet")
public void shouldCalculateOldAge() {
  // some work to do
}
```

JUnit Assertions

Test cases must assert that objects conform to an expected result, such as in Listing 289 where we assert that the age is greater than zero. For that, JUnit has an Assertions class that contains several methods. In order to use different assertions, you can either use the prefixed syntax (e.g. Assertions.assertEquals()) or import the Assertions class statically. Listing 292 shows a simplified subset of the methods defined in the Assertions class.

Listing 292. Subset of JUnit Assertions

```
public class Assertions {

  void assertTrue(boolean condition) { }
  void assertFalse(boolean condition) { }

  void assertNull(Object actual) { }
  void assertNotNull(Object actual) { }

  void assertEquals(Object expected, Object actual) { }
  void assertNotEquals(Object unexpected, Object actual) { }

  void assertArrayEquals(Object[] expected, Object[] actual) { }
  void assertLinesMatch(List<String> expectedLines, List<String> actualLines) { }

  void assertSame(Object expected, Object actual) { }
  void assertNotSame(Object unexpected, Object actual) { }
  void assertAll(Collection<Executable> executables) { }
  void assertTimeout(Duration timeout, Executable executable) { }

  <T extends Throwable> T assertThrows(Class<T> expectedType, Executable exec) { }
}
```

Executing Tests

JUnit is very well integrated with most IDEs (IntelliJ IDEA, Eclipse, NetBeans etc.). When working with these IDEs, in most cases, JUnit highlights in green to indicate successful tests and in red to indicate failures. Most IDEs also provide facilities to create test classes.

JUnit is also integrated with Maven through the Surefire[284] plugin used during the test phase of the build life cycle. It executes the JUnit test classes of an application and generates reports in XML and text file formats. That's mostly how we will be using JUnit in this fascicle: through Maven. To integrate JUnit in Maven, you just need the JUnit dependency and make sure to declare the Surefire plugin in the `pom.xml` as shown in Listing 293.

Listing 293. JUnit Dependencies in a Maven pom.xml

```xml
<dependencies>
  <dependency>
    <groupId>io.quarkus</groupId>
    <artifactId>quarkus-junit5</artifactId>
    <scope>test</scope>
  </dependency>
</dependencies>

<build>
  <plugins>
    <plugin>
      <artifactId>maven-surefire-plugin</artifactId>
      <configuration>
        <systemPropertyVariables>
          <java.util.logging.manager>
org.jboss.logmanager.LogManager</java.util.logging.manager>
          <maven.home>${maven.home}</maven.home>
        </systemPropertyVariables>
      </configuration>
    </plugin>
  </plugins>
</build>
```

The following Maven command runs the JUnit tests through the Surefire plugin:

```
$ mvn test
```

Then JUnit executes the tests and gives the number of executed tests, the number of failures and the number of disabled tests (through warnings).

```
[INFO] ----------------------------------------
[INFO] Building Quarkus :: Testing :: JVM Mode
[INFO] ----------------------------------------
[INFO]
[INFO] --- maven-surefire-plugin:test
[INFO]
[INFO] ----------
[INFO]  T E S T S
[INFO] ----------
[INFO] Running ArtistResourceTest
[INFO] [io.quarkus] (main) Quarkus on JVM started in 1.169s
[INFO] [io.quarkus] (main) Profile test activated.
[INFO] [io.quarkus] (main) Installed features: [cdi, resteasy, resteasy-jsonb]
[INFO] Tests run: 2, Failures: 0, Errors: 0, Skipped: 1, Time elapsed: 3.827 s
[INFO] [io.quarkus] (main) Quarkus stopped in 0.026s
[INFO]
[INFO] Results:
[INFO]
[INFO] Tests run: 2, Failures: 0, Errors: 0, Skipped: 1
[INFO]
[INFO] ------------
[INFO] BUILD SUCCESS
[INFO] ------------
```

A.6. cURL 7.x

To invoke the REST Web Services described in this fascicle, we often use cURL. cURL[285] is a command line tool for transferring files with url syntax via protocols such as HTTP, FTP, SFTP, SCP, and many more. It is free, open source (available under the MIT Licence) and has been ported to several operating systems. You can send HTTP commands, change HTTP headers, and so on. It is a good tool for simulating a user's actions in a web browser.

A.6.1. A Brief History of cURL

cURL was first released in 1997. The name stands for *Client URL*, that's why you can stumble on the spelling *cURL* instead of *Curl* or *CURL*. The original author and lead developer is the Swedish developer Daniel Stenberg[286].

A.6.2. Installing cURL on macOS

Usually macOS already provides cURL and installing another version in parallel can cause all kinds of trouble. So first, double check if cURL is already installed just by executing the following cURL command:

```
$ curl --version
```

If cURL is not installed, then it is just a matter of installing it with a single Homebrew command:

```
$ brew install curl
```

A.6.3. Checking for cURL Installation

Once installed, check for cURL by running `curl --version` in the terminal. It should display cURL version:

```
$ curl --version

curl 7.64.1 (x86_64-apple-darwin18.0) libcurl/7.64.1 LibreSSL/2.6.5 zlib/1.2.11
nghttp2/1.24.1
Protocols: dict file ftp ftps gopher http https imap imaps ldap ldaps pop3 pop3s rtsp
smb smbs smtp smtps telnet tftp
Features: AsynchDNS IPv6 Largefile GSS-API Kerberos SPNEGO NTLM NTLM_WB SSL libz HTTP2
UnixSockets HTTPS-proxy
```

A.6.4. Some cURL Commands

cURL is a command line utility where you can use several parameters and options to invoke URLs. You invoke `curl` with zero, one or several command lines and a URL (or set of URLs) to which the data should be transferred. cURL supports over two hundred different options and I would recommend reading the documentation for more help. To get some help on the commands[287] and options, you can use the following command:

```
$ curl --help

Usage: curl [options...] <url>
```

You can also opt to use `curl --manual` which will output the entire man page for cURL plus an appended tutorial for the most common use cases.

Here are some sample cURL commands that you will be using to invoke the RESTful web service examples in this fascicle.

- `curl http://localhost:8080/authors`: HTTP GET on a given URL.
- `curl -X GET http://localhost:8080/authors`: Same effect as the previous command, an HTTP GET on a given URL.
- `curl -v http://localhost:8080/authors`: HTTP GET on a given URL with verbose mode on.
- `curl -H 'Content-Type: application/json' http://localhost:8080/authors`: HTTP GET on a given URL passing the JSON Content Type in the HTTP Header.
- `curl -X DELETE http://localhost:8080/authors/1`: HTTP DELETE on a given URL.

A.6.5. Formatting the cURL JSON Output with JQ

Very often when using cURL to invoke a RESTful web service, we get some JSON payload in reply. cURL does not format this JSON, so you will get a flat String such as:

```
$ curl http://localhost:8080/vintage-store/artists
[{"id":"1","firstName":"John","lastName":"Lennon"},{"id":"2","firstName":"Paul","lastN
ame":"McCartney"},{"id":"3","firstName":"George","lastName":"Harrison"},{"id":"4","fir
stName":"Ringo","lastName":"Starr"}]
```

But what we really want is to format the JSON payload to make it easier to read. For that, there is a neat utility tool called jq[288]. It is a tool for processing JSON inputs, applying the given filter on them and producing the filtered results as JSON on standard output. You can install it on macOS with a simple brew install jq. Once installed, it's just a matter of piping the cURL output to jq like this:

```
$ curl http://localhost:8080/vintage-store/artists | jq
[
  {
    "id": "1",
    "firstName": "John",
    "lastName": "Lennon"
  },
  {
    "id": "2",
    "firstName": "Paul",
    "lastName": "McCartney"
  },
  {
    "id": "3",
    "firstName": "George",
    "lastName": "Harrison"
  },
  {
    "id": "4",
    "firstName": "Ringo",
    "lastName": "Starr"
  }
]
```

A.7. Docker

Docker[289] is a set of *Platform-as-a-Service* (PaaS) products that use OS-level virtualisation to deliver software. It makes it easier to create, deploy and run applications by using containers. Containers are isolated from one another and bundle their own software, libraries and configuration files; they can communicate with each other through well-defined channels. Containers allow developers to package an application with all its dependencies and ship it all out as one package.

A.7.1. A Brief History of Docker

Docker was founded by Solomon Hykes and Sebastien Pahl during the Y Combinator Summer 2010 startup incubator group and launched in 2011[290]. Hykes started the Docker project in France as an internal project within dotCloud (a *Platform-as-a-Service* company). Docker debuted to the public in Santa Clara at PyCon in 2013. It was released as open source in March 2013. At the time, it used LXC as its default execution environment. One year later, with the release of version 0.9, Docker replaced LXC with its own component, which was written in the Go programming language.

A.7.2. Installing Docker on macOS

The infrastructure in this fascicle uses Docker to ease the installation of the different technical services (database, monitoring, etc.). So for this, we need to install the docker command line. First of all, check if you already have the Docker formula installed on your machine:

```
$ brew cask list docker
Error: Cask 'docker' is not installed.
```

If the Docker formula is not installed, execute the following Homebrew command to install it:

```
$ brew cask install docker
...
docker was successfully installed!
```

You should now see the Docker formula in Homebrew:

```
$ brew cask list docker
==> App
/Applications/Docker.app
```

A.7.3. Checking for Docker Installation

After installing Docker, you should have docker available in your PATH. But the command docker should not be able to connect to the Docker daemon. You should have the following error:

```
$ docker version

Cannot connect to the Docker daemon at unix:///var/run/docker.sock.
        Is the docker daemon running?
```

That's because you need to launch the Docker Desktop application. To do that, you can either click on the Docker.app icon located under /Applications, launch it using Spotlight or execute the following command:

```
$ open -a Docker
```

On your Mac top menu bar you should see the logo of a whale. Click on it and you should see a menu that looks like Figure 70.

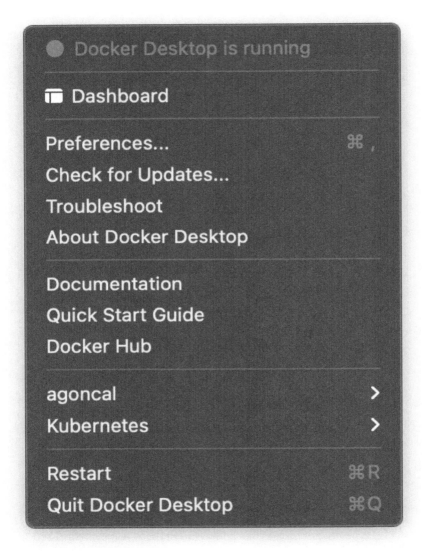

Figure 70. Docker icon on the menu bar

Click on the **About** menu, a window that looks like Figure 71 should give you the versions of the installed Docker tools.

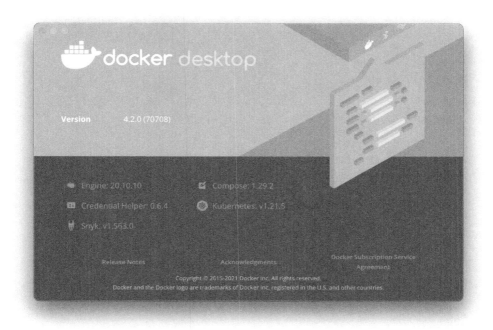

Figure 71. About Docker desktop

Now, if you type the same Docker command, it should connect to the daemon:

```
$ docker version

Client:
 Cloud integration: v1.0.20
 Version:           20.10.10
 API version:       1.41
 Go version:        go1.16.9
 Git commit:        b485636
 Built:             Mon Oct 25 07:43:15 2021
 OS/Arch:           darwin/amd64
 Context:           default
 Experimental:      true

Server: Docker Engine - Community
 Engine:
  Version:          20.10.10
  API version:      1.41 (minimum version 1.12)
  Go version:       go1.16.9
  Git commit:       e2f740d
  Built:            Mon Oct 25 07:41:30 2021
  OS/Arch:          linux/amd64
  Experimental:     true
 containerd:
  Version:          1.4.11
  GitCommit:        5b46e404f6b9f661a205e28
 runc:
  Version:          1.0.2
  GitCommit:        v1.0.2-0-g52b36a2
 docker-init:
  Version:          0.19.0
  GitCommit:        de40ad0
```

Finally, you can run your first container. The `docker container run` command will execute a container that is located on your computer. If not, it will pull the image from the Docker Hub[291] registry and then execute it. That's what happens when you execute an image for the very first time.

Below, the `docker container run` method wants to execute the Docker image called `hello-world`. It doesn't find the image locally, therefore it pulls the image from the default Docker Hub registry: https://hub.docker.com/_/hello-world. Then it executes it:

```
$ docker container run hello-world

Unable to find image 'hello-world:latest' locally
latest: Pulling from library/hello-world
Pull complete
Status: Downloaded newer image for hello-world:latest

Hello from Docker!
This message shows that your installation appears to be working correctly.

To generate this message, Docker took the following steps:
 1. The Docker client contacted the Docker daemon.
 2. The Docker daemon pulled the "hello-world" image from the Docker Hub.
 3. The Docker daemon created a new container from that image which runs the
    executable that produces the output you are currently reading.
 4. The Docker daemon streamed that output to the Docker client, which sent it
    to your terminal.

To try something more ambitious, you can run an Ubuntu container with:
 $ docker run -it ubuntu bash

Share images, automate workflows, and more with a free Docker ID:
 https://hub.docker.com/

For more examples and ideas, visit:
 https://docs.docker.com/get-started/
```

A.7.4. Building, Running, Pushing and Pulling Images

Let's now see the typical flow on how to get started on using docker images and containers. Basically you create a Dockerfile, build it into a local Docker image and run it inside a container. To make your local image available to others (external team developers but also tools such as Kubernetes), push the image to a remote Docker registry (the default one being Docker Hub). Then, if your local image has been removed, just pull it from the remote repository and execute it again.

But first, you need to create an account on a remote Docker repository. Let's take the default one: Docker Hub.

Remote Docker Repository

Docker Hub[292] is a service provided by Docker for finding and sharing container images. It will be used to push and pull our Docker images.

To create a Docker account, sign up on https://hub.docker.com/signup. The name of the account is very important as it will be used to name the Docker images so they can be pushed to your remote repository (the image name and account name have to be the same). Figure 72 shows a Docker hub account called agoncal (you should have your own).

agoncal

👤 User   🕐 Joined November 13, 2014

Figure 72. Docker hub account

Now back to your local computer. You should be able to login to your newly created Docker hub account with the following command:

```
$ docker login

Login with your Docker ID to push and pull images from Docker Hub.
Username: agoncal
Password:
Login Succeeded
```

Dockerfile

Now, let's create a very simple Dockerfile. The Dockerfile below is based on the Alpine image which is a very lightweight Linux (only 5 MB in size). Then, it uses the echo command to display the message *Hello Fascicle*. Take any text editor, create a file called Dockerfile and add the following:

```
FROM alpine
CMD echo "Hello Fascicle"
```

Building the Docker Image

Now, using this Dockerfile, build the Docker image using the following command:

```
$ docker image build -t agoncal/hello-fascicle .

Sending build context to Docker daemon  2.048kB
Step 1/2 : FROM alpine
Step 2/2 : CMD echo "Hello Fascicle"
Successfully built a896f9983057
Successfully tagged agoncal/hello-fascicle:latest
```

The last message of the trace indicates that the Docker image has been successfully built and is called agoncal/hello-fascicle:latest. Notice that the prefix agoncal is the name of the Docker hub account (change it accordingly to yours). To check that this image is now locally installed, type the following command:

```
$ docker image ls --filter "reference=agoncal/hello-fascicle"

REPOSITORY               TAG       IMAGE ID        SIZE
agoncal/hello-fascicle   latest    d036b3b86cd4    5.57MB
```

Running the Docker Image

Now that the image is available locally, let's execute it. The following command executes our image which echoes a message to the console:

```
$ docker container run agoncal/hello-fascicle

Hello Fascicle
```

Pushing to a Docker Registry

Now that we know that our image runs as expected, let's make it available to others by pushing it to the remote Docker registry. This is done with a simple push command. For consuming existing public images from Docker Hub, you don't need to be authenticated. But for publishing your own images, you need to be authenticated. The docker image push command assumes that you've already authenticated with the remote registry (otherwise execute docker login before hand):

```
$ docker image push agoncal/hello-fascicle

The push refers to repository [docker.io/agoncal/hello-fascicle]
50644c29ef5a: Mounted from library/alpine
latest: digest: sha256:608aa60a8d32b6b3 size: 528
```

Go back to the Docker Hub website to see the newly-pushed image. It should look like the repository shown in Figure 73.

Figure 73. Docker image available on Docker Hub

Pulling from a Docker Registry

Now let's remove our image from our local system:

```
$ docker image rm agoncal/hello-fascicle -f

Untagged: agoncal/hello-fascicle:latest
Untagged: agoncal/hello-fascicle@sha256:608aa60a8d32b6b3
Deleted: sha256:d036b3b86cd4a2a82234202dac26ebbf39f8aae2

$ docker image ls --filter "reference=agoncal/hello-fascicle"
REPOSITORY                  TAG               IMAGE ID        SIZE
```

The `docker image ls` command confirms that the `rm` command has been successful and that the image `agoncal/hello-fascicle` has been removed. This means that we can't execute our image anymore. Well, this is not exactly true. If we run our image again, Docker automatically downloads (pulls) the images that don't yet exist locally, creates a container, and starts it.

```
$ docker container run agoncal/hello-fascicle

Unable to find image 'agoncal/hello-fascicle:latest' locally
latest: Pulling from agoncal/hello-fascicle
df20fa9351a1: Already exists
Digest: sha256:608aa60a8d32b6b36ef595e1bf81c046bcf3504b06da787d1cbfe848e31da8db
Status: Downloaded newer image for agoncal/hello-fascicle:latest

Hello Fascicle
```

This has exactly the same effect as pulling the image first, and executing it after:

```
$ docker image pull agoncal/hello-fascicle

Using default tag: latest
latest: Pulling from agoncal/hello-fascicle
df20fa9351a1: Already exists
Digest: sha256:608aa60a8d32b6b36ef595e1bf81c046bcf3504b06da787d1cbfe848e31da8db
Status: Downloaded newer image for agoncal/hello-fascicle:latest
docker.io/agoncal/hello-fascicle:latest

$ docker container run agoncal/hello-fascicle

Hello Fascicle
```

A.7.5. Some Docker Commands

Docker is a command line utility where you can use several parameters and options to start/stop a container. You invoke `docker` with zero, one or several command line options with the container or image ID you want to work with. Docker comes with several options that are described in the documentation if you need more help. To get some help on the commands[293] and options, you can use the following command:

```
$ docker help

Usage:  docker [OPTIONS] COMMAND

$ docker help attach

Usage:  docker attach [OPTIONS] CONTAINER

Attach local standard input, output, and error streams to a running container
```

Here are some commands that you will be using to start/stop containers in this workshop.

- docker login: Logs into a Docker registry.
- docker image ls: Lists images.
- docker image push: Pushes a local Docker image to the remote Docker repository.
- docker image pull: Pulls a Docker image from the remote Docker repository to the local repository.
- docker container ls: Lists containers.
- docker container run <CONTAINER>: Starts one or more stopped containers.
- docker container stop <CONTAINER>: Stops one or more running containers.
- docker compose -f docker-compose.yaml up -d: Starts all containers defined in a Docker Compose file.
- docker compose -f docker-compose.yaml down: Stops all containers defined in a Docker Compose file.

A.8. VirtualBox

Depending on the version of Minikube or Docker that you have installed, you might need VirtualBox to make Minikube work on your machine. Recent versions of Minikube can work straight with Docker, but older versions need a hypervisor to be installed. There are several hypervisors running on macOS (xhyve, VMware Fusion or Parallels Desktop) but VirtualBox is the most popular one. *VirtualBox*[294] is an open source virtualization product that runs on Windows, Linux, Macintosh, and Solaris hosts and supports a large number of guest operating systems.

A.8.1. A Brief History of VirtualBox

VirtualBox[295] was first offered by the German company Innotek GmbH under a proprietary software license. In January 2007, Innotek GmbH released VirtualBox Open Source Edition (OSE) as free and open source software. Sun Microsystems acquired Innotek in February 2008. Oracle Corporation acquired Sun in January 2010 and re-branded the product as "*Oracle VM VirtualBox*".

A.8.2. Installing VirtualBox on macOS

First of all, check if you already have the VirtualBox formula installed on your machine:

```
$ brew cask list virtualbox
Error: Cask 'virtualbox' is not installed.
```

If the VirtualBox formula is not installed, execute the following Homebrew command to install it:

```
$ brew cask install virtualbox
...
virtualbox was successfully installed!
```

You should now see the VirtualBox formula in Homebrew:

```
$ brew cask list virtualbox
==> Pkg
VirtualBox.pkg (Pkg)
```

A.8.3. Checking for VirtualBox Installation

To check that VirtualBox is installed you can invoke the VBoxManage command (which is the command line interface for VirtualBox) and also VirtualBox itself:

```
$ VBoxManage -version
6.1.12r139181

$ VirtualBox -help
Oracle VM VirtualBox VM Selector v6.1.12

$ ll /Applications/VirtualBox.app/
```

Now, to execute VirtualBox, you can either click on the VirtualBox.app icon located under /Applications, launch it using Spotlight or execute the following command:

```
$ VirtualBox
```

You should see a user interface that looks like Figure 74.

Figure 74. Launching VirtualBox

A.9. Kubernetes

Kubernetes[296] (a.k.a. K8s) is an orchestrator for containerised applications. It takes its name from a Greek word meaning *helmsman*, or *captain*: if Docker packages applications inside containers, Kubernetes is the captain sailing those containers. Kubernetes can schedule, scale, heal, update, start or stop several containers.

A.9.1. A Brief History of Kubernetes

Back in the beginning, Google was already using containers way before Docker. They built in-house tools to orchestrate their millions of containers: Borg and Omega[297]. They opened source their orchestration technology and called it Kubernetes. It is now maintained by the *Cloud Native Computing Foundation*[298] (CNCF).

A.9.2. Different Kubernetes Flavours

There are several ways to jump into Kubernetes. You can install it manually from scratch on your Linux machines with tools such as kubeadm[299]. But this is pretty advanced and you might want to use already packaged Kubernetes distributions for local development (Minikube, Minishift, Kind, etc.) or hosted for a production environment (Google Container Engine, OpenShift, Amazon Elastic Container Service for Kubernetes, Azure Kubernetes Service, etc.). In this fascicle, I use Minikube as it is the most widely used Kubernetes distribution for local development.

A.9.3. Installing Minikube on macOS

Minikube[300] allows you to run Kubernetes locally on a developer's machine. It focuses on making Kubernetes easy to learn and develop by easily setting up and managing a local Kubernetes cluster.

Minikube is a single node Kubernetes cluster that runs on a hypervisor on your local machine. All you need is Docker, a hypervisor and Kubernetes. So before installing Minikube, make sure you have Docker and VirtualBox up and running. Then, it's just a matter of installing Minikube and kubectl, the command line interacting with Minikube.

Installing Kubectl

kubectl is the command line interface that lets you interact with your Minikube Kubernetes cluster. It sends requests to the Kubernetes API server running on the cluster to manage your Kubernetes environment.

Before installing kubectl, let's check if you already have it on your machine:

```
$ brew list kubectl
Error: No such keg: /usr/local/Cellar/kubernetes-cli
```

If the kubectl formula is not installed, execute the following Homebrew command to install it:

```
$ brew install kubectl
...
kubectl was successfully installed!
```

You should now see the kubectl formula in Homebrew:

```
$ brew list kubectl
/usr/local/Cellar/kubernetes-cli/1.22.3/bin/kubectl
/usr/local/Cellar/kubernetes-cli/1.22.3/etc/bash_completion.d/kubectl
/usr/local/Cellar/kubernetes-cli/1.22.3/share/man/ (224 files)
/usr/local/Cellar/kubernetes-cli/1.22.3/share/zsh/site-functions/_kubectl
```

Installing Minikube

Now that we have the client interface installed to interact with Minikube, let's install Minikube with Homebrew. Again, let's first check if it's already installed on your machine:

```
$ brew list minikube
Error: No such keg: /usr/local/Cellar/minikube
```

If the Minikube formula is not installed, execute the following Homebrew command to install it:

```
$ brew install minikube
...
minikube was successfully installed!
```

You should now see the Minikube formula in Homebrew:

```
$ brew list minikube
/usr/local/Cellar/minikube/1.24.0/bin/minikube
/usr/local/Cellar/minikube/1.24.0/etc/bash_completion.d/minikube
/usr/local/Cellar/minikube/1.24.0/share/zsh/site-functions/_minikube
```

A.9.4. Checking for Kubernetes Installation

After installing Minikube and the client interface, you should have both minikube and kubectl available in your PATH. But the command kubectl should not be able to connect to the Minikube cluster if it has not been started. You should have the following error:

```
$ kubectl version

Client Version: version.Info {Major:"1", Minor:"22", Platform:"darwin/amd64"}
Unable to connect to the server: dial tcp 192.168.64.2:8443: i/o timeout
```

That's because you need to start Minikube. Do so with the following command:

```
$ minikube start

minikube v1.24.0 on Darwin 10.15.6
Using the virtualbox driver based on user configuration
Starting control plane node minikube in cluster minikube
Creating virtualbox VM (CPUs=2, Memory=6000MB, Disk=20000MB) ...
Preparing Kubernetes v1.19.3 on Docker 19.03.8 ...
Verifying Kubernetes components...
Enabled addons: default-storageclass, storage-provisioner
Done! kubectl is now configured to use "minikube"
```

If it's the first time that you're starting Minikube, the command will download all the packages required and this can take a while. The last line indicates that "*kubectl is now configured to use minikube*", so you can now execute the kubectl command again and you should have a different output: a client version, as well as the server version this time. Notice that the server (Minikube) runs a Linux platform (not a macOS):

```
$ kubectl version

Client Version: version.Info {Major:"1", Minor:"22", Platform:"darwin/amd64"}
Server Version: version.Info {Major:"1", Minor:"22", Platform:"linux/amd64"}
```

You can check the status of Minikube:

```
$ minikube status
minikube
type: Control Plane
host: Running
kubelet: Running
apiserver: Running
kubeconfig: Configured
```

Minikube has a powerful feature called profiles. This allows you to create different virtual machines based on a name. When you start Minikube, the name of the default profile is `minikube` (you could start Minikube with a different profile using `minikube start --profile fascicle-profile` for example). Execute `minikube profile list` to check the available profiles. As you can see, VirtualBox is used as the hypervisor and Docker as the runtime:

```
$ minikube profile list
|----------|------------|---------|----------------|------|---------|
| Profile  | VM Driver  | Runtime |       IP       | Port | Status  |
|----------|------------|---------|----------------|------|---------|
| minikube | virtualbox | docker  | 192.168.99.107 | 8443 | Running |
|----------|------------|---------|----------------|------|---------|
```

If you launch the VirtualBox user interface (see Figure 75) you will notice that the `minikube` cluster is up and running.

Figure 75. Launching VirtualBox

If VirtualBox is not installed and you want to start the Minikube cluster, you will get the following error:

```
$ minikube start

minikube v1.12.3 on Darwin 10.15.6
'virtualbox' driver reported an issue: unable to find VBoxManage in $PATH
Suggestion: Install VirtualBox
virtualbox does not appear to be installed
```

To fix it, just install VirtualBox and set the vm-driver configuration. You can also use this configuration if you have several hypervisors installed on your machine and you want to make sure that VirtualBox is used. Change the configuration with the following command if needed:

```
$ minikube config set vm-driver virtualbox
```

A.9.5. Deploying a Docker Image to a Kubernetes Cluster

Now that you have Docker, VirtualBox, Minikube and kubectl configured and running, let's deploy and execute a remote Docker image into a Minikube cluster. But first we need to start the Minikube cluster, and set the deployment, pods and services so we can execute the Docker image.

 The Docker image is called agoncal/hello-fascicle and is available on Docker Hub [301]. It just displays a "*Hello Fascicle*" message when invoking a /hello URL. So nothing too fancy. Feel free to use another image if you want.

Starting the Kubernetes Cluster

If the Minikube cluster is not already started, start it with the following command:

```
$ minikube start
...
Done! kubectl is now configured to use "minikube"
```

Once the cluster is started, you can invoke the Minikube dashboard to have a visual representation of the cluster. Executing the following command will open the dashboard on your default browser:

```
$ minikube dashboard

Enabling dashboard ...
Verifying dashboard health ...
Launching proxy ...
Verifying proxy health ...
Opening http://127.0.0.1:64465/api/v1/namespaces/kubernetes-
dashboard/services/http:kubernetes-dashboard:/proxy/ in your default browser...
```

Figure 76 shows the *Overview* tab of the Minikube dashboard.

Figure 76. Minkube dashboard

Creating a Deployment

In Kubernetes, the idea is to describe a desired state of the cluster. Here, we want to have a single instance of a Java application running somewhere on a node. This desired state is called a *Deployment*. And a deployment manages one or several *Pods*. A Kubernetes pod is a group of one or more containers (in our case, it is the container running the `agoncal/hello-fascicle` image), tied together for the purposes of administration and networking. The deployment checks on the health of the pods and restarts the pod's container if it terminates. Deployments are the recommended way to manage the creation and scaling of pods.

The following kubectl command creates a deployment called `fascicle-deployment`. This deployment manages a pod that runs a container based on the provided Docker image.

```
$ kubectl create deployment fascicle-deployment --image=agoncal/hello-fascicle

deployment.apps/fascicle-deployment created
```

View the Deployment:

```
$ kubectl get deployments

NAME                  READY   UP-TO-DATE   AVAILABLE   AGE
fascicle-deployment   0/1     1            0           13s
```

View the Pod:

```
$ kubectl get pods

NAME                                     READY   STATUS    RESTARTS   AGE
fascicle-deployment-6b6db4b547-mm9d9     1/1     Running   0          24s
```

Now that we have the name of the pod, we can invoke a Linux command into this pod. For example, the following ls command lists the files under the deployments directory. This is where you'll find the Java application of the agoncal/hello-fascicle image.

```
$ kubectl exec fascicle-deployment-6b6db4b547-mm9d9 -- ls -l deployments

-rw-r--r-- 1 root root 245449  app.jar
drwxr-xr-x 2 root root   4096  lib
-r-xr----- 1 1001 root  20218  run-java.sh

$ kubectl exec fascicle-deployment-6b6db4b547-mm9d9 -- ls -l deployments/lib

-rw-r--r-- 1 root root  276413  commons-io.commons-io-2.7.jar
-rw-r--r-- 1 root root  613466  io.netty.netty-codec-http-4.1.49.Final.jar
-rw-r--r-- 1 root root  164638  io.quarkus.arc.arc-2.5.0.Final.jar
-rw-r--r-- 1 root root   28101  io.quarkus.quarkus-bootstrap-runner-2.5.0.Final.jar
-rw-r--r-- 1 root root    3032  io.quarkus.quarkus-container-image-docker-
2.5.0.Final.jar
-rw-r--r-- 1 root root  204316  io.quarkus.quarkus-core-2.5.0.Final.jar
...
```

Creating a Service

By default, the pod is only accessible by its internal IP address within the Kubernetes cluster. To make the container accessible from outside the Kubernetes virtual network, you have to expose the pod as a Kubernetes service. Expose the pod by using the kubectl expose command:

```
$ kubectl expose deployment fascicle-deployment --type=NodePort --port=8080

service/fascicle-deployment exposed
```

The --type=NodePort flag indicates that you want to expose the service port. View the Service you just created:

```
$ kubectl get services

NAME                   TYPE        CLUSTER-IP      EXTERNAL-IP   PORT(S)
fascicle-deployment    NodePort    10.103.14.182   <none>        8080:31699/TCP
kubernetes             ClusterIP   10.96.0.1       <none>        443/TCP
```

Running the Docker Image

To get the URL and port to access our application, we use:

```
~ $ minikube service list
|-------------|----------------------|---------------|-----------------------------|
|  NAMESPACE  |         NAME         |  TARGET PORT  |             URL             |
|-------------|----------------------|---------------|-----------------------------|
|  default    |  fascicle-deployment |          8080 | http://192.168.99.114:31699 |
|  default    |  kubernetes          |  No node port |                             |
|  kube-system|  kube-dns            |  No node port |                             |
|-------------|----------------------|---------------|-----------------------------|
```

So, to execute the `agoncal/hello-fascicle` image it's just a matter of invoking the service's URL. You can now point the browser (or cURL command) to http://192.168.99.114:31699/hello so it invokes the REST endpoint and displays "*Hello Fascicle*".

Now, you can go back to the dashboard. This time, you will see all the available resources, as in Figure 77. You can check the status of the deployments, pods, and services.

Figure 77. Minkube dashboard with available resources

Cleaning Up

Now you can clean up the resources you created in your cluster:

```
$ kubectl delete service fascicle-deployment
service "fascicle-deployment" deleted

$ kubectl delete deployment fascicle-deployment
deployment.apps "fascicle-deployment" deleted
```

Optionally, stop the Minikube virtual machine (VM):

```
$ minikube stop

Stopping node "minikube"  ...
1 nodes stopped.
```

Optionally, delete the Minikube VM:

```
$ minikube delete

Deleting "minikube" in virtualbox ...
Removed all traces of the "minikube" cluster.
```

A.9.6. Kubernetes Manifest Files

So far, we've been working exclusively on the command line to create a deployment with a service and a pod. But imagine doing so when you have several pods and complex deployments? There is an easier and more useful way to do it: creating configuration files using YAML and applying the entire file to a Minikube cluster (using the kubectl command).

For example, Listing 294 shows the YAML file that describes our fascicle-deployment. This file first describes some metadata (apiVersion, kind and metadata) and then the object spec describes the desired state of the deployment. This is basically deploying the agoncal/hello-fascicle Docker image and setting the port 8080.

Listing 294. Deployment Definition

```
apiVersion: apps/v1
kind: Deployment
metadata:
  labels:
    app.kubernetes.io/name: fascicle-deployment
    app.kubernetes.io/version: latest
  name: fascicle-deployment
spec:
  replicas: 1
  selector:
    matchLabels:
      app.kubernetes.io/name: fascicle-deployment
      app.kubernetes.io/version: latest
  template:
    metadata:
      labels:
        app.kubernetes.io/name: fascicle-deployment
        app.kubernetes.io/version: latest
    spec:
      containers:
        - env:
            - name: KUBERNETES_NAMESPACE
              valueFrom:
                fieldRef:
                  fieldPath: metadata.namespace
          image: agoncal/hello-fascicle:latest
          imagePullPolicy: IfNotPresent
          name: fascicle-deployment
          ports:
            - containerPort: 8080
              name: http
              protocol: TCP
```

Then we have another YAML file to describe the service. As you can see in Listing 295, the file starts with some metadata again, and describes the desired state of the service (the spec object). It sets the type of service to NodePort (which opens a port on the node of the cluster) and configures the external (30574) and internal port (8080 is the port Quarkus listens to).

Listing 295. Service Definition

```
apiVersion: v1
kind: Service
metadata:
  labels:
    app.kubernetes.io/name: fascicle-deployment
    app.kubernetes.io/version: latest
  name: fascicle-deployment
spec:
  ports:
    - name: http
      nodePort: 30574
      port: 8080
      targetPort: 8080
  selector:
    app.kubernetes.io/name: fascicle-deployment
    app.kubernetes.io/version: latest
  type: NodePort
```

When you create a Kubernetes object (Deployment, Service, Pod, etc.), either with commands or manifest files, you can always get its YAML description with the following commands:

```
$ kubectl get deployments/fascicle-deployment -o yaml
```

A.9.7. Some Kubernetes Commands

Minikube and kubectl are commands that use several parameters and options. To get some help on the commands and options, you can use the following commands:

```
$ minikube help
$ minikube start --help

$ kubectl help
$ kubectl config --help
```

Here are some commands that you will be using to start/stop containers in this workshop.

- minikube start: Starts a local Kubernetes cluster.

- minikube status: Gets the status of a local Kubernetes cluster.

- minikube stop: Stops a local Kubernetes cluster running in VirtualBox.

- minikube delete: Deletes a local Kubernetes cluster.

- minikube dashboard: Accesses the Kubernetes dashboard running within the minikube cluster.

- kubectl apply: Applies a configuration to a resource.

- kubectl create: Creates a resource (deployment, service, role, namespace, etc.).

- kubectl get: Displays one or many resources.

A.10. Kafka

Kafka[302] (or *Apache Kafka*) is an open source distributed event streaming platform. It provides a unified, high-throughput, low-latency platform for handling real-time data feeds thanks to its optimised binary TCP-based protocol. Kafka uses ZooKeeper to manage and coordinate the cluster topology. *ZooKeeper*[303] is a centralised service for maintaining configuration information, naming, providing distributed synchronization, and providing group services. All of these kinds of services are used in some form or another by distributed applications. ZooKeeper enables this distributed coordination in a highly reliable way.

A.10.1. A Brief History of Kafka

Kafka was originally developed by Jay Kreps at LinkedIn, and was subsequently open sourced in early 2011[304]. Graduation from the Apache Incubator occurred in 2012. Jay Kreps chose to name the software after the author Franz Kafka because it is "*a system optimised for writing*", and he liked Kafka's work. He then created the company Confluent in 2014 to give support and professional resources around Kafka.

A.10.2. Installing Kafka on macOS

First of all, check if you already have the Kafka and the ZooKeeper formulae installed on your machine:

```
$ brew list kafka
Error: No such keg: /usr/local/Cellar/kafka

$ brew list zookeeper
Error: No such keg: /usr/local/Cellar/zookeeper
```

If both formulae are not installed, just install Kafka with the following Homebrew command. Kafka depending on ZooKeeper, Homebrew will automatically install it:

```
$ brew install kafka
==> Installing dependencies for kafka: zookeeper
==> Installing kafka dependency: zookeeper
...
==> Installing kafka
...
```

You should now see both formulae in Homebrew:

```
$ brew list kafka
/usr/local/Cellar/kafka/3.0.0/.bottle/etc/ (19 files)

$ brew list zookeeper
/usr/local/Cellar/zookeeper/3.7.0_1/.bottle/etc/ (4 files)
```

A.10.3. Checking for Kafka Installation

After installing Kafka and ZooKeeper, you should have several binaries available in your PATH. If
you have completion in your shell, you can type kafka- and then press TAB. You should see all these
Kafka commands:

```
$ kafka- [PRESS TAB]
kafka-acls                    kafka-delete-records             kafka-replica-
verification
kafka-broker-api-versions     kafka-dump-log                   kafka-run-class
kafka-configs                 kafka-leader-election            kafka-server-start
kafka-console-consumer        kafka-log-dirs                   kafka-server-stop
kafka-console-producer        kafka-mirror-maker               kafka-streams-
application-reset
kafka-consumer-groups         kafka-preferred-replica-election kafka-topics
kafka-consumer-perf-test      kafka-producer-perf-test         kafka-verifiable-consumer
kafka-delegation-tokens       kafka-reassign-partitions        kafka-verifiable-producer

$ kafka-broker-api-versions --version
3.0.0
```

As for ZooKeeper, you can check its version with the following command:

```
$ zkServer version
ZooKeeper JMX enabled by default
Using config: /usr/local/etc/zookeeper/zoo.cfg
Apache ZooKeeper, version 3.7.0 2021-05-24 01:59 UTC
```

A.10.4. Publishing and Receiving Events

Now that you have Kafka and ZooKeeper up and running, let's publish and receive messages. But
before that, we need to start the Kafka cluster and create the topics.

Starting Kafka

Before starting Kafka we need to start ZooKeeper. You can do so using the zookeeper-server-start
command and passing a property file. Let's use the default zookeeper.properties file that is
available under the Kafka directory. The following command starts ZooKeeper in a standalone
mode, listening on port 2181 (as configured in the zookeeper.properties file):

```
$ zookeeper-server-start /usr/local/etc/kafka/zookeeper.properties
...
[INFO] Reading configuration from: /usr/local/etc/kafka/zookeeper.properties
[INFO] clientPortAddress is 0.0.0.0:2181
[INFO] Starting server
[INFO] binding to port 2181

$ zkServer status
Client port found: 2181. Client address: localhost.
Mode: standalone
```

Now that ZooKeeper is running, start the Kafka broker service with the `kafka-server-start` and the default configuration file:

```
$ kafka-server-start /usr/local/etc/kafka/server.properties
...
[INFO] starting
[INFO] Connecting to zookeeper on localhost:2181
[INFO] Initializing a new session to localhost:2181
[INFO] Initiating client connection
[INFO] Waiting until connected
[INFO] Socket connection established
[INFO] Starting
[INFO] [KafkaServer id=0] started
```

If ZooKeeper has not started, Kafka will refuse to start as well, displaying these kind of error messages:

```
[INFO] Opening socket connection to server localhost:2181
[INFO] Socket error occurred: localhost:2181: Connection refused
[INFO] Opening socket connection to server localhost:2181
[INFO] Socket error occurred: localhost:2181: Connection refused
```

Creating Topics

Messages (also called events or records) are durably stored in topics. A topic is a feed to which messages are published. Topics are always multi-producer and multi-subscriber: a topic can have zero, one or many producers that write messages to it, as well as zero, one, or many consumers that subscribe to these messages. Topics have a name and are partitioned, meaning that one topic is spread over a number of "*buckets*" located on different Kafka brokers.

The set of commands below list the available topics and creates one topic called `vinyl-topic` that has three partitions:

```
$ kafka-topics --zookeeper localhost:2181 --list

$ kafka-topics --zookeeper localhost:2181 --create --topic vinyl-topic --partitions 3
--replication-factor 1
Created topic vinyl-topic.

$ kafka-topics --zookeeper localhost:2181 --list
vinyl-topic
```

The kafka-topics command has a --describe parameter to get all the details and configuration of a topic:

```
$ kafka-topics --zookeeper localhost:2181 --describe --topic vinyl-topic

Topic: vinyl-topic  PartitionCount: 3   ReplicationFactor: 1   Configs:
    Topic: vinyl-topic  Partition: 0    Leader: 0   Replicas: 0 Isr: 0
    Topic: vinyl-topic  Partition: 1    Leader: 0   Replicas: 0 Isr: 0
    Topic: vinyl-topic  Partition: 2    Leader: 0   Replicas: 0 Isr: 0
```

Publishing Events

Now, time to send some messages to the topic. For that we use the kafka-console-producer that allows us to type messages on the console and send them to the topic. Open one terminal, execute the command and start typing some messages (here I use JSON but you can send any format to a topic):

```
$ kafka-console-producer --bootstrap-server localhost:9092 --topic vinyl-topic
> { "id": 1, "artist": "Ella Fitzgerald", "album": "Sings the Cole Porter Song Book" }
> { "id": 2, "artist": "Billie Holiday", "album": "Lady In Satin" }
> { "id": 3, "artist": "Sarah Vaughan", "album": "In the Land of Hi-Fi" }
> { "id": 4, "artist": "Nina Simone", "album": "Pastel Blues" }
```

Receiving Events

Open a second terminal and use the kafka-console-consumer to consume the messages. The --from -beginning parameter allows us to start consuming with the earliest message present in the topic rather than the latest message. You should see the following:

```
$ kafka-console-consumer --bootstrap-server localhost:9092 --topic vinyl-topic --from
-beginning

{ "id": 1, "artist": "Ella Fitzgerald", "album": "Sings the Cole Porter Song Book" }
{ "id": 2, "artist": "Billie Holiday", "album": "Lady In Satin" }
{ "id": 3, "artist": "Sarah Vaughan", "album": "In the Land of Hi-Fi" }
{ "id": 4, "artist": "Nina Simone", "album": "Pastel Blues" }
```

Keep sending messages on the first terminal and you'll see the messages arriving in the second terminal.

Cleaning Up

To clean up, we can delete our topic. For that just use the `--delete` parameter. Once you issue the delete command, the topic will be "*marked for deletion*," and you'll have to wait till it gets deleted.

```
$ kafka-topics --zookeeper localhost:2181 --delete --topic vinyl-topic
Topic vinyl-topic is marked for deletion.

$ kafka-topics --zookeeper localhost:2181 --list
```

Stopping Kafka

To stop Kafka you need to do it with two commands: one to stop Kafka itself, and another one to stop ZooKeeper.

```
$ kafka-server-stop
$ zookeeper-server-stop
```

A.10.5. Some Kafka Commands

Kafka has several commands where you can use several parameters and options. To get some help you can use the following commands:

- `kafka-configs --help`: Manipulates and describes the configuration for a topic, client, user or broker.
- `kafka-console-consumer --help`: Reads data from Kafka topics and outputs it to standard output.
- `kafka-console-producer --help`: Reads data from standard input and publishes it to Kafka.
- `kafka-topics --help`: Creates, deletes, describes, or changes a topic.

A.11. Git

Git[305] is a free and open source distributed version control system designed for tracking changes in computer files and coordinating work on those files among multiple people. It is primarily used for source code management in software development, but it can be used to keep track of changes in any set of files. Git was created by Linus Torvalds in 2005 for the development of the Linux kernel, with other kernel developers contributing to its initial development.

Git is not really needed to run the samples in this fascicle. Even if the code is hosted on a public Git repository (https://github.com/agoncal/agoncal-fascicle-quarkus/tree/2.0), you can either download the code as a zip file, or clone the repository. Only if you clone the repository will you need to have Git installed.

A.11.1. A Brief History of Git

Git development began in April 2005, after many developers in the Linux kernel gave up access to BitKeeper, a proprietary source-control management (SCM). Linus Torvalds wanted a distributed system that he could use, like BitKeeper, but none of the available free systems met his needs. So, Linus started the development of Git on 3rd April 2005, announced the project on 6th April and the first merge of multiple branches took place on 18th April. On 29th April, the nascent Git was benchmarked, recording patches to the Linux kernel tree at the rate of 6.7 patches per second[306].

A.11.2. Installing Git on macOS

On macOS, if you have installed Homebrew[307], then installing Git is just a matter of a single command. Open your terminal and install Git with the following command:

```
$ brew install git
```

A.11.3. Checking for Git Installation

Once installed, check for Git by running `git --version` in the terminal. It should display the git version:

```
$ git --version
git version 2.33.1
```

A.11.4. Cloning Repository

Once Git is installed, you can clone the code of the repository with a `git clone` on https://github.com/agoncal/agoncal-fascicle-quarkus.git.

[267] Homebrew https://brew.sh

[268] Homebrew History https://en.wikipedia.org/wiki/Homebrew_(package_manager)#History

[269] Homebrew Cask https://github.com/Homebrew/homebrew-cask

[270] Java http://www.oracle.com/technetwork/java/javase

[271] Visual VM https://visualvm.github.io

[272] The Java HotSpot Performance Engine Architecture https://www.oracle.com/technetwork/java/whitepaper-135217.html

[273] Java History https://en.wikipedia.org/wiki/Java_(programming_language)#History

[274] Java Website http://www.oracle.com/technetwork/java/javase/downloads/index.html

[275] GraalVM https://www.graalvm.org

[276] SubstrateVM https://github.com/oracle/graal/tree/master/substratevm

[277] GraalVM Download https://www.graalvm.org/downloads

[278] GraalVM GitHub https://github.com/graalvm/graalvm-ce-builds/tags

[279] Native Image https://www.graalvm.org/reference-manual/native-image

[280] Maven https://maven.apache.org

[281] Maven History https://en.wikipedia.org/wiki/Apache_Maven#History

[282] Maven Central https://search.maven.org

[283] JUnit https://junit.org/junit5

[284] Maven Surefire Plugin https://maven.apache.org/surefire/maven-surefire-plugin

[285] **cURL** https://curl.haxx.se

[286] **Daniel Stenberg** https://en.wikipedia.org/wiki/Daniel_Stenberg

[287] **cURL commands** https://ec.haxx.se/cmdline.html

[288] **jq** https://stedolan.github.io/jq

[289] **Docker** https://www.docker.com

[290] **Docker History** https://en.wikipedia.org/wiki/Docker_(software)#History

[291] **Docker Hub** https://hub.docker.com

[292] **Docker Hub** https://hub.docker.com

[293] **Docker commands** https://docs.docker.com/engine/reference/commandline/cli

[294] **VirtualBox** https://www.virtualbox.org

[295] **VirtualBox History** https://en.wikipedia.org/wiki/VirtualBox#History

[296] **Kubernetes** https://kubernetes.io

[297] **Borg, Omega, and Kubernetes** https://research.google/pubs/pub44843

[298] **Cloud Native Computing Foundation** https://www.cncf.io

[299] **kubeadm** https://github.com/kubernetes/kubeadm

[300] **Minikube** https://minikube.sigs.k8s.io

[301] **hello-fascicle Docker Image** https://hub.docker.com/r/agoncal/hello-fascicle

[302] **Kafka** https://kafka.apache.org

[303] **ZooKeeper** https://zookeeper.apache.org

[304] **Kafka History** https://en.wikipedia.org/wiki/Apache_Kafka#History

[305] **Git** https://git-scm.com

[306] **History of Git** https://en.wikipedia.org/wiki/Git#History

[307] **Homebrew** https://brew.sh

Appendix B: Quarkus Versions

Quarkus[308] evolves at a fast pace. Below you will find a short recap of the latest major versions and their content. If you want to have more details on each release, you can browse the GitHub account.

B.1. Quarkus 2.5 (*November 2021*)

Quarkus 2.5.0.Final[309] comes with the following main improvements:

- Upgrade to GraalVM/Mandrel 21.3
- Support for JPA entity listeners for Hibernate ORM in native mode
- Ability to add HTTP headers to responses
- Various usability improvements in extensions and our dev mode/testing infrastructure

B.2. Quarkus 2.4 (*October 2021*)

Quarkus 2.4.0.Final[310] brings the following new features:

- Hibernate Reactive 1.0.0.Final
- Introducing Kafka Streams DevUI
- Support continuous testing for multi module projects
- Support AWT image resize via new AWT extension

B.3. Quarkus 2.3 (*October 2021*)

Version 2.3.0.Final[311] includes a lot of refinements and improvements and some new features:

- Dev Service for Neo4J
- Logging with Panache
- Testing support for CLI applications
- MongoDB Liquibase extension
- Support for Hibernate ORM interceptors

B.4. Quarkus 2.2.1 (*August 2021*)

Version 2.2.0.Final wasn't fully released because it suffered from a bug preventing dev mode to work on Windows. Thus 2.2.1.Final[312] was announced with the following changes:

- Upgrade to GraalVM 21.2
- Add global flag to disable Dev Services
- Change the default thread model for RESTEasy Reactive
- Introduce support for MongoDB service binding

- Extension for running Narayana LRA participants

B.5. Quarkus 2.1 (*July 2021*)

Quarkus 2.1[313] stabilizes the 2.0 version and brings new features:

- Add Dev Services support for Keycloak
- Add reactive MS SQL client extension
- Upgrade Kotlin dependency to 1.5.21
- Split out the WebSocket client

B.6. Quarkus 2.0 (*June 2021*)

Quarkus 2.0[314] with a ton of exciting new features. There is a migration guide[315] you can follow to make sure your code is up to date:

- JDK 11 as the minimum Java runtime
- Support for GraalVM 21.1
- Vert.x 4
- Eclipse MicroProfile 4 and updated SmallRye components
- Continuous Testing
- Quarkus CLI

B.7. Quarkus 1.13 (*March 2021*)

Quarkus 1.13[316] brings several new features:

- Dev Services simplifies testing with containers (automatically start containers for when testing so no need to configure anything).
- OpenTelemetry is now supported via two new extensions.
- Kubernetes Service Binding simplifies the deployment on Kubernetes.
- MicroProfile REST Client is now based on RESTEasy Reactive.
- quarkus-jacoco can generate test coverage reports.

B.8. Quarkus 1.12 (*February 2021*)

Quarkus 1.12[317] comes with some significant changes:

- Fast-JAR is now the default packaging when you build a jar.
- RESTEasy Reactive keeps improving and it now has support for multipart.
- Vert.x Axle and RX Java managed instances have been dropped.
- We upgraded to GraalVM 21.0.

B.9. Quarkus 1.11 (*January 2021*)

Quarkus 1.11[318] is a very important release because it brings reactive programming to RESTEasy. The major new features are:

- RESTEasy Reactive[319]
- Development console
- Improved Micrometer support
- Spring Data REST extension
- Non application endpoints moved to /q/ path
- jbang dev mode & platform support
- Recommended version of GraalVM is 20.3

B.10. Quarkus 1.10 (*December 2020*)

Quarkus 1.10[320] comes with a lot of improvements and new features:

- Default media type is now JSON
- The Micrometer extension got its fair share of improvements (e.g. new registries)
- New Qute error pages
- Swagger/GraphQL/Health/OpenAPI UIs and Swagger UI configuration
- Part of the Hibernate ORM configuration is now overridable at runtime
- SmallRye Reactive Messaging 2.5.0 and Mutiny 0.11.0
- Reactive SQL Clients support multiple datasources
- New Amazon IAM extension

B.11. Quarkus 1.9 (*October 2020*)

Quarkus 1.9[321] comes with a lot of improvements on top of our existing feature set:

- The Micrometer extension is maturing
- Kafka now has metrics
- Multiple Redis clients are supported (as well as Sentinel connections)
- Bean Validation is supported by Reactive Routes
- SmallRye Reactive Messaging upgraded to 2.4.0 and Mutiny to 0.9.0
- Creation of the Quarkiverse initiative[322], the extension ecosystem.

B.12. Quarkus 1.8 (*September 2020*)

Quarkus 1.8[323] comes with bug fixes, improvements, as well as some notable new features:

- Multiple persistence units support for the Hibernate ORM extension
- A new Micrometer extension
- jbang integration for easy Quarkus-based scripting
- An update to GraalVM 20.2

B.13. Quarkus 1.7 (*August 2020*)

Quarkus 1.7[324], with more than 300 pull requests merged, was released with Elasticsearch and Redis clients, Reactive routes and Funqy improvements. The most prominent new features are:

- New extensions for the low-level and high level Elasticsearch REST clients
- An extension for the Vert.x Redis client
- An Hibernate Envers extension
- Support for the JDBC Db2 driver
- A lot of improvements to the Reactive routes feature
- The Funqy serverless framework got some interesting new features

B.14. Quarkus 1.6 (*July 2020*)

Quarkus 1.6[325] released with AppCDS, Google Cloud Functions, GraalVM 20.1.0 and more.

- Integrated generation of AppCDS archives to improve startup time in JVM mode
- Support for Google Cloud Functions - joining the existing Amazon Lambda and Azure Functions support
- Reactive IBM Db2 client (the Db2 JDBC driver is coming in 1.7)
- An Apache Cassandra client
- WebJars locator extension and Spring `@Scheduled` support
- Better tools to troubleshoot your applications
- Upgrade to GraalVM 20.1.0

B.15. Quarkus 1.5 (*June 2020*)

Quarkus 1.5[326] introduces the fast-jar packaging as an option.

- New fast-jar packaging format to bring faster startup times
- Quarkus 1.4 introduced command mode and 1.5 added a Picocli[327] extension
- Adds gRPC extension
- Implements Eclipse MicroProfile GraphQL extension
- Supports more Amazon Services (DynamoDB, KMS, S3, SES, SNS, SQS)
- Hibernate ORM REST Data with Panache extension

* Spring Cache compatibility layer

B.16. Quarkus 1.4 (*April 2020*)

Quarkus 1.4[328] brings some major updates.

* Deprecates support for Java 8 as Java 11 is recommended
* Introduces *Command mode* (how to build command line applications with Quarkus)
* Introduces *Funqy*, the new FaaS framework, to improve function front (AWS Lambdas and Azure Functions)
* Adds support for HTTP/2
* Quarkus Security 1.1.0.Final
* Moves the Security API to Mutiny
* Improved mocking (add support for `@InjectMock` and Mockito)
* Adds support for SmallRye Reactive Messaging 2.0
* Update to SmallRye Health 2.2.0

B.17. Quarkus 1.3 (*March 2020*)

Quarkus 1.3[329] passed the TCKs of all Eclipse MicroProfile 3.3 specifications. MicroProfile 3.3 includes the following specification updates:

* Config 1.4
* Fault Tolerance 2.1
* Health 2.2
* Metrics 2.3
* REST Client 1.4

In addition to the specifications within the MicroProfile platform, Quarkus also includes implementations of Reactive Streams Operators, Reactive Messaging, and Context Propagation. This version also brings GraalVM 20.0 support and a new class loader infrastructure[330].

B.18. Quarkus 1.2 (*January 2020*)

Quarkus 1.2[331] was released with GraalVM 19.3.1 support, Metrics, Cache extension, and much more.

* Supports three flavors of GraalVM:
  * GraalVM 19.2.1 - JDK 8
  * GraalVM 19.3.1 - JDK 8
  * GraalVM 19.3.1 - JDK 11
* Adds a brand new Cache extension

- Adds metrics for Agroal (the database connection pool) and Hibernate ORM
- New SmallRye Fault Tolerance v4.0.0 that replaces Hystrix

B.19. Quarkus 1.1 (*December 2019*)

Quarkus 1.1[332] released with a template engine and YAML configuration.

- Adds Qute template engine
- YAML support for configuration file
- Adds health checks for Kafka, Kafka Streams, MongoDB, Neo4j and Artemis
- Adds Quartz extension

B.20. Quarkus 1.0 (*November 2019*)

First final version[333] of Quarkus.

- Creation of a Platform BOM
- Upgrades SmallRye OpenAPI and Swagger UI
- Updates to GraalVM SDK 19.2.1
- Replace usage of java.util.logging by JBoss logging
- Upgrade to Hibernate ORM 5.4.9.Final
- Quarkus HTTP 3.0.0.Final
- Quarkus Security 1.0.0.Final

B.21. Quarkus 0.0.1 (*November 2018*)

Very first commit[334] of the Quarkus code. Tag 0.0.1 was created[335].

[308] Quarkus Releases https://github.com/quarkusio/quarkus/releases
[309] Quarkus 2.5 https://quarkus.io/blog/quarkus-2-5-0-final-released
[310] Quarkus 2.4 https://quarkus.io/blog/quarkus-2-4-0-final-released
[311] Quarkus 2.3 https://quarkus.io/blog/quarkus-2-3-0-final-released
[312] Quarkus 2.2.1 https://quarkus.io/blog/quarkus-2-2-1-final-released
[313] Quarkus 2.1 https://quarkus.io/blog/quarkus-2-1-0-final-released
[314] Quarkus 2.0 https://quarkus.io/blog/quarkus-2-0-0-final-released
[315] Migration Guide Quarkus 2.0 https://github.com/quarkusio/quarkus/wiki/Migration-Guide-2.0
[316] Quarkus 1.13 https://quarkus.io/blog/quarkus-1-13-0-final-released
[317] Quarkus 1.12 https://quarkus.io/blog/quarkus-1-12-0-final-released
[318] Quarkus 1.11 https://quarkus.io/blog/quarkus-1-11-0-final-released
[319] RESTEasy Reactive https://quarkus.io/blog/resteasy-reactive
[320] Quarkus 1.10 https://quarkus.io/blog/quarkus-1-10-2-final-released
[321] Quarkus 1.9 https://quarkus.io/blog/quarkus-1-9-0-final-released
[322] Quarkiverse https://github.com/quarkiverse
[323] Quarkus 1.8 https://quarkus.io/blog/quarkus-1-8-0-final-released
[324] Quarkus 1.7 https://quarkus.io/blog/quarkus-1-7-0-final-released

[325] **Quarkus 1.6** https://quarkus.io/blog/quarkus-1-6-0-final-released

[326] **Quarkus 1.5** https://quarkus.io/blog/quarkus-1-5-final-released

[327] **Picocli** https://picocli.info

[328] **Quarkus 1.4** https://quarkus.io/blog/quarkus-1-4-final-released

[329] **Quarkus 1.3** https://quarkus.io/blog/quarkus-eclipse-microprofile-3-3

[330] **Quarkus Class Loader** https://quarkus.io/guides/class-loading-reference

[331] **Quarkus 1.2** https://quarkus.io/blog/quarkus-1-2-0-final-released

[332] **Quarkus 1.1** https://quarkus.io/blog/quarkus-1-1-0-final-released

[333] **Quarkus 1.0** https://quarkus.io/blog/quarkus-1-0-0-Final-bits-are-here

[334] **Quarkus 1st commit** https://github.com/quarkusio/quarkus/commit/161cfa303b4ea366dbd07e54bf4fe5a67ddec497

[335] **Quarkus Tag 0.0.1** https://github.com/quarkusio/quarkus/commits/0.0.1?after=1200367b8ddbe5605d8219c4994205f6c1d7af50+1084

Appendix C: Eclipse MicroProfile Specification Versions

The MicroProfile[136] specification evolves at a fast pace. Below you will find a short recap of the latest versions and which sub-specification has been updated for a specific version. If you want to have more details on each specification, you can browse the GitHub account.

C.1. MicroProfile 4.1 (*July 2021*)

MicroProfile 4.1[137] brings the following updates:

- Health 3.1

C.2. MicroProfile 4.0 (*December 2020*)

MicroProfile 4.0[138] is a major release. It is the first version released by the recently-formed *MicroProfile Working Group*[139] within the Eclipse Foundation. It includes updates to:

- Configuration 2.0
- Health 3.0
- Eclipse MicroProfile JWT Auth 1.2
- Metrics 3.0
- REST Client 2.0
- Fault Tolerance 3.0
- Eclipse MicroProfile OpenAPI 2.0
- OpenTracing 2.0

C.3. MicroProfile 3.3 (*February 2020*)

MicroProfile 3.3[140] is an incremental release. It includes an update to:

- Configuration 1.4
- Fault Tolerance 2.1
- Health 2.2
- Metrics 2.3
- REST Client 1.4

C.4. MicroProfile 3.2 (*November 2019*)

MicroProfile 3.2[141] is an incremental release. It includes an update to:

- Metrics 2.2

- Health 2.1

C.5. MicroProfile 3.1 (*October 2019*)

MicroProfile 3.1[342] is an incremental release. It includes an update to:

- Health 2.1
- Metrics 2.1

C.6. MicroProfile 3.0 (*June 2019*)

MicroProfile 3.0[343] is a major release. It consists of:

- Eclipse MicroProfile Configuration 1.3
- Eclipse MicroProfile Fault Tolerance 2.0
- Eclipse MicroProfile Health 2.0
- Eclipse MicroProfile JWT Auth 1.1
- Eclipse MicroProfile Metrics 2.0
- Eclipse MicroProfile OpenAPI 1.1
- Eclipse MicroProfile OpenTracing 1.3
- Eclipse MicroProfile REST Client 1.3
- Context and Dependency Injection 2.0
- Common Annotations 1.3
- Java API for RESTful Web Services 2.1
- JSON Binding 1.0
- JSON Processing 1.1

C.7. MicroProfile 2.2 (*February 2019*)

MicroProfile 2.2[344] is an incremental release. It includes an update to:

- Fault Tolerance 2.0
- OpenAPI 1.1
- OpenTracing 1.3
- REST Client 1.2

C.8. MicroProfile 2.1 (*October 2018*)

MicroProfile 2.1[345] is an incremental release. It includes an update to:

- OpenTracing 1.2

C.9. MicroProfile 2.0.1 (*July 2018*)

MicroProfile 2.0.1[346] is a patch release to correct an issue with the JSON-B maven dependency in the pom.xml. The defined content for MicroProfile 2.0 did not change.

C.10. MicroProfile 2.0 (*June 2018*)

MicroProfile 2.0[347] is a major release since the subset of Java EE dependencies are now based on Java EE 8. It consists of:

- Eclipse MicroProfile Configuration 1.3
- Eclipse MicroProfile Fault Tolerance 1.1
- Eclipse MicroProfile Health 1.0
- Eclipse MicroProfile JWT Auth 1.1
- Eclipse MicroProfile Metrics 1.1
- Eclipse MicroProfile OpenAPI 1.0
- Eclipse MicroProfile OpenTracing 1.1
- Eclipse MicroProfile REST Client 1.1
- Context and Dependency Injection 2.0
- Common Annotations 1.3
- Java API for RESTful Web Services 2.1
- JSON Binding 1.0
- JSON Processing 1.1

C.11. MicroProfile 1.4 (*June 2018*)

MicroProfile 1.4[348] is an incremental release. It includes an update to:

- Configuration 1.3
- Fault Tolerance 1.1
- JWT 1.1
- OpenTracing 1.1
- REST Client 1.1

C.12. MicroProfile 1.3 (*January 2018*)

MicroProfile 1.3[349] is an incremental release. It includes an update to:

- Configuration 1.2
- Metrics 1.1

It adds:

- OpenAPI 1.0
- OpenTracing 1.0
- REST Client 1.0

C.13. MicroProfile 1.2 (*September 2017*)

MicroProfile 1.2[350] is an incremental release. It includes an update to:

- Common Annotations 1.2
- Configuration 1.1

It adds:

- Fault Tolerance 1.0
- Health 1.0
- Metrics 1.0
- JWT 1.0

C.14. MicroProfile 1.1 (*August 2017*)

MicroProfile 1.1[351] is an incremental release. It adds:

- Configuration 1.0

C.15. MicroProfile 1.0

MicroProfile 1.0 is the first major release and is based on Java EE 7 specifications. It consists of:

- Context and Dependency Injection 1.2
- Java API for RESTful Web Services 2.0
- JSON Processing 1.0

[336] **MicroProfile Releases** https://github.com/eclipse/microprofile/releases

[337] **MicroProfile 4.1** https://github.com/eclipse/microprofile/releases/tag/4.1

[338] **MicroProfile 4.0** https://github.com/eclipse/microprofile/releases/tag/4.0

[339] **MicroProfile Working Group 4.0** https://microprofile.io/workinggroup

[340] **MicroProfile 3.3** https://github.com/eclipse/microprofile/releases/tag/3.3

[341] **MicroProfile 3.2** https://github.com/eclipse/microprofile/releases/tag/3.2

[342] **MicroProfile 3.1** https://github.com/eclipse/microprofile/releases/tag/3.1

[343] **MicroProfile 3.0** https://github.com/eclipse/microprofile/releases/tag/3.0

[344] **MicroProfile 2.2** https://github.com/eclipse/microprofile/releases/tag/2.2

[345] **MicroProfile 2.1** https://github.com/eclipse/microprofile/releases/tag/2.1

[346] **MicroProfile 2.0.1** https://github.com/eclipse/microprofile/releases/tag/2.0.1

[347] **MicroProfile 2.0** https://github.com/eclipse/microprofile/releases/tag/2.0

[348] MicroProfile 1.4 https://github.com/eclipse/microprofile/releases/tag/1.4

[349] MicroProfile 1.3 https://github.com/eclipse/microprofile-bom/releases/tag/1.3

[350] MicroProfile 1.2 https://github.com/eclipse/microprofile-bom/releases/tag/1.2

[351] MicroProfile 1.1 https://github.com/eclipse/microprofile-bom/releases/tag/1.1.0

Appendix D: References

- Quarkus https://quarkus.io
- Quarkus developers' guides https://quarkus.io/guides
- Quarkus Super Hero Workshop https://quarkus.io/quarkus-workshops/super-heroes
- Merry Christmas And Happy Fallback With Microprofile https://antoniogoncalves.org/2021/01/12/merry-chistmas-and-happy-fallback-with-microprofile/
- SmallRye https://github.com/smallrye
- MicroProfile https://microprofile.io
  - Config https://github.com/eclipse/microprofile-config
  - Fault Tolerance https://github.com/eclipse/microprofile-fault-tolerance
  - Health https://github.com/eclipse/microprofile-health
  - JWT https://github.com/eclipse/microprofile-jwt-auth
  - Metrics https://github.com/eclipse/microprofile-metrics
  - OpenApi https://github.com/eclipse/microprofile-open-api
  - OpenTracing https://github.com/eclipse/microprofile-opentracing
  - Reactive Messaging https://github.com/eclipse/microprofile-reactive-messaging
  - Reactive Streams Operators https://github.com/eclipse/microprofile-reactive-streams-operators
  - REST-Client https://github.com/eclipse/microprofile-rest-client

Appendix E: Revisions of the Fascicle

E.1. 2021-11-29

- Content
  - Updated book title to "Understanding Quarkus 2.x"
  - Fixed typos
  - Improved footnote references
  - Added a What's New in Quarkus 2.x section
  - Added Continuous Testing
  - Updated to Quarkus 2.x
  - Updated to MicroProfile 4.1
  - Removed deprecated `@ConfigProperties` in favour of new `@ConfigMapping`
  - Added Dev UI
  - Added Dev Services
  - Added how to access the entity manager within Panache
  - Updated all the Quarkus internal paths (e.g. from `/swagger-ui`, `/openapi` to `/q/swagger-ui`, `/q/openapi`)
  - Added a section on QSON
  - Fixed Reactive Messaging subpackages
  - Added Startup health check
  - Added new Quarkus specific health checks
  - Added Metrics API table
  - Updated JAR packaging format (JAR, Fast-JAR, Legacy-JAR, etc.)
  - Added Kubernetes graphics
  - Moved JUnit section from chapter Testing to the Appendixes
- Code
  - Bumped from Quarkus 1.13.x to 2.5.x
  - Bumped from Maven 3.6.x to 3.8.x
  - Bumped from GraalVM 21.0.x to 21.3.x
  - Bumped from Docker 19.x to 20.x
  - Bumped from Minikube 1.19.x to 1.22.x
  - Bumped from Kafka 2.6.x to 3.0.x
  - Removed Health UI external dependency as now it's bundle within Quarkus
  - Added JBoss Logger injection

- ◦ Added Startup health check
- ◦ Added `@TestTransaction`
- ◦ Replace `/mp-rest/url` property with `quarkus.rest-client." ".uri`

E.2. 2021-05-03

- eBook published on agoncal.teachable.com
- Paper book published on Amazon KDP[352] (*Kindle Direct Publishing*)
- Content
  - ◦ Added MicroProfile 4.x
  - ◦ Added *Understanding Quarkus 2.x* and *Practising Quarkus 2.x* Appendix F
  - ◦ Added online trainings section Appendix F
- Code
  - ◦ Bumped from Quarkus 1.9.x to 1.13.x
  - ◦ Bumped from GraalVM 20.x to 21.x

E.3. 2020-11-02

- Book published on Red Hat Developer Portal[353]

[352] KDP https://kdp.amazon.com
[353] Red Hat Developer Portal https://developers.redhat.com

Appendix F: Resources by the Same Author

F.1. Fascicles

The *agoncal fascicle* series contains two types of fascicles. The *Understanding* collection is about fascicles that dive into a specific technology, explain it, and show different aspects of it as well as integrating it with other external technologies. On the other hand, the *Practising* collection is all about coding. So you are supposed to already know a little bit of this technology and be ready to code in order to build a specific application. Below the list of fascicles I have written.

F.1.1. Understanding Bean Validation 2.0

Validating data is a common task that Java developers have to do and it is spread throughout all layers (from client to database) of an application. This common practice is time-consuming, error prone, and hard to maintain in the long run. Besides, some of these constraints are so frequently used that they could be considered standard (checking for a null value, size, range, etc.). It would be good to be able to centralise these constraints in one place and share them across layers.

That's when Bean Validation comes into play.

In this fascicle, you will learn Bean Validation and use its different APIs to apply constraints on a bean, validate all sorts of constraints, write your own constraints and a few advanced topics such as integrating Bean Validation with other frameworks (JPA, JAX-RS, CDI, Spring).

You can find two different formats of this fascicle:

- eBooks (PDF/EPUB) at https://agoncal.teachable.com/p/ebook-understanding-bean-validation
- Paper book (ISBN: 9781980399025) and eBooks at https://www.amazon.com/gp/product/B07B2KJ41R

F.1.2. Understanding JPA 2.2

Applications are made up of business logic, interaction with other systems, user interfaces etc. and data. Most of the data that our applications manipulate have to be stored in datastores, retrieved, processed and analysed. If this datastore is a relational database and you use an object-oriented programming language such as Java, then you might want to use an Object-Relational Mapping tool.

That's when Java Persistence API comes into play.

In this fascicle, you will learn JPA, the standard ORM that maps Java objects to relational databases. You will discover its annotations for mapping entities, as well as the Java Persistence Query Language, entity life cycle and a few advanced topics such as integrating JPA with other frameworks (Bean Validation, JTA, CDI, Spring).

You can find two different formats of this fascicle:

- eBooks (PDF/EPUB) at https://agoncal.teachable.com/p/ebook-understanding-jpa
- Paper book (ISBN: 9781093918977) and eBooks at https://www.amazon.com/gp/product/B0993R88N3

F.1.3. Understanding Quarkus 2.x

Microservices is an architectural style that structures an application as a collection of distributed services. Microservices are certainly appealing but there are many questions that should be asked prior to diving into this architectural style: How do I deal with an unreliable network in a distributed architecture? How do I test my services? How do I monitor them? How do I package and execute them?

That's when Quarkus comes into play.

In this fascicle, you will learn Quarkus but also its ecosystem. You will discover Quarkus internals and how you can use it to build REST and reactive microservices, bind and process JSON or access datastores in a transactional way. With Cloud Native and GraalVM in mind, Quarkus makes packaging and orchestrating your microservices with Docker and Kubernetes easy.

This fascicle has a good mix of theory and practical examples. It is the companion book of *Practising Quarkus 2.x* where you learn how to develop an entire microservice architecture.

You can find two different formats of this fascicle:

- eBooks (PDF/EPUB) at https://agoncal.teachable.com/p/ebook-understanding-quarkus
- Paper book (ISBN: 9798775773083) and eBooks at https://www.amazon.com/gp/product/B0993R88N3

F.1.4. Practising Quarkus 2.x

Microservices is an architectural style that structures an application as a collection of distributed services. Microservices are certainly appealing but there are many questions that should be asked prior to diving into this architectural style: How do I deal with an unreliable network in a distributed architecture? How do I test my services? How do I monitor them? How do I package and execute them?

That's when Quarkus comes into play.

In this fascicle you will develop an entire microservice application using Quarkus as well as MicroProfile. You will expose REST endpoints using JAX-RS and OpenAPI, customise the JSON output thanks to JSON-B and deal with persistence and transaction with Hibernate ORM with

Panache and JTA. Having distributed microservices, you will implement health checks and add some metrics so you can monitor your microservice architecture. Finally, thanks to GraalVM you will build native executables, and package and execute them with Docker.

This fascicle is very practical. It is the companion book of the more theoretical *Understanding Quarkus 2.x* where you'll learn more about Quarkus, MicroProfile, REST and reactive microservices, as well as Cloud Native and GraalVM.

You can find two different formats of this fascicle:

- eBooks (PDF/EPUB) at https://agoncal.teachable.com/p/ebook-practising-quarkus

- Paper book (ISBN: 9798629562115) and eBooks at https://www.amazon.com/gp/product/B0993RBKKR

F.2. Online Courses

Online courses are a great way to learn a new technology or dive into one that you already know. Below the list of online courses I have created.

F.2.1. Starting With Quarkus

This course[354] is for Java developers who want to discover Quarkus. It's a mixture of slides and code so you can "Understand and Practice" at the same time. This way, you learn the theory, and then put it into practice by developing an application step by step.

In this course you will go through an entire development cycle. After introducing Quarkus, you will make sure your development environment is set up, and you will go from bootstrapping a Quarkus application, to running it as a Docker container.

F.2.2. Building Microservices With Quarkus

This course[355] is for Quarkus developers who want to discover how Quarkus and MicroProfile handle microservices. It's a mixture of slides and code so you can "Understand and Practice" at the same time. This way, you learn the theory, and then put it into practice by developing a microservice architecture step by step.

In this course you will develop two microservices that talk to each other. After introducing Microservices and MicroProfile, you will make sure your development environment is set up, and you will go from bootstrapping two Quarkus microservices, to running them as Docker containers.

F.2.3. Accessing Relational Databases with Quarkus

This course[356] is for Quarkus developers who want to discover how Quarkus handles relational databases. It's a mixture of slides and code so you can "Understand and Practice" at the same time. This way, you learn the theory, and then put it into practice by developing a microservice architecture step by step.

In this course you will develop a Quarkus applications maps and queries different kind of persistent objects to several relational databases. After introducing JDBC, JPA and Panache ORM, you will make sure your development environment is set up, and you will go from bootstrapping three Quarkus applications, developing and refactoring a rich business model, map and query these objects to a PostgreSQL database.

F.2.4. Quarkus: Fundamentals (*PluralSight*)

Quarkus is said to be a Supersonic Subatomic Java toolkit. But what does this mean? This course[357] explains what Quarkus is so you can decide if it's suited for your project.

F.2.5. Microservices: The Big Picture (*PluralSight*)

Microservices are quickly being adopted by companies worldwide. This course[358] teaches you the basics of microservice architectures from a 10,000-foot high view.

F.2.6. Java EE: The Big Picture (*PluralSight*)

This course[359] functions as a technical and business overview of Java Enterprise Edition.

F.2.7. Java EE: Getting Started (*PluralSight*)

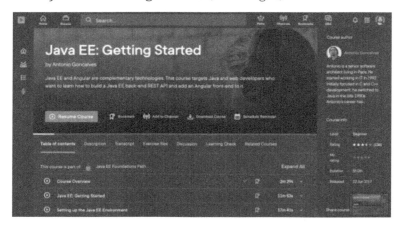

Java EE and Angular are complementary technologies. This course[360] targets Java and web developers who want to learn how to build a Java EE back-end REST API and add an Angular front-end to it.

F.2.8. Java EE 7 Fundamentals (*PluralSight*)

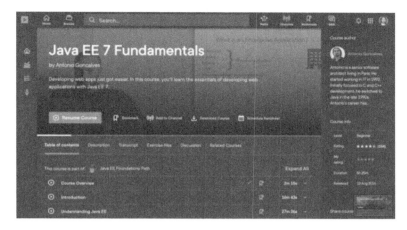

Developing web apps just got easier. In this course[361], you'll learn the essentials of developing web applications with Java EE 7.

F.2.9. Java Persistence API 2.2 (*PluralSight*)

In this course[362] you will learn how to map and query Java objects to a relational database in your Java SE and Java EE applications.

F.2.10. Context and Dependency Injection 1.1 (*PluralSight*)

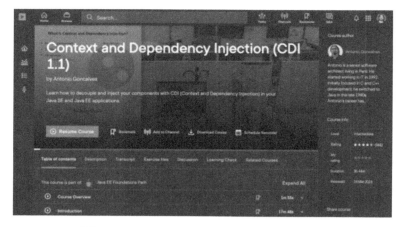

In this course[363] you will learn how to decouple and inject your components with CDI (Context and Dependency Injection) in your Java SE and Java EE applications.

F.2.11. Bean Validation 1.1 (*PluralSight*)

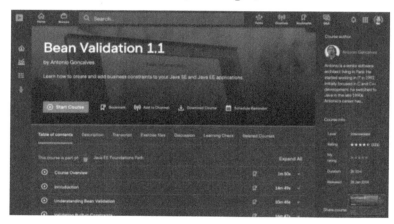

In this course[364] you will learn how to create and add business constraints to your Java SE and Java EE applications.

[354] Starting With Quarkus https://agoncal.teachable.com/p/course-starting-with-quarkus

[355] Building Microservices With Quarkus https://agoncal.teachable.com/p/course-building-microservices-with-quarkus

[356] Accessing Relational Databases with Quarkus https://agoncal.teachable.com/p/course-accessing-databases-with-jpa-and-panache-in-quarkus

[357] Quarkus: Fundamentals https://app.pluralsight.com/library/courses/quarkus-fundamentals/table-of-contents

[358] Microservices: The Big Picture https://app.pluralsight.com/library/courses/microservices-big-picture/table-of-contents

[359] Java EE: The Big Picture https://app.pluralsight.com/library/courses/java-ee-big-picture/table-of-contents

[360] Java EE: Getting Started https://app.pluralsight.com/library/courses/java-ee-getting-started/table-of-contents

[361] Java EE 7 Fundamentals https://app.pluralsight.com/library/courses/java-ee-7-fundamentals/table-of-contents

[362] Java EE: The Big Picture https://app.pluralsight.com/library/courses/java-persistence-api-21/table-of-contents

[363] Context and Dependency Injection 1.1 https://app.pluralsight.com/library/courses/context-dependency-injection-1-1/table-of-contents

[364] Bean Validation 1.1 https://app.pluralsight.com/library/courses/bean-validation/table-of-contents

Appendix G: Printed Back Cover

Antonio Goncalves is a senior software architect and Java Champion. Having been focused on Java development since the late 1990s, his career has taken him to many different countries and companies. For the last few years, Antonio has given talks at international conferences, mainly on Java, distributed systems and microservices. This fascicle stems from his extensive experience in writing books, blogs and articles.

Microservices is an architectural style that structures an application as a collection of distributed services. Microservices are certainly appealing but there are many questions that should be asked prior to diving into this architectural style: How do I deal with an unreliable network in a distributed architecture? How do I test my services? How do I monitor them? How do I package and execute them?

That's when Quarkus comes into play.

In this fascicle, you will learn Quarkus but also its ecosystem. You will discover Quarkus internals and how you can use it to build REST and reactive microservices, bind and process JSON or access datastores in a transactional way. With Cloud Native and GraalVM in mind, Quarkus makes packaging and orchestrating your microservices with Docker and Kubernetes easy.

This fascicle has a good mix of theory and practical examples. It is the companion book of *Practising Quarkus 2.x* where you learn how to develop an entire microservice architecture.

You can find two different formats of this fascicle:

- eBooks (PDF/EPUB) at https://agoncal.teachable.com/p/ebook-understanding-quarkus
- Paper book (ISBN: 9798775773083) and eBooks at https://www.amazon.com/gp/product/B0993R88N3